taste of home WINNING RECIPES

REIMAN MEDIA GROUP, LLC • GREENDALE, WI

A TASTE OF HOME/READER'S DIGEST BOOK

For other Taste of Home books and products, visit us at **tasteofhome.com.**

For more Reader's Digest products and information, visit **rd.com** (in the United States) or see **rd.ca** (in Canada).

International Standard Book Number: **978-1-61765-101-4**
Library of Congress Control Number: **2012932718**

Cover Photographers: Dan Roberts, Rob Hagen, Jim Wieland
Food Styling Manager: Sarah Thompson
Food Stylists: Kathryn Conrad (senior), Alynna Malson, Kaitlyn Besasie, Sue Draheim, Leah Rekau, Shannon Roum
Set Styling Manager: Stephanie Marchese
Set Stylists: Melissa Haberman, Dee Dee Jacq, Grace Natoli Sheldon, Jennifer Bradley Vent

Pictured on front cover:
(Top) Penne Gorgonzola with Chicken, page 147;
Neapolitan Cheesecake, page 251;
Peppered Filets with Tomato-Mushroom Salsa, page 103;
(Main) Worth It Lasagna, page 110.

Pictured on back cover:
Grilled Italian Meatball Burgers, page 75;
Frosted Walnut Brownie Cups, page 287;
Thai Chicken Lettuce Wraps, page 145.

Printed in China.
1 3 5 7 9 10 8 6 4 2

contents

Do you have a dish you're ALWAYS asked to bring? We can't wait to hear about it! Enter one of our many national recipe contests online at **TASTEOFHOME.COM/CONTESTS** and you may win BIG!

LIKE US ON FACEBOOK!
facebook.com/tasteofhome

TWEET US!
Follow @tasteofhome on Twitter

VISIT OUR BLOG
loveandhomemaderecipes.com

MORE GREAT COOKBOOKS!
shoptasteofhome.com

You'll be a *winner* when you serve these **417** *top-rated recipes.*

There is no greater **compliment** than being **that person** that family and friends think of when they **need a great-tasting dish**. How do you become that go-to cook? **It's easy!** Just turn to any of the **proven ribbon-winning recipes** inside the all new **Winning Recipes.**

Whatever the occasion...whatever the meal...with **Winning Recipes** in hand, you'll have an endless repertoire of **top-honor recipes**. Each one was **submitted by a cook like you**, then sorted, tested and judged in **national cooking contests** by the **Taste of Home food editors**. It's a recipe for **guaranteed success!**

page 251 Sue's Neapolitan Cheesecake

Page through this **top-notch collection** to discover...

417 RIBBON-WINNING RECIPES that use basic ingredients and **easy-to-follow steps** for no-fail results. Watch for the **"Grand Prize"** icon showcasing the grand champion recipes.

PREP & COOK TIMES that **eliminate the guesswork.** You'll know exactly how long it will take to get each lip-smacking dish on the table.

COLOR PHOTOS to **tempt your taste buds** and show what you can expect from each finished dish.

16 JAM-PACKED, ENTICING CHAPTERS brimming with **delicious selections** for every meal and any occasion, from **weeknight suppers** to **festive holiday desserts** and everything in between.

AN AT-A-GLANCE ICON that highlights **quick-to-fix winners** you can have on the table in **30 minutes or less**.

With the **best-of-the-best recipes** in **one convenient collection**, it's never been easier to prepare **crowd-pleasing fare**. The only thing that might prove difficult is finding the time to **make them all**!

page 90 Bridget's Broccoli Quiche

"My mother passed down this quiche recipe to me. She has been making it for more than 30 years. It's versatile enough to serve at any meal, and leftovers can be frozen and reheated in the microwave."

–Bridget Corbett *Valdosta, Georgia*

WINNERS
CIRCLE

appetizers & beverages

Nosh, snack, graze...drink, sip, guzzle..whatever you call it, find the perfect appetizers and beverages here to suit every occasion and craving. Whether you're fixing a little something for yourself or the whole gang, these contest-winning recipes will not disappoint!

SUN-DRIED TOMATO DIP, 12

Buffalo Wing Cheese Mold

PREP: 40 MIN. + CHILLING • YIELD: 24 SERVINGS

I took a baked version of a hot wing dip and turned it into a cheese ball appetizer for summertime parties. My family thinks this variation is ideal warm weather snacking material.

Deborah Helser *Attica, New York*

- **2 packages (8 ounces each) cream cheese, softened**
- **2 celery ribs, finely chopped**
- **2 cups (8 ounces) crumbled blue cheese**
- **1 cup (4 ounces) shredded Monterey Jack cheese**
- **1½ cups finely chopped cooked chicken breasts**
- **3 tablespoons buffalo wing sauce**
- **1 French bread baguette (16 ounces)**
- **¼ cup olive oil**
- **½ cup shredded carrots, optional**

1 In a large bowl, combine the cream cheese, celery, blue and Monterey Jack cheeses. In a small bowl, combine chicken and wing sauce.

2 Line a 1-qt. bowl with plastic wrap, overlapping the sides of the bowl. Spread 1½ cups of cream cheese mixture over the bottom and up the sides in prepared bowl. Layer with chicken mixture and remaining cream cheese mixture. Bring plastic wrap over cheese; press down gently. Refrigerate for at least 4 hours or until firm.

3 Just before serving, cut baguette into ¼-in. slices. Place on an ungreased baking sheet; brush with oil. Bake at 375° for 10-12 minutes or until lightly browned.

4 Remove mold from the refrigerator and invert onto a serving plate. Remove bowl and plastic wrap. Garnish with carrots if desired. Serve with toasted baguette slices.

CHICKEN BREAST BASICS

>> Buying skinned and boned chicken breasts can cut up to 15 minutes off your cooking time. Save money by buying larger size packages, then rewrap individually or in family-size portions and freeze.

Turkey Sliders with Chili Cheese Mayo

PREP: 25 MIN. • COOK: 10 MIN. • YIELD: 1 DOZEN

Serve these juicy sliders with an assortment of toppings as a fun family dinner or a scrumptious appetizer. The chili cheese mayo adds at tasty kick!

Lisa Hundley *Aberdeen, North Carolina*

- **4 bacon strips**
- **1 medium onion, finely chopped**
- **2 garlic cloves, minced**
- **2 tablespoons Worcestershire sauce**
- **½ teaspoon salt**
- **¼ teaspoon pepper**
- **1 pound ground turkey**
- **2 tablespoons olive oil**
- **12 heat-and-serve rolls**

MAYO:

- **1 cup mayonnaise**
- **1 jar (5 ounces) sharp American cheese spread**
- **1 teaspoon onion powder**
- **1 teaspoon garlic powder**
- **1 teaspoon chili powder**

TOPPINGS:

- **12 small lettuce leaves**
- **2 plum tomatoes, thinly sliced**

1 In a large skillet, cook bacon over medium heat until crisp. Remove to paper towels; drain. Crumble bacon and set aside. In the same skillet, saute onion in the drippings until tender. Add garlic; cook 1 minute longer.

2 Transfer to a large bowl. Add the bacon, Worcestershire sauce, salt and pepper. Crumble turkey over mixture and mix well. Shape into 12 patties.

3 Cook in a large skillet in oil over medium heat for 3-4 minutes on each side or until a meat thermometer reads 165° and juices run clear. Meanwhile, bake rolls according to package directions.

4 For mayo, in a small bowl, combine the mayonnaise, cheese spread, onion powder, garlic powder and chili powder. Split rolls; spread with mayo. Top each burger with lettuce and tomato.

Chipotle Pea Spread

30 min.

PREP/TOTAL TIME: 20 MIN. • YIELD: 1½ CUPS

I love hummus and bacon, but needed to make something green for a contest. It took a few tries to come up with a recipe everyone loves. Hope you do, too!

Frances "Kay" Bouma *Trail, British Columbia*

- **2 cups frozen peas**
- **⅓ cup grated Parmesan cheese**
- **3 cooked bacon strips, chopped**
- **¼ cup reduced-fat sour cream**
- **2 tablespoons olive oil**
- **1 tablespoon lime juice**
- **2 garlic cloves**
- **1 to 2 teaspoons minced chipotle pepper in adobo sauce**
- **¼ teaspoon pepper**

Assorted fresh vegetables or crackers

1 In a small saucepan, bring 4 cups water to a boil. Add peas; cover and cook for 1 minute. Drain and immediately place peas in ice water. Drain and pat dry.

2 Place peas in a food processor; add the cheese, bacon, sour cream, oil, lime juice, garlic, chipotle pepper and pepper. Cover and process until smooth. Serve with vegetables or crackers.

Strawberry Melon Fizz 

PREP/TOTAL TIME: 30 MIN. • YIELD: 8-10 SERVINGS

Experimenting in the kitchen is fun for me. I came up with this by combining two different recipes—one was for a melon ball basket and the other for a sparkling beverage.

Teresa Messick *Montgomery, Alabama*

- **2 cups sugar**
- **1 cup water**
- **5 fresh mint sprigs**
- **1 quart fresh strawberries, halved**
- **2 cups cubed honeydew**
- **1¾ cups cubed cantaloupe**

Ginger ale or sparkling white grape juice

1 In a large saucepan, combine the sugar, water and mint; bring to a boil. Boil and stir until a candy thermometer reads 240° (soft-ball stage). Remove from the heat; allow to cool. Discard mint.

2 Combine strawberries and melon. Just before serving, fill tall glasses with fruit and drizzle with 1 tablespoon syrup. Add ginger ale to each.

Goat Cheese Spread in Roasted Pepper Cups

PREP: 40 MIN. • BAKE: 25 MIN. • YIELD: 8 SERVINGS

I had a similar dish in a restaurant in Seattle, and when I returned home I just had to try my hand at making it. This is the fantastic result. I've taken it to work for parties and my boss once commented, "It's so good, it must be illegal."

Jenny Rodriquez *Pasco, Washington*

- **4 medium sweet red peppers**
- **3 tablespoons olive oil, divided**
- **1 medium onion, finely chopped**
- **4 garlic cloves, minced**
- **1 package (8 ounces) cream cheese, softened**
- **8 ounces fresh goat cheese, softened**
- **1 cup grated Parmesan cheese**
- **2 to 3 medium tomatoes, seeded and finely chopped**
- **2 tablespoons minced fresh cilantro**
- **1 tablespoon minced fresh parsley**
- **½ teaspoon hot pepper sauce**
- **⅛ teaspoon salt**
- **⅛ teaspoon pepper**

HERBED GARLIC TOASTS:

- **½ cup butter, softened**
- **1 tablespoon minced fresh parsley**
- **2 garlic cloves, minced**
- **24 slices French bread baguette (¼ inch thick)**

1 Remove tops and seeds from peppers; rub with 1 tablespoon oil. Place in an ungreased 8-in. square baking dish. Bake, uncovered, at 350° for 15-20 minutes. Remove from oven; turn peppers upside down in baking dish to drain.

2 In a small skillet, saute onion in remaining oil until tender. Add garlic; cook 1 minute longer. Transfer to a large bowl. Stir in the cheeses, tomatoes, cilantro, parsley, pepper sauce, salt and pepper. Spoon into pepper cups; return to baking dish.

3 Bake filled cups, uncovered, at 350° for 25-30 minutes or until heated through.

4 Meanwhile, in a small bowl, combine the butter, parsley and garlic; spread over baguette slices. Place on an ungreased baking sheet. Bake for 10-12 minutes or until lightly browned. Serve with cheese spread.

Jalapeno Popper Dip

PREP: 15 MIN. • BAKE: 20 MIN.
YIELD: 16 SERVINGS (¼ CUP EACH)

Here's a fantastic way to deliver all that blazing jalapeno popper taste without the work. Whenever I bring it to a party, I tote along notecards to hand out the ever-popular recipe. Serve with corn chips, tortilla chips or butter crackers.

Jennifer Wilke *Collinsville, Illinois*

- **2 packages (8 ounces each) cream cheese, softened**
- **1 cup mayonnaise**
- **½ cup shredded cheddar cheese**
- **1 can (4 ounces) chopped green chilies**
- **1 can (4 ounces) diced jalapeno peppers**
- **½ cup shredded Parmesan cheese, divided**
- **½ cup seasoned bread crumbs**
- **1 tablespoon olive oil**

Corn chips, tortilla chips *or* assorted crackers

1 In a large bowl, beat the cream cheese, mayonnaise, cheddar, chilies, peppers and ¼ cup Parmesan until blended. Spoon into an ungreased 1½-qt. baking dish.

2 In a small bowl, combine the bread crumbs, oil and remaining Parmesan. Sprinkle over cheese mixture. Bake, uncovered, at 350° for 20-25 min. or until golden brown. Serve with chips or crackers.

Tropical Guacamole 30 min.

PREP/TOTAL TIME: 20 MIN. • YIELD: 3½ CUPS

Fresh pineapple stars in this fruity guacamole that sure hits the spot! I have seen both kids and adults enjoy it as a poolside snack or as a satisfying appetizer at a summer barbecue.

Sarah White *Salt Lake Cty, Utah*

- **3 medium ripe avocados, peeled**
- **2 cups finely chopped fresh pineapple**
- **1 medium tomato, seeded and chopped**
- **2 jalapeno peppers, seeded and chopped**
- **⅓ cup minced fresh cilantro**
- **2 tablespoons lime juice**
- **3 garlic cloves, minced**
- **1 teaspoon salt**
- **½ teaspoon pepper**

Tortilla chips

1 In a small bowl, mash two avocados. Stir in the pineapple, tomato, jalapenos, cilantro, lime juice, garlic, salt and pepper. Coarsely chop remaining avocado; gently stir into guacamole. Serve with chips.

EDITOR'S NOTE: Wear disposable gloves when cutting hot peppers; the oils can burn skin. Avoid touching your face.

Terrific Tomato Tart

PREP: 15 MIN. • BAKE: 20 MIN. • YIELD: 8 SERVINGS

Fresh, colorful tomatoes, feta cheese and prepared pesto perfectly complement the crispy phyllo dough crust. One slice is never enough!

Diane Halferty *Corpus Christi, Texas*

- **12 sheets phyllo dough (14 inches x 9 inches)**
- **2 tablespoons olive oil**
- **2 tablespoons dry bread crumbs**
- **2 tablespoons prepared pesto**
- **¾ cup crumbled feta cheese, divided**
- **1 medium tomato, cut into ¼-inch slices**
- **1 large yellow tomato, cut into ¼-inch slices**
- **¼ teaspoon pepper**
- **5 to 6 fresh basil leaves, thinly sliced**

1 Place one sheet of phyllo dough on a baking sheet lined with parchment paper; brush with ½ teaspoon oil and sprinkle with ½ teaspoon bread crumbs. (Keep remaining phyllo covered with plastic wrap and a damp towel to prevent it from drying out.) Repeat layers, being careful to brush oil all the way to edges.

2 Fold each side ¾ in. toward center to form a rim. Spread with pesto and sprinkle with half of the feta cheese. Alternately arrange the red and yellow tomato slices over cheese. Sprinkle with pepper and remaining feta.

3 Bake at 400° for 20-25 minutes or until crust is golden brown and crispy. Cool on a wire rack for 5 minutes. Remove parchment paper before cutting. Garnish with basil.

Sun-Dried Tomato Dip

30 min.

PREP/TOTAL TIME: 10 MIN. • YIELD: 2 CUPS

I love to serve this dip for just about any occasion. It's so quick and easy to pull together and full of robust flavor!

Andrea Reynolds *Rocky River, Ohio*

- **1 package (8 ounces) cream cheese, softened**
- **½ cup sour cream**
- **½ cup mayonnaise**
- **¼ cup oil-packed sun-dried tomatoes, drained and patted dry**
- **½ teaspoon salt**
- **¼ teaspoon pepper**
- **¼ teaspoon hot pepper sauce**
- **2 green onions, sliced**

Assorted crackers and/or fresh vegetables

1 Place the first seven ingredients in a food processor; cover and process until blended. Add green onions; cover and pulse until finely chopped. Serve with crackers and/or vegetables.

Fire-Roasted Salsa 

PREP/TOTAL TIME: 15 MIN. • YIELD: 1½ CUPS

Here's the pleasantly spicy treat friends and family won't be able to stray from at your Cinco de Mayo buffet. Canned tomatoes speed preparation in this restaurant-quality salsa that's table-ready in just 15 minutes.

Missy Kampling *Mountain View, California*

- **1 can (14½ ounces) fire-roasted diced tomatoes, drained**
- **½ cup sliced onion**
- **⅓ cup fresh cilantro leaves**
- **1 tablespoon lime juice**
- **1 teaspoon sugar**
- **¼ teaspoon salt**

1 In a food processor, combine the tomatoes, onion, cilantro, lime juice, sugar and salt. Cover and process until desired consistency.

Movie Theater Pretzel Rods

PREP: 70 MIN. + RISING • BAKE: 10 MIN.
YIELD: 32 PRETZEL RODS

My kids and all of their friends can't get enough of these large, chewy pretzel rods. They are especially good when eaten fresh from the oven.

Lisa Shaw *Burnettsville, Indiana*

- **1 package (¼ ounce) active dry yeast**
- **1½ cups warm water (110° to 115°)**
- **2 tablespoons sugar**
- **2 tablespoons butter, melted**
- **1½ teaspoons salt**
- **4 to 4½ cups all-purpose flour**
- **8 cups water**
- **½ cup baking soda**
- **1 egg yolk**
- **1 tablespoon cold water**

Coarse salt, optional

1 In a large bowl, dissolve yeast in warm water. Add the sugar, butter, salt and 2 cups flour. Beat until smooth. Stir in enough remaining flour to form a soft dough (dough will be sticky).

2 Turn dough onto a floured surface; knead until smooth and elastic, about 6-8 minutes. Place in a greased bowl, turning once to grease top. Cover and let rise in a warm place until doubled, about 1 hour.

3 In a large saucepan, bring 8 cups water and baking soda to a boil. Punch dough down; divide into 32 portions. Roll each into a 5-in. log. Add to boiling water, a few at a time, for 30 seconds. Remove with a slotted spoon; drain on paper towels. Place on greased baking sheets.

4 Lightly beat egg yolk and cold water; brush over pretzels. Sprinkle with coarse salt if desired. Bake 425° for 9-11 minutes or until golden brown. Remove from pans to wire racks. Serve warm.

Topsy-Turvy Sangria 

PREP/TOTAL TIME: 10 MIN.
YIELD: 10 SERVINGS (¾ CUP EACH)

I got this recipe from a friend a few years ago. It's perfect for relaxed get-togethers. It tastes best when you make it the night before and let the flavors steep. But be careful—it goes down easy!

Tracy Field *Bremerton, Washington*

- **1 bottle (750 milliliters) merlot**
- **1 cup sugar**
- **1 cup orange liqueur**
- **½ to 1 cup brandy**
- **3 cups lemon-lime soda, chilled**
- **1 cup sliced fresh strawberries**
- **1 medium lemon, sliced**
- **1 medium orange, sliced**
- **1 medium peach, sliced**

Ice cubes

1 In a pitcher, stir the wine, sugar, orange liqueur and brandy until sugar is dissolved. Stir in soda and fruit. Serve over ice.

EASY DINNER PARTY

>> For an appetizer buffet that serves as the meal, offer five or six different appetizers (including some substantial selections) and plan on eight to nine pieces per guest. If you'll also be serving a meal, two to three pieces per person is sufficient.

Barbecue Wings 

PREP/TOTAL TIME: 30 MIN. • YIELD: 6 SERVINGS

I was exposed to the famous buffalo wing when I grew up in Buffalo, New York. In search of a version that would make the hot sauce my own, I created this delectable starter. These wings are spicy and sweet with a hint of celery, and always go fast at parties.

Sara Yarrington *Salem, New Hampshire*

Oil for deep-fat frying
- **1 package (40 ounces) fresh or frozen chicken wingettes, thawed**
- **½ cup barbecue sauce**
- **1 tablespoon butter**
- **1 teaspoon celery seed**
- **1 teaspoon hot pepper sauce**

1 In an electric skillet or deep-fat fryer, heat oil to 375°. Fry chicken wings, a few at a time, for 8 minutes or until golden brown and juices run clear, turning occasionally. Drain on paper towels.

2 In a small microwave-safe bowl, combine the barbecue sauce, butter, celery seed and hot pepper sauce. Cover and microwave on high for 1 minute or until heated through. Place the chicken wings in a large bowl; add sauce and toss to coat.

Tomato-Jalapeno Granita

PREP: 15 MIN. + FREEZING • YIELD: 6 SERVINGS

Everyone will say "Wow!" after one taste of this refreshing, icy dessert. Even my grandchildren enjoy the tomato, mint and lime flavors.

Paula Marchesi *Lenhartsville, Pennsylvania*

- **2 cups tomato juice**
- **⅓ cup sugar**
- **4 mint sprigs**
- **1 jalapeno pepper, sliced**
- **2 tablespoons lime juice**

Fresh mint leaves, optional

1 In a small saucepan, bring the tomato juice, sugar, mint sprigs and jalapeno to a boil. Cook and stir until sugar is dissolved. Remove from the heat, cover and let stand for 15 minutes.

2 Strain and discard solids. Stir in lime juice. Transfer to a 1-qt. dish; cool to room temperature. Freeze for 1 hour; stir with a fork.

3 Freeze 2-3 hours longer or until completely frozen, stirring every 30 minutes. Scrape granita with a fork just before serving; spoon into dessert dishes. Garnish with additional mint if desired.

EDITOR'S NOTE: Wear disposable gloves when cutting hot peppers; the oils can burn skin. Avoid touching your face.

Bacon and Fontina Stuffed Mushrooms

PREP: 30 MIN. • BAKE: 10 MIN. • YIELD: 2 DOZEN

For me, it doesn't get better than lots of bacon and cheese in a mushroom cap. They'll be a hit with your guests, too.

Tammy Rex *New Tripoli, Pennsylvania*

- **24 large fresh mushrooms**
- **4 ounces cream cheese, softened**
- **1 cup (4 ounces) shredded fontina cheese**
- **8 bacon strips, cooked and crumbled**
- **4 green onions, chopped**
- **¼ cup chopped oil-packed sun-dried tomatoes**
- **3 tablespoons minced fresh parsley**
- **1 tablespoon olive oil**

1 Remove stems from mushrooms and set caps aside; discard stems or save for another use. In a small bowl, combine the cream cheese, fontina cheese, bacon, onions, sun-dried tomatoes and parsley. Fill each mushroom cap with about 1 tablespoon of filling.

2 Place on a greased baking sheet. Drizzle with oil. Bake, uncovered, at 425° for 8-10 minutes or until mushrooms are tender.

Watermelon Spritzer

PREP: 5 MIN. + CHILLING • YIELD: 5 SERVINGS

It couldn't get much easier than this bright spritzer! Watermelon blended with limeade is cool and refreshing. It's a wonderful thirst-quencher on a hot summer day.

Geraldine Saucier *Albuquerque, New Mexico*

- **4 cups cubed seedless watermelon**
- **¾ cup frozen limeade concentrate, thawed**
- **2½ cups carbonated water**

Lime slices

1 Place watermelon in a blender. Cover and process until blended. Strain and discard pulp; transfer juice to a pitcher. Stir in limeade concentrate. Refrigerate for 6 hours or overnight.

2 Just before serving, stir in carbonated water. Garnish servings with lime slices.

Roasted Grape Tomatoes 

PREP/TOTAL TIME: 25 MIN. • YIELD: 4 CUPS

Everyone loves this mouthwatering starter that requires just a few ingredients. We appreciate that it's a fast, simple way to use up extra tomatoes from our garden.

Linda Green *Ardmore, Oklahoma*

- **½ cup cider vinegar**
- **¼ cup packed brown sugar**
- **2 tablespoons canola oil**
- **4 garlic cloves, minced**
- **½ teaspoon salt**
- **½ teaspoon pepper**
- **1 pound grape tomatoes**
- **1 tablespoon minced fresh parsley**

Assorted crackers and Gouda cheese slices

3 In a large bowl, whisk the first six ingredients. Add tomatoes; toss to coat. Transfer to a greased 15-in. x 10-in. x 1-in. baking pan. Sprinkle with parsley.

4 Bake, uncovered, at 375° for 12-14 minutes or until softened, stirring occasionally. Serve with crackers and cheese.

Polenta Parmigiana 

PREP/TOTAL TIME: 30 MIN. • YIELD: 16 APPETIZERS

This warm, Italian-flavored appetizer also makes a quick, filling lunch. I prefer this veggie version, but my kids like to add pepperoni or sausage to create mini pizzas.

Carolyn Kumpe *El Dorado, California*

- **1 tube (1 pound) polenta, cut into 16 slices**
- **¼ cup olive oil**
- **1 cup tomato basil pasta sauce, warmed**
- **½ pound fresh mozzarella cheese, cut into 16 slices**
- **¼ cup grated Parmesan cheese**
- **½ teaspoon salt**
- **⅛ teaspoon pepper**

Fresh basil leaves, optional

1 Place polenta in a greased 15-in. x 10-in. x 1-in. baking pan; brush with olive oil. Bake at 425° for 15-20 minutes or until edges are golden brown.

2 Spoon pasta sauce over polenta slices. Top each with a mozzarella cheese slice; sprinkle with Parmesan cheese, salt and pepper. Bake 3-5 minutes longer or until cheese is melted. Garnish with basil if desired.

Brie Cherry Pastry Cups

30 min.

PREP/TOTAL TIME: 30 MIN. • YIELD: 3 DOZEN

Golden brown and flaky, these bite-size puff pastries with creamy Brie and sweet cherry preserves could double as a dessert.

Marilyn McSween *Mentor, Ohio*

- **1 sheet frozen puff pastry, thawed**
- **½ cup cherry preserves**
- **4 ounces Brie cheese, cut into ½-inch cubes**
- **¼ cup chopped pecans *or* walnuts**
- **2 tablespoons minced chives**

1 Unfold puff pastry; cut into 36 squares. Gently press squares onto the bottoms of 36 greased miniature muffin cups.

2 Bake at 375° for 10 minutes. Using the end of a wooden spoon handle, make a ½-in.-deep indentation in the center of each. Bake 6-8 minutes longer or until golden brown. With spoon handle, press squares down again.

3 Spoon a rounded ½ teaspoonful of preserves into each cup. Top with cheese; sprinkle with nuts and chives. Bake for 3-5 minutes or until cheese is melted.

Chorizo-Queso Egg Rolls

PREP: 45 MIN. + CHILLING • COOK: 5 MIN./BATCH
YIELD: 4 DOZEN

Little bites deliver big flavor in this combination of tangy sausage and creamy cheese in crisp wontons. The recipe is an appetizing take-off on my favorite Mexican entree.

Kari Wheaton *South Beloit, Illinois*

- **½ cup mayonnaise**
- **½ cup sour cream**
- **2 ounces cream cheese, softened**
- **2 tablespoons minced fresh cilantro**
- **1 tablespoon chopped chipotle pepper in adobo sauce**
- **6 ounces uncooked chorizo or bulk spicy pork sausage**
- **2 cups crumbled queso fresco**
- **¼ cup enchilada sauce**
- **¼ cup chopped green chilies**
- **1 package (12 ounces) wonton wrappers**

Oil for frying

1 For dipping sauce, in a small bowl, combine the mayonnaise, sour cream, cream cheese, cilantro and chipotle peppers. Cover and refrigerate until serving.

2 Crumble chorizo into a large skillet; cook for 6-8 minutes over medium heat or until fully cooked. Drain. Stir in the queso fresco, enchilada sauce and chilies.

3 Position a wonton wrapper with one point toward you. Place 2 teaspoons of filling in the center. (Keep remaining wrappers covered with a damp paper towel until ready to use.) Fold bottom corner over filling; fold sides toward center over filling. Roll toward the remaining point. Moisten top corner with water; press to seal. Repeat with remaining wrappers and filling.

4 In an electric skillet, heat 1 in. of oil to 375°. Fry egg rolls in batches for 1-2 minutes on each side or until golden brown. Drain on paper towels. Serve warm with dipping sauce.

Teacher's Caviar 

PREP/TOTAL TIME: 25 MIN. • YIELD: 8 CUPS

I love the fresh flavors, colors and convenience of this dish. It adds fun to a workday lunch without adding inches to the waistline or putting a dent in the food budget. The salsa can be served immediately or chilled in the morning and eaten at lunch time! Try it with baked tortilla chips or spooned over chicken.

Ellen Finger *Lancaster, Pennsylvania*

- **2 cans (15 ounces each) black beans, rinsed and drained**
- **2 medium tomatoes, seeded and chopped**
- **1½ cups frozen corn, thawed**
- **1 medium ripe avocado, peeled and cubed**
- **1 can (8 ounces) unsweetened pineapple chunks, drained and quartered**
- **1 medium sweet orange pepper, chopped**
- **6 green onions, thinly sliced**
- **½ cup minced fresh cilantro**
- **⅓ cup lime juice**
- **2 tablespoons olive oil**
- **2 tablespoons honey**
- **½ teaspoon salt**
- **⅛ teaspoon cayenne pepper**

Baked tortilla chip scoops

1 In a large bowl, combine the first eight ingredients.

2 In a small bowl, whisk the lime juice, oil, honey, salt and cayenne. Pour over bean mixture; toss to coat. Serve with baked chips.

Mocha Cappuccino Punch

PREP: 15 MIN. + CHILLING
YIELD: 13 SERVINGS (¾ CUP EACH)

Coffee, meet ice cream. An inventive way to indulge a crowd, this luscious java punch will quench the urgent chocolate cravings.

Fancheon Resler *Bluffton, Indiana*

- **1 cup hot water**
- **2 tablespoons instant coffee granules**
- **¼ teaspoon ground cinnamon**
- **1 can (14 ounces) fat-free sweetened condensed milk**
- **½ cup chocolate syrup**
- **1 quart half-and-half cream**
- **1 quart chocolate ice cream**
- **2 cups club soda, chilled**

Baking cocoa

1 In a small bowl, whisk the water, coffee granules and cinnamon until coffee granules are dissolved. Stir in milk and chocolate syrup. Cover and refrigerate until chilled.

2 Transfer milk mixture to a punch bowl; stir in half-and-half cream. Add scoops of ice cream; gradually pour in club soda. Dust top with cocoa. Serve immediately.

Berry Smoothies

30 min.

PREP/TOTAL TIME: 5 MIN. • YIELD: 5 SERVINGS

Smooth out the morning rush with a boost of berries. Tart, tangy and sweet, there's no reason to add any extra sugar to this delightfully balanced beverage.

Elisabeth Larsen *Pleasant Grv, Utah*

- **2 cups cranberry juice**
- **2 containers (6 ounces *each*) raspberry yogurt**
- **1 cup frozen unsweetened raspberries**
- **1 cup frozen unsweetened blueberries**
- **8 ice cubes**

1 In a blender, combine all ingredients; cover and process for 30-45 seconds or until blended. Pour into chilled glasses; serve immediately.

Grilled Steak Appetizers with Stilton Sauce

PREP: 25 MIN. • GRILL: 10 MIN. • YIELD: 20 APPETIZERS (3/4 CUP SAUCE)

Here's a hearty appetizer that will get any gathering off to a delicious start. The rich, creamy cheese sauce complements the grilled steak to perfection.

Radelle Knappenberger *Oviedo, Florida*

- **2 boneless beef top loin steaks (8 ounces each)**
- **1/4 teaspoon salt**
- **1/4 teaspoon pepper**
- **1/2 cup white wine or chicken broth**
- **1/3 cup heavy whipping cream**
- **3 tablespoons sour cream**
- **2 ounces Stilton cheese, cubed**

1 Sprinkle steaks with salt and pepper. Grill steaks, covered, over medium heat for 4-6 minutes on each side or until meat reaches desired doneness (for medium-rare, a thermometer should read 145°; medium, 160°; well-done, 170°). Remove meat to a cutting board and keep warm.

2 In a small saucepan, bring wine to a boil; cook until reduced by half. Add cream. Bring to a gentle boil. Reduce heat; simmer, uncovered, until thickened, stirring occasionally. Remove from the heat. Add sour cream and cheese; stir until cheese is melted.

3 Cut steaks into 1-in. cubes; skewer with toothpicks. Serve with sauce.

EDITOR'S NOTES: Top loin steak may be labeled as strip steak, Kansas City steak, New York strip steak, ambassador steak or boneless club steak in your region. You may substitute 1/3 cup crumbled blue cheese for the Stilton cheese.

Smoky Grilled Corn Salsa

PREP/TOTAL TIME: 30 MIN. • YIELD: 6 CUPS

Our backyard grill is the perfect place to cook up the ingredients for homemade corn salsa. It's yummy with tortilla chips and as a topping for meat, poultry and fish.

Alicia DeWolfe *Gloucester, Massachusetts*

- **6 plum tomatoes, halved**
- **4 medium ears sweet corn, husks removed**
- **2 medium sweet yellow peppers, halved**
- **2 medium green peppers, halved**
- **3 jalapeno peppers, halved and seeded**
- **1 medium red onion, cut into ½-inch slices**
- **¼ cup minced fresh cilantro**
- **3 tablespoons olive oil**
- **3 tablespoons red wine vinegar**
- **5 garlic cloves, minced**
- **1 teaspoon salt**
- **½ teaspoon sugar**
- **½ teaspoon pepper**

1 Grill the tomatoes, corn, peppers and onion, covered, over medium heat for 10-12 minutes or until tender, turning occasionally. Allow vegetables to cool slightly. Remove corn from cobs; transfer to a large bowl. Chop the remaining vegetables and add to corn.

2 In a small bowl, whisk the cilantro, oil, vinegar, garlic, salt, sugar and pepper. Pour over vegetables; toss to coat. Serve warm or cold.

EDITOR'S NOTE: Wear disposable gloves when cutting hot peppers; the oils can burn skin. Avoid touching your face.

Sparkling Kiwi Lemonade

PREP: 20 MIN. + FREEZING • YIELD: 6 SERVINGS

Keep some kiwi ice cubes in the freezer so they're ready whenever you crave a tall glass of this dressed-up summertime favorite.

Emily Seidel *Ainsworth, Nebraska*

- **8 medium kiwifruit, peeled, divided**
- **¾ cup sugar**
- **¾ cup lemon juice**
- **1 liter carbonated water**

1 Slice two kiwi into small pieces. Place in ice cube trays and fill with water. Freeze.

2 Cut remaining kiwi into fourths; place in a food processor. Cover and process until smooth. Strain; discard pulp. In a 2-qt. pitcher, stir sugar and lemon juice until sugar is dissolved. Stir in kiwi puree. Refrigerate until chilled. Just before serving, stir in carbonated water. Serve over kiwi ice cubes.

WINNERS CIRCLE

Grilled Corn Dip

PREP: 30 MIN. • BAKE: 25 MIN. • YIELD: 5 CUPS

Great for summer, this tasty appetizer is a must-have on weekend family gatherings at our cottage on Sandusky Bay. It's well worth the time it takes to grill the corn and cut from the cob.

Cathy Myers *Monroeville, Ohio*

- **6 medium ears sweet corn, husks removed**
- **1 large onion, chopped**
- **1 jalapeno pepper, finely chopped**
- **2 tablespoons butter**
- **2 garlic cloves, minced**
- **1 cup mayonnaise**
- **½ cup sour cream**
- **½ teaspoon chili powder**
- **2 cups (8 ounces) shredded Monterey Jack cheese**
- **1 can (2¼ ounces) sliced ripe olives, drained**
- **2 tablespoons sliced green onions**

Tortilla chips

1 Grill corn, covered, over medium heat for 10-12 minutes or until tender, turning occasionally.

2 Cut corn from cobs. In a large skillet, saute the onion and jalapeno in butter for 2-3 minutes or until almost tender. Add corn and garlic; saute 1-2 minutes longer or until vegetables are tender. Remove from the heat.

3 In a large bowl, combine the mayonnaise, sour cream and chili powder. Stir in cheese and corn mixture. Transfer to a greased 2-qt. baking dish.

4 Bake, uncovered, at 400° for 25-30 minutes or until bubbly and golden brown. Sprinkle with olives and green onions; serve with chips.

EDITOR'S NOTE: Wear disposable gloves when cutting hot peppers; the oils can burn skin. Avoid touching your face.

Mini Muffuletta

PREP: 25 MIN. + CHILLING • YIELD: 3 DOZEN

Guests love the Mediterranean flavor in these mini sandwich wedges. The recipe is great for a party and can be made a day in advance.

Gareth Craner *Minden, Nevada*

- **1 jar (10 ounces) pimiento-stuffed olives, drained and chopped**
- **2 cans (4¼ ounces each) chopped ripe olives**
- **2 tablespoons balsamic vinegar**
- **1 tablespoon red wine vinegar**
- **1 tablespoon olive oil**
- **3 garlic cloves, minced**
- **1 teaspoon dried basil**
- **1 teaspoon dried oregano**
- **6 French rolls, split**
- **½ pound thinly sliced hard salami**
- **¼ pound sliced provolone cheese**
- **½ pound thinly sliced cotto salami**
- **¼ pound sliced part-skim mozzarella cheese**

1 In a large bowl, combine the first eight ingredients; set aside. Hollow out tops and bottoms of rolls, leaving ¾-in. shells (discard removed bread or save for another use).

2 Spread olive mixture over tops and bottoms of rolls. On roll bottoms, layer with hard salami, provolone cheese, cotto salami and mozzarella cheese. Replace tops.

3 Wrap tightly in plastic wrap. Refrigerate overnight. Cut each into six wedges; secure with toothpicks.

Pina Colada Slush

PREP: 10 MIN. + FREEZING
YIELD: 12 SERVINGS (3 QUARTS)

Try this fruity cooler for a special treat on a steamy day. I'm asked to bring it to family gatherings all year long, so I always keep a batch or two in my freezer.

Alisa Allred *Vernal, Utah*

- **3 cans (6 ounces each) unsweetened pineapple juice**
- **2 cups water**
- **1 can (10 ounces) frozen non-alcoholic pina colada mix**
- **1 tablespoon lime juice**
- **3½ teaspoons Crystal Light lemonade drink mix**
- **6 cups lemon-lime soda, chilled**

1 In a large bowl, combine the pineapple juice, water, pina colada mix, lime juice and soft drink mix; stir until drink mix is dissolved. Transfer to a 2-qt. freezer container. Freeze for 6 hours or overnight.

2 Remove from the freezer 45 minutes before serving. For each serving, combine ½ cup slush mixture with ½ cup lemon-lime soda.

WINNERS
CIRCLE

salads & sides

It's a priceless feeling to have a tried-and-true recipe that makes any meal a success. Delight your dinner guests anytime—Thursday to Thanksgiving—with this spread of real cooks' faves for rounding out lunch and dinner.

QUINOA AND BLACK BEAN SALAD, 34

Chunky Cranberry Salad

PREP: 25 MIN. + CHILLING • YIELD: 12 SERVINGS

I first tried this recipe while taking a cooking class. Full of mixed fruit, celery and nuts, it's a lively alternative to jellied cranberry sauce. When cranberries are in season, I buy extra and freeze them so I can make this salad year-round.

Joyce Butterfield *Nancy, Kentucky*

- **4 cups fresh *or* frozen cranberries**
- **3½ cups unsweetened pineapple juice**
- **2 envelopes unflavored gelatin**
- **½ cup cold water**
- **2 cups sugar**
- **1 can (20 ounces) unsweetened pineapple tidbits, drained**
- **1 cup chopped pecans**
- **1 cup green grapes, chopped**
- **½ cup finely chopped celery**
- **2 teaspoons grated orange peel**

1 In a large saucepan, combine the cranberries and pineapple juice. Cook over medium heat until berries pop, about 15 minutes.

2 Meanwhile, in a small bowl, sprinkle gelatin over cold water; let stand for 5 minutes. In a large bowl, combine the berry mixture, sugar and softened gelatin. Chill until partially set.

3 Fold in the pineapple, pecans, grapes, celery and orange peel. Pour into individual serving dishes. Chill until firm.

CHICKEN BREAST BASICS

>> Buy and freeze extra bags of cranberries during the holiday season when they are on sale so you can make your favorite berry dishes—like Chunky Cranberry Salad—all year long.

Curried Fried Rice with Pineapple

PREP/TOTAL TIME: 30 MIN. • YIELD: 8 SERVINGS

This is a special fried rice popular in Thai restaurants and called Khao Pad. It has a bit of heat, a little sweetness and the best little touch of crunch.

Joanna Yuen *San Jose, California*

- **4 tablespoons canola oil, divided**
- **2 eggs, beaten**
- **1 small onion, finely chopped**
- **2 shallots, finely chopped**
- **3 garlic cloves, minced**
- **4 cups cold cooked rice**
- **1 can (8 ounces) unsweetened pineapple chunks, drained**
- **½ cup lightly salted cashews**
- **½ cup frozen peas**
- **⅓ cup minced fresh cilantro**
- **¼ cup raisins**
- **3 tablespoons chicken broth**
- **2 tablespoons fish sauce**
- **1½ teaspoons curry powder**
- **1 teaspoon sugar**
- **¼ teaspoon crushed red pepper flakes**

1 In a large skillet or wok, heat 1 tablespoon oil over medium-high heat; add eggs. As eggs set, lift edges, letting uncooked portion flow underneath. When eggs are completely cooked, remove to a plate and keep warm.

2 In the same pan, stir-fry onion and shallots in remaining oil until tender. Add garlic; cook 1 minute longer. Stir in the rice, pineapple, cashews, peas, cilantro, raisins, broth, fish sauce, curry, sugar and pepper flakes; heat through. Chop egg into small pieces; add to rice mixture.

Mango-Chutney Chicken Salad

PREP: 15 MIN. + CHILLING • YIELD: 6 SERVINGS

I often make this recipe and eat it at school for lunch. It makes me feel like I've ordered out from a fancy restaurant. It is wonderful as a salad or as a gourmet lunch wrap.

Michelle Sichak *Meridian, Idaho*

- **1 carton (6 ounces) plain yogurt**
- **¼ cup light coconut milk**
- **1½ teaspoons curry powder**
- **2 cups cubed cooked chicken**
- **2 cups green grapes, halved**
- **6 green onions, chopped**
- **½ cup dried cranberries**
- **⅓ cup mango chutney**
- **¼ cup slivered almonds, toasted**

1 In a small bowl, whisk the yogurt, milk and curry until smooth.

2 In a large bowl, combine the chicken, grapes, onions and cranberries. Drizzle with yogurt dressing and toss to coat. Fold in mango chutney. Refrigerate for at least 1 hour.

3 Just before serving, sprinkle with almonds.

Spicy Sweet Potato Fries

PREP: 25 MIN. • BAKE: 30 MIN. • YIELD: 5 SERVINGS

Better pile these sweet and spicy orange fries high on the plate. Served with a thick dipping sauce, they create a craving for more.

Mary Jones *Williamstown, West Virginia*

- **1 teaspoon coriander seeds**
- **½ teaspoon fennel seed**
- **½ teaspoon dried oregano**
- **½ teaspoon crushed red pepper flakes**
- **½ teaspoon salt**
- **2 pounds sweet potatoes (about 4 medium), peeled and cut into wedges**
- **2 tablespoons canola oil**

SPICY MAYONNAISE DIP:

- **1¼ cups mayonnaise**
- **2 tablespoons lime juice**
- **2 tablespoons minced fresh cilantro**
- **2 garlic cloves, minced**
- **1 teaspoon ground mustard**
- **¼ teaspoon cayenne pepper**
- **⅛ teaspoon salt**

1 In a spice grinder or with a mortar and pestle, combine the coriander, fennel, oregano and pepper flakes; grind until mixture becomes a fine powder. Stir in salt.

2 In a large bowl, combine the potatoes, oil and ground spices; toss to coat. Transfer to a greased 15-in. x 10-in. x 1-in. baking pan.

3 Bake, uncovered, at 400° for 30-35 minutes or until crisp and golden brown, turning occasionally. Meanwhile, in a small bowl, combine the dip ingredients; chill until serving. Serve with fries.

Marvelous Mediterranean Vegetables

PREP: 25 MIN. + MARINATING • GRILL: 10 MIN.
YIELD: 9 SERVINGS

With so many barbecues in the summer, I created this simple, tasty dish to complement any entree. I like to prepare it earlier in the day and let it marinate, then I just throw it on the grill.

Cathy Godberson *Oakville, Ontario*

- **3 large portobello mushrooms, sliced**
- **1 each medium sweet red, orange and yellow peppers, sliced**
- **1 medium zucchini, sliced**
- **10 fresh asparagus spears, cut into 2-inch lengths**
- **1 small onion, sliced and separated into rings**
- **¾ cup grape tomatoes**
- **½ cup fresh sugar snap peas**
- **½ cup fresh broccoli florets**
- **½ cup pitted Greek olives**
- **1 bottle (14 ounces) Greek vinaigrette**
- **½ cup crumbled feta cheese**

1 In a large resealable plastic bag, combine the mushrooms, peppers and zucchini. Add the asparagus, onion, tomatoes, peas, broccoli and olives. Pour vinaigrette into bag; seal bag and turn to coat. Refrigerate for at least 30 minutes.

2 Discard marinade. Transfer vegetables to a grill wok or basket. Grill, uncovered, over medium heat for 8-12 minutes or until tender, stirring frequently. Place on a serving plate; sprinkle with cheese.

EDITOR'S NOTE: If you do not have a grill wok or basket, use a disposable foil pan. Poke holes in the bottom of the pan with a meat fork to allow liquid to drain.

Grilled Romaine Toss

PREP: 25 MIN. • GRILL: 10 MIN. • YIELD: 10 SERVINGS

I often double this fantastic salad, and it's always history by the end of the night. Prepare it indoors by using the broiler.

Trisha Kruse *Eagle, Idaho*

- **¼ cup olive oil**
- **3 tablespoons sugar**
- **1 teaspoon dried rosemary, crushed**
- **1 teaspoon dried thyme**
- **¼ teaspoon salt**
- **¼ teaspoon pepper**
- **8 plum tomatoes, quartered**
- **2 large sweet onions, thinly sliced**

GRILLED ROMAINE:

- **4 romaine hearts**
- **2 tablespoons olive oil**
- **¼ teaspoon salt**
- **¼ teaspoon pepper**

DRESSING:

- **¼ cup olive oil**
- **¼ cup balsamic vinegar**
- **3 garlic cloves, peeled and halved**
- **2 tablespoons brown sugar**
- **¼ cup grated Parmesan cheese**

1 In a large bowl, combine the first six ingredients. Add tomatoes and onions; toss to coat. Transfer to a grill wok or basket. Grill, covered, over medium heat for 8-12 minutes or until tender, stirring frequently. Set aside.

2 For grilled romaine, cut romaine hearts in half lengthwise, leaving ends intact. Brush with oil; sprinkle with salt and pepper. Place romaine halves cut sides down on grill. Grill, covered, over medium heat for 3-4 minutes on each side or until slightly charred and wilted.

3 For dressing, place the oil, vinegar, garlic and brown sugar in a food processor; cover and process until smooth.

4 Coarsely chop romaine; divide among 10 salad plates. Top with tomato mixture; drizzle with dressing. Sprinkle with cheese.

EDITOR'S NOTE: If you do not have a grill wok or basket, use a disposable foil pan. Poke holes in the bottom of the pan with a meat fork to allow liquid to drain.

Spicy Pepper Slaw

PREP: 20 MIN. + CHILLING • YIELD: 8 SERVINGS

I love coleslaw, but I wanted to jazz it up and make it just a little healthier. This recipe not only makes a good side dish, but it's also great as a relish on a chicken sandwich or burger. Jalapenos give it just the right kick.

Cheryl McCleary *Kansas City, Kansas*

- **3 cups shredded cabbage**
- **2 celery ribs, chopped**
- **1 medium green pepper, julienned**
- **1 cup cut fresh green beans (1-inch pieces)**
- **1 cup cut fresh asparagus (1-inch pieces)**
- **1 bunch green onions, chopped**
- **1 banana pepper, seeded and chopped**
- **2 jalapeno peppers, seeded and chopped**
- **2 serrano peppers, seeded and chopped**
- **½ cup cider vinegar**
- **3 tablespoons olive oil**
- **1 tablespoon lime juice**
- **1 tablespoon minced fresh thyme**
- **1 tablespoon snipped fresh dill**
- **1 tablespoon minced fresh cilantro**
- **1 teaspoon salt**
- **1 teaspoon pepper**

1 In a large bowl, combine the first nine ingredients. In a small bowl, whisk the remaining ingredients; pour over salad and toss to coat. Refrigerate for at least 1 hour before serving.

EDITOR'S NOTE: Wear disposable gloves when cutting hot peppers; the oils can burn skin. Avoid touching your face.

Strawberry Salad with Mojito Vinaigrette

30 min.

PREP/TOTAL TIME: 20 MIN.
YIELD: 5 SERVINGS

Mojitos are a fun summery drink and the inspiration behind this refreshing side salad. No rum was used in my recipe, but it certainly could be added to the vinaigrette.

Donna Marie Ryan *Topsfield, Massachusetts*

- **¼ cup white wine vinegar**
- **4 fresh strawberries, hulled**
- **2 tablespoons water**
- **2 tablespoons lime juice**
- **2 tablespoons coarsely chopped fresh mint**
- **2 tablespoons honey**
- **¼ teaspoon salt**

Dash pepper

- **2 tablespoons olive oil**

SALAD:

- **1 package (5 ounces) spring mix salad greens**
- **2 cups fresh strawberries, hulled and sliced**
- **1 small red onion, thinly sliced**
- **3 ounces fresh goat cheese, crumbled**
- **¼ cup chopped walnuts**

1 In a blender, combine the first eight ingredients. While processing, gradually add oil in a steady stream. Set aside.

2 Divide salad greens among five salad plates; top with strawberries, onion, cheese and walnuts. Drizzle with vinaigrette.

Caramelized Grapefruit Salad

PREP/TOTAL TIME: 25 MIN. • YIELD: 4 SERVINGS

Grapefruit segments are treated to a slight caramelization in a hot skillet just before topping this colorful salad. It's finished with a light honey mustard dressing, bacon and avocado.

Maria Davis *Flower Mound, Texas*

- **⅓ cup pecan halves**
- **2 tablespoons plus ¼ cup sugar, divided**
- **1 medium grapefruit, peeled and cut into segments**
- **4 cups spring mix salad greens**
- **¾ cup chopped cucumber**
- **2 green onions, sliced**
- **½ medium ripe avocado, peeled and cubed**
- **2 bacon strips, cooked and crumbled**
- **3 tablespoons reduced-fat honey mustard salad dressing**
- **¼ teaspoon coarsely ground pepper**

1 In a small nonstick skillet over medium heat, cook and stir pecans and 2 tablespoons sugar for 2-4 minutes or until sugar is melted. Spread on foil to cool.

2 Coat grapefruit segments with remaining sugar. Coat the same skillet with cooking spray; cook grapefruit over medium heat for 2-3 minutes on each side or until browned.

3 In a large bowl, combine the salad greens, cucumber, onions, avocado and bacon. Drizzle with salad dressing and toss to coat.

4 Divide salad among four serving plates. Top with grapefruit and pecans; sprinkle with pepper.

Balsamic Arugula Salad 

PREP/TOTAL TIME: 5 MIN. • YIELD: 4 SERVINGS

With four simple ingredients, this arugula salad comes together in a flash and makes a sophisticated side.

Lisa Speer *Palm Beach, Florida*

- **6 cups fresh arugula or baby spinach**
- **½ cup cherry tomatoes, halved**
- **¼ cup grated Parmesan cheese**
- **¼ cup balsamic vinaigrette**

1 In a large bowl, combine the arugula, tomatoes and cheese. Drizzle with the vinaigrette; toss to coat. Serve immediately.

Confetti Jicama Salad

PREP: 35 MIN. + CHILLING • YIELD: 6 SERVINGS

I love jicama dipped in citrus and sprinkled with salt and jalapenos, so I created this salad with the same flavors.

Jan Lysak-Ruiz *Yucaipa, California*

- **½ medium jicama, peeled and julienned**
- **1⅓ cups julienned seedless cucumber**
- **1 each small sweet red, orange and yellow pepper, julienned**
- **½ cup thinly sliced red onion**
- **3 green onions, chopped**

DRESSING:

- **⅓ cup minced fresh cilantro**
- **1 jalapeno pepper, seeded and finely chopped**
- **2 tablespoons lime juice**
- **2 tablespoons orange juice concentrate**
- **2 tablespoons olive oil**
- **1 garlic clove, minced**
- **1 teaspoon sugar**
- **½ teaspoon salt**
- **¼ teaspoon pepper**
- **⅛ teaspoon cayenne pepper**

1 In a large bowl, combine the jicama, cucumber, peppers and onions.

2 In a small bowl, whisk the cilantro, jalapeno, lime juice, juice concentrate, oil, garlic and seasonings. Pour over salad; toss to coat. Cover and refrigerate for at least 1 hour. Stir before serving.

EDITOR'S NOTE: Wear disposable gloves when cutting hot peppers; the oils can burn skin. Avoid touching your face.

Spinach Souffle

PREP: 20 MIN. • BAKE: 35 MIN. • YIELD: 6 SERVINGS

You just can't make an easier, more delicious side dish than this. It's great with beef, pork and lamb, and I especially like serving it for a festive meal like New Year's Eve.

Bette Duffy *Kenmore, Washington*

- **2 packages (10 ounces each) frozen chopped spinach, thawed and squeezed dry**
- **1 package (8 ounces) cream cheese, cubed**
- **1½ cups (6 ounces) shredded Monterey Jack cheese**
- **4 eggs, lightly beaten**
- **¼ cup butter, melted**
- **1 garlic clove, minced**
- **½ teaspoon salt**

1 In a large bowl, combine all ingredients. Transfer to a greased 1½-qt. baking dish. Bake at 350° for 35-40 minutes or until edges are lightly browned.

THAWING FROZEN SPINACH

>> When a recipe calls for frozen spinach, thawed and squeezed dry, use a salad spinner. It makes it easy to get rid of the excess water—and gives your hands a welcome break!

Blue Cheese Bread Pudding

PREP: 30 MIN. + STANDING • BAKE: 40 MIN. + STANDING • YIELD: 12 SERVINGS

You can play with the flavor of this recipe by changing the type of blue cheese you use, from sharp Stilton to saltier Gorgonzola.

Crystal Bruns *Iliff, Colorado*

- **¼ cup butter, cubed**
- **1 medium onion, chopped**
- **3 garlic cloves, minced**
- **2 French bread baguettes (10½ ounces each), cut into 1-inch cubes**
- **4 cups (16 ounces) crumbled blue cheese**
- **5 eggs**
- **5 egg yolks**
- **3 cups heavy whipping cream**
- **1 teaspoon salt**
- **½ teaspoon pepper**

1 In a small skillet over medium heat, melt butter. Add onion; cook and stir until softened. Reduce heat to medium-low; cook, stirring occasionally, for 20 minutes or until onion is golden brown. Add garlic; cook 2 minutes longer.

2 Place half of the bread in a greased 13-in. x 9-in. baking dish. Layer with onion mixture and half of blue cheese. Top with remaining bread and blue cheese.

3 In a large bowl, whisk the eggs, egg yolks, cream, salt and pepper. Pour over bread; let stand for 15 minutes or until bread is softened.

4 Bake, uncovered, at 375° for 40-45 minutes or until a knife inserted near the center comes out clean. Let stand 10 minutes before serving. Serve warm.

Asian Quinoa

PREP: 20 MIN. • COOK: 20 MIN. + STANDING
YIELD: 4 SERVINGS

I love to cook and come up with new recipes. I serve this dish at least once a month and sometimes more. For a different twist, I'll occasionally add a scrambled egg or use soy sauce instead of the rice vinegar.

Sonya Labbe *West Hollywood, California*

- **1 cup water**
- **2 tablespoons rice vinegar**
- **2 tablespoons plum sauce**
- **2 garlic cloves, minced**
- **1 teaspoon minced fresh gingerroot**
- **1 teaspoon sesame oil**
- **¼ teaspoon salt**
- **¼ teaspoon crushed red pepper flakes**
- **½ cup quinoa, rinsed**
- **1 medium sweet red pepper, chopped**
- **½ cup sliced water chestnuts, chopped**
- **½ cup fresh sugar snap peas, trimmed and halved**
- **2 green onions, thinly sliced**

1 In a large saucepan, combine the first eight ingredients; bring to a boil. Add quinoa. Reduce heat; cover and simmer for 12-15 minutes or until water is absorbed.

2 Remove from the heat. Add the red pepper, water chestnuts, peas and onions; fluff with a fork. Cover and let stand for 10 minutes.

EDITOR'S NOTE: Look for quinoa in the cereal, rice or organic food aisle.

Quinoa and Black Bean Salad

PREP: 20 MIN. • COOK: 15 MIN. • YIELD: 8 SERVINGS

This good-for-you dish can be served either cold as a salad side dish for eight people or warm as an entree for four people. The Lime Vinaigrette adds a punch of flavor.

Yvonne Compton *Elkton, Oregon*

- **1 cup vegetable broth**
- **1 cup water**
- **1 cup quinoa, rinsed**
- **1 medium sweet orange pepper, chopped**
- **1 small red onion, chopped**
- **1 garlic clove, minced**
- **1 can (15 ounces) black beans, rinsed and drained**
- **1 cup frozen corn, thawed**
- **2 cups cherry tomatoes, halved**
- **¼ cup olive oil**
- **2 tablespoons lime juice**
- **1 teaspoon balsamic vinegar**
- **½ teaspoon salt**
- **¼ teaspoon pepper**
- **¼ teaspoon chili powder**
- **1 medium ripe avocado, peeled and cubed**
- **2 tablespoons minced fresh cilantro**

1 In a small saucepan, bring broth and water to a boil. Add quinoa. Reduce heat; cover and simmer for 12-16 minutes or until liquid is absorbed. Remove from the heat; fluff with a fork.

2 In a large nonstick skillet coated with cooking spray, cook the orange pepper, onion and garlic for 2 minutes. Stir in beans and corn; cook 2-3 minutes longer or until onion is tender. Remove from the heat; cool for 5 minutes. Stir in the tomatoes.

3 In a small bowl, whisk the oil, lime juice, vinegar, salt, pepper and chili powder. Pour over tomato mixture; toss to coat.

4 Spoon quinoa onto a serving platter. Top with tomato mixture, avocado and cilantro.

EDITOR'S NOTE: Look for quinoa in the cereal, rice or organic food aisle.

Curried Egg Lettuce Cups

PREP: 20 MIN. + CHILLING • YIELD: 6 SERVINGS

Guests will love the combination of crisp, cold lettuce leaves and flavorful egg salad. Peanuts add crunchy texture to the dish that makes it even more fun to eat.

Patricia Nieh *Portola Valley, California*

- **4 ounces cream cheese, softened**
- **¼ cup sour cream**
- **2 teaspoons curry powder**
- **¼ teaspoon salt**
- **6 hard-cooked eggs, chopped**
- **¼ cup finely chopped green pepper**
- **¼ cup finely chopped green onions**
- **4 tablespoons chopped salted peanuts, divided**
- **6 Bibb or Boston lettuce leaves**
- **½ cup mango chutney**

1 In a large bowl, combine the first four ingredients. Stir in the eggs, pepper and onions. Cover and refrigerate for at least 1 hour.

2 Just before serving, stir in 3 tablespoons peanuts. Place a rounded ⅓ cupful on each lettuce leaf. Top with chutney; sprinkle with remaining peanuts.

Strawberry & Pecan Salad

PREP/TOTAL TIME: 30 MIN. • YIELD: 8 SERVINGS

Sweet strawberries and crunchy pecans make this salad a guaranteed crowd-pleaser. I never bring leftovers home.

Sharon Meyer *Fulton, Missouri*

- **⅓ cup canola oil**
- **¼ cup plus 3 tablespoons sugar, divided**
- **2 tablespoons white vinegar**
- **2 tablespoons grated onion**
- **½ teaspoon ground mustard**
- **¼ teaspoon salt**
- **½ cup pecan halves**
- **2 heads leaf lettuce, torn**
- **1 cup sliced fresh strawberries**
- **½ cup shredded Monterey Jack cheese**
- **⅓ cup sunflower kernels**

1 In a small bowl, whisk the oil, ¼ cup sugar, vinegar, onion, mustard and salt until sugar is completely dissolved; set aside.

2 Place pecans in a small heavy skillet. Cook over medium heat for 1-2 minutes until nuts are toasted. Sprinkle with remaining sugar. Cook and stir for 2-4 minutes or until sugar is melted. Spread on foil to cool. Break apart.

3 In a large serving bowl, combine the lettuce, strawberries, cheese, sunflower kernels and sugared pecans. Drizzle with vinaigrette; toss to coat.

South-of-the-Border Caprese Salad

30 min.

PREP/TOTAL TIME: 30 MIN.
YIELD: 6 SERVINGS (1 CUP DRESSING)

Plump heirloom tomatoes star in this garden-fresh medley, topped with a sweet-tart dressing and crumbled cheese.

Kathleen Merkley *Layton, Utah*

CILANTRO VINAIGRETTE:

- **⅓ cup white wine vinegar**
- **½ cup fresh cilantro leaves**
- **3 tablespoons sugar**
- **1 jalapeno pepper, seeded and chopped**
- **1 garlic clove, peeled and quartered**
- **¾ teaspoon salt**
- **⅔ cup olive oil**

SALAD:

- **4 cups torn mixed salad greens**
- **3 large heirloom or other tomatoes, sliced**
- **½ cup crumbled queso fresco or diced part-skim mozzarella cheese**
- **¼ teaspoon salt**
- **⅛ teaspoon pepper**
- **1½ teaspoons fresh cilantro leaves**

1 In a blender, combine the first six ingredients. While processing, gradually add oil in a steady stream.

2 Arrange greens on a serving platter; top with tomatoes. Sprinkle with cheese, salt and pepper.

3 Just before serving, drizzle salad with ½ cup dressing; garnish with cilantro leaves. Refrigerate leftover dressing.

EDITOR'S NOTE: Wear disposable gloves when cutting hot peppers; the oils can burn skin. Avoid touching your face.

Antipasto Picnic Salad

PREP: 30 MIN. • COOK: 15 MIN.
YIELD: 25 SERVINGS (1 CUP EACH)

With a tempting blend of meats, veggies and pasta, how can you go wrong? The recipe goes together in no time, has easily adjustable ingredients for any crowd and tastes as good at room temperature as it does chilled.

Michele Larson *Baden, Pennsylvania*

- **1 package (16 ounces) medium pasta shells**
- **2 jars (16 ounces each) giardiniera**
- **1 pound fresh broccoli florets**
- **½ pound cubed part-skim mozzarella cheese**
- **½ pound hard salami, cubed**
- **½ pound deli ham, cubed**
- **2 packages (3½ ounces each) sliced pepperoni, halved**
- **1 large green pepper, cut into chunks**
- **1 can (6 ounces) pitted ripe olives, drained**

DRESSING:

- **½ cup olive oil**
- **¼ cup red wine vinegar**
- **2 tablespoons lemon juice**
- **1 teaspoon Italian seasoning**
- **1 teaspoon coarsely ground pepper**
- **½ teaspoon salt**

1 Cook pasta according to package directions. Meanwhile, drain giardiniera, reserving ¾ cup liquid. In a large bowl, combine the giardiniera, broccoli, mozzarella, salami, ham, pepperoni, green pepper and olives. Drain pasta and rinse in cold water; stir into meat mixture.

2 For dressing, in a small bowl, whisk the oil, vinegar, lemon juice, Italian seasoning, pepper, salt and reserved giardiniera liquid. Pour over salad and toss to coat. Refrigerate until serving.

EDITOR'S NOTE: Giardiniera, a pickled vegetable mixture, is available in mild and hot varieties and can be found in the Italian or pickle section of your grocery store.

Baked German Potato Salad

PREP: 50 MIN. • BAKE: 30 MIN. • YIELD: 8-10 SERVINGS

What makes this German potato salad so different is that it's sweet instead of tangy. During the holidays, my family has an annual ham dinner, and I always prepare it. In fact, it's so popular I usually make a double batch!

Julie Myers *Lexington, Ohio*

- **12 medium red potatoes (about 3 pounds)**
- **8 bacon strips**
- **2 medium onions, chopped**
- **¾ cup packed brown sugar**
- **⅔ cup water, divided**
- **⅓ cup white vinegar**
- **⅓ cup sweet pickle juice**
- **2 teaspoons dried parsley flakes**
- **1 teaspoon salt**
- **½ to ¾ teaspoon celery seed**
- **4½ teaspoons all-purpose flour**

1 In a saucepan, cook potatoes until just tender; drain. Peel and slice into an ungreased 2-qt. baking dish; set aside.

2 In a skillet, cook bacon until crisp; drain, reserving 2 tablespoons drippings. Crumble bacon and set aside. Saute onions in drippings until tender. Stir in the brown sugar, ½ cup water, vinegar, pickle juice, parsley, salt and celery seed. Simmer, uncovered, for 5-10 minutes.

3 Meanwhile, combine flour and remaining water until smooth; stir into onion mixture. Bring to a boil. Cook and stir for 2 minutes or until thickened. Pour over potatoes. Add bacon; gently stir to coat. Bake, uncovered, at 350° for 30 minutes or until heated through.

Calico Cranberry Couscous Salad

PREP/TOTAL TIME: 20 MIN.
YIELD: 6 SERVINGS

A simple homemade Dijon dressing jazzes up couscous, dried cranberries and green onions.

Rosemarie Matheus *Germantown, Wisconsin*

- **1 cup water**
- **¾ cup uncooked couscous**
- **½ cup dried cranberries**
- **½ cup chopped celery**
- **½ cup shredded carrot**
- **¼ cup chopped green onions**
- **¼ cup slivered almonds, toasted**

DRESSING:

- **3 tablespoons red wine vinegar**
- **1 tablespoon olive oil**
- **1 tablespoon Dijon mustard**
- **¼ teaspoon salt**
- **¼ teaspoon pepper**

1 In a small saucepan, bring water to a boil. Stir in couscous; cover and remove from the heat. Let stand for 5 minutes. Fluff with a fork; cool.

2 In a serving bowl, combine the couscous, cranberries, celery, carrot, onions and almonds.

3 In a small bowl, whisk the dressing ingredients. Pour over salad; toss to coat. Serve at room temperature or chilled.

Potato and Mushroom Gratin

PREP: 20 MIN. • BAKE: 55 MIN.
YIELD: 8 SERVINGS

Rich, cheesy and indulgent, this creamy recipe is laced with wine and makes a perfect take-along side dish for potlucks or open houses.

Laurie LaClair *North Richland Hills, Texas*

- **2 jars (4½ ounces each) sliced mushrooms, drained**
- **3 shallots, finely chopped**
- **1 tablespoon olive oil**
- **2 tablespoons Marsala wine**
- **3 large potatoes (about 1½ pounds), peeled and thinly sliced**
- **1 cup (4 ounces) shredded Swiss cheese**
- **½ cup shredded Parmesan cheese**
- **2 tablespoons minced fresh basil or 2 teaspoons dried basil**
- **1½ cups heavy whipping cream**
- **1 tablespoon butter, cubed**
- **⅛ teaspoon salt**
- **⅛ teaspoon pepper**

1 In a large skillet, saute mushrooms and shallots in oil until tender. Add wine; cook and stir for 2 minutes.

2 Arrange a third of the potatoes in a greased 10-in. round shallow baking dish. Layer with half of the mushroom mixture, cheeses, basil and another third of potatoes. Repeat layers. Pour cream over top. Dot with butter; sprinkle with salt and pepper.

3 Bake, uncovered, at 350° for 55-65 minutes or until potatoes are tender.

Orzo with Spinach and Pine Nuts

PREP: 10 MIN. • COOK: 25 MIN. • YIELD: 12 SERVINGS (¾ CUP EACH)

I have shared this salad many times with the teachers at my school. They enjoy it so much that they request it. It's best to put the tomatoes on the salad just before serving so they won't wilt from the heat and moisture. In my opinion, the dish wouldn't be as tasty if you substituted another vinegar for the balsamic vinegar.

Kate Whitehead *Lindenhurst, Illinois*

- **1 package (16 ounces) orzo pasta**
- **1 cup pine nuts**
- **1 garlic clove, minced**
- **½ teaspoon dried basil**
- **½ teaspoon crushed red pepper flakes**
- **¼ cup olive oil**
- **1 tablespoon butter**
- **2 packages (6 ounces each) fresh baby spinach**
- **1 teaspoon salt**
- **¼ teaspoon pepper**
- **¼ cup balsamic vinegar**
- **2 cups (8 ounces) crumbled feta cheese**
- **1 large tomato, finely chopped**

1 In a large saucepan, cook pasta according to package directions.

2 Meanwhile, in a Dutch oven over medium heat, cook the pine nuts, garlic, basil and pepper flakes in oil and butter just until nuts are lightly browned.

3 Add the spinach, salt and pepper; cook and stir 4-5 minutes longer or just until spinach is wilted. Transfer to a large bowl.

4 Drain pasta. Stir into spinach mixture. Drizzle with vinegar; sprinkle with cheese and tomato.

Cilantro Couscous Salad 

PREP/TOTAL TIME: 25 MIN.
YIELD: 12 SERVINGS (⅔ CUP EACH)

Since this serves 12, I always make it for potlucks, where it's always appreciated. My 11-year-old daughter likes it so much we served it at her birthday tea party.

Cindy Gifford *Cedar City, Utah*

- **1 package (10 ounces) couscous**
- **1 medium cucumber, finely chopped**
- **2 medium tomatoes, seeded and finely chopped**
- **⅔ cup minced fresh cilantro**
- **⅓ cup olive oil**
- **¼ cup lemon juice**
- **3 garlic cloves, minced**
- **1 package (8 ounces) feta cheese, crumbled**

1 Prepare couscous according to package directions; let cool to room temperature.

2 In a large serving bowl, combine the cucumber, tomatoes, cilantro and couscous. In a small bowl, whisk the oil, lemon juice and garlic. Drizzle over salad; toss to coat. Add cheese and toss gently to combine. Chill until serving.

Cowboy Baked Beans

PREP: 25 MIN. • BAKE: 50 MIN
YIELD: 12 SERVINGS (¾ CUP EACH)

Baked beans are a perennial favorite at barbecues and potlucks. My meaty recipe uses a variety of beans and has a great smoky taste.

Joe Sherwood *Tryon, Nebraska*

- **1 pound ground beef**
- **1 pound bacon, cooked and crumbled**
- **2 cups barbecue sauce**
- **1 can (16 ounces) butter beans, rinsed and drained**
- **1 can (15¾ ounces) pork and beans**
- **1 can (15½ ounces) navy beans, rinsed and drained**
- **1 can (15 ounces) black beans, rinsed and drained**
- **2 medium onions, chopped**
- **¼ cup packed brown sugar**
- **¼ cup molasses**
- **2 tablespoons balsamic vinegar**
- **2 teaspoons ground mustard**
- **2 teaspoons Worcestershire sauce**
- **1 teaspoon salt**
- **1 teaspoon garlic powder**
- **1 teaspoon pepper**

1 In a Dutch oven, cook beef over medium heat until no longer pink; drain. Stir in the remaining ingredients. Transfer to a greased 13-in. x 9-in. baking dish. Bake, uncovered, at 350° for 50-60 minutes or until heated through.

Fiesta Grilled Corn

PREP: 25 MIN. + SOAKING • GRILL: 25 MIN.
YIELD: 6 SERVINGS

We love Mexican food and corn on the cob, so I combined them into something fresh and spicy. For Italian flair, I make this corn with basil and oregano butter and Parmesan cheese.

MacKenzie Severson *Germantown, Maryland*

- **½ cup butter, softened**
- **¼ cup minced fresh cilantro**
- **2 teaspoons grated lime peel**
- **½ teaspoon garlic powder**
- **6 large ears sweet corn in husks**
- **½ cup mayonnaise**
- **1 tablespoon chili powder**
- **½ teaspoon paprika**
- **½ cup queso fresco or fresh goat cheese, crumbled**

1 In a small bowl, combine the butter, cilantro, lime peel and garlic powder. Shape into a log; wrap in plastic wrap. Refrigerate for 30 minutes or until firm.

2 Carefully peel back corn husks to within 1 in. of bottoms; remove silk. Place in a Dutch oven; cover with cold water. Soak for 20 minutes; drain. In a small bowl, combine the mayonnaise, chili powder and paprika. Spread over corn. Rewrap corn in husks and secure with kitchen string.

3 Grill corn, covered, over medium heat for 25-30 minutes or until tender, turning often. Serve with butter slices and sprinkle with cheese.

Summer Bounty Potato Salad

PREP: 35 MIN. • COOK 25 MIN. + CHILLING
YIELD: 20 SERVINGS (¾ CUP EACH)

A parent from a school where I previously taught gave me this recipe, and I think of her every time I make this potato salad. It's dressed in a fresh basil vinaigrette.

Dee Dee Calow *Warren, Illinois*

- **3 pounds small red potatoes, quartered**
- **1 pound fresh green beans, trimmed and cut in half**
- **⅓ cup olive oil**
- **¼ cup red wine vinegar**
- **¼ cup minced fresh basil**
- **2 tablespoons minced fresh parsley**
- **1½ teaspoons salt**
- **½ teaspoon pepper**
- **6 hard-cooked eggs, sliced**
- **1 cup grape tomatoes**

1 Place potatoes in a large saucepan and cover with water. Bring to a boil. Reduce heat; cover and cook for 4 minutes. Stir in beans; cover and cook 10-12 minutes longer or vegetables are tender. Drain.

2 In a small bowl, whisk the oil, vinegar, basil, parsley, salt and pepper. Pour over potato mixture; toss to coat. Cover and refrigerate for at least 1 hour.

3 Stir before serving; top with eggs and tomatoes.

Garden Mashed Potatoes

PREP: 20 MIN. • COOK: 15 MIN.
YIELD: 8 SERVINGS

Here is a great way to perk up mashed potatoes. With lots of veggies and full flavor, it will be a delectable complement to many meals.

Brenda Budler *Chadron, Nebraska*

- **1 pound medium Yukon Gold potatoes, cubed**
- **1 pound medium red potatoes, cubed**
- **1 pound medium carrots, chopped**
- **4 garlic cloves, peeled and halved**
- **1 jalapeno pepper, seeded and chopped**
- **¼ cup butter, cubed**
- **½ teaspoon salt**
- **¼ teaspoon pepper**
- **1½ cups frozen white corn, thawed**
- **½ cup shredded Monterey Jack cheese**

1 Place the potatoes, carrots, garlic and jalapeno in a large saucepan; cover with water. Bring to a boil. Reduce heat; cover and cook for 15-20 minutes or until tender. Drain.

2 Mash vegetables with butter, salt and pepper; stir in corn and cheese.

EDITOR'S NOTE: Wear disposable gloves when cutting hot peppers; the oils can burn skin. Avoid touching your face.

Herbed Garlic Potatoes

PREP/TOTAL TIME: 30 MIN. • YIELD: 8 SERVINGS

My mom cooks from scratch and rarely uses a recipe. That's how I learned to use a pinch of this, a dash of that. But it was actually my dad who invented these mouthwatering potatoes. The spuds fit any kind of meal—from fancy to burgers—and becomes a favorite of all who try them.

Sherry DesJardin *Fairbanks, Alaska*

- **15 small red potatoes (about 2 pounds), cut in half**
- **⅓ cup butter**
- **¼ cup minced fresh parsley**
- **2 tablespoons minced chives**
- **1½ teaspoons minced fresh tarragon or ½ teaspoon dried tarragon**
- **2 to 3 garlic cloves, minced**
- **3 bacon strips, cooked and crumbled**
- **½ teaspoon salt**
- **¼ teaspoon pepper**

1 Place potatoes in a large saucepan and cover with water. Bring to a boil. Reduce heat; cover and cook for 15-20 minutes or until tender. Drain well.

2 In a large skillet, melt butter. Add the parsley, chives, tarragon and garlic; cook and stir over low heat for 1-2 minutes. Add the potatoes, bacon, salt and pepper; toss to coat. Cook until heated through, about 5 minutes.

Blueberry Spinach Salad

30 min

PREP/TOTAL TIME: 10 MIN.
YIELD: 8 SERVINGS

I came up with this recipe while trying to use up blueberries that I didn't want to go to waste. The combination of flavors and textures is delightful.

Jan Lysak-Ruiz *Yucaipa, California*

- **½ cup olive oil**
- **¼ cup white balsamic vinegar**
- **2 teaspoons Dijon mustard**
- **1 teaspoon sugar**
- **¼ teaspoon salt**
- **1 package (10 ounces) fresh spinach, trimmed**
- **1 cup (4 ounces) crumbled feta cheese**
- **1 cup fresh blueberries**
- **½ cup pine nuts, toasted**

1 Place the first five ingredients in a jar with a tight-fitting lid; shake well. Refrigerate until serving.

2 In a large bowl, combine the spinach, cheese, blueberries and nuts. Just before serving, shake dressing and drizzle over salad; toss to coat.

Au Gratin Potatoes with Green Chilies

PREP: 50 MIN. • BAKE: 40 MIN.
YIELD: 13 SERVINGS (3/4 CUP EACH)

These cheesy and zippy potatoes are quite popular at holiday meals and potlucks. I like to serve them with my trademark holiday ham.

Cathy Rau *Newport, Oregon*

- **8 medium Yukon Gold potatoes (about 4 pounds), peeled and cut into 1/4-inch slices**
- **1 small onion, thinly sliced**
- **1 tablespoon butter**
- **1 tablespoon olive oil**
- **1/4 cup all-purpose flour**
- **1 teaspoon salt**
- **1 teaspoon pepper**
- **1 can (14 1/2 ounces) chicken broth**
- **3/4 cup 2% milk**
- **3/4 cup half-and-half cream**
- **2 cans (4 ounces each) chopped green chilies**
- **1 cup (4 ounces) shredded cheddar cheese**
- **1 cup (4 ounces) shredded Swiss cheese**
- **1/2 cup plus 2 tablespoons shredded Parmesan cheese divided**
- **1 teaspoon Dijon mustard**
- **1/2 teaspoon garlic powder**
- **3 to 4 drops hot pepper sauce**

Dash ground nutmeg

1 Place potatoes in a Dutch oven; cover with water. Bring to a boil. Cover and cook for 2-3 minutes. Drain and pat dry; set aside.

2 In a large saucepan, saute onion in butter and oil until tender. Stir in the flour, salt and pepper until blended. Gradually stir in the broth, milk and cream. Bring to a boil; cook and stir for 2-3 minutes or until thickened.

3 Stir in the chilies, cheddar cheese, Swiss cheese, 1/2 cup Parmesan cheese, mustard, garlic powder, pepper sauce and nutmeg until cheese is melted.

4 In a greased 13-in. x 9-in. baking dish, arrange half of the potatoes and cheese sauce. Repeat (dish will be full).

5 Cover and bake at 350° for 30 minutes. Uncover; sprinkle with remaining Parmesan cheese. Bake 10-15 minutes longer or until potatoes are tender and top is lightly browned. Let stand for 5 minutes before serving.

WINNERS CIRCLE

soups & chilis

Warm up on a chilly winter evening or cool down on a hot summer day with these must-try soups and chilis. Have your stockpot (or slow cooker) ready... your soup cravings are about to begin.

PEPPERONI PIZZA CHILI, 47

Pea Soup with Mushroom Cream Sauce

PREP: 25 MIN. • COOK: 15 MIN. • YIELD: 6 SERVINGS

Fresh garden peas combine with a hint of basil for a delightfully light spring soup. A unique mushroom drizzle adds extra depth to this beautiful creation.

Sally Sibthorpe *Shelby Township, Michigan*

- **½ pound sliced baby portobello mushrooms, divided**
- **1 tablespoon butter**
- **¼ cup chopped onion**
- **1 garlic clove, minced**
- **½ cup half-and-half cream**
- **3 tablespoons sherry or reduced-sodium chicken broth**
- **1 tablespoon minced fresh thyme or 1 teaspoon dried thyme**
- **¾ teaspoon salt, divided**
- **5 cups fresh or frozen peas, divided**
- **3 cups reduced-sodium chicken broth**
- **2 tablespoons lemon juice**
- **4½ teaspoons minced fresh basil or 1½ teaspoons dried basil**

1 Set aside 3 tablespoons mushrooms for garnish. In a large skillet, saute remaining mushrooms in butter until tender.

2 Add onion to skillet; saute until tender. Add garlic; cook 1 minute longer. Stir in the cream, sherry, thyme and ¼ teaspoon salt. Bring to a boil. Reduce heat; simmer, uncovered, for 2 minutes. Cool slightly. Transfer to a blender; process until smooth. Set aside.

3 In a Dutch oven, combine 4½ cups peas, chicken broth and remaining salt. Bring to a boil. Reduce heat; simmer, uncovered, for 4 minutes or until peas are tender. Stir in lemon juice and basil; heat through. Transfer to a blender; process in batches until blended.

4 Ladle soup into serving bowls; top with mushroom cream sauce. Garnish with reserved mushrooms and remaining peas.

Pepperoni Pizza Chili

PREP: 20 MIN. • COOK: 30 MIN. • YIELD: 12 SERVINGS (3 QUARTS)

Pizza and chili go together like Monday night and football in this must-try game food that really delivers at halftime.

Jennifer Gelormino *Pittsburgh, Pennsylvania*

- **2 pounds ground beef**
- **1 pound bulk hot Italian sausage**
- **1 large onion, chopped**
- **1 large green pepper, chopped**
- **4 garlic cloves, minced**
- **1 jar (16 ounces) salsa**
- **1 can (16 ounces) hot chili beans, undrained**
- **1 can (16 ounces) kidney beans, rinsed and drained**
- **1 can (12 ounces) pizza sauce**
- **1 package (8 ounces) sliced pepperoni, halved**
- **1 cup water**
- **2 teaspoons chili powder**
- **½ teaspoon salt**
- **½ teaspoon pepper**
- **3 cups (12 ounces) shredded part-skim mozzarella cheese**

1 In a Dutch oven, cook the beef, sausage, onion, green pepper and garlic over medium heat until meat is no longer pink; drain.

2 Stir in the salsa, beans, pizza sauce, pepperoni, water, chili powder, salt and pepper. Bring to a boil. Reduce heat; cover and simmer for 20 minutes or until heated through. Sprinkle servings with cheese.

30 min.

Chicken Tortilla Chowder

PREP/TOTAL TIME: 20 MIN.
YIELD: 8-10 SERVINGS (2½ QUARTS)

As a student attending college full-time, I find my time in the kitchen is limited. This recipe helps me have a hot meal on the table when my husband gets home. He's a real meat-and-potatoes man, but he absolutely loves this thick, creamy chowder with tortilla strips that puff up like homemade noodles.

Jennifer Gouge *Lubbock, Texas*

- **1 can (14½ ounces) chicken broth**
- **1 can (10¾ ounces) condensed cream of chicken soup, undiluted**
- **1 can (10¾ ounces) condensed cream of potato soup, undiluted**
- **1½ cups milk**
- **2 cups cubed cooked chicken**
- **1 can (11 ounces) Mexicorn**
- **1 jar (4½ ounces) sliced mushrooms, drained**
- **1 can (4 ounces) chopped green chilies**
- **¼ cup thinly sliced green onions**
- **4 flour tortillas (6 to 7 inches), cut into ½-inch strips**
- **1½ cups (6 ounces) shredded cheddar cheese**

1 In a Dutch oven, combine the broth, soups and milk. Stir in the chicken, corn, mushrooms, chilies and onions. Bring to a boil. Add the tortilla strips. Reduce heat; simmer, uncovered, for 8-10 minutes or until heated through. Add cheese; stir just until melted. Serve immediately.

Golden Squash Soup

PREP: 35 MIN. • COOK: 30 MIN. + COOLING
YIELD: 12-14 SERVINGS (3½ QUARTS)

This special recipe from my mother-in-law is one that I enjoy making as part of our fall meals. The soup is so pretty that it dresses up the table. We especially enjoy it on crisp evenings.

Mary Ann Klein
Washington Township, New Jersey

- **3 leeks (white portion only), sliced**
- **4 medium carrots, chopped**
- **5 tablespoons butter**
- **3 pounds butternut squash, peeled and cubed**
- **6 cups chicken broth**
- **3 medium zucchini, peeled and sliced**
- **2 teaspoons salt**
- **½ teaspoon dried thyme**
- **¼ teaspoon white pepper**
- **1 cup half-and-half cream**
- **½ cup 2% milk**

Grated Parmesan cheese and chives, optional

1 In a Dutch oven, saute leeks and carrots in butter for 5 minutes, stirring occasionally. Add the squash, broth, zucchini, salt, thyme and pepper; bring to a boil. Reduce heat; cover and simmer for 30-35 minutes or until vegetables are tender. Cool until lukewarm.

2 In a blender, puree soup in small batches until smooth; return to pan. Stir in cream and milk; heat through (do not boil). Sprinkle with cheese and chives if desired.

Hot and Sour Soup

PREP: 20 MIN. • COOK: 25 MIN. • YIELD: 6 SERVINGS (ABOUT 2 QUARTS)

We've tried several recipes for this soup and couldn't find one that resembled the one we liked at a restaurant. So, I made my own and I must say it is on par with what you'll find when dining out. Regular or hot chili sauce can be used, according to taste.

Vera Leitow *Mancelona, Michigan*

- **¾ pound pork tenderloin, cut into 1½-inch x ¼-inch strips**
- **1 tablespoon olive oil**
- **½ pound sliced fresh mushrooms**
- **6 cups chicken broth**
- **¼ cup soy sauce**
- **2 tablespoons chili garlic sauce**
- **¾ teaspoon pepper**
- **1 package (14 ounces) extra-firm tofu, drained and cut into ¼-inch cubes**
- **1 can (8 ounces) bamboo shoots, drained**
- **1 can (8 ounces) sliced water chestnuts, drained**
- **½ cup white vinegar**
- **⅓ cup cornstarch**
- **⅓ cup cold water**
- **2 teaspoons sesame oil**

Finely chopped green onions

1 In a Dutch oven, brown pork in oil until no longer pink; remove meat and keep warm. Add mushrooms; saute until tender. Set aside and keep warm.

2 Add the broth, soy sauce, chili garlic sauce and pepper to the pan. Bring to a boil. Reduce heat; cover and simmer for 10 minutes. Return the meat and mushrooms to the pan. Stir in the tofu, bamboo shoots, water chestnuts and vinegar. Simmer, uncovered, for 10 minutes.

3 In a small bowl, combine cornstarch and water until smooth; gradually stir into soup. Bring to a boil; cook and stir for 2 minutes or until thickened. Remove from the heat; stir in sesame oil. Garnish servings with onions.

Chicken Chorizo Posole

PREP: 40 MIN. • COOK: 40 MIN. • YIELD: 9 SERVINGS

I first tasted posole while visiting a friend in Santa Fe. It was a revelation! I have since been experimenting with many versions, and this one has become a much-loved tradition for my family. The leftovers are fantastic!

Jennifer Beckman *Falls Church, Virginia*

- **1 pound tomatillos, husks removed, cut in half**
- **1 large onion, quartered**
- **2 jalapeno peppers, halved and seeded**
- **4 garlic cloves, peeled**
- **4 cups water**
- **1 cup reduced-sodium chicken broth**
- **1 whole garlic bulb, loose paper removed, cut in half**
- **5 whole cloves**
- **2 bay leaves**
- **2 boneless skinless chicken breast halves (6 ounces each)**
- **1 pound uncooked chorizo or bulk spicy pork sausage**
- **2 cans (15 ounces each) hominy, rinsed and drained**
- **3 teaspoons lime juice, divided**
- **1 teaspoon dried oregano**
- **1 teaspoon ground cumin**
- **½ teaspoon salt, divided**

SALSA:

- **1 cup minced fresh cilantro, divided**
- **1 medium mango, peeled and cubed**
- **1 medium ripe avocado, peeled and cubed**
- **5 radishes, chopped**

GARNISH:

- **6 cups tortilla chips**

1 Place the tomatillos, onion, jalapenos and garlic cloves on a greased baking sheet. Bake at 425° for 25-30 minutes or until tomatillos are tender. Cool slightly. Transfer to a food processor; cover and process until blended.

2 In a Dutch oven, bring the water, broth, garlic bulb, cloves and bay leaves to a boil. Reduce heat; add chicken breasts and poach, uncovered, for 15-20 minutes or until no longer pink.

3 Remove chicken from broth and shred. Strain broth, discarding seasonings. Crumble chorizo into Dutch oven; cook over medium heat for 6-8 minutes or until fully cooked. Drain. Return broth to Dutch oven. Stir in the hominy, 2 teaspoons lime juice, oregano, cumin, ¼ teaspoon salt, tomatillo mixture and shredded chicken; heat through. Stir in ½ cup cilantro.

4 For salsa, in a small bowl, combine the mango, avocado, radishes and remaining cilantro, lime juice and salt. Serve with soup. Garnish with chips.

EDITOR'S NOTE: Wear disposable gloves when cutting hot peppers; the oils can burn skin. Avoid touching your face.

Tuscan Sausage and Potato Soup

PREP: 20 MIN. • COOK: 45 MIN.
YIELD: 10 SERVINGS (3¾ QUARTS)

This outstanding soup will be popular with the whole family. Though it looks special, it's actually quick to make. I like serving it with fresh hot rolls.

Lisa Sinicki *Erie, Pennsylvania*

- **1½ pounds bulk Italian sausage**
- **3 pounds potatoes, peeled and sliced**
- **3 cans (14½ ounces each) chicken broth**
- **2 cups water**
- **1 cup chopped sweet onion**
- **2 garlic cloves, minced**
- **¼ teaspoon salt**
- **⅛ teaspoon pepper**
- **3 cups chopped Swiss chard**
- **2 cups heavy whipping cream**
- **8 bacon strips, cooked and crumbled**

1 In a large skillet, cook sausage over medium heat until no longer pink. Drain; set aside.

2 In a Dutch oven, combine the potatoes, broth, water, onion, garlic, salt and pepper. Bring to a boil. Reduce heat; cover and simmer for 18-22 minutes or until potatoes are tender.

3 Stir in the Swiss chard, cream, bacon and sausage. Bring to a boil. Reduce heat; simmer, uncovered, for 5 to 10 minutes or until chard is tender.

BUYING AND STORING BACON

>> Check the date stamp on packages of vacuum-sealed bacon to make sure it's fresh. The date reflects the last date of sale. Once the package is opened, bacon should be used within a week.

Four-Onion Soup

PREP: 35 MIN. • COOK: 50 MIN. • YIELD: 6 SERVINGS

This mellow, rich-tasting onion soup is such a mainstay for our family that I felt compelled to share the recipe. Topped with toasted French bread and melted cheese, it's special to serve.

Margaret Adams *Pacific Grove, California*

- **1 medium yellow onion**
- **1 medium red onion**
- **1 medium leek (white portion only)**
- **5 green onions with tops**
- **1 garlic clove, minced**
- **2 tablespoons butter**
- **2 cans (14½ ounces each) beef broth**
- **1 can (10½ ounces) condensed beef consomme, undiluted**
- **1 teaspoon Worcestershire sauce**
- **½ teaspoon ground nutmeg**
- **1 cup (4 ounces) shredded Swiss cheese**
- **6 slices French bread (¾ inch thick), toasted**
- **6 tablespoons grated Parmesan cheese, optional**

1 Slice all onions and leek ¼ in. thick. In a large saucepan over medium-low heat, saute onions and garlic in butter for 15 minutes or until tender and golden, stirring occasionally. Add broth, consomme, Worcestershire sauce and nutmeg; bring to a boil. Reduce heat; cover and simmer for 30 minutes.

2 Sprinkle 1 tablespoon of Swiss cheese in the bottom of six oven-proof 8-oz. bowls. Ladle hot soup into bowls. Top each with a slice of bread. Sprinkle with remaining Swiss cheese and Parmesan cheese if desired.

3 Broil 6-8 in. from the heat or until cheese melts. Serve immediately.

Cheese Tortellini and Kale Soup

PREP: 30 MIN. • COOK: 45 MIN.
YIELD: 12 SERVINGS (3 QUARTS)

A steaming bowl of this hearty soup is always welcomed by both my family and neighbors. I often serve it when we get together during the cold months to watch football games. Add crusty bread to round out the meal.

Marlena Liimatainen *Denton, Maryland*

- **3 Italian sausage links (4 ounces each), sliced**
- **1 medium onion, finely chopped**
- **1 cup chopped fennel bulb**
- **4 garlic cloves, minced**
- **1½ teaspoons minced fresh thyme**
- **½ teaspoon crushed red pepper flakes**
- **2 tablespoons olive oil**
- **2 cartons (32 ounces each) reduced-sodium chicken broth**
- **1 cup water**
- **4 cups chopped fresh kale**
- **1 can (15 ounces) white kidney or cannellini beans, rinsed and drained**
- **1 package (9 ounces) refrigerated cheese tortellini**

1 In a large saucepan, cook the sausage, onion, fennel, garlic, thyme and pepper flakes in oil until sausage is no longer pink; drain. Add broth and water; bring to a boil.

2 Stir in kale and beans; return to a boil. Reduce heat; simmer, uncovered, until kale is tender. Add tortellini; simmer, uncovered, for 7-9 minutes or until tender.

Basil Tomato Soup With Orzo

PREP: 15 MIN. • COOK: 25 MIN.
YIELD: 16 SERVINGS (4½ QUARTS)

This soup is so scrumptious that it's worth the time it takes to cut up the fresh basil. I believe it is even better the next day, after the flavors have had a chance to blend in the refrigerator overnight.

Tonia Billbe *Elmira, New York*

- **1 large onion, chopped**
- **¼ cup butter, cubed**
- **2 garlic cloves, minced**
- **3 cans (28 ounces each) crushed tomatoes**
- **1 carton (32 ounces) chicken broth**
- **1 cup loosely packed basil leaves, chopped**
- **1 tablespoon sugar**
- **½ teaspoon pepper**
- **1¼ cups uncooked orzo pasta**
- **1 cup heavy whipping cream**
- **½ cup grated Romano cheese**

1 In a Dutch oven, saute onion in butter for 3 minutes. Add garlic; cook 1-2 minutes longer or until onion is tender. Stir in the tomatoes, broth, basil, sugar and pepper. Bring to a boil. Reduce heat; cover and simmer for 15 minutes.

2 Meanwhile, cook the orzo according to package directions; drain. Add orzo and cream to soup; heat through (do not boil). Sprinkle servings with cheese.

Mediterranean Chicken Soup

PREP: 25 MIN. • COOK: 40 MIN. • YIELD: 8 SERVINGS (2 QUARTS)

This is my go-to soup when I'm under the weather because it always makes me feel better. This filling dish is also delicious for lunch or dinner, even when you're feeling great.

Angie Pitts *Charleston, South Carolina*

- **1½ pounds boneless skinless chicken breasts, cut into ¾-inch cubes**
- **1 tablespoon Greek seasoning**
- **1 teaspoon pepper**
- **1 tablespoon olive oil**
- **4 green onions, thinly sliced**
- **1 garlic clove, minced**
- **¼ cup white wine or chicken broth**
- **7 cups reduced-sodium chicken broth**
- **¼ cup chopped sun-dried tomatoes (not packed in oil)**
- **¼ cup pitted Greek olives, sliced**
- **1 tablespoon capers, drained**
- **1½ teaspoons minced fresh basil or ½ teaspoon dried basil**
- **1½ teaspoons minced fresh oregano or ½ teaspoon dried oregano**
- **1½ cups uncooked orzo pasta**
- **2 tablespoons lemon juice**
- **1½ teaspoons minced fresh parsley**

1 Season chicken with Greek seasoning and pepper. In a Dutch oven, saute chicken in oil until no longer pink; remove and set aside. Add green onions and garlic to the pan; saute for 1 minute. Add wine, stirring to loosen browned bits from pan.

2 Stir in the broth, tomatoes, olives, capers, basil, oregano and chicken. Bring to a boil. Reduce heat; cover and simmer for 15 minutes. Return to a boil. Stir in orzo. Cook 8-10 minutes longer or until pasta is tender. Stir in lemon juice and parsley.

Roasted Tomato Soup

PREP: 30 MIN. • COOK: 30 MIN.
YIELD: 6 SERVINGS(1½ QUARTS)

Just before the first frost of the season, we gather up all of the tomatoes from my mom's garden to create this flavor-packed soup. Although it sounds like a lot of garlic, when it's roasted, the garlic becomes mellow and almost sweet. We serve this soup with toasted bread spread with pesto.

Kaitlyn Lerdahl *Madison, Wisconsin*

- **15 large tomatoes (5 pounds), seeded and quartered**
- **¼ cup plus 2 tablespoons canola oil, divided**
- **8 garlic cloves, minced**
- **1 large onion, chopped**
- **2 cups water**
- **1 teaspoon salt**
- **½ teaspoon crushed red pepper flakes, optional**
- **½ cup heavy whipping cream**

Fresh basil leaves, optional

1 Place tomatoes in a greased 15-in. x 10-in. x 1-in. baking pan. Combine ¼ cup oil and garlic; drizzle over tomatoes. Toss to coat. Bake at 400° for 15-20 minutes or until softened, stirring occasionally. Remove and discard skins.

2 Meanwhile, in a Dutch oven, saute onion in remaining oil until tender. Add the tomatoes, water, salt and pepper flakes if desired. Bring to a boil. Reduce heat; cover and simmer for 30 minutes or until flavors are blended. Cool slightly.

3 In a blender, process soup in batches until smooth. Stir in cream; heat through. Cool; transfer to freezer containers. Cover and freeze for up to 3 months.

TO USE FROZEN SOUP: Thaw in the refrigerator overnight. Place in a large saucepan; heat through. Garnish with basil if desired.

SAVING SUMMER'S BOUNTY

>> Put extra garden tomatoes in a plastic freezer bag and store in your freezer. To use in soup, stew or sauce, just hold the frozen tomatoes under warm water, and the skins will slip right off. Drop the whole skinless tomatoes into the pot—they'll break up during cooking, which also saves time chopping.

Crouton-Topped Garlic Soup

PREP: 20 MIN. • COOK: 1 HOUR • YIELD: 4 SERVINGS

Pan roasting the garlic gives this soup a rich flavor, while a touch of cream lends body. The herbed croutons enhance the soup's taste and add texture, but it's the freshly grated cheese that makes this dish taste like heaven!

Carolyn Kumpe *El Dorado, California*

- **20 garlic cloves, peeled**
- **1 tablespoon olive oil**
- **2 large onions, halved and sliced**
- **2 tablespoons butter**
- **2½ cups reduced-sodium chicken broth**
- **1 tablespoon minced fresh thyme or 1 teaspoon dried thyme**
- **1 bay leaf**
- **1 cup heavy whipping cream**

CROUTONS:

- **2 cups cubed sourdough bread, crusts removed**
- **2 tablespoons olive oil**
- **1 teaspoon minced fresh rosemary or ¼ teaspoon dried rosemary, crushed**
- **¼ teaspoon salt**
- **⅛ teaspoon pepper**

TOPPINGS:

- **½ cup shredded Gruyere or Swiss cheese**
- **2 tablespoons minced fresh parsley**

1 In a small skillet, cook garlic in oil over low heat for 3-5 minutes or until golden brown. Remove from the heat; set aside.

2 In a Dutch oven over medium-high heat, cook onions in butter until softened. Reduce heat to medium-low; cook, stirring occasionally, for 30 minutes or until deep golden brown. Add the broth, thyme, bay leaf and reserved garlic. Bring to a boil. Reduce heat; cover and simmer for 20 minutes to allow flavors to blend. Stir in cream; heat through. Discard bay leaf.

3 For croutons, place bread in a small bowl. Combine the oil, rosemary, salt and pepper; drizzle over bread and toss to coat. Place in an ungreased 15-in. x 10-in. x 1-in. baking pan. Bake at 400° for 15-20 minutes or until golden brown, stirring occasionally.

4 Divide soup among four bowls. Top with croutons, cheese and parsley.

Tomato Dill Soup

PREP/TOTAL TIME: 30 MIN. • YIELD: 4 SERVINGS (1 QUART)

Most often, I make this soup ahead and keep it in the fridge. It's particularly good to heat up and serve with tuna or grilled cheese sandwiches, hard rolls or a salad.

Patricia Kile *Elizabethtown, Pennsylvania*

- **1 medium onion, thinly sliced**
- **1 garlic clove, minced**
- **2 tablespoons canola oil**
- **1 tablespoon butter**
- **3 large tomatoes, sliced**
- **½ teaspoon salt**
- **Pinch pepper**
- **1 can (6 ounces) tomato paste**
- **¼ cup all-purpose flour**
- **2 cups water, divided**
- **¾ cup heavy whipping cream, whipped**
- **1 to 2 tablespoons finely minced fresh dill or 1 to 2 teaspoons dill weed**

1 In a large saucepan, saute onion and garlic in oil and butter until tender. Add the tomatoes, salt and pepper; cook over medium-high heat for 3 minutes or until heated through. Remove from the heat and stir in tomato paste.

2 In a small bowl, combine flour and ½ cup of water; stir until smooth. Stir into saucepan. Gradually stir in remaining water until smooth; bring to a boil over medium heat. Cook and stir for 2 minutes or until thickened.

3 Place mixture in a sieve over a large bowl. With the back of a spoon, press vegetables through the sieve to remove seeds and skin; return puree to pan. Add cream and dill; cook over low heat just until heated through (do not boil).

Creamy White Chili

PREP: 10 MIN. • COOK: 40 MIN. • YIELD: 7 SERVINGS

I got this wonderful recipe from my sister-in-law, who made a big batch and served a crowd one night. It was a hit. Plus, it's easy and quick, which is helpful since I'm a college student. In all my years of 4-H cooking, I've never had another dish get so many compliments.

Laura Brewer *Lafayette, Indiana*

- **1 pound boneless skinless chicken breasts, cut into ½-inch cubes**
- **1 medium onion, chopped**
- **1½ teaspoons garlic powder**
- **1 tablespoon canola oil**
- **2 cans (15½ ounces each) great northern beans, rinsed and drained**
- **1 can (14½ ounces) chicken broth**
- **2 cans (4 ounces each) chopped green chilies**
- **1 teaspoon salt**
- **1 teaspoon ground cumin**
- **1 teaspoon dried oregano**
- **½ teaspoon pepper**
- **¼ teaspoon cayenne pepper**
- **1 cup (8 ounces) sour cream**
- **½ cup heavy whipping cream**

1 In a large saucepan, saute the chicken, onion and garlic powder in oil until chicken is no longer pink. Add the beans, broth, chilies and seasonings. Bring to a boil. Reduce heat; simmer, uncovered, for 30 minutes.

2 Remove from the heat; stir in sour cream and whipping cream.

TEST KITCHEN TIP: You can make this using half-and-half cream instead of heavy cream with great success.

Curried Chicken Soup

PREP: 25 MIN. • COOK: 45 MIN. • YIELD: 8 SERVINGS

My German mother would occasionally cook dishes that were not traditional German recipes. One of my favorites was her Curried Chicken Soup. I've added my own touches to it, such as the chickpeas, coconut milk and fresh cilantro.

Deanna Hindenach *Paw Paw, Michigan*

- **4 teaspoons curry powder**
- **½ teaspoon salt**
- **½ teaspoon pepper**
- **½ teaspoon cayenne pepper**
- **1 pound boneless skinless chicken breasts, cut into 1-inch cubes**
- **3 medium carrots, chopped**
- **1 medium sweet red pepper, chopped**
- **1 small onion, chopped**
- **2 tablespoons olive oil**
- **1 garlic clove, minced**
- **1 can (15 ounces) garbanzo beans or chickpeas, rinsed and drained**
- **1 can (14½ ounces) chicken broth**
- **1 can (14½ ounces) diced tomatoes, drained**
- **1 cup water**
- **1 can (13.66 ounces) coconut milk**
- **¾ cup minced fresh cilantro**

1 In a large resealable plastic bag, combine the curry, salt, pepper and cayenne. Add chicken, a few pieces at a time, and shake to coat.

2 In a large saucepan over medium heat, cook the chicken, carrots, red pepper and onion in oil for 4 minutes. Add garlic; cook 1-2 minutes longer or until chicken is browned and vegetables are tender; drain.

3 Stir in the garbanzo beans, broth, tomatoes and water. Bring to a boil. Reduce heat; cover and simmer for 30 minutes. Stir in coconut milk; heat through. Garnish servings with cilantro.

Stuffing Dumpling Soup

PREP: 20 MIN. • COOK: 25 MIN. • YIELD: 5 SERVINGS

Stuffing adds delicious seasonings and flavor to this favorite day-after-Thanksgiving soup. It's a delicious way to use all those holiday leftovers.

Relina Shirley *Reno, Nevada*

- **1 cup sliced fresh mushrooms**
- **1 medium onion, chopped**
- **1 tablespoon olive oil**
- **3 garlic cloves, minced**
- **4 cups reduced-sodium chicken broth**
- **1½ cups chopped fresh carrots**
- **2 teaspoons Creole seasoning**
- **2 eggs**
- **½ cup all-purpose flour**
- **2 cups cooked stuffing**
- **2 cups cubed cooked turkey**
- **1½ cups cut fresh green beans**

1 In a Dutch oven, saute mushrooms and onion in oil until tender. Add garlic; cook 1 minute longer. Add the broth, carrots and Creole seasoning. Bring to a boil. Reduce heat; simmer, uncovered for 5-8 minutes or until carrots are tender.

2 Meanwhile, in a large bowl, whisk eggs and flour until smooth. Crumble stuffing over mixture; mix well. If necessary, add water, 1 teaspoon at a time, until mixture holds its shape.

3 Add the turkey and green beans; return to a boil. Drop stuffing mixture by heaping tablespoonfuls onto simmering soup. Cover and simmer for 8-10 minutes or until a toothpick inserted in a dumpling comes out clean (do not lift the cover while simmering).

EDITOR'S NOTE: The following spices may be substituted for 1 teaspoon Creole seasoning: ¼ teaspoon each salt, garlic powder and paprika; and a pinch each of dried thyme, ground cumin and cayenne pepper.

Sweet Potato Soup

PREP: 25 MIN. • COOK: 20 MIN. • YIELD: 8 SERVINGS (2 QUARTS)

Subtle ginger and peanut butter flavor make this dazzling orange soup unique. It has a mildly hot and spicy taste with an Asian flair.

Hilda Fallas *Kirkland, Washington*

- **1 large onion, chopped**
- **1 medium sweet red pepper, chopped**
- **2 medium carrots, chopped**
- **2 teaspoons canola oil**
- **1 teaspoon minced fresh gingerroot**
- **1 garlic clove, minced**
- **½ teaspoon cayenne pepper**
- **½ teaspoon coarsely ground pepper**
- **1 carton (32 ounces) plus 1 can (14½ ounces) reduced-sodium chicken broth**
- **1 can (14½ ounces) diced tomatoes, undrained**
- **1 large sweet potato, peeled and cubed**
- **⅔ cup creamy peanut butter**
- **2 teaspoons honey**
- **4 green onions, chopped**

1 In a large saucepan, saute the onion, red pepper and carrots in oil for 3 minutes. Stir in the ginger, garlic, cayenne and pepper; cook 2 minutes longer. Add the broth, tomatoes and sweet potato. Bring to a boil. Reduce heat; cover and simmer for 15-20 minutes or until potatoes are tender.

2 Cool slightly. In a blender, cover and process soup in batches until smooth. Return all to pan and heat through. Stir in peanut butter and honey. Cook and stir until peanut butter is melted. Garnish servings with green onions.

Harvest Squash Soup

PREP: 15 MIN. • COOK: 30 MIN.
YIELD: 10 SERVINGS (2½ QUARTS)

Hosting an autumn gathering? I recommend this hearty soup. The combination of squash, applesauce and spices gives it appealing flavor.

Mrs. H.L. Sosnowski *Grand Island, New York*

- **1½ cups chopped onions**
- **1 tablespoon vegetable oil**
- **4 cups mashed cooked butternut squash**
- **3 cups chicken broth**
- **2 cups unsweetened applesauce**
- **1½ cups milk**
- **1 bay leaf**
- **1 tablespoon sugar**
- **1 tablespoon lime juice**
- **1 teaspoon curry powder**
- **½ teaspoon salt, optional**
- **½ teaspoon ground cinnamon**
- **¼ teaspoon ground nutmeg**
- **¼ teaspoon pepper**

1 In a Dutch oven, saute onions in oil until tender. Add the remaining ingredients. Bring to a boil. Reduce heat; simmer, uncovered, for 30 minutes. Discard bay leaf before serving.

Hearty Split Pea Soup

PREP: 30 MIN. • COOK: 7 HOURS
YIELD: 6 SERVINGS (2¼ QUARTS)

Inspired by the reality show "Survivor," we started a 39-day Soup Challenge to eat healthier. We figured if "Survivor" contestants could last 39 days on so little food, surely we could survive on soup! This was a family favorite.

Debra Keil *Owasso, Oklahoma*

- **1 large onion, chopped**
- **1 cup chopped celery**
- **1 cup chopped fresh carrots**
- **1 teaspoon dried thyme**
- **2 tablespoons olive oil**
- **1 package (16 ounces) dried green split peas, rinsed**
- **4 cups vegetable broth**
- **2 cups water**
- **6 ounces Canadian bacon, chopped**
- **¼ teaspoon pepper**

1 In a large skillet, saute the onion, celery, carrots and thyme in oil until tender.

2 Transfer to a 5-qt. slow cooker. Add the peas, broth and water. Cover and cook on low for 7-8 hours or until peas are tender.

3 Cool slightly. In a blender, process half of the soup until smooth. Return all to the slow cooker. Add bacon and pepper; heat through.

Hungarian Mushroom Soup

PREP: 20 MIN. • COOK: 30 MIN. • YIELD: 4 SERVINGS

You'd think you were enjoying a first course at a fine restaurant when you taste this cream soup. It's so delicious!

Sandy Vaughn *Central Point, Oregon*

- **1 large sweet onion, chopped**
- **¼ cup butter, cubed**
- **¾ pound sliced fresh mushrooms**
- **3 tablespoons all-purpose flour**
- **1 tablespoon paprika**
- **1 teaspoon dill weed**
- **¾ teaspoon salt**
- **¼ teaspoon coarsely ground pepper**
- **1 can (14½ ounces) chicken broth**
- **1 cup 2% milk**
- **1 tablespoon soy sauce**
- **½ cup sour cream**
- **2 teaspoons lemon juice**

1 In a large saucepan, saute onion in butter for 2 minutes. Add mushrooms; cook 4-5 minutes longer or until mushrooms are tender.

2 Stir in the flour, paprika, dill, salt and pepper until blended. Gradually stir in the broth, milk and soy sauce. Bring to a boil; cook and stir for 2 minutes or until thickened. Reduce heat; cover and simmer for 15 minutes.

3 Just before serving, stir in sour cream and lemon juice (do not boil).

Easy Minestrone

PREP: 25 MIN. • COOK: 40 MIN.
YIELD: 11 SERVINGS (2¾ QUARTS)

My recipe is special because it's one of the few dinners my entire family loves. And I can feel good about serving it because it's full of nutrition and low in fat.

Lauren Brennan *Hood River, Oregon*

- **2 large carrots, diced**
- **2 celery ribs, chopped**
- **1 medium onion, chopped**
- **1 tablespoon olive oil**
- **1 tablespoon butter**
- **2 garlic cloves, minced**
- **2 cans (14½ ounces each) reduced-sodium chicken broth**
- **2 cans (8 ounces each) no-salt-added tomato sauce**
- **1 can (16 ounces) kidney beans, rinsed and drained**
- **1 can (15 ounces) garbanzo beans or chickpeas, rinsed and drained**
- **1 can (14½ ounces) diced tomatoes, undrained**
- **1½ cups shredded cabbage**
- **1 tablespoon dried basil**
- **1½ teaspoons dried parsley flakes**
- **1 teaspoon dried oregano**
- **½ teaspoon pepper**
- **1 cup uncooked whole wheat elbow macaroni**
- **11 teaspoons grated Parmesan cheese**

1 In a large saucepan, saute the carrots, celery and onion in oil and butter until tender. Add garlic; cook 1 minute longer.

2 Stir in the broth, tomato sauce, beans, tomatoes, cabbage, basil, parsley, oregano and pepper. Bring to a boil. Reduce heat; cover and simmer for 20 minutes. Meanwhile, cook pasta according to package directions; drain.

3 Return soup to a boil. Stir in pasta; heat through. Ladle into bowls. Sprinkle with cheese.

Chipotle Butternut Squash Soup

PREP: 35 MIN. • COOK: 40 MIN.
YIELD: 12 SERVINGS (3 QUARTS)

Autumn has always been my favorite time of year, and the combination of butternut squash and apples reminds me of the season. The spicy chipotle peppers add some heat and zip. Using two chipotle peppers will make a spicy soup. If you prefer less heat, add only one pepper or no peppers at all.

Andrea Gilkenson *Wausau, Wisconsin*

- **1 medium butternut squash (3½ to 4 pounds), peeled, seeded and cubed**
- **2 medium carrots, chopped**
- **1 large onion, chopped**
- **2 celery ribs, chopped**
- **3 tablespoons butter**
- **2 medium tart apples, peeled and cubed**
- **3 garlic cloves, minced**
- **3 cans (14½ ounces each) chicken broth**
- **1 cup unsweetened apple cider or juice**
- **1 chipotle pepper in adobo sauce, seeded and chopped**
- **½ teaspoon salt**
- **½ cup sour cream**

1 In a Dutch oven, saute the squash, carrots, onion and celery in butter for 5 minutes.

2 Add apples and garlic; cook 3 minutes longer. Stir in the broth, apple cider, chipotle pepper and salt. Bring to a boil. Reduce heat; cover and simmer for 20-25 minutes or until vegetables are tender.

3 Cool slightly. In a blender, process soup in batches until smooth. Return all to pan and heat through. Stir in sour cream (do not boil).

Parmesan Artichoke Soup

PREP: 25 MIN. • COOK: 30 MIN. • YIELD: 12 SERVINGS (3 QUARTS)

For a unique cream soup that has a splendid flavor, try this combination of artichokes, sun-dried tomatoes and Parmesan cheese.

Malee Jergensen *Murray, Utah*

- **4 celery ribs, finely chopped**
- **1 medium onion, finely chopped**
- **½ cup finely chopped carrot**
- **½ cup butter, cubed**
- **3 garlic cloves, minced**
- **1 cup all-purpose flour**
- **4½ teaspoons minced fresh thyme or 1½ teaspoons dried thyme**
- **¾ teaspoon salt**
- **½ teaspoon pepper**
- **2 cartons (32 ounces each) reduced-sodium chicken broth**
- **3 bay leaves**
- **1 quart heavy whipping cream**
- **1½ cups shredded Parmesan cheese**
- **1 jar (7½ ounces) marinated quartered artichoke hearts, drained and coarsely chopped**
- **¼ cup sun-dried tomatoes (not packed in oil), chopped**

1 In a large saucepan, saute the celery, onion and carrot in butter until tender. Add the garlic; cook 1 minute longer. Stir in the flour, thyme, salt and pepper until blended; gradually add broth. Add bay leaves. Bring to a boil. Cook and stir for 2 minutes or until thickened.

2 Reduce heat; whisk in the cream, cheese, artichokes and tomatoes. Bring to a gentle boil. Simmer, uncovered, for 5-10 minutes or until flavors are blended. Discard bay leaves.

Hearty Hamburger Soup

PREP: 10 MIN. • COOK: 30 MIN.
YIELD: 8 SERVINGS (2 QUARTS)

At family get-togethers, our children always request this spirit-warming soup along with a fresh loaf of homemade bread and tall glasses of milk. It has robust flavor, plenty of fresh-tasting vegetables and is easy to make.

Barbara Brown *Janesville, Wisconsin*

- **1 pound ground beef**
- **4 cups water**
- **1 can (14½ ounces) diced tomatoes, undrained**
- **3 medium carrots, sliced**
- **2 medium potatoes, peeled and cubed**
- **1 medium onion, chopped**
- **½ cup chopped celery**
- **4 teaspoons beef bouillon granules**
- **1½ teaspoons salt**
- **¼ teaspoon pepper**
- **¼ teaspoon dried oregano**
- **1 cup cut fresh or frozen green beans**

1 In a large saucepan, brown beef; drain. Add the next 10 ingredients; bring to a boil.

2 Reduce heat; cover and simmer for 15 minutes or until potatoes and carrots are tender. Add beans. Cover and simmer 15 minutes longer or until the beans are tender.

WINNERS CIRCLE

sandwiches

Mmm...sandwiches. Served cold or hot, layered with meat or veggies, they're a classic standby. The simple satisfaction created by two pieces of bread and an endless array of fillings is one reason we had to include a section devoted solely to these scrumptious hoagies, burgers, wraps and more.

BACON CHEESEBURGER MEATBALL SUBS , 71

Barbecued Burgers

PREP: 25 MIN. • GRILL: 15 MIN. • YIELD: 6 SERVINGS

I can't take all the credit for these winning burgers. My husband's uncle passed down the special barbecue sauce recipe. We love it on everything—it seemed only natural to try it on, and in, burgers!

Rhoda Troyer *Glenford, Ohio*

SAUCE:

- **1 cup ketchup**
- **½ cup packed brown sugar**
- **⅓ cup sugar**
- **¼ cup honey**
- **¼ cup molasses**
- **2 teaspoons prepared mustard**
- **1½ teaspoons Worcestershire sauce**
- **¼ teaspoon salt**
- **¼ teaspoon liquid smoke**
- **⅛ teaspoon pepper**

BURGERS:

- **1 egg, lightly beaten**
- **⅓ cup quick-cooking oats**
- **¼ teaspoon onion salt**
- **¼ teaspoon garlic salt**
- **¼ teaspoon pepper**
- **⅛ teaspoon salt**
- **1½ pounds ground beef**
- **6 hamburger buns, split**

Toppings of your choice

1 In a small saucepan, combine the first 10 ingredients. Bring to a boil. Remove from the heat. Set aside 1 cup barbecue sauce to serve with burgers.

2 In a large bowl, combine the egg, oats, ¼ cup of the remaining barbecue sauce, onion salt, garlic salt, pepper and salt. Crumble beef over mixture and mix well. Shape into six patties.

3 Grill, covered, over medium heat for 6-8 minutes on each side or until a thermometer reads 160°, basting with ½ cup barbecue sauce during the last 5 minutes. Serve on buns with toppings of your choice and reserved barbecue sauce.

Cuban-Style Pork Sandwiches

PREP: 20 MIN. • COOK: 6 HOURS + STANDING • YIELD: 10 SERVINGS

Loaded with tangy flavor, this is a lighter version of a favorite restaurant-style sandwich. If you don't have a panini maker, tuck the sandwiches under the broiler until the bread is browned and the cheese is melted.

Robin Haas *Cranston, Rhode Island*

- **1 large onion, cut into wedges**
- **¾ cup reduced-sodium chicken broth**
- **1 cup minced fresh parsley**
- **7 garlic cloves, minced and divided**
- **2 tablespoons cider vinegar**
- **1 tablespoon plus 1½ teaspoons lemon juice, divided**
- **2 teaspoons ground cumin**
- **1 teaspoon ground mustard**
- **1 teaspoon dried oregano**
- **½ teaspoon salt**
- **½ teaspoon pepper**
- **1 boneless pork shoulder butt roast (3 to 4 pounds)**
- **1¼ cups fat-free mayonnaise**
- **2 tablespoons Dijon mustard**
- **10 whole wheat hamburger buns, split**
- **1¼ cups (5 ounces) shredded reduced-fat Swiss cheese**
- **1 medium onion, thinly sliced and separated into rings**
- **2 whole dill pickles, sliced**

1 Place onion wedges and broth in a 5-qt. slow cooker. In a small bowl, combine the parsley, 5 garlic cloves, vinegar, 1 tablespoon lemon juice, cumin, mustard, oregano, salt and pepper; rub over pork. Add to slow cooker. Cover and cook on low for 6-8 hours or until meat is tender.

2 Remove meat; let stand for 10 minutes before slicing. In another small bowl, combine the mayonnaise, mustard and remaining garlic and lemon juice; spread over buns. Layer bun bottoms with pork, cheese, sliced onion and pickles; replace tops.

3 Cook on a panini maker or indoor grill for 2-3 minutes or until buns are browned and cheese is melted.

Greek Turkey Pitas

PREP: 25 MIN. + CHILLING • YIELD: 2 SERVINGS

We like to fix these generous sandwiches whenever we have leftover turkey in the house. They're easy to make and a perfect choice for a light meal on the deck or patio.

Jean Graf-Joyce *Albany, Oregon*

- **¼ cup plain yogurt**
- **¼ cup chopped seeded peeled cucumber**
- **¼ teaspoon lemon-pepper seasoning**
- **¼ teaspoon dried oregano**
- **⅛ teaspoon garlic powder**
- **¼ pound cooked turkey breast, cubed**
- **2 whole pita breads, warmed**
- **1 small tomato, sliced**
- **2 slices red onion, halved**
- **2 pitted Greek olives, sliced**
- **2 pepperoncini, sliced**
- **½ cup shredded lettuce**
- **2 tablespoons crumbled feta cheese**

1 In a small bowl, combine the first five ingredients. Stir in the turkey. Cover and refrigerate for at least 1 hour.

2 Spoon turkey mixture onto each pita; top with tomato, onion, olives, pepperoncini, lettuce and feta cheese. Fold in half.

Chicken Pesto Clubs

30 min.

PREP/TOTAL TIME: 10 MIN.
YIELD: 2 SERVINGS

This colorful sandwich is a crisp golden-brown on the outside, with a fresh-tasting, full-flavored filling the whole family will love. It's supper in 10 minutes flat!

Terri Crandall *Gardnerville, Nevada*

- **4 slices ready-to-serve fully cooked bacon**
- **4 slices sourdough bread**
- **2 tablespoons prepared pesto**
- **1 cup ready-to-use grilled chicken breast strips**
- **2 slices cheddar cheese**
- **1 medium tomato, sliced**
- **1 cup fresh arugula or baby spinach**
- **1 tablespoon olive oil**

1 Heat bacon according to package directions. Meanwhile, spread bread slices with pesto. Layer two slices with chicken, cheese, tomato, arugula and bacon; top with remaining bread slice.

2 Brush outsides of sandwiches with oil. Cook on an indoor grill for 3-4 minutes or until bread is browned and cheese is melted.

Mahogany-Glazed Mushroom Burgers

PREP: 30 MIN. • GRILL: 10 MIN. • YIELD: 6 SERVINGS

This burger is covered with a few of my favorite things: portobello mushrooms, goat cheese, basil and mascarpone. These burgers are quite juicy, so serve them with extra napkins.

Lisa Keys *Kennet Square, Pennsylvania*

- **¼ cup maple syrup**
- **¼ cup Kahlua (coffee liqueur)**
- **¼ cup reduced-sodium soy sauce**
- **10 ounces sliced baby portobello mushrooms**
- **½ cup thinly sliced red onion**
- **2 tablespoons olive oil**
- **¼ teaspoon kosher salt**
- **⅛ teaspoon pepper**

CHEESE SPREAD:

- **½ cup mascarpone cheese**
- **½ cup crumbled goat cheese**
- **¼ cup minced fresh parsley**
- **2 tablespoons minced fresh basil or 2 teaspoons dried basil**
- **⅛ teaspoon pepper**

BURGERS:

- **1½ pounds ground beef**
- **1 teaspoon kosher salt**
- **½ teaspoon pepper**
- **6 hard rolls, split**

1 In a small saucepan, combine the maple syrup, Kahlua and soy sauce. Bring to a boil; cook for 8 minutes or until liquid is reduced by half.

2 In a large skillet, saute mushrooms and onion in oil until tender. Add the salt, pepper and ¼ cup of the Kahlua mixture. Cook and stir until liquid is almost evaporated.

3 In a small bowl, combine the cheese spread ingredients; cover and refrigerate until serving.

4 Crumble beef into a large bowl. Sprinkle with salt and pepper; mix well. Shape into six patties.

5 Grill burgers, covered, over medium heat for 6 minutes. Turn; grill 5-8 minutes longer or until a thermometer reads 160° and juices run clear, basting occasionally with remaining Kahlua mixture. Grill rolls, uncovered, for 1-2 minutes or until toasted.

6 Spread rolls with cheese spread; top with burgers and mushroom mixture. Replace tops.

Buffalo Chicken Burgers with Tangy Slaw

PREP: 25 MIN. • BROIL: 10 MIN. • YIELD: 4 SERVINGS

These burgers are my way of enjoying the flavors of buffalo chicken wings while avoiding some of the fat and calories.

Jeanne Holt *Mendota Heights, Minnesota*

SLAW:

- **¼ cup thinly sliced celery**
- **¼ cup shredded peeled apple**
- **2 tablespoons fat-free blue cheese salad dressing**
- **1 teaspoon finely chopped walnuts**

SAUCE:

- **3 tablespoons Louisiana-style hot sauce**
- **2 teaspoons ketchup**
- **2 teaspoons reduced-fat butter, melted**

BURGERS:

- **2 tablespoons chopped sweet red pepper**
- **2 tablespoons plus 4 teaspoons thinly sliced green onions, divided**
- **1 tablespoon unsweetened applesauce**
- **¼ teaspoon salt**
- **¼ teaspoon garlic salt**
- **¼ teaspoon pepper**
- **1 pound ground chicken**
- **4 lettuce leaves**
- **4 hamburger buns, split**

1 In a small bowl, combine the celery, apple, salad dressing and walnuts. In another small bowl, combine the hot sauce, ketchup and butter; set aside.

2 In a large bowl, combine the red pepper, 2 tablespoons green onion, applesauce, salt, garlic salt and pepper. Crumble chicken over mixture and mix well. Shape into four burgers.

3 Broil 6 in. from the heat for 5-7 minutes on each side or until a thermometer reads 165° and juices run clear, basting occasionally with reserved sauce.

4 Serve on lettuce-lined buns; top each with 2 tablespoons slaw and sprinkle with remaining green onion.

EDITOR'S NOTE: This recipe was tested with Land O' Lakes light stick butter.

Roast Pork Sandwiches with Peach Chutney

PREP: 15 MIN. • BAKE: 35 MIN. • YIELD: 4 SERVINGS

The combination of roast pork with peach chutney used to be a favorite Sunday dinner. Since my children are on their own now, I cut the original recipe down for sandwiches.

Lily Julow *Gainesville, Florida*

- **1 pork tenderloin (1 pound)**
- **2 tablespoons spicy brown mustard**

PEACH CHUTNEY:

- **¼ cup peach preserves**
- **3 tablespoons finely chopped onion**
- **2 tablespoons red wine vinegar**
- **1 small garlic clove, minced**
- **¼ teaspoon mustard seed**
- **⅛ teaspoon salt**
- **⅛ teaspoon ground ginger**
- **⅛ teaspoon ground cinnamon**
- **Dash cayenne pepper**
- **Dash ground cloves**
- **¼ cup fat-free mayonnaise**
- **4 onion rolls, split and toasted**
- **4 lettuce leaves**

1 Brush pork with mustard; place on a rack in a shallow roasting pan. Bake at 425° for 35-40 minutes or until a thermometer reads 160°. Let stand for 5 minutes before slicing.

2 Meanwhile, for chutney, in a small saucepan, combine the preserves, onion, vinegar, garlic and seasonings. Bring to a boil. Reduce heat; simmer, uncovered, for 7-8 minutes or until thickened. Set aside to cool. Spread mayonnaise over roll bottoms. Layer with lettuce, pork slices and chutney. Replace tops.

Triple Pepper Steak Sandwiches

PREP: 40 MIN. • COOK: 5 MIN./BATCH • YIELD: 4 SERVINGS

Separate parts of this recipe can be made ahead of time and the sandwich assembled quickly for a weeknight meal. This fork-and-knife sandwich works very well with leftover fajita meat and peppers, or as a way to use leftover grilled steak or chicken. The chipotle cream sauce can be made up to 3 days in advance.

Robert Taylor *Shawnee, Kansas*

- **2 boneless beef top loin steaks (1 inch thick and 8 ounces each)**
- **¼ teaspoon salt**
- **⅛ teaspoon pepper**
- **1 large sweet onion, thinly sliced**
- **1 cup sliced fresh mushrooms**
- **1 poblano pepper, thinly sliced**
- **2 tablespoons plus 2 teaspoons butter, divided**
- **2 tablespoons chopped onion**
- **1 garlic clove, minced**
- **½ cup heavy whipping cream**
- **1 chipotle pepper in adobo sauce, minced**
- **½ teaspoon ground cumin**
- **¼ teaspoon chicken bouillon granules**
- **1 loaf (14 ounces) ciabatta bread**
- **4 slices pepper jack cheese**

1 Sprinkle steaks with salt and pepper. Grill, covered, over medium heat or broil 3-4 in. from the heat for 7-9 minutes on each side or until meat reaches desired doneness (for medium-rare, a thermometer should read 145°; medium, 160°; well-done, 170°). Let stand for 5 minutes before slicing.

2 Meanwhile, in a large skillet, saute sliced onion, mushrooms and poblano pepper in 2 tablespoons butter until tender. Remove from the heat; stir in sliced steak.

3 In a small saucepan, saute chopped onion in remaining butter until tender. Add garlic; cook 1 minute longer. Stir in the cream, chipotle, cumin and bouillon; cook and stir until thickened.

4 Cut ciabatta in half horizontally, then cut into four equal portions. Place cheese on bottom bread slices; top with steak mixture, chipotle cream sauce and remaining bread. Cook on a panini maker or indoor grill for 3-4 minutes or until bread is browned and cheese is melted.

EDITOR'S NOTE: Wear disposable gloves when cutting hot peppers; the oils can burn skin. Avoid touching your face.

Turkey Sandwich with Pineapple Salsa

PREP: 25 MIN. • BAKE: 15 MIN. • YIELD: 6 SERVINGS

Pineapple salsa adds tropical flair to these fresh-tasting hoagies that are great for a quick dinner or entertaining a few guests.

Andrea Boyer *Lenore, Idaho*

- **1¼ cups finely chopped fresh pineapple**
- **2 roma tomatoes, finely chopped**
- **½ cup finely chopped onion**
- **⅓ cup minced fresh cilantro**
- **1 loaf (1 pound) French bread**
- **1 pound thinly sliced cooked turkey**
- **6 slices part-skim mozzarella cheese**

AIOLI:

- **¾ cup mayonnaise**
- **2 tablespoons lemon juice**
- **2 garlic cloves, minced**
- **½ teaspoon pepper**

1 In a small bowl, combine the pineapple, tomatoes, onion and cilantro; set aside.

2 Cut bread in half horizontally; place cut sides up on an ungreased baking sheet. Bake at 350° for 4-5 minutes or until toasted; remove top half from pan. Layer bottom half with turkey and cheese. Bake 10-13 minutes longer or until turkey is heated through and cheese is melted.

3 Meanwhile, combine the aioli ingredients in a small bowl. Carefully spread over cheese; top with salsa. Replace bread top; cut into six slices.

30 min.

Zesty Garlic-Avocado Sandwiches

PREP/TOTAL TIME: 30 MIN. • YIELD: 6 SERVINGS

Here's a tasty meatless sandwich I concocted by combining some of our family's favorite ingredients: garlic, avocado, cream cheese and bagels. For a variation, add fresh chives or minced sun-dried tomato to the cream cheese. Any leftover spread makes an excellent veggie dip.

Tricia Farnum *Branson West, Missouri*

- **1 package (8 ounces) cream cheese, softened**
- **2 medium ripe avocados, peeled**
- **1 garlic clove, minced**
- **⅛ teaspoon salt**
- **6 whole grain bagels, split and toasted**
- **6 slices tomato**
- **½ cup sliced cucumber**
- **6 slices red onion**
- **6 sweet red pepper rings**
- **6 lettuce leaves**

1 In a small bowl, beat the cream cheese, avocados, garlic and salt until smooth. Spread on bagels; top with tomato, cucumber, onion, pepper rings and lettuce.

Slow-Cooked Pulled Pork

PREP: 20 MIN. + CHILLING • COOK: 8 HOURS
YIELD: 10 SERVINGS

Every time I bring this dish to a potluck I get asked, "Where did you get the pork?" People are surprised to hear me say that I made it. When I tell them how simple the recipe is, they are doubly surprised. The process fits the demands of any busy schedule: easy to make and easy to serve.

Betsy Rivas *Chesterfield, Missouri*

- **2 tablespoons brown sugar**
- **4½ teaspoons paprika**
- **2 tablespoons coarsely ground pepper, divided**
- **1 tablespoon kosher salt**
- **1 teaspoon chili powder**
- **½ teaspoon cayenne pepper**
- **1 boneless pork shoulder butt roast (3 to 4 pounds), cut in half**
- **1 cup cider vinegar**
- **¼ cup beef broth**
- **¼ cup barbecue sauce**
- **2 tablespoons Worcestershire sauce**
- **1½ teaspoons hickory liquid smoke, optional**
- **10 kaiser rolls, split**

1 In a small bowl, combine the brown sugar, paprika, 1 tablespoon pepper, salt, chili powder and cayenne. Rub over roast; cover and refrigerate for 8 hours or overnight.

2 Place roast in a 4- or 5-qt. slow cooker. Combine the vinegar, broth, barbecue sauce, Worcestershire sauce, liquid smoke, if desired, and remaining pepper; pour over roast. Cover and cook on low for 8-10 hours or until meat is tender.

3 Remove meat from slow cooker; cool slightly. Shred meat with two forks and return to the slow cooker; heat through. Using a slotted spoon, place ½ cup meat on each roll.

Bacon Cheeseburger Meatball Subs

PREP: 40 MIN. • BAKE: 20 MIN. • YIELD: 8 SANDWICHES

I love combining some of my favorite dishes into a brand new creation. Here, I took a meatball and a bacon cheeseburger and literally rolled the recipes into one. The hearty dish will please the meat lovers in your gang.

Cyndy Gerken *Naples, Florida*

- **2 eggs, lightly beaten**
- **1 tablespoon Worcestershire sauce**
- **2 medium onions, finely chopped**
- **⅔ cup seasoned bread crumbs**
- **⅓ cup grated Parmesan cheese**
- **3 tablespoons minced fresh parsley or 1 tablespoon dried parsley flakes**
- **8 garlic cloves, minced**
- **2 tablespoons minced fresh basil or 2 teaspoons dried basil**
- **1 tablespoon minced fresh oregano or 1 teaspoon dried oregano**
- **⅛ teaspoon kosher salt**
- **⅛ teaspoon pepper**
- **⅛ teaspoon crushed red pepper flakes**
- **¾ pound ground beef**
- **⅔ pound ground veal**
- **⅔ pound ground pork**
- **24 cubes cheddar cheese (½-inch each)**
- **8 cooked bacon strips, cut into thirds**
- **8 lettuce leaves**
- **8 submarine buns, split and toasted**
- **1 cup barbecue sauce, warmed**

1 In a large bowl, combine the first 12 ingredients. Crumble the meats over the mixture and mix well; divide into 24 portions.

2 Wrap each cheese cube with a cut bacon strip. Shape one portion of meat mixture around each bacon-wrapped cheese cube. Place meatballs on a greased rack in a shallow baking pan.

3 Bake, uncovered, at 400° for 20-25 minutes or until a thermometer reads 160°. Drain on paper towels. Serve on lettuce-lined buns with barbecue sauce.

French Cheeseburger Loaf

PREP: 25 MIN. • BAKE: 25 MIN.
YIELD: 6 SERVINGS

Once you prepare this impressive-looking yet simple-to-make sandwich, you'll probably never look at refrigerated bread dough the same way. It's just too easy!

Nancy Daugherty *Cortland, Ohio*

- **¾ pound lean ground beef (90% lean)**
- **½ cup chopped sweet onion**
- **1 small green pepper, chopped**
- **2 garlic cloves, minced**
- **2 tablespoons all-purpose flour**
- **2 tablespoons Dijon mustard**
- **1 tablespoon ketchup**
- **1 tube (11 ounces) refrigerated crusty French loaf**
- **4 slices reduced-fat process American cheese product**
- **1 egg white, lightly beaten**
- **3 tablespoons shredded Parmesan cheese**

1 In a large skillet, cook the beef, onion and pepper over medium heat until meat is no longer pink. Add garlic; cook 1 minute longer. Stir in the flour, mustard and ketchup; set aside.

2 Unroll dough starting at the seam. Pat into a 14-in. x 12-in. rectangle. Spoon meat mixture lengthwise down the center of the dough; top with cheese slices. Bring long sides of dough to the center over filling; pinch seams to seal.

3 Place seam side down on a baking sheet coated with cooking spray. Brush with egg white. Sprinkle with Parmesan cheese.

4 With a sharp knife, cut diagonal slits in top of loaf. Bake at 350° for 25-30 minutes or until golden brown. Serve warm.

Meat-atarian Sub

PREP: 20 MIN. • BAKE: 25 MIN.
YIELD: 6 SERVINGS

According to contest judges, it's meaty but not overly salty. But according to me, it's the ultimate food for football season.

Shanon Mayer *Mountain View, Wyoming*

- **1 cup (4 ounces) shredded part-skim mozzarella cheese**
- **½ cup grated Parmesan cheese**
- **½ cup butter, softened**
- **½ cup mayonnaise**
- **2 garlic cloves, minced**
- **1 teaspoon Italian seasoning**
- **¼ teaspoon crushed red pepper flakes**
- **¼ teaspoon pepper**
- **1 loaf (1 pound) French bread, halved lengthwise**
- **1 pound sliced deli ham**
- **2 packages (2.1 ounces each) ready-to-serve fully cooked bacon, warmed**
- **4 ounces sliced pepperoni**
- **½ cup pizza sauce**

1 In a small bowl, combine the first eight ingredients. Spread over cut sides of bread. Layer with ham, bacon, pepperoni and pizza sauce; replace top.

2 Wrap in foil; place on a large baking sheet. Bake at 350° for 25-30 minutes or until heated through. Cut into slices.

Summer Veggie Subs

PREP: 30 MIN. + STANDING • YIELD: 12 SERVINGS

Every Sunday night during the summer, a park near our home holds free outdoor concerts. We've been going for years. These subs are perfect for picnics, and I've taken them to the park several times.

Jennie Todd *Lancaster, Pennsylvania*

- **4 medium sweet red peppers**
- **½ cup fat-free mayonnaise**
- **2 tablespoons minced fresh basil**
- **1 tablespoon minced fresh parsley**
- **1 tablespoon minced fresh tarragon**
- **2 loaves French bread (1 pound each), halved lengthwise**
- **2 cups fresh baby spinach**
- **2 cups thinly sliced cucumbers**
- **2 cups alfalfa sprouts**
- **4 medium tomatoes, sliced**
- **2 medium ripe avocados, peeled and sliced**
- **¾ pound thinly sliced deli turkey**
- **6 slices reduced-fat Swiss cheese, halved**

1 Broil peppers 4 in. from the heat until skins blister, about 5 minutes. With tongs, rotate peppers a quarter turn. Broil and rotate until all sides are blistered and blackened. Immediately place peppers in a large bowl; cover and let stand for 15-20 minutes.

2 Peel off and discard charred skin. Remove stems and seeds. Julienne the peppers.

3 Combine the mayonnaise, basil, parsley and tarragon; spread over bread bottoms. Top with spinach, cucumbers, sprouts, roasted peppers, tomatoes, avocados, turkey and cheese. Replace tops. Cut each loaf into six slices.

Grilled Veggie Wraps

PREP: 15 MIN. + MARINATING • GRILL: 15 MIN.
YIELD: 4 SERVINGS

I love this vegetable marinade, but the key to this recipe's success is the three-cheese spread.

Britani Sepanski *Indianapolis, Indiana*

- **2 tablespoons balsamic vinegar**
- **1½ teaspoons minced fresh basil**
- **1½ teaspoons olive oil**
- **1½ teaspoons molasses**
- **¾ teaspoon minced fresh thyme**
- **⅛ teaspoon salt**
- **⅛ teaspoon pepper**
- **1 medium zucchini, cut lengthwise into ¼-inch slices**
- **1 medium sweet red pepper, cut into 1-inch pieces**
- **1 medium red onion, cut into ½-inch slices**
- **4 ounces whole fresh mushrooms, cut into ½-inch pieces**
- **4 ounces fresh sugar snap peas**
- **½ cup crumbled feta cheese**
- **3 tablespoons reduced-fat cream cheese**
- **2 tablespoons grated Parmesan cheese**
- **1 tablespoon reduced-fat mayonnaise**
- **4 flour tortillas (8 inches)**
- **4 romaine leaves**

1 In a large resealable plastic bag, combine the first seven ingredients; add vegetables. Seal bag and turn to coat; refrigerate for 2 hours, turning once.

2 Drain and reserve marinade. Transfer vegetables to a grill wok or basket. Grill, uncovered, over medium-high heat for 5 minutes, stirring frequently.

3 Set aside 1 teaspoon marinade. Turn vegetables; baste with remaining marinade. Grill 5-8 minutes longer or until tender, stirring frequently. Meanwhile, in a small bowl, combine cheeses and mayonnaise; set aside.

4 Brush one side of each tortilla with reserved marinade. Place tortillas, marinade side down, on grill for 1-3 minutes or until lightly toasted. Spread 3 tablespoons of cheese mixture over ungrilled side of each tortilla. Top with romaine and 1 cup grilled vegetables; roll up.

EDITOR'S NOTE: If you do not have a grill wok or basket, use a disposable foil pan. Poke holes in the bottom of the pan with a meat fork to allow liquid to drain.

Tuscan Burgers with Pesto Mayo

PREP: 25 MIN. • GRILL: 20 MIN. • YIELD: 4 SERVINGS

Everyone needs to bring their appetite when you serve these big-bite burgers. Each bite has a bit of Italy in it with the use of pancetta, pesto and mozzarella cheese. Try them—you'll never order an ordinary burger again!

Rita Combs *Valdosta, Georgia*

- **¼ cup mayonnaise**
- **¼ cup prepared pesto, divided**
- **3 ounces sliced pancetta, finely chopped**
- **¼ teaspoon pepper**
- **⅛ teaspoon kosher salt**
- **1 pound ground beef**
- **1 small red onion, cut into 4 slices**
- **1 large tomato, cut into 4 slices**
- **1 tablespoon olive oil**
- **8 ounces fresh mozzarella cheese, cut into 4 slices**
- **4 Italian rolls, split**
- **1 cup fresh arugula or fresh baby spinach**

1 In a small bowl, combine mayonnaise and 2 tablespoons pesto; cover and chill until serving. In a large bowl, combine the pancetta, pepper, salt and remaining pesto. Crumble beef over mixture and mix well. Shape into four patties.

2 Brush onion and tomato slices with oil. Grill onion over medium heat for 4-6 minutes on each side or until crisp-tender. Grill tomato for 1-2 minutes on each side or until lightly browned.

3 Grill burgers, covered, over medium heat for 5-7 minutes on each side or until a thermometer reads 160° and juices run clear. Top burgers with mozzarella cheese. Grill 1 minute longer or until cheese is melted. Spread cut sides of rolls with pesto mayonnaise; top with burgers, onion, tomato and arugula.

Grilled Italian Meatball Burgers

PREP: 25 MIN. • GRILL: 15 MIN. • YIELD: 8 SERVINGS

I just love these grilled patties! They're a big hit with kids and adults. I serve them with sliced green peppers, tomato and onions and a jar of crushed red peppers on the side for adults. Kids seem to enjoy them best "as-is."

Priscilla Gilbert *Indian Harbour Beach, Florida*

- **1 egg, lightly beaten**
- **⅓ cup seasoned bread crumbs**
- **3 garlic cloves, minced**
- **1 teaspoon dried oregano**
- **1 teaspoon dried basil**
- **¼ teaspoon salt**
- **¼ teaspoon dried thyme**
- **1½ pounds lean ground beef (90% lean)**
- **½ pound Italian turkey sausage links, casings removed**
- **¾ cup shredded part-skim mozzarella cheese**
- **8 kaiser rolls, split**
- **1 cup roasted garlic Parmesan spaghetti sauce, warmed**

1 In a large bowl, combine the first seven ingredients. Crumble beef and sausage over mixture and mix well. Shape into eight burgers.

2 Using long-handled tongs, moisten a paper towel with cooking oil and lightly coat the grill rack. Grill burgers, covered, over medium heat or broil 4 in. from the heat for 5-7 minutes on each side or until a thermometer reads 165° and juices run clear.

3 Sprinkle burgers with cheese; cook 2-3 minutes longer or until cheese is melted. Remove and keep warm.

4 Grill or broil rolls for 1-2 minutes or until toasted. Serve burgers on rolls with spaghetti sauce.

Pesto Chicken Salad Sandwiches

30 min.

PREP/TOTAL TIME: 20 MIN.
YIELD: 6 SERVINGS

Sandwiches are a teacher's lunchtime staple. The pesto and roasted peppers add a welcome twist to the traditional chicken salad.

Ellen Finger *Lancaster, Pennsylvania*

- **⅔ cup reduced-fat mayonnaise**
- **⅓ cup prepared pesto**
- **2 tablespoons lemon juice**
- **¼ teaspoon garlic powder**
- **¼ teaspoon pepper**
- **3 cups cubed cooked chicken**
- **1 jar (7 ounces) roasted sweet red peppers, drained and chopped**
- **1 celery rib, finely chopped**
- **6 romaine leaves**
- **6 ciabatta rolls, split**

1 In a large bowl, combine the first five ingredients. Add the chicken, red peppers and celery; toss to coat. Serve on lettuce-lined rolls.

Sweet & Tangy Pulled Pork

PREP: 15 MIN. • COOK: 8 HOURS • YIELD: 12 SERVINGS

The slow cooker makes these super sandwiches a snap to put together on a busy weeknight. By the incredible flavor, you'd think I'd slaved over them all day! I like to serve them with a side of creamy coleslaw or corn on the cob.

Megan Klimkewicz *Kaiser, Missouri*

- **1 boneless pork shoulder butt roast (3 to 4 pounds)**
- **1 jar (18 ounces) apricot preserves**
- **1 large onion, chopped**
- **2 tablespoons reduced-sodium soy sauce**
- **2 tablespoons Dijon mustard**

Hamburger buns, split, optional

1 Cut pork roast in half; place in a 4- or 5-qt. slow cooker. Combine the preserves, onion, soy sauce and mustard; pour over roast. Cover and cook on low for 8-10 hours or until meat is tender.

2 Remove meat; cool slightly. Skim fat from cooking juices. Shred pork with two forks and return to slow cooker; heat through. Serve on buns, if desired.

Curried Chicken Sloppy Joes

PREP: 20 MIN. • COOK: 30 MIN. • YIELD: 10 SERVINGS

These delicious sloppy joes pack a burst of unexpected flavors in every bite. They'll surely jazz up your sloppy joe repertoire. For potlucks, keep the chicken mixture warm in a slow cooker and let everyone fill their own buns.

Jamie Miller *Maple Grove, Minnesota*

- **1¼ pounds ground chicken**
- **1 cup chopped sweet onion**
- **½ cup chopped sweet orange pepper**
- **2 garlic cloves, minced**
- **1 tablespoon olive oil**
- **2 teaspoons curry powder**
- **1 teaspoon minced fresh gingerroot**
- **½ teaspoon coarsely ground pepper**
- **¼ teaspoon salt**
- **1 can (14½ ounces) petite diced tomatoes, undrained**
- **1 medium tart apple, peeled and diced**
- **½ cup golden raisins**
- **3 tablespoons mango chutney**
- **¼ cup reduced-fat mayonnaise**
- **1 tablespoon Dijon mustard**
- **10 whole wheat hamburger buns, split**

1 In a large nonstick skillet, cook chicken over medium heat until no longer pink; drain and set aside.

2 In the same skillet, cook the onion, pepper and garlic in oil until tender. Stir in the curry, ginger, pepper and salt; cook 1 minute longer.

3 Stir in the tomatoes, apple and raisins; bring to a boil. Reduce heat; simmer, uncovered, for 6-8 minutes. Stir in the chutney, mayonnaise, mustard and chicken; heat through. Serve on buns.

Jalapeno Popper Burgers

PREP: 30 MIN. • GRILL: 15 MIN. • YIELD: 4 SERVINGS

What do you get when you combine a jalapeno popper and a great burger? This fantastic recipe! It takes the classic components of a popper and encases them in a juicy patty, for a burst of flavor in every bite.

Jo Davison *Naples, Florida*

- **3 jalapeno peppers, halved lengthwise and seeded**
- **1 teaspoon olive oil**
- **6 bacon strips, cooked and crumbled**
- **1 package (3 ounces) cream cheese, softened**
- **2 garlic cloves, minced**
- **1 teaspoon salt**
- **1 teaspoon lemon-pepper seasoning**
- **½ teaspoon pepper**
- **¼ teaspoon paprika**
- **2 pounds ground beef**
- **4 slices pepper jack cheese**
- **4 hamburger buns, split**
- **4 lettuce leaves**
- **1 large tomato, sliced**
- **¾ cup guacamole**

1 Brush jalapenos with oil. Grill, covered, over medium heat for 3-5 minutes or until tender, turning occasionally. When cool enough to handle, finely chop. In a small bowl, combine the bacon, cream cheese and jalapeno until blended.

2 In a large bowl, combine the garlic, salt, lemon pepper, pepper and paprika. Crumble beef over mixture and mix well. Shape into eight thin patties. Spoon bacon mixture onto center of four patties; top with remaining patties and press edges firmly to seal.

3 Grill burgers, covered, over medium heat or broil 4 in. from heat for 6-7 minutes on each side or until a thermometer reads 160° and juices run clear. Top with pepper jack cheese. Cover and cook 1-2 minutes longer or until cheese is melted.

4 Grill buns, cut side down, over medium heat for 30-60 seconds or until toasted. Serve burgers on buns with lettuce, tomato and guacamole.

EDITOR'S NOTE: Wear disposable gloves when cutting hot peppers; the oils can burn skin. Avoid touching your face.

Sweet and Sassy Turkey Burgers

PREP: 25 MIN. • GRILL: 15 MIN. • YIELD: 6 SERVINGS

If you think turkey burgers are dry and tasteless, you haven't tried this scrumptious recipe! Cranberry sauce with turkey is a match made in heaven.

Marla Clark *Moriarty, New Mexico*

- **6 turkey bacon strips, diced and cooked**
- **¼ cup dried cranberries**
- **1 tablespoon maple syrup**
- **1 teaspoon rubbed sage**
- **⅛ teaspoon pepper**
- **1¼ pounds extra-lean ground turkey**
- **1 Italian turkey sausage link (4 ounces), casing removed**
- **3 slices part-skim mozzarella cheese, cut in half**
- **6 onion rolls, split**
- **6 tablespoons jellied cranberry sauce**
- **6 tablespoons fat-free mayonnaise**
- **6 lettuce leaves**

1 In a large bowl, combine the first five ingredients. Crumble turkey and sausage over mixture and mix well. Shape into six burgers.

2 Using long-handled tongs, moisten a paper towel with cooking oil and lightly coat the grill rack. Grill burgers, covered, over medium heat or broil 4 in. from the heat for 5-7 minutes on each side or until a thermometer reads 165° and juices run clear. Top with cheese; cook 1-2 minutes longer or until cheese is melted.

3 Toast the rolls; spread warm rolls with cranberry sauce and mayonnaise. Serve burgers on rolls with lettuce.

WINNERS CIRCLE

breakfast & brunch

Make your day a winner by starting it with a satisfying breakfast. From fast fuel for busy mornings to leisurely weekend brunches, the daybreak delights featured here make getting up in the morning a little easier.

BAKED BREAKFAST BURRITOS, 93

Tiramisu Crepes

PREP: 30 MIN. + CHILLING • COOK: 5 MIN./BATCH
YIELD: 22 CREPES

Delicate crepes, filled with creamy mascarpone cheese and laced with vanilla and a hint of coffee liqueur, make for a mouthwatering morning treat.

Karen Shelton *Collierville, Tennessee*

- **4 eggs**
- **¾ cup 2% milk**
- **¼ cup club soda**
- **3 tablespoons butter, melted**
- **2 tablespoons strong brewed coffee**
- **1 teaspoon vanilla extract**
- **1 cup all-purpose flour**
- **3 tablespoons sugar**
- **2 tablespoons baking cocoa**
- **¼ teaspoon salt**

FILLING:

- **1 carton (8 ounces) mascarpone cheese**
- **1 package (8 ounces) cream cheese, softened**
- **1 cup sugar**
- **¼ cup coffee liqueur or strong brewed coffee**
- **2 tablespoons vanilla extract**

Optional toppings: chocolate syrup, whipped cream and baking cocoa

1 In a large bowl, beat the eggs, milk, soda, butter, coffee and vanilla. Combine the flour, sugar, cocoa and salt; add to milk mixture and mix well. Cover and refrigerate for 1 hour.

2 Heat a lightly greased 8-in. nonstick skillet over medium heat; pour 2 tablespoons batter into the center of skillet. Lift and tilt pan to coat bottom evenly. Cook until top appears dry; turn and cook 15-20 seconds longer. Remove to a wire rack. Repeat with remaining batter, greasing skillet as needed. When cool, stack crepes with waxed paper or paper towels in between.

3 For filling, in a large bowl, beat the cheeses and sugar until fluffy. Add liqueur and vanilla; beat until smooth. Spoon about 2 tablespoons filling down the center of each crepe; roll up. Top with chocolate syrup, whipped cream and cocoa if desired.

Chicken Club Brunch Ring

PREP: 20 MIN. • BAKE: 20 MIN. • YIELD: 16 SERVINGS

A few tubes of crescent rolls make this impressive recipe a snap. I fill the ring with chicken salad and serve warm slices with mustard-flavored mayonnaise.

Rebecca Clark *Warrior, Alabama*

- **½ cup mayonnaise**
- **1 tablespoon minced fresh parsley**
- **2 teaspoons Dijon mustard**
- **1½ teaspoons finely chopped onion**
- **1¾ cups cubed cooked chicken breast (½-inch cubes)**
- **2 bacon strips, cooked and crumbled**
- **1 cup (4 ounces) shredded Swiss cheese, divided**
- **2 tubes (8 ounces each) refrigerated crescent rolls**
- **2 plum tomatoes**
- **2 cups shredded lettuce**

1 In a large bowl, combine the mayonnaise, parsley, mustard and onion. Stir in the chicken, bacon and ¾ cup cheese.

2 Unroll crescent dough; separate into 16 triangles. Arrange on an ungreased 12-in. round pizza pan, forming a ring with pointed ends facing outer edge of pan and wide ends overlapping.

3 Spoon chicken mixture over wide ends; fold points over filling and tuck under wide ends (filling will be visible). Chop half of a tomato; set aside. Slice remaining tomatoes; place over filling and tuck into dough.

4 Bake at 375° for 20-25 minutes or until golden brown. Sprinkle with remaining cheese. Let stand for 5 minutes. Place lettuce in center of ring; sprinkle with chopped tomato.

30 min.

Baked Fruit Compote

PREP/TOTAL TIME: 30 MIN.
YIELD: 11 SERVINGS

Put canned fruit in a fancy, festive mood with a splash of Madeira wine. This dish brightens any winter brunch. Mix and match canned fruits to suit your family's tastes.

Myrt Pfannkuche *Pell City, Alabama*

- **1 can (29 ounces) sliced peaches, drained**
- **1 can (20 ounces) pineapple chunks, drained**
- **2 cans (8 ounces each) grapefruit sections, drained**
- **1 can (15¼ ounces) sliced pears, drained**
- **1 can (11 ounces) mandarin oranges, drained**
- **1 cup pitted dried plums**
- **½ cup butter, cubed**
- **½ cup packed brown sugar**
- **¼ cup Madeira wine, optional**

Fresh mint leaves, optional

1 In a 13-in. x 9-in. baking dish, combine the first six ingredients.

2 In a small saucepan, combine butter and brown sugar. Bring to a boil over medium heat; cook and stir for 2-3 minutes or until sugar is dissolved. Remove from the heat; stir in wine if desired. Pour over fruit and toss to coat.

3 Bake, uncovered, at 350° for 20-25 minutes or until heated through. Garnish with mint if desired.

Blueberry Sour Cream Pancakes

PREP: 20 MIN. • COOK: 5MIN./BATCH
YIELD: ABOUT 20 PANCAKES (3½ CUPS TOPPING)

When our family of 10 goes blueberry picking, we have a bounty of berries in no time. We especially enjoy them in these melt-in-your-mouth pancakes topped with a satisfying sauce.

Paula Hadley *Somerville, Louisiana*

- **½ cup sugar**
- **2 tablespoons cornstarch**
- **1 cup cold water**
- **4 cups fresh or frozen blueberries**

PANCAKES:

- **2 cups all-purpose flour**
- **¼ cup sugar**
- **4 teaspoons baking powder**
- **½ teaspoon salt**
- **2 eggs, lightly beaten**
- **1½ cups 2% milk**
- **1 cup (8 ounces) sour cream**
- **⅓ cup butter, melted**
- **1 cup fresh or frozen blueberries**

1 In a large saucepan, combine sugar and cornstarch. Stir in water until smooth. Add blueberries. Bring to a boil over medium heat; cook and stir for 2 minutes or until thickened. Remove from the heat; cover and keep warm.

2 For pancakes, in a large bowl, combine the flour, sugar, baking powder and salt. Combine the eggs, milk, sour cream and butter. Stir into dry ingredients just until moistened. Fold in blueberries.

3 Pour batter by ¼ cupful onto a greased hot griddle. Turn when bubbles form on top; cook until the second side is golden brown. Serve with blueberry topping.

EDITOR'S NOTE: If using frozen blueberries, use without thawing to avoid discoloring the batter.

Fajita Frittata

PREP/TOTAL TIME: 25 MIN.
YIELD: 8 SERVINGS

Why settle for a bowl of cereal when you can have this super flavorful and quick entree. It takes me just a few minutes to prepare. Though it's ideal for breakfast and brunch, it is also a popular dinner request at my house.

Mary Ann Gomez *Lombard, Illinois*

- **½ pound boneless skinless chicken breast, cut into strips**
- **1 small onion, cut into thin strips**
- **½ medium green pepper, cut into thin strips**
- **1 teaspoon lime juice**
- **½ teaspoon salt**
- **½ teaspoon ground cumin**
- **½ teaspoon chili powder**
- **2 tablespoons canola oil**
- **8 eggs, lightly beaten**
- **1 cup (4 ounces) shredded Colby-Monterey Jack cheese**

Salsa and sour cream, optional

1 In a large ovenproof skillet, saute the chicken, onion, green pepper, lime juice, salt, cumin and chili powder in oil until chicken is no longer pink.

2 Pour eggs over chicken mixture. Cover and cook over medium-low heat for 8-10 minutes or until eggs are nearly set. Uncover; broil 6 in. from the heat for 2-3 minutes or until eggs are set.

3 Sprinkle with cheese. Cover and let stand for 1 minute or until cheese is melted. Serve with salsa and sour cream if desired.

Tomato Onion Quiche

**PREP: 20 MIN. • BAKE: 45 MIN. + STANDING
YIELD: 3 SERVINGS**

This pretty quiche is best fresh out of the oven when the cheese is wonderfully gooey. I especially enjoy it in summer with vine-ripe tomatoes and fresh basil.

Sherri Crews *St. Augustine, Florida*

- **1 sheet refrigerated pie pastry**
- **1 cup (4 ounces) shredded part-skim mozzarella cheese**
- **½ cup sliced sweet onion**
- **2 small plum tomatoes, seeded and thinly sliced**
- **3 medium fresh mushrooms, thinly sliced**
- **¼ cup shredded Parmesan cheese**
- **3 eggs**
- **½ cup half-and-half cream**
- **½ teaspoon ground mustard**
- **½ teaspoon dried basil**
- **½ teaspoon dried oregano**
- **½ teaspoon dried thyme**

1 Cut pastry sheet in half. Repackage and refrigerate one half for another use. On a lightly floured surface, roll out remaining half into an 8-in. circle. Transfer to a 7-in. pie plate; flute edges.

2 Layer half of the mozzarella cheese, onion and tomato in pastry. Top with mushrooms; layer with remaining mozzarella cheese, onion and tomato. Sprinkle with Parmesan cheese. In a small bowl, combine the eggs, cream, mustard and herbs; pour over top.

3 Bake at 350° for 45-55 minutes or until a knife inserted near the center comes out clean. Let stand for 10 minutes before cutting.

Caramel-Pecan French Toast Bake

PREP: 20 MIN. + CHLLING • BAKE: 30 MIN. • YIELD: 8 SERVINGS

For a sensational Sunday brunch specialty, try this French toast. You make it up the night before, so you only need to bake it and make the syrup the following day.

Brad Shue *Harper, Kansas*

- **1 cup packed brown sugar**
- **½ cup butter, cubed**
- **2 tablespoons light corn syrup**
- **1 cup chopped pecans, divided**
- **8 slices French bread (¾ inch thick)**
- **6 eggs**
- **1½ cups 2% milk**
- **1½ teaspoons ground cinnamon**
- **1 teaspoon ground nutmeg**
- **1 teaspoon vanilla extract**
- **¼ teaspoon salt**

SAUCE:

- **½ cup packed brown sugar**
- **¼ cup butter, cubed**
- **1 tablespoon light corn syrup**

1 In a small saucepan, combine the brown sugar, butter and corn syrup. Bring to a boil. Reduce heat; cook and stir for 3-4 minutes or until thickened. Pour into a greased 13-in. x 9-in. baking dish. Sprinkle with ½ cup pecans; top with bread slices.

2 In a large bowl, whisk the eggs, milk, cinnamon, nutmeg, vanilla and salt; pour evenly over bread. Sprinkle with remaining pecans. Cover and refrigerate for 8 hours or overnight.

3 Remove from the refrigerator 30 minutes before baking. Bake, uncovered, at 350° for 30-35 minutes or until a knife inserted near the center comes out clean.

4 Meanwhile, in a small saucepan, combine sauce ingredients. Bring to a boil. Reduce heat; cook and stir for 2 minutes or until thickened. Serve with French toast.

Scrambled Eggs with Chorizo 

PREP/TOTAL TIME: 15 MIN. • YIELD: 2 SERVINGS

Sometimes I serve this egg breakfast for lunch or dinner with a tossed salad or green vegetable such as steamed spinach. For even more variety, replace the tortillas with taco chips.

Donna Marie Ryan *Topsfield, Massachusetts*

- **3 flour tortillas (6 inches)**
- **2 tablespoons butter, divided**
- **3 ounces uncooked chorizo or bulk spicy pork sausage**
- **1 tablespoon diced seeded jalapeno pepper**
- **2 garlic cloves, minced**
- **2 plum tomatoes, seeded and chopped**
- **½ teaspoon Cajun seasoning**
- **4 eggs, lightly beaten**
- **3 tablespoons picante sauce**

1 Cut tortillas into quarters; place on a baking sheet coated with cooking spray. Bake at 400° for 3-5 minutes or until crisp.

2 Meanwhile, in a small skillet, heat 1 tablespoon butter. Crumble chorizo into the pan; add jalapeno and garlic. Cook and stir over medium heat until meat is fully cooked; drain. Stir in tomatoes and Cajun seasoning.

3 In another skillet, heat remaining butter until hot. Add eggs; cook and stir over medium heat until completely set. Divide scrambled eggs between two plates. Serve with chorizo mixture, tortillas and picante sauce.

EDITOR'S NOTE: Wear disposable gloves when cutting hot peppers; the oils can burn skin. Avoid touching your face.

CAJUN SEASONING

>> Look for Cajun seasoning in the spice section of your grocery store. You can also make your own Cajun seasoning. Although there are many different blends, a typical mix includes salt, onion powder, garlic powder, cayenne pepper, ground mustard, celery seed and pepper.

I'm Stuffed French Toast

PREP: 30 MIN. • COOK: 5 MIN. • YIELD: 4 SERVINGS

I was able to remake this dish I first enjoyed at a restaurant. The fruit adds a special touch to this morning delight.

Melissa Kerrick *Auburn, New York*

- **2 medium ripe bananas, sliced**
- **2 tablespoons brown sugar**
- **1 teaspoon banana or vanilla extract**
- **1 package (8 ounces) reduced-fat cream cheese**
- **8 slices oat bread (½ inch thick)**
- **2 eggs**
- **⅔ cup evaporated milk**
- **1¼ teaspoons ground cinnamon**
- **1¼ teaspoons vanilla extract**
- **1 tablespoon butter**
- **1 cup sliced fresh strawberries or frozen unsweetened sliced strawberries, thawed**
- **½ cup fresh blueberries or frozen unsweetened blueberries**
- **1 tablespoon sugar**
- **Confectioners' sugar**

1 In a large skillet coated with cooking spray, saute bananas with brown sugar. Stir in banana extract. In a small bowl, beat cream cheese until smooth. Add banana mixture; beat well. Spread on four slices of bread; top with remaining bread.

2 In a shallow bowl, whisk the eggs, milk, cinnamon and vanilla. Dip both sides of sandwiches in egg mixture.

3 In a large skillet, toast sandwiches in butter for 2-3 minutes on each side or until golden brown.

4 Meanwhile, in a saucepan, combine the strawberries, blueberries and sugar; heat through. Serve with French toast; sprinkle with confectioners' sugar.

30 min.

Pecan-Stuffed Waffles

PREP/TOTAL TIME: 15 MIN.
YIELD: 4 SERVINGS

Look no further for an easy yet impressive recipe that's perfect for guests. No one will believe it only takes minutes to prepare. The creamy brown sugar and pecan filling between the waffles is delectable!

Jenny Flake *Newport Beach, California*

- **8 frozen waffles**
- **2 packages (3 ounces each) cream cheese, softened**
- **½ cup packed brown sugar**
- **1½ teaspoons ground cinnamon**
- **1 teaspoon vanilla extract**
- **½ cup chopped pecans**
- **1 cup maple syrup**
- **Confectioners' sugar**
- **4 fresh strawberries, cut in half**

1 Toast waffles according to package directions. In a small bowl, beat the cream cheese, brown sugar, cinnamon and vanilla until smooth. Stir in pecans.

2 Spread over four waffles; top with remaining waffles. Drizzle with syrup. Sprinkle with confectioners' sugar; garnish with a strawberry.

Strawberry Puff Pancake

30 min.

PREP/TOTAL TIME: 30 MIN.
YIELD: 4 SERVINGS

I've cut this recipe to 2 eggs and 1/2 cup milk for my husband and me, and it works just fine. It's yummy with strawberry or blueberry topping. You could even garnish it with whipped topping for a light dessert.

Brenda Morton *Hale Center, Texas*

- **2 tablespoons butter**
- **3 eggs**
- **¾ cup fat-free milk**
- **1 teaspoon vanilla extract**
- **¾ cup all-purpose flour**
- **⅛ teaspoon salt**
- **⅛ teaspoon ground cinnamon**
- **¼ cup sugar**
- **1 tablespoon cornstarch**
- **½ cup water**
- **1 cup sliced fresh strawberries**

Confectioners' sugar

1 Place butter in a 9-in. pie plate; place in a 400° oven for 4-5 minutes or until melted. Meanwhile, in a small bowl, whisk the eggs, milk and vanilla. In another small bowl, combine the flour, salt and cinnamon; whisk into egg mixture until blended.

2 Pour into prepared pie plate. Bake for 15-20 minutes or until sides are crisp and golden brown.

3 In a small saucepan, combine sugar and cornstarch. Stir in water until smooth; add strawberries. Cook and stir over medium heat until thickened. Coarsely mash strawberries. Serve with pancake. Dust with confectioners' sugar.

Spring Morning Casserole

PREP: 25 MIN. + CHILLING • BAKE: 40 MIN. + STANDING • YIELD: 12 SERVINGS

My mom gave me this recipe, and it has quickly become my favorite breakfast casserole. I love that it can be made the night before and popped in the oven for a stress-free morning.

Melody Holland *Lebanon, Pennsylvania*

- **2 cups cut fresh asparagus (1-inch pieces)**
- **1 small sweet red pepper, chopped**
- **1 small onion, chopped**
- **3 tablespoons butter**
- **8 cups cubed day-old French bread**
- **1 cup cubed fully cooked ham**
- **2 cups (8 ounces) shredded cheddar cheese**
- **8 eggs, beaten**
- **2 cups 2% milk**
- **⅓ cup honey**
- **½ teaspoon salt**
- **⅓ teaspoon pepper**

1 In a large skillet, saute the asparagus, red pepper and onion in butter until tender; set aside.

2 Place bread in a greased 13-in. x 9-in. baking dish. Layer with ham, 1 cup cheese and vegetable mixture. Sprinkle with remaining cheese. In a large bowl, combine the eggs, milk, honey, salt and pepper. Pour over the top of casserole. Cover and refrigerate overnight.

3 Remove from the refrigerator 30 minutes before baking. Bake, uncovered, at 350° for 40-45 minutes or until a knife inserted near the center comes out clean. Let stand for 10 minutes before cutting.

Ham & Cheese Breakfast Strudels

PREP: 25 MIN. • BAKE: 15 MIN. • YIELD: 6 SERVINGS

Make any morning special with these savory breakfast strudels. Sometimes I assemble the strudels ahead and freeze them individually before baking.

Jo Groth *Plainfield, Iowa*

- **3 tablespoons butter, divided**
- **2 tablespoons all-purpose flour**
- **1 cup milk**
- **⅓ cup shredded Swiss cheese**
- **2 tablespoons grated Parmesan cheese**
- **¼ teaspoon salt**
- **5 eggs, lightly beaten**
- **¼ pound ground fully cooked ham (about ¾ cup)**
- **6 sheets phyllo dough**
- **½ cup butter, melted**
- **¼ cup dry bread crumbs**

TOPPING:

- **2 tablespoons grated Parmesan cheese**
- **2 tablespoons minced fresh parsley**

1 In a small saucepan, melt 2 tablespoons butter. Stir in flour until smooth; gradually add milk. Bring to a boil; cook and stir for 2 minutes or until thickened. Stir in cheeses and salt. Set aside.

2 In a large nonstick skillet, melt remaining butter over medium heat. Add eggs to the pan; cook and stir until almost set. Stir in ham and reserved cheese sauce; heat through. Remove from the heat.

3 Place one sheet of phyllo dough on a work surface. (Keep remaining phyllo covered with plastic wrap and a damp towel to prevent it from drying out.) Brush with melted butter. Sprinkle with 2 teaspoons bread crumbs. Fold in half lengthwise; brush again with butter. Spoon ⅓ cup filling onto phyllo about 2 in. from a short side. Fold side and edges over filling and roll up.

4 Brush with butter. Repeat. Place desired number of strudels on a greased baking sheet; sprinkle each with 1 teaspoon cheese and 1 teaspoon parsley. Bake at 375° for 10-15 minutes or until golden brown. Serve immediately.

TO FREEZE AND BAKE STRUDELS: Individually wrap uncooked strudels in waxed paper and foil. Freeze for up to 1 month. Place 2 in. apart on a greased baking sheet; sprinkle with cheese and parsley. Bake at 375° for 30-35 minutes or until golden brown.

Ginger Fruit Crisp

PREP: 20 MIN. • BAKE: 30 MIN. • YIELD: 9 SERVINGS

Our B&B guests tell us this fun breakfast crisp is one of the most enjoyable parts of their stay. There is seldom a crumb of it left.

Elinor Stabile *Canmore, Alberta*

- **⅓ cup packed brown sugar**
- **2 tablespoons plus 1½ teaspoons cornstarch**
- **2 cups sliced fresh plums**
- **1 cup sliced peeled peaches**
- **1 cup sliced nectarines**

TOPPING:

- **1 cup crushed gingersnap cookies (about 20 cookies)**
- **½ cup old-fashioned oats**
- **⅓ cup packed brown sugar**
- **½ teaspoon ground ginger**
- **½ teaspoon ground cinnamon**
- **¼ teaspoon salt**
- **⅓ cup cold butter, cubed**
- **½ cup sliced almonds**

Whipped cream, optional

1 In a large bowl, combine brown sugar and cornstarch. Add the plums, peaches and nectarines; gently toss to coat. Transfer to a greased 8-in. square baking dish.

2 For topping, in a small bowl, combine the gingersnap crumbs, oats, brown sugar, ginger, cinnamon and salt. Cut in butter until crumbly. Stir in almonds; sprinkle over fruit.

3 Bake at 350° for 30-35 minutes or until filling is bubbly and topping is browned. Serve warm with whipped cream, if desired.

QUICK-COOKING OATS

>> Before quick-cooking or old-fashioned oats are processed, the hull is removed and they're cleaned, toasted and cleaned again. At this point, they are referred to as groats. Old-fashioned oats are groats that are steamed and flattened with huge rollers. They take about 15 minutes to cook. Quick-cooking oats are groats that have been cut into two or three pieces before being steamed and rolled. They cook in about 5 minutes. Use them interchangeably, but old-fashioned oats may add more texture.

Oatmeal Brulee with Ginger Cream

PREP: 30 MIN. • BROIL: 10 MIN. • YIELD: 4 SERVINGS

This is an awesome dish for a chilly morning. I love the crispy, caramelized top and raspberry surprise at the bottom.

Yvonne Starlin *Hermitage, Tennessee*

GINGER CREAM:

- **½ cup heavy whipping cream**
- **2 slices fresh gingerroot (about ¾-inch diameter)**
- **1 cinnamon stick (3 inches)**
- **1 tablespoon grated orange peel**
- **3 tablespoons maple syrup**
- **⅛ teaspoon ground nutmeg**

OATMEAL:

- **4 cups water**
- **2 cups old-fashioned oats**
- **¼ cup chopped dried apricots**
- **¼ cup dried cherries, chopped**
- **½ teaspoon salt**
- **3 tablespoons brown sugar**
- **2 tablespoons butter**
- **1 cup fresh or frozen unsweetened raspberries, thawed**
- **¼ cup sugar**

1 In a small saucepan, bring the cream, ginger, cinnamon and orange peel to a boil. Reduce heat; cover and simmer for 10 minutes. Remove from the heat; strain and discard the solids. Stir in syrup and nutmeg; set aside.

2 In a large saucepan over medium heat, bring water to a boil. Add the oats, apricots, cherries and salt; cook and stir for 5 minutes. Remove from the heat; stir in brown sugar and ¼ cup ginger cream. Cover and let stand for 2 minutes.

3 Grease four 10-oz. ramekins with the butter; add raspberries. Spoon oatmeal over the top; sprinkle with sugar. Place on a baking sheet. Broil 4-6 in. from the heat for 7-9 minutes or until sugar is caramelized. Serve with remaining ginger cream.

Ham and Avocado Scramble

30 min.

PREP/TOTAL TIME: 15 MIN.
YIELD: 4 SERVINGS

Hearty ham, creamy avocado and a hint of garlic; this winning egg dish works any time, breakfast, lunch or dinner.

Elisabeth Larsen *Pleasant Grove, Utah*

- **8 eggs**
- **¼ cup 2% milk**
- **1 teaspoon garlic powder**
- **¼ teaspoon pepper**
- **1 cup cubed fully cooked ham**
- **1 tablespoon butter**
- **1 medium ripe avocado, peeled and cubed**
- **1 cup (4 ounces) shredded Colby-Monterey Jack cheese**

1 In a large bowl, whisk the eggs, milk, garlic powder and pepper; stir in ham. In a large skillet, melt butter over medium-high heat. Add egg mixture; cook and stir until almost set. Stir in avocado and cheese. Cook and stir until completely set.

Southwest Breakfast Tart

PREP: 30 MIN. • BAKE: 25 MIN. + STANDING
YIELD: 6 SERVINGS

Give your breakfast crowd a stick-to-the-ribs jump start in the morning with this cheesy tart. It's packed with sausage, plenty of heat, color and hearty Tex-Mex flavor.

Pamela Shank *Parkersburg, West Virginia*

- **½ pound bulk spicy pork sausage**
- **4 teaspoons chopped seeded jalapeno pepper**
- **1 tablespoon finely chopped red onion**
- **1 can (4 ounces) chopped green chilies**
- **1 sheet refrigerated pie pastry**
- **1¼ cups shredded Monterey Jack cheese, divided**
- **6 eggs**
- **⅓ cup half-and-half cream**
- **½ teaspoon salt**
- **¼ teaspoon pepper**
- **1 tablespoon finely chopped sweet red pepper**
- **1 tablespoon finely chopped green pepper**

Optional toppings: sour cream, salsa, chopped tomatoes and sliced green onions

1 In a large skillet, cook the sausage, jalapeno and onion over medium heat until meat is no longer pink; drain. Stir in chilies.

2 Press pastry onto the bottom and up the sides of an ungreased 9-in. tart pan with removable bottom; trim edges. Sprinkle ½ cup cheese over crust; top with sausage mixture.

3 In a large bowl, whisk the eggs, cream, salt and pepper. Pour over sausage mixture. Sprinkle with red and green peppers and ½ cup cheese.

4 Bake at 350° for 25-30 minutes or until eggs are set and a knife inserted near the center comes out clean. Sprinkle with remaining cheese. Let stand for 10 minutes before cutting. Serve with toppings of your choice.

EDITOR'S NOTE: Wear disposable gloves when cutting hot peppers; the oils can burn skin. Avoid touching your face.

Broccoli Quiche

PREP: 30 MIN. • BAKE: 35 MIN. + STANDING
YIELD: 6 SERVINGS

My mother passed down this quiche recipe to me. She has been making it for more than 30 years. It's versatile enough to serve at any meal. Leftovers can be frozen and reheated in the microwave.

Bridget Corbett *Valdosta, Georgia*

- **1 refrigerated pie pastry**
- **1 package (9 ounces) frozen broccoli cuts, thawed and chopped**
- **1 small onion, finely chopped**
- **2 tablespoons butter**
- **1 cup heavy whipping cream**
- **3 eggs**
- **½ cup mayonnaise**
- **1 tablespoon all-purpose flour**
- **1 tablespoon chicken broth**
- **½ teaspoon salt**
- **⅛ teaspoon ground nutmeg**
- **⅛ teaspoon pepper**
- **1½ cups (6 ounces) shredded cheddar cheese**

1 Unroll pastry into a 9-in. deep-dish pie plate; flute edges. Line unpricked pastry with a double thickness of heavy-duty foil. Bake at 450° for 8 minutes. Remove foil; bake 5 minutes longer. Cool on a wire rack.

2 In a large skillet, saute broccoli and onion in butter until onion is tender. Remove from the heat. In a large bowl, whisk the cream, eggs, mayonnaise, flour, broth, salt, nutmeg and pepper; stir in the cheese and broccoli mixture. Pour into crust.

3 Bake at 350° for 35-40 minutes or until a knife inserted near the center comes out clean. Let stand for 10 minutes before cutting.

Baked Apple French Toast

PREP: 20 MIN. + CHILLING • BAKE: 35 MIN.
YIELD: 10 SERVINGS

My wonderful brunch recipe tastes special and will have your guests asking for seconds. I serve it with whipped topping, maple syrup and additional nuts.

Beverly Johnston *Rubicon, Wisconsin*

- **20 slices French bread (1 inch thick)**
- **1 can (21 ounces) apple pie filling**
- **8 eggs, lightly beaten**
- **2 cups 2% milk**
- **2 teaspoons vanilla extract**
- **½ teaspoon ground cinnamon**
- **½ teaspoon ground nutmeg**

TOPPING:

- **1 cup packed brown sugar**
- **½ cup cold butter, cubed**
- **1 cup chopped pecans**
- **2 tablespoons corn syrup**

1 Arrange 10 slices of bread in a greased 13-in. x 9-in. baking dish. Spread with pie filling; top with remaining bread. In a large bowl, whisk the eggs, milk, vanilla, cinnamon and nutmeg. Pour over bread. Cover and refrigerate overnight.

2 Remove from the refrigerator 30 minutes before baking. Meanwhile, place brown sugar in a small bowl. Cut in butter until mixture resembles coarse crumbs. Stir in pecans and corn syrup. Sprinkle over French toast.

3 Bake, uncovered, at 350° for 35-40 minutes or until a knife inserted near the center comes out clean.

Mushroom-Artichoke Brunch Bake

PREP: 30 MIN. • BAKE: 40 MIN. • YIELD: 12 SERVINGS

While the potatoes are baking the rest of the prep can be done; there's not much slicing or measuring. You can also add a layer of little smoked sausages cut in half lengthwise over the artichokes if you want a more substantial meal.

Suzanne Francis *Marysville, Washington*

- **3 cups frozen shredded hash brown potatoes, thawed**
- **2 tablespoons butter, melted, divided**
- **½ teaspoon salt**
- **2½ cups sliced fresh mushrooms**
- **1 can (14 ounces) water-packed artichoke hearts, rinsed, drained and quartered**
- **3 cups (12 ounces) shredded cheddar cheese**
- **12 eggs**
- **1¾ cups 2% milk**
- **1 can (4 ounces) chopped green chilies, drained**

1 Place potatoes in a greased 13-in. x 9-in. baking dish; drizzle with 1 tablespoon butter and sprinkle with salt. Bake at 350° for 20-25 minutes or until lightly browned.

2 Meanwhile, in a small skillet, saute mushrooms in remaining butter until tender. Place artichokes on paper towels; pat dry. Sprinkle the mushrooms, artichokes and cheese over the potatoes. In a large bowl, whisk the eggs, milk and green chilies; pour over cheese.

3 Bake, uncovered, for 40-45 minutes or until a knife inserted near the center comes out clean. Let stand for 5 minutes before serving.

Crisp 'n' Tender Corn Waffles

PREP: 15 MIN. + STANDING • COOK: 20 MIN.
YIELD: 16 WAFFLES

I like to serve these crisp, golden-brown waffles with honey and applesauce. For a savory change of pace, serve them topped with creamed chicken.

Maxine Reese *Candler, North Carolina*

- **2 eggs, separated**
- **2 cups all-purpose flour**
- **2½ teaspoons baking powder**
- **½ teaspoon salt**
- **1½ cups milk**
- **1 can (8¼ ounces) cream-style corn**
- **½ cup canola oil**

1 Place egg whites in a small bowl; let stand at room temperature for 30 minutes.

2 In a large bowl, combine the flour, baking powder and salt. Combine the milk, corn, egg yolks and oil; stir into dry ingredients just until combined.

3 Beat reserved egg whites until stiff peaks form; fold into batter. Pour batter by ¼ cupfuls into a preheated waffle iron; bake according to manufacturer's directions until golden brown.

Cranberry Orange Pancakes

PREP: 20 MIN. • COOK: 5 MIN./BATCH • YIELD: 12 PANCAKES (1¼ CUPS SYRUP)

These fluffy pancakes are drop-dead gorgeous, ready in just minutes and brimming with sweet, tart and tangy flavor.

Nancy Zimmerman *Cape May Court House, New Jersey*

SYRUP:

- **1 cup fresh or frozen cranberries**
- **⅔ cup orange juice**
- **½ cup sugar**
- **3 tablespoons maple syrup**

PANCAKES:

- **2 cups biscuit/baking mix**
- **2 tablespoons sugar**
- **2 teaspoons baking powder**
- **2 eggs**
- **1 egg yolk**
- **1 cup evaporated milk**
- **2 tablespoons orange juice**
- **1 teaspoon grated orange peel**
- **⅓ cup chopped fresh or frozen cranberries**

Orange peel strips, optional

1 In a saucepan, bring the cranberries, orange juice and sugar to a boil. Reduce heat; simmer, uncovered, for 5 minutes. Cool slightly. With a slotted spoon, remove ¼ cup cranberries; set aside.

2 In a blender, process cranberry mixture until smooth. Transfer to a small bowl; stir in maple syrup and reserved cranberries. Keep warm.

3 In a large bowl, combine the biscuit mix, sugar and baking powder. In another bowl, whisk the eggs, egg yolk, milk, orange juice and peel. Stir into dry ingredients just until blended. Fold in chopped cranberries.

4 Drop batter by ¼ cupfuls onto a greased hot griddle; turn when bubbles form on top. Cook until second side is golden brown. Serve with syrup. Garnish with orange peel strips if desired.

Baked Breakfast Burritos 

PREP/TOTAL TIME: 30 MIN. • YIELD: 4 SERVINGS

Every week, I try a minimum of three new recipes. This is one I clipped from the paper. When I served it to my five grown children, not a morsel was left!

Carol Towey *Pasadena, California*

- **6 to 8 bacon strips**
- **8 fresh mushrooms, sliced**
- **6 green onions, sliced**
- **1/3 cup chopped green pepper**
- **1 garlic clove, minced**
- **8 eggs**
- **1/4 cup sour cream**
- **3/4 cup shredded cheddar cheese, divided**
- **3 tablespoons enchilada sauce**
- **1 tablespoon butter**
- **4 large flour tortillas (10 inches)**

Sour cream and additional enchilada sauce, optional

1 In a skillet, cook bacon until crisp; remove to paper towel to drain. Reserve 1 tablespoon of drippings. Saute mushrooms, onions, green pepper and garlic in drippings until tender; set aside and keep warm.

2 In a bowl, beat eggs and sour cream. Stir in 1/4 cup cheese and enchilada sauce. In a skillet, melt butter; add egg mixture. Cook over low heat, stirring occasionally until eggs are set. Remove from heat.

3 Crumble the bacon; add to eggs with mushroom mixture. Spoon down center of tortillas; roll up.

4 Place, seam side down, in an 11-in. x 7-in. baking dish. Sprinkle with remaining cheese. Bake at 350° for 5 minutes or until cheese melts. Serve with sour cream and enchilada sauce if desired.

Croissant French Toast

PREP/TOTAL TIME: 30 MIN. • YIELD: 4 SERVINGS

More like a scrumptious dessert than a main dish, this rich French toast is topped with a tangy raspberry sauce and a vanilla sauce that includes ice cream. I cut the croissants into shapes with a cookie cutter for my 4-year-old grandson, Patrick. He even asks for the "ice cream sauce" on pancakes.

June Dickerson *Philippi, West Virginia*

- **½ cup sugar**
- **1 tablespoon all-purpose flour**
- **2 cups heavy whipping cream**
- **4 egg yolks, beaten**
- **2 scoops vanilla ice cream**
- **1 tablespoon vanilla extract**

BERRY SAUCE:

- **2 cups fresh or frozen raspberries**
- **2 tablespoons sugar**

FRENCH TOAST:

- **3 eggs**
- **4 croissants, split**
- **2 tablespoons butter**

1 In a large saucepan, combine the sugar and flour. Stir in cream until smooth. Cook and stir over medium-high heat until thickened and bubbly. Reduce heat; cook and stir 2 minutes longer. Remove from the heat. Stir a small amount of hot filling into egg yolks; return all to the pan, stirring constantly. Cook and stir until mixture reaches 160°.

2 Remove from the heat. Gently stir in ice cream and vanilla until ice cream is melted. Place plastic wrap over the surface of the sauce; cool.

3 For berry sauce, combine raspberries and sugar in a saucepan. Simmer, uncovered, for 2-3 minutes. Remove from the heat; set aside.

4 In a shallow bowl, beat eggs. Dip both sides of croissants in egg. On a griddle, brown croissants on both sides in butter. Serve with vanilla and berry sauces.

FLAVORFUL FRENCH TOAST

>> When making French toast, try giving it a boost by using a flavored nondairy coffee creamer instead of milk in the egg-milk mixture. French vanilla is especially yummy.

Eggs Benedict Brunch Braid

PREP: 45 MIN. • BAKE: 20 MIN. • YIELD: 8 SERVINGS

A Christmas morning staple at our house, this pretty braid has all the ingredients of a classic eggs Benedict dish, encased in puff pastry to create a beautiful loaf.

Sarah Strohl *Commerce Township, Michigan*

- **3 egg yolks**
- **1 tablespoon lemon juice**
- **¼ teaspoon salt**
- **¼ teaspoon Dijon mustard**
- **Dash cayenne pepper**
- **½ cup unsalted butter, melted**

BRAID:

- **1 tablespoon unsalted butter**
- **6 eggs**
- **½ teaspoon salt**
- **¼ teaspoon pepper**
- **1 sheet frozen puff pastry, thawed**
- **6 slices Canadian bacon**
- **2 tablespoons minced chives, divided**
- **1 teaspoon water**

1 In a blender, combine the first five ingredients. Cover and process on high. While processing, gradually add butter in a steady stream until combined. Set aside.

2 In a large skillet, melt butter over medium-high heat. Whisk five eggs, salt and pepper; add to skillet. Cook and stir until barely set; stir in sauce.

3 On a lightly greased baking sheet, roll out pastry into a 12-in. x 10-in. rectangle. Layer the Canadian bacon and egg mixture down the center of rectangle; sprinkle with 1 tablespoon chives.

4 On each long side, cut ½-in.-wide strips. Starting at one end, fold alternating strips at an angle across filling; pinch ends to seal. Whisk remaining egg and water; brush over braid.

5 Bake at 375° for 20-25 minutes or until golden brown and eggs are completely set. Let stand for 5 minutes before cutting. Sprinkle with remaining chives.

EDITOR'S NOTE: Refrigerate the assembled braid overnight, or freeze it for up to two weeks. Cover tightly with plastic wrap so the pastry doesn't dry out. Before baking, brush with egg wash. Add 20 minutes to baking time if frozen.

Golden Corn Quiche

PREP: 20 MIN. • BAKE: 35 MIN. + STANDING
YIELD: 8 SERVINGS

I serve cut-up fresh fruit with this comforting quiche, which my vegetarian son really enjoys. You could also pair it with a slice or two of ham.

Donna Gonda *North Canton, Ohio*

- **1 unbaked pastry shell (9 inches)**
- **1⅓ cups half-and-half cream**
- **3 eggs**
- **3 tablespoons butter, melted**
- **½ small onion, cut into wedges**
- **1 tablespoon all-purpose flour**
- **1 tablespoon sugar**
- **1 teaspoon salt**
- **2 cups frozen corn, thawed**

1 Let pastry shell stand at room temperature for 10 minutes. Line unpricked pastry shell with a double thickness of heavy-duty foil. Bake at 375° for 5 minutes. Remove foil; bake 5 minutes longer.

2 In a blender, combine the cream, eggs, butter, onion, flour, sugar and salt; cover and process until blended. Stir in corn; pour into crust.

3 Bake for 35-40 minutes or until a knife inserted near the center comes out clean. Let stand for 10 minutes before cutting.

WINNERS
CIRCLE

beef

Add it to a casserole, throw it on the grill or savor it in a home-style stew... beef boosts the appeal and heartiness of any entree. So the next time your hungry crew asks what's for dinner, wow them by serving any one of these ribbon-winning beef specialties.

PEPPERED FILETS WITH TOMATO-MUSHROOM SALSA, 103

Maple-Glazed Corned Beef

PREP: 25 MIN. • COOK: 2½ HOURS
YIELD: 12 SERVINGS

Corned beef gets a touch of sweetness thanks to a maple syrup glaze. Even people who say they don't care for corned beef will ask for seconds when served this one. This recipe was passed down from my great-grandmother.

Gayle Macklin *Vail, Arizona*

- **2 corned beef briskets with spice packets (3 pounds each)**
- **1 large sweet onion, sliced**
- **12 garlic cloves, peeled and halved**
- **¼ cup kosher salt**
- **¼ cup whole peppercorns**
- **8 bay leaves**
- **2 tablespoons dried basil**
- **2 tablespoons dried oregano**
- **4 quarts water**
- **3 cups beef broth**
- **¼ cup maple syrup**
- **⅓ cup packed brown sugar**

1 Place briskets and contents of the spice packets in a stockpot. Add onion, garlic, salt, peppercorns, bay leaves, basil and oregano. Pour in water and beef broth. Bring to a boil. Reduce heat; cover and simmer for 2½ to 3 hours or until meat is tender.

2 Transfer meat to a broiler pan. Brush with maple syrup; sprinkle with brown sugar. Broil 4-6 in. from the heat for 2-3 minutes or until beef is glazed. Thinly slice across the grain.

CORNED BEEF COVER-UP

>> When you cook a corned beef and cabbage dinner, save the broth. The next day, chop up the leftover beef, carrots, cabbage and potatoes and simmer them in the broth with any other leftover vegetables you have on hand to make a hearty and enjoyable soup.

French Beef Stew

PREP: 40 MIN. • COOK: 2¼ HOURS • YIELD: 20 SERVINGS (1 CUP EACH)

"Special" and "sensational" are words that come to mind to describe this stew. One bite and you'll know why. It makes a lot, but can easily be halved.

John Maxson *Mason City, Illinois*

- **5 pounds beef sirloin tip roast, cut into 1-inch cubes**
- **1½ teaspoons salt**
- **½ teaspoon pepper**
- **3 tablespoons olive oil**
- **2 large sweet onions, chopped**
- **3 medium carrots, sliced**
- **5 tablespoons butter, divided**
- **6 garlic cloves, minced**
- **2 pounds assorted fresh mushrooms, such as portobello, shiitake or oyster, sliced**
- **4 large Yukon Gold potatoes, cubed**
- **1 carton (32 ounces) beef broth**
- **1 cup dry red wine or additional beef broth**
- **1 tablespoon minced fresh basil or 1 teaspoon dried basil**
- **3 tablespoons all-purpose flour**
- **1 cup heavy whipping cream**
- **⅔ cup crumbled blue cheese**

1 Sprinkle beef with salt and pepper. In a stockpot, brown the beef in oil in batches. Remove and keep warm.

2 In the same pan, saute onions and carrots in 2 tablespoons butter for 4 minutes. Add garlic; cook 2 minutes longer. Stir in mushrooms, potatoes, broth, wine, basil and beef. Bring to a boil. Reduce heat; cover and simmer for 1¼ hours. Uncover; simmer 20-30 minutes longer or until beef is tender.

3 In a small saucepan, melt remaining butter. Stir in flour until smooth; gradually add cream. Bring to a boil; cook and stir for 2 minutes or until thickened. Stir into stew; heat through. Sprinkle with cheese.

BBQ Hoedown Tacos

PREP: 20 MIN. • COOK: 15 MIN.
YIELD: 4 SERVINGS

Here's a family-friendly twist on traditional tacos. They're easy to make after a long day at work. I use toasted flour tortillas, which are a healthy alternative to fried shells. To toast the tortillas, fold them in half without creasing the bottom. Pop into a long slotted toaster and toast to golden brown. They will be in a natural taco shape and ready to eat.

Denise Pounds *Hutchinson, Kansas*

- **1 pound ground beef**
- **1 small onion, chopped**
- **¾ cup barbecue sauce**
- **1 can (4 ounces) chopped green chilies**
- **1 teaspoon ground coriander**
- **1 teaspoon ground cumin**
- **½ teaspoon salt**
- **2 cups angel hair coleslaw mix**
- **¼ cup green goddess salad dressing**
- **8 flour tortillas (6 inches), warmed**
- **8 slices pepper jack cheese**

1 In a large nonstick skillet, cook beef and onion over medium heat until meat is no longer pink; drain. Stir in the barbecue sauce, chilies, coriander, cumin and salt. Bring to a boil. Reduce heat; simmer, uncovered, for 5-7 minutes or until heated through.

2 In a small bowl, combine coleslaw mix and salad dressing; toss to coat. On each tortilla, layer cheese, beef mixture and coleslaw; fold to close.

Creamy Beef Enchiladas

PREP: 25 MIN. • BAKE: 20 MIN.
YIELD: 12 SERVINGS

People rave over the comforting home-style twist I added to traditional beef enchiladas. A can of cream of mushroom soup is the trick!

Belinda Moran *Woodbury, Tennessee*

- **2 pounds lean ground beef (90% lean)**
- **1 cup chopped onion**
- **1 can (10¾ ounces) condensed cream of mushroom soup, undiluted**
- **1 cup (8 ounces) sour cream**
- **1 can (4 ounces) chopped green chilies**
- **3 cups (12 ounces) shredded cheddar cheese, divided**
- **3 cans (10 ounces each) enchilada sauce, divided**
- **12 flour tortillas (8 inches), warmed**

1 In a Dutch oven, cook beef and onion over medium heat until meat is no longer pink; drain. Add the soup, sour cream, chilies, 1 cup cheese and ½ cup enchilada sauce; heat through.

2 Spread ¼ cup enchilada sauce into each of two ungreased 13-in. x 9-in. baking dishes. Place ½ cup beef mixture down the center of each tortilla. Roll up and place seam side down in each prepared dish.

3 Pour remaining enchilada sauce over top; sprinkle with remaining cheese. Bake, uncovered, at 350° for 20-25 minutes or until heated through.

Caribbean Beef Short Ribs

PREP: 30 MIN. • COOK: 5½ HOURS • YIELD: 8 SERVINGS

Fresh pineapple and mango add a subtle sweetness to these fall-off-the-bone tender ribs. Slow cooker preparation makes it a great no-fuss meal.

Loanne Chiu *Fort Worth, Texas*

- **3 pounds boneless beef short ribs, cut into 1½-inch pieces**
- **¼ cup olive oil**
- **⅔ cup thawed pineapple juice concentrate**
- **⅔ cup reduced-sodium soy sauce**
- **½ cup water**
- **⅓ cup rum**
- **⅓ cup honey**
- **2 tablespoons minced fresh gingerroot**
- **6 garlic cloves, minced**
- **2 teaspoons pepper**
- **1 teaspoon ground allspice**
- **½ teaspoon salt**
- **2 large sweet red peppers, chopped**
- **2 cups cubed fresh pineapple**
- **2 cups cubed peeled mango**
- **6 green onions, cut into 1-inch pieces**
- **2 tablespoons cornstarch**
- **2 tablespoons cold water**

Lettuce leaves

1 In a large skillet, brown ribs in oil in batches on all sides. Transfer to a 4-qt. slow cooker.

2 Add the pineapple juice concentrate, soy sauce, water, rum, honey, ginger, garlic, pepper, allspice and salt to the skillet. Bring to a boil; reduce heat and simmer for 5 minutes. Pour over ribs.

3 Cover and cook on low for 5-6 hours or until meat is tender. Stir in red peppers. Top with the pineapple, mango and onions (do not stir). Cover and cook 30 minutes longer or until heated through.

4 Remove beef mixture to a large bowl; keep warm. Transfer cooking juices to a small saucepan. Combine cornstarch and cold water until smooth; gradually stir into pan. Bring to a boil; cook and stir for 2 minutes or until thickened. Serve beef mixture on lettuce; drizzle with gravy.

Bacon & Tomato-Topped Meat Loaf

PREP: 30 MIN. • BAKE: 1 HOUR • YIELD: 6 SERVINGS

I started with a meat loaf recipe that included horseradish and I added a few other complementary flavors. The results were a moist meat loaf with visible bits of veggies and plenty of savory flavor.

Cheryl Moring *New Edinburg, Arkansas*

- **1 small onion, finely chopped**
- **1 celery rib, finely chopped**
- **1 small green pepper, finely chopped**
- **1 tablespoon canola oil**
- **1 garlic clove, minced**
- **1 egg, lightly beaten**
- **1 tablespoon prepared horseradish**
- **1 tablespoon dry red wine or beef broth**
- **1 teaspoon prepared mustard**
- **1 teaspoon Worcestershire sauce**
- **1 cup soft bread crumbs**
- **1 tablespoon all-purpose flour**
- **1 tablespoon brown sugar**
- **1 teaspoon salt**
- **1 teaspoon Cajun seasoning**
- **1 teaspoon pepper**
- **½ teaspoon chili powder**
- **1 pound lean ground beef (90% lean)**
- **½ pound bulk pork sausage**
- **½ pound bacon strips**

TOPPING:

- **1 can (14½ ounces) diced tomatoes, drained**
- **1 can (8 ounces) tomato sauce**

1 In a large skillet, saute the onion, celery and green pepper in oil until tender. Add garlic; cook 1 minute longer. Transfer to a large bowl; cool slightly.

2 Add the egg, horseradish, wine, mustard, Worcestershire sauce, bread crumbs, flour, brown sugar and seasonings. Crumble beef and sausage over mixture and mix well. Pat into an ungreased 9-in. x 5-in. loaf pan. Place bacon strips over meat loaf; tuck in ends.

3 Bake, uncovered, at 350° for 55 minutes. Combine tomatoes and tomato sauce; spoon over loaf. Bake 5-10 minutes longer or until no pink remains and a thermometer reads 160°.

Steak and Rice Roll-Ups

PREP: 25 MIN. • COOK: 1¼ HOURS • YIELD: 6 SERVINGS

I have been making this family-favorite recipe since the 1960s. It still gets many compliments and makes any meal special.

Elaine Solander *Littleton, Colorado*

- **1 cup finely chopped fresh mushrooms**
- **2 green onions, finely chopped**
- **¼ cup finely chopped green pepper**
- **2 tablespoons butter**
- **1½ cups cooked long grain rice**
- **2 tablespoons diced pimientos**
- **¼ teaspoon dried thyme**
- **¼ teaspoon dried marjoram**
- **2 pounds beef top round steak (½ inch thick)**
- **2 tablespoons canola oil**
- **2 tablespoons plus 1 teaspoon onion soup mix**
- **1 cup water**

1 In a large skillet, saute the mushrooms, onions and pepper in butter until tender. Transfer to a small bowl; stir in the rice, pimientos, thyme and marjoram.

2 Cut steak into six pieces; flatten to ½-in. thickness. Spread evenly with mushroom mixture; roll up and secure with toothpicks.

3 In the same skillet, brown roll-ups in oil on all sides. Add soup mix and water; cover and simmer for 1 to 1¼ hours or until meat is tender, occasionally spooning cooking liquid over roll-ups.

4 Thicken cooking juices if desired; serve with roll-ups. Discard toothpicks.

Mongolian Beef

PREP/TOTAL TIME: 25 MIN. • YIELD: 4 SERVINGS

My family just loves this meal-in-one, including my husband, who is truly a meat-and-potatoes guy. The dish uses inexpensive ingredients to produce big flavor in a small amount of time.

Heather Blum *Coleman, Wisconsin*

- **1 tablespoon cornstarch**
- **¾ cup reduced-sodium chicken broth**
- **2 tablespoons reduced-sodium soy sauce**
- **1 tablespoon hoisin sauce**
- **2 teaspoons sesame oil**
- **1 pound beef top sirloin steak, cut into thin strips**
- **1 tablespoon olive oil, divided**
- **5 green onions, cut into 1-inch pieces**
- **2 cups hot cooked rice**

1 In a small bowl, combine cornstarch and broth until smooth. Stir in the soy sauce, hoisin sauce and sesame oil; set aside. In a large nonstick skillet or wok, stir-fry beef in 1½ teaspoons hot olive oil until no longer pink. Remove and keep warm.

2 In the same skillet, stir-fry the onions in remaining olive oil for 3-4 minutes or until crisp-tender. Stir cornstarch mixture and add to the pan. Bring to a boil; cook and stir for 2 minutes or until thickened. Reduce heat; add beef and heat through. Serve with rice.

Peppered Filets with Tomato-Mushroom Salsa

PREP: 30 MIN. • COOK: 15 MIN. • YIELD: 6 SERVINGS

The secret to these marvelous filets is in the salsa. It's full of fresh veggies and seasonings that bring a true taste of summer at any time of the year.

Ann Hillmeyer *Sandia Park, New Mexico*

- **6 plum tomatoes, seeded and chopped**
- **1 cup chopped fresh mushrooms**
- **¼ cup minced fresh Italian parsley**
- **2 tablespoons finely chopped shallot**
- **2 teaspoons minced garlic, divided**
- **5 teaspoons olive oil, divided**
- **1 tablespoon lime juice**
- **½ teaspoon salt**
- **¼ teaspoon pepper**
- **6 beef tenderloin steaks (4 ounces each)**
- **2 teaspoons lemon-pepper seasoning**
- **⅓ cup balsamic vinegar**
- **¼ cup beef broth**
- **4 teaspoons butter**
- **6 lime slices**

1 For salsa, in a small bowl, combine the tomatoes, mushrooms, parsley, shallot, 1 teaspoon garlic, 3 teaspoons oil, lime juice, salt and pepper; set aside.

2 Sprinkle steaks with lemon pepper. In a large skillet, cook steaks in remaining oil for 4-5 minutes on each side or until meat reaches desired doneness (for medium-rare, a thermometer should read 145°; medium, 160°; well-done, 170°). Remove and keep warm.

3 Combine the vinegar, broth and remaining garlic; stir into skillet. Bring to a boil; cook until liquid is reduced by half, about 2-3 minutes. Stir in butter.

4 Spoon sauce over steaks. Serve with salsa. Garnish with lime slices.

Pizza Tot Casserole

PREP: 10 MIN. • BAKE: 30 MIN. • YIELD: 6-8 SERVINGS

This upside-down pizza casserole requires ground beef and only a handful of other ingredients. The Tater Tots make this simple supper a guaranteed kid-pleaser.

Chris Stukel *Des Plaines, Illinois*

- **1 pound ground beef**
- **1 medium green pepper, chopped**
- **1 medium onion, chopped**
- **1 can (10¾ ounces) condensed tomato soup, undiluted**
- **1 jar (4½ ounces) sliced mushrooms, drained**
- **1 teaspoon Italian seasoning**
- **2 cups (8 ounces) shredded part-skim mozzarella cheese**
- **1 package (32 ounces) frozen Tater Tots**

1 In a large skillet, cook the beef, pepper and onion over medium heat until meat is no longer pink; drain. Add the soup, mushrooms and Italian seasoning.

2 Transfer to a greased 13-in. x 9-in. baking dish. Top with cheese and potatoes. Bake, uncovered, at 400° for 30-35 minutes or until golden brown.

Italian Strip Steaks with Focaccia

PREP: 15 MIN. • COOK: 25 MIN. • YIELD: 4 SERVINGS

Tender, juicy steaks are dressed up with roasted sweet peppers, baby portobellos, shallots, onions, olives and cheese. It's a magnificent meal that is surprisingly simple to prepare.

Patricia Harmon *Baden, Pennsylvania*

- **4 boneless beef top loin steaks (8 ounces each)**
- **3 tablespoons olive oil, divided**
- **½ pound sliced baby portobello mushrooms**
- **1 shallot, finely chopped**
- **3 tablespoons chopped red onion**
- **2 garlic cloves, minced**
- **2 teaspoons minced fresh rosemary**
- **½ cup roasted sweet red peppers, cut into strips**
- **¼ cup dry red wine or beef broth**
- **¼ teaspoon salt**
- **¼ teaspoon coarsely ground pepper**
- **1 focaccia bread (12 ounces), cut into quarters**
- **⅔ cup shredded Asiago cheese**
- **¼ cup sliced pimiento-stuffed olives**

1 In a large skillet, cook steaks in 2 tablespoons oil over medium heat for 5-6 minutes on each side or until meat reaches desired doneness (for medium-rare, a thermometer should read 145°; medium, 160°; well-done, 170°). Remove and keep warm.

2 In the same skillet, saute the mushrooms, shallot and onion in remaining oil. Add garlic and rosemary; saute 1-2 minutes longer. Stir in the red peppers, wine, salt and pepper; heat through.

3 Place focaccia on serving plates; top each with a steak and ½ cup mushroom mixture. Sprinkle with cheese and olives.

EDITOR'S NOTE: Top loin steak may be labeled as strip steak, Kansas City steak, New York strip steak, ambassador steak or boneless club steak in your region.

Slow-Cooked Caribbean Pot Roast

PREP: 30 MIN. • COOK: 6 HOURS • YIELD: 10 SERVINGS

I put this dish together throughout the fall and winter seasons, but considering how simple it is to prepare, anytime is a great time to enjoy it!

Jenn Tidwell *Fair Oaks, California*

- **2 medium sweet potatoes, cubed**
- **2 large carrots, sliced**
- **¼ cup chopped celery**
- **1 boneless beef chuck roast (2½ pounds)**
- **1 tablespoon canola oil**
- **1 large onion, chopped**
- **2 garlic cloves, minced**
- **1 tablespoon all-purpose flour**
- **1 tablespoon sugar**
- **1 tablespoon brown sugar**
- **1 teaspoon ground cumin**
- **¾ teaspoon salt**
- **¾ teaspoon ground coriander**
- **¾ teaspoon chili powder**
- **½ teaspoon dried oregano**
- **⅛ teaspoon ground cinnamon**
- **¾ teaspoon grated orange peel**
- **¾ teaspoon baking cocoa**
- **1 can (15 ounces) tomato sauce**

1 Place potatoes, carrots and celery in a 5-qt. slow cooker. In a large skillet, brown meat in oil on all sides. Transfer meat to slow cooker.

2 In the same skillet, saute onion in drippings until tender. Add garlic; cook 1 minute longer. Combine the flour, sugar, brown sugar, seasonings, orange peel and cocoa. Stir in tomato sauce; add to skillet and heat through. Pour over beef.

3 Cover and cook on low for 6-8 hours or until beef and vegetables are tender.

Chipotle-Honey Grilled T-Bones

PREP: 20 MIN. + MARINATING • GRILL: 10 MIN. YIELD: 4 SERVINGS

If you like to kick things up on the grill, this is the steak for you.

Donna Goutermont *Juneau, Alaska*

- **½ cup minced fresh cilantro**
- **½ cup lime juice**
- **½ cup honey**
- **2 tablespoons adobo sauce**
- **3 garlic cloves, minced**
- **1 tablespoon chopped chipotle pepper in adobo sauce**
- **1 teaspoon salt**
- **1 teaspoon ground cumin**
- **½ teaspoon ground allspice**
- **½ teaspoon pepper**
- **¼ teaspoon Dijon mustard**
- **4 beef T-bone steaks (12 ounces each)**

1 In a small bowl, combine the first 11 ingredients. Pour ½ cup marinade into a large resealable plastic bag. Add the steaks; seal bag and turn to coat. Refrigerate for up to 1 hour. Cover and refrigerate remaining marinade.

2 Drain meat and discard marinade. Grill steaks, covered, over medium heat or broil 4 in. from the heat for 5-6 minutes on each side or until meat reaches desired doneness (for medium-rare, a thermometer should read 145°; medium, 160°; well-done, 170°), basting occasionally with ½ cup reserved marinade. Serve with remaining marinade.

Loaded Flank Steak

30 min.

PREP/TOTAL TIME: 30 MIN.
YIELD: 6 SERVINGS

For a delicious steak dinner, try this super easy recipe. The stuffing mixture filling makes the entree elegant enough to serve to guests.

Tammy Thomas *Mustang, Oklahoma*

- **½ cup butter, softened**
- **6 bacon strips, cooked and crumbled**
- **3 green onions, chopped**
- **2 tablespoons ranch salad dressing mix**
- **½ teaspoon pepper**
- **1 beef flank steak (1½ to 2 pounds)**

1 In a small bowl, combine the first five ingredients. Cut a deep slit in steak, forming a pocket. Stuff butter mixture into slit.

2 Grill steak, covered, over medium heat or broil 4-6 in. from the heat for 6-7 minutes on each side or until meat reaches desired doneness (for medium-rare, a thermometer should read 145°; medium, 160°; well-done, 170°). Let stand 5 minutes before serving. To serve, thinly slice across the grain.

Santa Maria Roast Beef

PREP: 20 MIN. + MARINATING • GRILL: 1 HOUR + STANDING
YIELD: 6 SERVINGS

It just isn't summer until I enjoy this succulent roast beef hot from the grill. The tender slices are wonderful paired with potatoes and carrots or as a sandwich.

Allison Ector *Ardmore, Pennsylvania*

- **4 tablespoons paprika**
- **3 tablespoons brown sugar**
- **2 tablespoons chili powder**
- **1 tablespoon garlic powder**
- **1 tablespoon white pepper**
- **1 tablespoon celery salt**
- **1 tablespoon ground cumin**
- **1 tablespoon dried oregano**
- **1 tablespoon pepper**
- **2 teaspoons cayenne pepper**
- **1 teaspoon ground mustard**
- **1 beef tri-tip roast or beef sirloin tip roast (2 to 3 pounds)**
- **2 cups soaked hickory wood chips or chunks**
- **2 tablespoons canola oil**

1 Combine the first 11 ingredients; rub desired amount over roast. Wrap in plastic and refrigerate overnight. Store leftover dry rub in an airtight container for up to 6 months.

2 Remove roast from the refrigerator 1 hour before grilling. Prepare grill for indirect heat, using a drip pan. Add wood chips according to manufacturer's directions.

3 Unwrap roast and brush with oil; place over drip pan. Grill, covered, over medium-low indirect heat for 1 to 1½ hours or until meat reaches desired doneness (for medium-rare, a thermometer should read 145°; medium, 160°; well-done, 170°). Let stand for 10-15 minutes before slicing.

BAKED SANTA MARIA ROAST BEEF: Prepare roast and refrigerate as directed. Unwrap roast and brush with oil and ½ teaspoon liquid smoke. Place on a rack in a shallow roasting pan. Bake, uncovered, at 425° for 55-75 minutes or until meat reaches desired doneness.

Shepherd's Pie Twice-Baked Potatoes

PREP: 1¾ HOURS • BAKE: 25 MIN. • YIELD: 6 SERVINGS

My spin on stuffed potatoes makes for a filling meal. Serve with a green salad, and satisfaction is guaranteed even for hearty appetites.

Cyndy Gerken *Naples, Florida*

- **6 large russet potatoes**
- **2 tablespoons olive oil**
- **1 pound ground beef**
- **1 medium onion, chopped**
- **1 medium green pepper, chopped**
- **1 medium sweet red pepper, chopped**
- **4 garlic cloves, minced**
- **1 package (16 ounces) frozen mixed vegetables**
- **3 tablespoons Worcestershire sauce**
- **1 tablespoon tomato paste**
- **1 tablespoon steak seasoning**
- **¼ teaspoon salt**
- **⅛ teaspoon pepper**

Dash cayenne pepper

- **2 teaspoons paprika, divided**
- **½ cup butter, cubed**
- **¾ cup heavy whipping cream**
- **¼ cup sour cream**
- **1 cup shredded Monterey Jack cheese**
- **1 cup shredded cheddar cheese**
- **¼ cup shredded Parmesan cheese**
- **2 tablespoons minced chives**

TOPPINGS:

- **½ cup shredded cheddar cheese**
- **1 teaspoon paprika**
- **1 tablespoon minced chives**

1 Scrub and pierce potatoes; rub with oil. Bake at 375° for 1 hour or until tender.

2 In a large skillet, cook the beef, onion, peppers and garlic over medium heat until beef is no longer pink; drain. Add the mixed vegetables, Worcestershire sauce, tomato paste, steak seasoning, salt, pepper, cayenne and 1 teaspoon paprika. Cook and stir until vegetables are tender.

3 When cool enough to handle, cut a thin slice off the top of each potato and discard. Scoop out the pulp, leaving thin shells.

4 In a large bowl, mash the pulp with butter. Add the whipping cream, sour cream, cheeses and chives; mash until combined. Spoon 1 cup meat mixture into each potato shell; top with ½ cup potato mixture. Sprinkle with remaining paprika.

5 Place on a baking sheet. Bake at 375° for 20 minutes. Sprinkle with cheese and paprika; bake 5 minutes longer or until melted. Sprinkle with chives.

Favorite Mexican Lasagna

PREP: 25 MIN. • BAKE: 40 MIN. + STANDING
YIELD: 12 SERVINGS

I love lasagna and I love Mexican food, so it only seemed appropriate that I create a dish that combines the two. Here are the delicious results. Feel free to change up the toppings to suit your family's taste.

Tina Newhauser *Peterborough, New Hampshire*

- **1¼ pounds ground beef**
- **1 medium onion, chopped**
- **4 garlic cloves, minced**
- **2 cups salsa**
- **1 can (16 ounces) refried beans**
- **1 can (15 ounces) black beans, rinsed and drained**
- **1 can (10 ounces) enchilada sauce**
- **1 can (4 ounces) chopped green chilies**
- **1 envelope taco seasoning**
- **¼ teaspoon pepper**
- **6 flour tortillas (10 inches)**
- **3 cups (12 ounces) shredded Mexican cheese blend, divided**
- **2 cups crushed tortilla chips**

Sliced ripe olives, guacamole, chopped tomatoes and sour cream, optional

1 In a large skillet, cook beef and onion over medium heat until meat is no longer pink. Add garlic; cook 1 minute longer. Drain. Stir in the salsa, beans, enchilada sauce, chilies, taco seasoning and pepper; heat through.

2 Spread 1 cup meat mixture in a greased 13-in. x 9-in. baking dish. Layer with two tortillas, a third of the remaining meat mixture and 1 cup cheese. Repeat layers. Top with remaining tortillas and meat mixture.

3 Cover and bake at 375° for 30 minutes. Uncover; sprinkle with remaining cheese and top with tortilla chips.

4 Bake 10-15 minutes longer or until cheese is melted. Let stand for 10 minutes before serving. Garnish with olives, guacamole, tomatoes and sour cream if desired.

Meatball Sub Casserole

PREP: 40 MIN. • BAKE: 30 MIN. • YIELD: 6 SERVINGS

If you like meatball subs, you'll love this tangy casserole that has all the rich flavor of the popular sandwiches with none of the mess.

Gina Harris *Seneca, South Carolina*

- **⅓ cup chopped green onions**
- **¼ cup seasoned bread crumbs**
- **3 tablespoons grated Parmesan cheese**
- **1 pound ground beef**
- **1 loaf (1 pound) Italian bread, cut into 1-inch slices**
- **1 package (8 ounces) cream cheese, softened**
- **½ cup mayonnaise**
- **1 teaspoon Italian seasoning**
- **¼ teaspoon pepper**
- **2 cups (8 ounces) shredded part-skim mozzarella cheese, divided**
- **3½ cups spaghetti sauce**
- **1 cup water**
- **2 garlic cloves, minced**

1 In a large bowl, combine the onions, bread crumbs and Parmesan cheese. Crumble beef over mixture and mix well. Shape into 1-in. balls; place on a greased rack in a shallow baking pan. Bake at 400° for 15-20 minutes or until no longer pink.

2 Meanwhile, arrange bread in a single layer in an ungreased 13-in. x 9-in. baking dish (all of the bread might not be used). Combine the cream cheese, mayonnaise, Italian seasoning and pepper; spread over the bread. Sprinkle with ½ cup mozzarella.

3 Combine the spaghetti sauce, water and garlic; add meatballs. Pour over cheese mixture; sprinkle with remaining mozzarella. Bake, uncovered, at 350° for 30 minutes or until heated through.

Melt-in-Your-Mouth Pot Roast

PREP: 10 MIN. • COOK: 6 HOURS
YIELD: 6-8 SERVINGS

Something about a pot roast dinner just says welcome home. And with the slow cooker doing most of the work, it's even more inviting for me!

Jeannie Klugh *Lancaster, Pennsylvania*

- **1 pound medium red potatoes, quartered**
- **1 cup fresh baby carrots**
- **1 boneless beef chuck roast (3 to 4 pounds)**
- **¼ cup Dijon mustard**
- **2 teaspoons dried rosemary, crushed**
- **1 teaspoon garlic salt**
- **½ teaspoon dried thyme**
- **½ teaspoon pepper**
- **⅓ cup chopped onion**
- **1½ cups beef broth**

1 Place potatoes and carrots in a 5-qt. slow cooker. Cut roast in half. In a small bowl, combine the mustard, rosemary, garlic salt, thyme and pepper; rub over roast.

2 Place in slow cooker; top with onion and broth. Cover and cook on low for 6-8 hours or until meat and vegetables are tender.

Merlot Filet Mignon

PREP/TOTAL TIME: 20 MIN. • YIELD: 2 SERVINGS

Although this filet is such a simple recipe, you can feel confident serving it to your guests. The rich sauce adds a touch of elegance. Just add a salad and rolls and enjoy!

Jauneen Hosking *Waterford, Wisconsin*

- **2 beef tenderloin steaks (8 ounces each)**
- **3 tablespoons butter, divided**
- **1 tablespoon olive oil**
- **1 cup merlot**
- **2 tablespoons heavy whipping cream**
- **⅛ teaspoon salt**

1 In a small skillet, cook steaks in 1 tablespoon butter and oil over medium heat for 4-6 minutes on each side or until meat reaches desired doneness (for medium-rare, a thermometer should read 145°; medium, 160°; well-done, 170°). Remove and keep warm.

2 In the same skillet, add wine, stirring to loosen browned bits from pan. Bring to a boil; cook until liquid is reduced to ¼ cup. Add the cream, salt and remaining butter; bring to a boil. Cook and stir for 1-2 minutes or until slightly thickened and butter is melted. Serve with steaks.

Worth It Lasagna

PREP: 1 HOUR • BAKE: 55 MIN. + STANDING
YIELD: 2 CASSEROLES (12 SERVINGS EACH)

I break out this lasagna recipe whenever I need to feed a crowd. It has such an abundance of tasty ingredients. Often I'll serve one pan to guests and freeze the other for a family meal later.

Joan Broxholme *Boulder City, Nevada*

- **2 jars (24 ounces each) meatless spaghetti sauce**
- **1 can (14½ ounces) diced tomatoes, drained**
- **½ cup Burgundy wine**
- **2 tablespoons brown sugar**
- **3 garlic cloves, minced**
- **2 pounds Italian turkey sausage links, casings removed**
- **¾ cup raisins**
- **2 teaspoons Italian seasoning**
- **1½ pounds sliced fresh mushrooms**
- **1 medium onion, chopped**
- **2 eggs, lightly beaten**
- **2 cartons (15 ounces each) ricotta cheese**
- **1 package (10 ounces) frozen chopped spinach, thawed and squeezed dry**
- **1 cup grated Parmesan cheese**
- **2 packages (24 ounces each) frozen cheese ravioli, thawed**
- **1 cup shredded Parmesan cheese**
- **18 slices provolone cheese, cut in half**
- **6 cups (24 ounces) shredded Monterey Jack cheese**
- **5 large tomatoes, sliced**

1 In a Dutch oven, bring first five ingredients to a boil. Reduce heat; simmer, uncovered, for 20 minutes or until desired thickness is achieved, stirring often.

2 In a large skillet, cook sausage over medium heat until no longer pink; drain. Stir in raisins and Italian seasoning; add to sauce. In the same skillet, saute mushrooms and onion until moisture has evaporated. Stir into sauce. In a large bowl, combine the eggs, ricotta, spinach and grated Parmesan cheese; set aside.

3 In each of two greased 13-in. x 9-in. baking dishes, layer with $1\frac{1}{3}$ cups sauce, half of a package of ravioli, $1\frac{1}{3}$ cups sauce, $\frac{1}{4}$ cup shredded Parmesan cheese, six half slices of provolone cheese, 1 cup Monterey Jack cheese and $2\frac{1}{2}$ cups spinach mixture.

4 Top each with six half slices of provolone cheese, 1 cup Monterey Jack cheese, $1\frac{1}{3}$ cups sauce, remaining ravioli and sauce, $\frac{1}{4}$ cup shredded Parmesan cheese, six half slices of provolone cheese, sliced tomatoes and remaining Monterey Jack cheese (dishes will be full).

5 Cover and bake at 375° for 45 minutes. Uncover; bake 10-15 minutes longer or until a thermometer reads 160°. Let stand 15 minutes before serving.

Peppered Filets with Cherry Port Sauce for 2

PREP/TOTAL TIME: 30 MIN. • YIELD: 2 SERVINGS

I like to serve my peppery beef steaks with a light vegetable side dish. You can substitute dried cranberries for the cherries and feta for blue cheese.

Barbara Lento *Houston, Pennsylvania*

- **2 beef tenderloin steaks (8 ounces each)**
- **2 teaspoons coarsely ground pepper**
- **1 cup dry red wine**
- **$\frac{1}{2}$ cup chopped red onion**
- **$\frac{1}{3}$ cup golden raisins**
- **$\frac{1}{3}$ cup dried cherries**
- **2 tablespoons sugar**
- **$1\frac{1}{2}$ teaspoons cornstarch**
- **$\frac{1}{4}$ teaspoon ground mustard**

Dash salt

- **2 teaspoons cold water**
- **$\frac{1}{4}$ cup crumbled blue cheese**

1 Sprinkle steaks with pepper. Grill, covered, over medium heat or broil 4 in. from the heat for 6-8 minutes on each side or until meat reaches desired doneness (for medium-rare, a thermometer should read 145°; medium, 160°; well-done, 170°).

2 Meanwhile, in a small saucepan, combine the wine, onion, raisins, cherries and sugar. Bring to a boil; cook until liquid is reduced by half.

3 Combine the cornstarch, mustard, salt and water until smooth. Gradually stir into the pan. Bring to a boil; cook and stir for 2 minutes or until thickened. Serve sauce with steaks; sprinkle with cheese.

WINNERS CIRCLE

Tuscan Steak Flatbreads

PREP: 25 MIN. • GRILL: 15 MIN. • YIELD: 4 SERVINGS

It was love at first taste when I discovered this flatbread sandwich. Here is my own creation starring tender strips of steak and Tuscan flavors.

Michael Cohen *Los Angeles, California*

SUN-DRIED TOMATO PESTO:

- **⅓ cup packed fresh parsley sprigs**
- **2 tablespoons fresh basil leaves**
- **1 garlic clove, quartered**
- **2 tablespoons grated Parmesan cheese**
- **2 tablespoons oil-packed sun-dried tomatoes, patted dry**
- **2 tablespoons sherry**
- **¼ teaspoon salt**
- **Dash pepper**
- **¼ cup olive oil**

STEAK FLATBREADS:

- **1 beef top sirloin steak (¾ inch thick and 1¼ pounds)**
- **¼ teaspoon salt**
- **¼ teaspoon pepper**
- **4 flatbreads or whole pita breads**
- **2 tablespoons olive oil**
- **1 cup (4 ounces) shredded fontina cheese**
- **¼ cup fresh basil leaves, thinly sliced**

1 For pesto, place the parsley, basil and garlic in a food processor; cover and pulse until chopped. Add the Parmesan cheese, tomatoes, sherry, salt and pepper; cover and process until blended. While processing, gradually add oil in a steady stream. Set aside.

2 Sprinkle steak with salt and pepper. Grill, covered, over medium heat for 6-10 minutes on each side or until meat reaches desired doneness (for medium-rare, a thermometer should read 145°; medium, 160°; well-done, 170°). Remove and keep warm.

3 Brush one side of each flatbread with oil; place oiled side down on grill rack. Grill, covered, over medium heat for 1-2 minutes or until heated through.

4 Spread pesto over grilled side of flatbreads. Cut steak into thin strips; place over pesto. Top with fontina cheese and basil.

Zippy Peanut Steak Kabobs

PREP: 40 MIN. + MARINATING • GRILL: 10 MIN. • YIELD: 8 SERVINGS

If you like your kabobs with a kick, you're sure to savor these meaty skewers seasoned with habanero pepper sauce. The zippy steak chunks are balanced with refreshing pineapple and red pepper. Sometimes I substitute chicken for the beef.

Sheri Nutter *Oneida, Kentucky*

- **¾ cup packed brown sugar**
- **¾ cup water**
- **1 cup chunky peanut butter**
- **1 cup reduced-sodium soy sauce**
- **¾ cup honey barbecue sauce**
- **⅓ cup canola oil**
- **1 to 2 tablespoons habanero pepper sauce**
- **3 garlic cloves, minced**
- **2 pounds beef top sirloin steak, cut into thin strips**
- **2 teaspoons ground ginger**
- **1 fresh pineapple, cut into 1-inch cubes**
- **2 large sweet red peppers, cut into 1-inch pieces**

Hot cooked jasmine rice

1 In a small saucepan, combine brown sugar and water. Cook and stir over low heat until sugar is dissolved. Remove from the heat. Whisk in peanut butter until blended. Stir in the soy sauce, barbecue sauce, oil, pepper sauce and garlic.

2 Pour 3 cups of the marinade into a large resealable plastic bag; add beef. Seal bag and turn to coat; refrigerate for 4 hours. Cover and refrigerate remaining marinade until serving.

3 Drain meat and discard marinade. Sprinkle ginger over pineapple. On 16 metal or soaked wooden skewers, alternately thread the beef, pineapple and red peppers.

4 Grill, covered, over medium heat for 5-7 minutes on each side or until meat reaches desired doneness. Serve with rice and reserved marinade for dipping.

Wild West Wellingtons

PREP: 15 MIN. • BAKE: 20 MIN.
YIELD: 2 SERVINGS

Traditional Beef Wellington is delicious...but add some southwestern flair and it becomes an incredible experience for the palate!

Jenni Dise *Phoenix, Arizona*

- **2 beef tenderloin steaks (6 ounces each)**
- **¼ teaspoon salt**
- **¼ teaspoon ground cumin**
- **¼ teaspoon pepper**
- **2 ounces cream cheese, softened**
- **¼ cup canned chopped green chilies**
- **½ sheet frozen puff pastry, thawed**
- **2 teaspoons beaten egg**
- **½ teaspoon water**

Salsa, optional

1 Sprinkle steaks with salt, cumin and pepper. In a large nonstick skillet coated with cooking spray, brown steaks on both sides; remove and keep warm. In a small bowl, combine cream cheese and chilies; set aside.

2 On a lightly floured surface, roll pastry into a 16-in. x 12-in. rectangle. Cut into two 12-in. x 8-in. rectangles. Place a steak on one side of each rectangle; top with cream cheese mixture. Fold pastry over meat; seal seams. Place seam side down on a rack in a shallow baking pan.

3 Combine egg and water; brush over pastry. Bake at 400° for 18-22 minutes or until meat reaches desired doneness (for medium-rare, a thermometer should read 145°; medium, 160°; well-done, 170°). Let stand for 5 minutes. Serve with salsa if desired.

WINNERS CIRCLE

pork

Chicken and beef are delicious, but when you've had your fill, turn to juicy, versatile pork. Spicy pork sausage jazzes up casseroles and pizzas, while chops and tenderloin make a first-class meal. Get your knife and fork ready—these outstanding recipes are sure to win the affection of your taste buds.

ASIAN BARBECUED PORK LOIN, 122

Bourbon Brat Skewers

PREP: 20 MIN. + MARINATING • GRILL: 15 MIN.
YIELD: 6 SKEWERS

These skewers of grilled bratwurst and veggies marinated in a tasty bourbon sauce have a permanent place on our tailgate party food list.

Mary Marlowe Leverette *Columbia, South Carolina*

- **½ cup reduced-sodium soy sauce**
- **½ cup bourbon**
- **3 tablespoons brown sugar**
- **1 teaspoon seasoned salt**
- **¼ teaspoon cayenne pepper**
- **2 cups whole mushrooms**
- **2 medium sweet red peppers, cut into 1-inch pieces**
- **1 medium green pepper, cut into 1-inch pieces**
- **1 medium onion, cut into wedges**
- **1 package (16 ounces) uncooked bratwurst links, cut into 1-inch slices**

1 In a large resealable plastic bag, combine the first five ingredients. Add the vegetables; seal bag and turn to coat. Refrigerate for at least 1 hour.

2 Drain and reserve marinade. On six metal or soaked wooden skewers, alternately thread the vegetables and bratwurst. Brush with reserved marinade. Grill, covered, over medium heat for 15-20 minutes or until bratwurst is no longer pink and vegetables are tender, turning and basting frequently with reserved marinade.

MINCING AND CHOPPING

>> To mince or chop, hold the handle of a chef's knife with one hand, and rest the finger of your other hand on the top of the blade near the tip. Using the handle to guide and apply pressure, move knife in an arc across the food with a rocking motion until pieces of food are the desired size. Mincing results in pieces no larger than 1/8 in., and chopping can produce 1/4-in. to 1/2-in. pieces.

Apple-Stuffed Pork Chops

PREP: 30 MIN. • BAKE: 15 MIN. • YIELD: 2 SERVINGS

My family has used apples for many great dishes, including this one from my grandmother that I adapted for two. It also makes use of apple butter and apple cider. We love this recipe served with a baked sweet potato and green salad.

Heather Kenney *Arlington, Virginia*

- **2 tablespoons apple butter**
- **2 tablespoons cider vinegar**
- **1 tablespoon Dijon mustard**
- **2 to 3 teaspoons minced fresh rosemary**
- **2 boneless butterflied pork chops (6 ounces each)**
- **¾ teaspoon salt**
- **¼ teaspoon pepper**
- **1 large tart apple, chopped**
- **⅓ cup chopped sweet onion**
- **2 tablespoons butter**
- **¾ cup apple cider or juice**

1 In a small bowl, combine the apple butter, vinegar, mustard and rosemary. Flatten pork chops to ½-in. thickness; sprinkle with salt and pepper. Brush with apple butter mixture.

2 Combine apple and onion; place over one side of each pork chop. Fold other side of pork over filling and secure with toothpicks.

3 In a small ovenproof skillet, brown chops in butter for 3-4 minutes on each side or until a thermometer reads 145°. Add cider.

4 Bake, uncovered, at 350° for 15-20 minutes or until apples and onions are tender. Remove chops and keep warm. Bring pan juices to a boil; cook until reduced by half. Discard toothpicks. Serve with sauce.

EDITOR'S NOTE: This recipe was tested with commercially prepared apple butter.

30 min.

Peanutty Pork Stir-Fry

PREP/TOTAL TIME: 25 MIN.
YIELD: 2 SERVINGS

This easy, colorful stir-fry with an Asian flavor will become a popular mainstay at your house. Leftovers even taste great cold.

Gina Berry *Chanhassen, Minnesota*

- **1 can (8 ounces) pineapple chunks**
- **½ pound pork tenderloin, cut into ½-inch strips**
- **1 tablespoon sesame oil**
- **¾ cup julienned sweet red pepper**
- **¾ cup chopped carrot**
- **2 green onions, chopped**
- **3 tablespoons reduced-sodium soy sauce**
- **3 tablespoons reduced-sodium teriyaki sauce**
- **1 tablespoon creamy peanut butter**
- **¼ cup unsalted dry roasted peanuts, finely chopped**

Hot cooked rice, optional

1 Drain pineapple, reserving juice; set aside. In a large skillet, stir-fry pork in oil until no longer pink. Add the red pepper, carrot and onions; cook and stir for 2-3 minutes or until crisp-tender.

2 Stir in the soy sauce, teriyaki sauce, peanut butter and reserved pineapple juice. Bring to a boil; cook and stir for 1-2 minutes or until thickened. Stir in peanuts and pineapple. Serve with rice if desired.

Andouille-Stuffed Pork Loin

PREP: 30 MIN. • BAKE: 40 MIN. • YIELD: 12 SERVINGS

My andouille-stuffed and bacon-wrapped pork loin is full of bold flavors and simple to prepare. It is a potluck favorite. The recipe may be prepared ahead, covered and refrigerated before baking.

Judy Armstrong *Prairieville, Louisiana*

- **¼ cup Dijon mustard**
- **2 tablespoons apricot preserves**
- **1 tablespoon minced fresh rosemary or 1 teaspoon dried rosemary, crushed**
- **1 tablespoon minced fresh thyme or 1 teaspoon dried thyme**
- **3 garlic cloves, minced**
- **2 boneless pork loin roasts (2 pounds each)**
- **1 teaspoon salt**
- **1 teaspoon pepper**
- **4 fully cooked andouille sausage links (about 1 pound)**
- **12 bacon strips**
- **½ cup chicken broth**
- **½ cup white wine or additional chicken broth**

1 In a small bowl, combine the first five ingredients. Set aside.

2 Make a lengthwise slit down the center of each roast to within ½ in. of bottom. Open roast so it lies flat; cover with plastic wrap. Flatten slightly. Remove plastic wrap. Season with salt and pepper.

3 Arrange two sausage links in center of each roast. Close roasts; brush with mustard mixture. Wrap each roast with bacon. Tie several times with kitchen string; secure ends with toothpicks. Place on a rack in a shallow roasting pan. Pour broth and wine into roasting pan.

4 Bake, uncovered, at 400° for 40-50 minutes or until a thermometer inserted into the pork loin reads 145°. Let stand 5 minutes before slicing. Discard string and toothpicks.

"Secret's in the Sauce" BBQ Ribs

PREP: 10 MIN. • COOK: 6 HOURS
YIELD: 5 SERVINGS

A sweet, rich sauce makes these ribs so tender the meat literally falls off the bones. And the aroma is simply wonderful. Yum!

Tanya Reid *Winston-Salem, North Carolina*

- **2 racks pork baby back ribs (about 4½ pounds)**
- **1½ teaspoons pepper**
- **2½ cups barbecue sauce**
- **¾ cup cherry preserves**
- **1 tablespoon Dijon mustard**
- **1 garlic clove, minced**

1 Cut ribs into serving-size pieces; sprinkle with pepper. Place in a 5- or 6-qt. slow cooker. Combine the remaining ingredients; pour over ribs. Cover and cook on low for 6-8 hours or until meat is tender. Serve with sauce.

Pepperoni Lasagna Roll-ups

PREP: 45 MIN. • BAKE: 55 MIN. • YIELD: 16 SERVINGS

Tastes like pizza, looks like manicotti and everyone loves it! I'm a teacher and usually make it for faculty meetings and potlucks because it can be made in advance and is very portable.

Jamie Miller *Maple Grove, Minnesota*

- **16 uncooked lasagna noodles**
- **½ pound bulk Italian sausage**
- **½ pound sliced baby portobello mushrooms**
- **¼ cup chopped sweet onion**
- **1 jar (24 ounces) tomato basil pasta sauce**
- **1½ teaspoons brown sugar**
- **1½ teaspoons fennel seed, crushed**
- **½ teaspoon dried tarragon**
- **1⅛ teaspoons salt, divided**
- **⅛ teaspoon crushed red pepper flakes, optional**
- **1 package (3½ ounces) sliced pepperoni**
- **2½ cups (10 ounces) shredded part-skim mozzarella cheese**
- **2½ cups part-skim ricotta cheese**
- **2 cups grated Parmesan cheese, divided**
- **2 eggs, lightly beaten**
- **6 tablespoons minced fresh parsley, divided**
- **3 tablespoons minced fresh basil or 1 tablespoon dried basil**
- **½ teaspoon pepper**

1 Cook noodles according to package directions.

2 Meanwhile, in a Dutch oven, cook the sausage, mushrooms and onion over medium heat until meat is no longer pink; drain and transfer to a large bowl. Stir in the pasta sauce, brown sugar, fennel seed, tarragon, ⅛ teaspoon salt and pepper flakes if desired.

3 In the same pan, cook pepperoni for 4-5 minutes or until lightly browned; remove to paper towels to drain.

4 In another large bowl, combine the mozzarella, ricotta, 1 cup Parmesan, eggs, 4 tablespoons parsley, basil, pepper and remaining salt.

5 Drain noodles. Spread 1 cup meat sauce in a greased 13-in. x 9-in. baking dish. Spread ¼ cup cheese mixture over each noodle; top with 3 or 4 pepperoni slices. Carefully roll up; place seam side down in prepared dish. Top with remaining meat sauce; sprinkle with remaining Parmesan.

6 Cover and bake at 350° for 55-60 minutes or until bubbly. Sprinkle with remaining parsley before serving.

Orange-Ginger Pork Chops

PREP: 10 MIN. + MARINATING • GRILL: 10 MIN.
YIELD: 4 SERVINGS

Basting chops with this tangy sauce makes them extremely tender and savory. My family requests this dish for the terrific taste.

Lynette Randleman *Buffalo, Wyoming*

- **4 teaspoons minced fresh gingerroot**
- **1 garlic clove, minced**
- **1 tablespoon canola oil**
- **½ cup sherry or chicken broth**
- **¼ cup honey**
- **¼ cup reduced-sodium soy sauce**
- **1 tablespoon sesame seeds**
- **1 tablespoon grated orange peel**
- **¾ teaspoon hot pepper sauce**
- **4 bone-in pork loin chop (6 ounces each)**
- **1 teaspoon cornstarch**
- **2 tablespoons water**

1 In a large saucepan, cook ginger and garlic in oil for 1 minute; remove from the heat. Stir in the sherry or broth, honey, soy sauce, sesame seeds, orange peel and hot pepper sauce. Pour ½ cup into a small bowl; set aside.

2 Pour remaining marinade into a large resealable plastic bag; add pork chops. Seal bag and turn to coat; refrigerate for at least 1 hour.

3 Meanwhile, in a small saucepan, combine cornstarch and water until smooth; add reserved marinade. Bring to a boil; cook and stir for 1 minute or until thickened.

4 Drain and discard marinade from pork. Using long-handled tongs, moisten a paper towel with cooking oil and lightly coat the grill rack.

5 Grill chops, covered, over medium heat for 4-5 minutes on each side or until a thermometer reads 145°; baste occasionally with sauce. Let stand for 5 minutes before serving. Serve with remaining sauce.

Tacoritos

PREP: 40 MIN. • BAKE: 20 MIN. • YIELD: 8 SERVINGS

This mild and meaty Southwestern dish combines the delicious flavor of tacos with the heartiness of burritos. Your family's going to love them!

Monica Flatford *Knoxville, Tennessee*

- **¼ cup butter, cubed**
- **¼ cup all-purpose flour**
- **4 cups water**
- **3 tablespoons chili powder**
- **1 teaspoon garlic salt**
- **1 pound ground beef**
- **1 pound bulk pork sausage**
- **¼ cup chopped onion**
- **1 cup refried beans**
- **8 flour tortillas (8 inches), warmed**
- **3 cups (12 ounces) shredded Monterey Jack cheese**
- **Optional toppings: shredded lettuce, chopped tomatoes, sliced ripe olives and sour cream**

1 In a large saucepan, melt butter. Stir in flour until smooth; gradually add water. Bring to a boil; cook and stir for 1 minute or until thickened. Stir in chili powder and garlic salt. Bring to a boil. Reduce heat; simmer, uncovered, for 10 minutes.

2 In a large skillet over medium heat, cook the beef, sausage and onion until meat is no longer pink; drain. Stir in refried beans; heat through.

3 Spread ¼ cup sauce in a greased 13-in. x 9-in. baking dish. Spread 1 tablespoon sauce over each tortilla; place ⅔ cup meat mixture down the center of each. Top each with ¼ cup cheese. Roll up and place seam side down in prepared dish. Pour remaining sauce over the top; sprinkle with remaining cheese.

4 Bake, uncovered, at 350° for 18-22 minutes or until bubbly and cheese is melted. Serve with optional toppings if desired.

Big Kahuna Pizza

30 min.

PREP/TOTAL TIME: 30 MIN.
YIELD: 6 SERVINGS

A prebaked pizza crust and refrigerated barbecued pork make this tasty supper idea super fast and super easy. Cut into bite-sized pieces, and it can double as a great last-minute appetizer, too!

Joni Hilton *Rocklin, California*

- **1 prebaked 12-inch pizza crust**
- **1 carton (18 ounces) refrigerated fully cooked barbecued shredded pork**
- **1 can (20 ounces) pineapple chunks, drained**
- **⅓ cup chopped red onion**
- **2 cups (8 ounces) shredded part-skim mozzarella cheese**

1 Place pizza crust on an ungreased 12-in. pizza pan. Spread shredded pork over crust; top with pineapple and onion. Sprinkle with cheese.

2 Bake at 350° for 20-25 minutes or until cheese is melted.

Pizza Quesadillas

30 min.

PREP/TOTAL TIME: 10 MIN.
YIELD: 2 SERVINGS

When my husband and I need a quick meal, I fix this using leftover ingredients. Unlike traditional Mexican quesadillas, it calls for Italian meats, cheeses and seasoning. Serve it with a green salad topped with Italian dressing for a simple dinner for two.

Barbara Rupert *Edgefield, South Carolina*

- **1 cup meatless spaghetti sauce**
- **2 teaspoons butter, softened**
- **4 flour tortillas (10 inches)**
- **1 cup (4 ounces) shredded part-skim mozzarella cheese**
- **8 thin slices hard salami**
- **12 slices pepperoni**
- **¼ cup shredded Parmesan cheese**
- **½ teaspoon dried oregano**

1 In a small saucepan, cook spaghetti sauce over medium-low heat for 3-4 minutes or until heated through.

2 Meanwhile, spread butter over one side of each tortilla. Sprinkle unbuttered side of two tortillas with mozzarella cheese; top with salami and pepperoni. Sprinkle with Parmesan cheese and oregano. Top with remaining tortillas, buttered side up.

3 Cook on a griddle over medium heat for 2-3 minutes on each side or until cheese is melted. Cut into wedges; serve with warmed spaghetti sauce.

Asian Barbecued Pork Loin

PREP: 15 MIN. • BAKE: 1 HOUR + STANDING • YIELD: 8-10 SERVINGS

A sweet and spicy glass tops this tender and juicy roast. I like serving it with jasmine rice and green beans amandine.

Melissa Carafa *Broomall, Pennsylvania*

- **1 boneless whole pork loin roast (3 to 4 pounds)**
- **½ teaspoon garlic salt**
- **¼ teaspoon pepper**
- **¼ cup finely chopped onion**
- **1 tablespoon butter**
- **½ cup ketchup**
- **⅓ cup honey**
- **1 tablespoon hoisin sauce**
- **1½ teaspoons Chinese-style mustard**
- **1 teaspoon reduced-sodium soy sauce**
- **½ teaspoon garlic powder**
- **¼ teaspoon ground ginger**
- **¼ teaspoon Chinese five-spice powder**

1 Sprinkle pork roast with garlic salt and pepper. Place in a shallow roasting pan lined with heavy-duty foil. Bake, uncovered, at 350° for 50 minutes.

2 Meanwhile, in a small saucepan, saute onion in butter until tender. Stir in the remaining ingredients. Bring to a boil. Reduce heat; simmer, uncovered, until sauce is reduced to ¾ cup, about 20-25 minutes, stirring often.

3 Brush sauce over pork. Bake 10-15 minutes longer or until a thermometer reads 145°. Let stand for 10 minutes before slicing.

Sausage Calzones

PREP: 35 MIN. + RISING • BAKE: 20 MIN.
YIELD: 6 SERVINGS

In these pizza turnovers, Italian sausage combines with ricotta, Parmesan and spinach.

Janine Colasurdo *Chesapeake, Virginia*

- **1 package (¼ ounce) active dry yeast**
- **½ cup warm water (110° to 115°)**
- **¾ cup warm milk (110° to 115°)**
- **2 tablespoons plus 2 teaspoons olive oil, divided**
- **1½ teaspoons salt**
- **1 teaspoon sugar**
- **3 to 3¼ cups all-purpose flour**
- **1 pound bulk Italian sausage**
- **1 package (10 ounces) frozen chopped spinach, thawed and squeezed dry**
- **1 carton (15 ounces) ricotta cheese**
- **½ cup grated Parmesan cheese**
- **1 tablespoon minced fresh parsley**
- **⅛ teaspoon pepper**
- **2 tablespoons cornmeal**
- **½ teaspoon garlic salt**
- **1½ cups pizza sauce, warmed**

1 In a large bowl, dissolve yeast in water. Add the milk, 2 tablespoons oil, salt, sugar and 2 cups flour; beat until smooth. Stir in enough remaining flour to form a soft dough.

2 Turn onto a floured surface; knead until smooth and elastic, about 6-8 minutes. Place in a greased bowl; turn once to grease top. Cover and let rise in a warm place until doubled, about 1 hour.

3 Meanwhile, in a large skillet, cook sausage over medium heat until no longer pink; drain. Add the spinach, cheeses, parsley and pepper; mix well.

4 Punch dough down; divide into six pieces. On a floured surface, roll each piece into an 8-in. circle. Top each with ⅔ cup filling. Fold dough over filling; pinch to seal.

5 Place on greased baking sheets sprinkled with cornmeal. Brush tops lightly with remaining oil; sprinkle with garlic salt. Bake at 400° for 20-25 minutes or until golden brown. Serve with pizza sauce.

Fruited Pork Chops

PREP: 10 MIN. • COOK: 3 HOURS 10 MIN. • YIELD: 6 SERVINGS

Here's one of my favorite slow-cooker recipes. I often prepare these tender chops with pineapple sauce and serve them with fluffy and nutritious brown rice.

Cindy Ragan *North Huntingdon, Pennsylvania*

- **3 tablespoons all-purpose flour**
- **1½ teaspoons dried oregano**
- **¾ teaspoon salt**
- **¼ teaspoon garlic powder**
- **¼ teaspoon pepper**
- **6 lean boneless pork loin chops (5 ounces each)**
- **1 tablespoon olive oil**
- **1 can (20 ounces) unsweetened pineapple chunks**
- **¾ cup unsweetened pineapple juice**
- **¼ cup water**
- **2 tablespoons brown sugar**
- **2 tablespoons dried minced onion**
- **2 tablespoons tomato paste**
- **¼ cup raisins**

1 In a large resealable plastic bag, combine the flour, oregano, salt, garlic powder and pepper; add the pork chops, one at a time, and shake to coat. In a nonstick skillet, brown chops on both sides in oil. Transfer to a 5-qt. slow cooker.

2 Drain pineapple, reserving juice; set pineapple aside. In a bowl, combine the ¾ cup pineapple juice with reserved pineapple juice. Stir in the water, brown sugar, onion and tomato paste; pour over chops. Sprinkle with raisins. Cover and cook on high for 3 to 3½ hours or until meat is tender and a thermometer reads 160°. Stir in reserved pineapple. Cover and cook 10 minutes longer or until heated through.

Hometown Pasty Pies

PREP: 70 MIN. + CHILLING • BAKE: 45 MIN. + STANDING
YIELD: 2 PIES (8 SERVINGS EACH)

I prepare these in advance and freeze them for a quick dinner later...or to share with a friend or neighbor. The meaty baked pies make a hot, filling meal.

Jen Hatlen *Edgerton, Wisconsin*

- **5 cups all-purpose flour**
- **1 tablespoon sugar**
- **1½ teaspoons salt**
- **2 cups butter-flavored shortening**
- **7 tablespoons cold water**
- **1 egg**
- **1 tablespoon white vinegar**

FILLING:

- **2 cups cubed peeled potatoes**
- **2 cups finely chopped fresh carrots**
- **1 pound ground beef**
- **1 pound bulk pork sausage**
- **1 cup sliced fresh mushrooms**
- **1 medium onion, chopped**
- **1 can (10¾ ounces) condensed cream of mushroom soup, undiluted**
- **1 can (10¾ ounces) condensed cream of chicken soup, undiluted**

- 1 **cup frozen peas**
- 1 **tablespoon sherry or chicken broth**
- ½ **teaspoon salt**
- ½ **teaspoon seasoned salt**
- ¼ **teaspoon pepper**
- ½ **cup shredded Colby cheese**
- ½ **cup sour cream**

1 In a large bowl, combine the flour, sugar and salt; cut in shortening until crumbly. Whisk water, egg and vinegar; gradually add to flour mixture, tossing with a fork until dough forms a ball. Divide dough in quarters so that two of the portions are slightly larger than the other two; wrap each in plastic wrap. Refrigerate for 1 hour or until easy to handle.

2 Meanwhile, place potatoes in a large saucepan and cover with water. Bring to a boil. Reduce heat; cover and cook for 5 minutes. Add carrots; cook 6-9 minutes longer or until vegetables are tender. Drain and set aside.

3 In a Dutch oven, cook beef and sausage over medium heat until meat is no longer pink. Remove from pan with a slotted spoon; drain, reserving 1 tablespoon drippings. Saute mushrooms and onion in drippings until tender. Add the soups, peas, sherry, salt, seasoned salt, pepper, beef mixture and potato mixture; heat through.

4 Roll out one of the larger portions of dough to fit a 9-in. pie plate. Transfer pastry to pie plate. Trim pastry even with edge. Fill with half of the meat mixture. Repeat with remaining larger portion of dough and filling.

5 Roll out smaller portions of dough to fit tops of pies. Place over filling. Trim, seal and flute edges. Cut slits in pastry.

6 Bake at 375° for 45-50 minutes or until crust is golden brown. Cover edges with foil during the last 15 minutes to prevent overbrowning if necessary. Sprinkle tops with cheese; let stand for 10 minutes. Serve with sour cream.

Horseradish Honey Ham

PREP: 15 MIN. • BAKE: 1 HOUR 40 MIN. • YIELD: 16 SERVINGS

When my husband and I first tasted this delicious ham, we were surprised to learn that the sauce included horseradish. That secret ingredient definitely is the key to its tangy taste. I serve it for Easter and Christmas.

Beverly Loomis *Ithaca, Michigan*

- 1 **boneless fully cooked ham (5 to 7 pounds)**
- ¼ **cup honey, warmed**
- ⅛ **teaspoon ground cloves**
- 1 **cup packed brown sugar**
- ½ **cup prepared horseradish**
- ¼ **cup lemon juice**

1 Cut ham into ¼-in. slices and tie with kitchen string. Place ham on a rack in a shallow roasting pan. Combine honey and cloves; drizzle over ham. Bake, uncovered, at 350° for 1¼ hours, basting often with drippings.

2 Meanwhile, combine the brown sugar, horseradish and lemon juice. Baste ham with brown sugar sauce, allowing sauce to drip down between the slices. Bake, uncovered, for 25-30 minutes or until a thermometer reads 140°.

Parmesan Pork Cutlets

PREP: 25 MIN. • COOK: 15 MIN. • YIELD: 4 SERVINGS

The aroma of the cutlets cooking on the stove makes my family eager to come to the dinner table. These easy-to-make cutlets are awesome and even my children like them.

Julie Ahern *Waukegan, Illinois*

- 1 **pork tenderloin (1 pound)**
- ⅓ **cup all-purpose flour**
- 2 **eggs, lightly beaten**
- 1 **cup dry bread crumbs**
- ¼ **cup grated Parmesan cheese**
- 1 **teaspoon salt**
- ¼ **cup olive oil**

Lemon wedges

1 Cut pork diagonally into eight slices; pound each to ¼-in. thickness. Place flour and eggs in separate shallow bowls. In another shallow bowl, combine the bread crumbs, cheese and salt. Dip pork in the flour, eggs, then bread crumb mixture.

2 In a large skillet, cook pork in oil in batches over medium heat for 2-3 minutes on each side or until crisp and meat juices run clear. Remove and keep warm. Serve with lemon wedges.

Pork Tenderloin with Cilantro-Lime Pesto

PREP: 30 MIN. + CHILLING • BAKE: 25 MIN. + STANDING
YIELD: 6 SERVINGS

Scrumptious, elegant, easy...what more could you want in a recipe? The homemade cilantro-jalapeno pesto has a wonderful blend of flavor and goes deliciously well with the pork.

Jerri Gradert *Lincoln, Nebraska*

- **¼ cup chopped green onions**
- **2 tablespoons minced fresh gingerroot**
- **2 tablespoons lime juice**
- **2 tablespoons orange juice**
- **1 tablespoon minced garlic**
- **1 tablespoon minced fresh cilantro**
- **1 teaspoon chopped seeded jalapeno pepper**
- **½ teaspoon pepper**
- **2 tablespoons olive oil**
- **2 pork tenderloins (1 pound *each*)**
- **½ cup shredded pepper jack cheese**
- **¼ cup sunflower kernels, toasted and chopped**
- **½ cup crumbled cooked bacon**

1 In a small food processor, combine the first eight ingredients; cover and process until blended. While processing, gradually add oil in a steady stream.

2 Make a lengthwise slit down the center of each tenderloin to within ½ in. of bottom. Open tenderloin so it lies flat; cover with plastic wrap. Flatten to ¾-in. thickness.

3 Remove plastic wrap; spread a fourth of the pesto mixture over each tenderloin. Sprinkle each with the cheese, sunflower kernels and bacon. Close tenderloins; tie at 1½-in. to 2-in. intervals with kitchen string and secure ends with toothpicks. Spread remaining pesto over tenderloins. Cover and refrigerate for several hours or overnight.

4 Place tenderloins on a rack in a shallow baking pan. Bake at 425° for 25-30 minutes or until a thermometer reads 160°. Cover and let stand for 10 minutes before slicing.

EDITOR'S NOTE: Wear disposable gloves when cutting hot peppers; the oils can burn skin. Avoid touching your face.

Calgary Stampede Ribs

PREP: 2½ HOURS + MARINATING • GRILL: 15 MIN. • YIELD: 4 SERVINGS

"More, please!" is what I hear when I serve these zippy, finger-licking ribs to family or guests. The first time my husband and I tried them, we pronounced them "the best ever." The recipe has its roots in the Calgary Stampede, an annual Western and agricultural fair and exhibition in our province.

Marian Misik *Sherwood Park, Alberta*

- **4 pounds pork baby back ribs, cut into serving-size pieces**
- **3 garlic cloves, minced**
- **1 tablespoon sugar**
- **1 tablespoon paprika**
- **2 teaspoons each salt, pepper, chili powder and ground cumin**

BARBECUE SAUCE:

- **1 small onion, finely chopped**
- **2 tablespoons butter**
- **1 cup ketchup**
- **¼ cup packed brown sugar**
- **3 tablespoons lemon juice**
- **3 tablespoons Worcestershire sauce**
- **2 tablespoons cider vinegar**
- **1½ teaspoons ground mustard**
- **1 teaspoon celery seed**
- **⅛ teaspoon cayenne pepper**

1 Rub ribs with garlic; place in a shallow roasting pan. Cover and bake at 325° for 2 hours. Cool slightly. Combine the seasonings and rub over ribs. Cover and refrigerate for 8 hours or overnight.

2 In a small saucepan, saute onion in butter until tender. Stir in the remaining ingredients. Bring to a boil. Reduce heat; cook and stir until thickened, about 10 minutes. Remove from the heat; set aside ¾ cup. Brush ribs with some of the remaining sauce.

3 Grill, covered, over medium heat for 12 minutes, turning and basting with sauce. Serve with reserved sauce.

Cranberry-Glazed Pork Roast

PREP: 15 MIN. • BAKE: 1 HOUR + STANDING
YIELD: 6-8 SERVINGS

Many pork recipes were too spicy for me, so I decided to try this sweeter alternative. That was 18 years ago, and it became a family favorite. It tastes great the day after in a cold sandwich, too. Today, our two grown daughters make this roast often.

Madeline Strauss *Clinton Township, Michigan*

- **1 teaspoon salt**
- **½ teaspoon pepper**
- **1 boneless rolled pork loin roast (3 pounds)**
- **1 cup jellied cranberry sauce**
- **½ cup orange juice**
- **¼ cup packed brown sugar**

1 Combine salt and pepper; rub over the roast. Place roast, fat side up, on a rack in a greased roasting pan. Bake, uncovered, at 350° for 40 minutes.

2 Meanwhile, combine the cranberry sauce, orange juice and brown sugar in a saucepan; cook over medium heat until cranberry sauce is melted. Drizzle a fourth of the glaze over roast.

3 Bake 20 minutes longer or until a thermometer reads 145°, drizzling frequently with glaze. Let stand for 10 minutes before slicing. Warm remaining glaze; serve with roast.

Pretty Penne Ham Skillet 

PREP/TOTAL TIME: 30 MIN. • YIELD: 6 SERVINGS

I enjoy experimenting with herbs and spices to cut down on salt and sugar. Parsley, basil and oregano season this tasty main dish.

Kathy Stephan *West Seneca, New York*

- **1 package (16 ounces) penne pasta**
- **3 cups cubed fully cooked ham**
- **1 large sweet red pepper, diced**
- **1 medium onion, chopped**
- **¼ cup minced fresh parsley**
- **1½ teaspoons minced fresh basil or ½ teaspoon dried basil**
- **1½ teaspoons minced fresh oregano or ½ teaspoon dried oregano**
- **¼ cup olive oil**
- **3 tablespoons butter**
- **2 garlic cloves, minced**
- **1 can (14½ ounces) chicken broth**
- **1 tablespoon lemon juice**
- **½ cup shredded Parmesan cheese**

1 Cook pasta according to package directions. Meanwhile, in a large skillet, saute the ham, red pepper, onion, parsley, basil and oregano in oil and butter for 4-6 minutes or until ham is browned and vegetables are tender. Add garlic; cook 1 minute longer.

2 Stir in broth and lemon juice. Bring to a boil. Reduce heat; simmer, uncovered, for 10-15 minutes or until liquid is reduced by half. Drain pasta; stir into ham mixture. Sprinkle with cheese.

Meat Lover's Pizza

30 min.

PREP/TOTAL TIME: 30 MIN. • YIELD: 8 SLICES

My hefty, cheesy "meal-on-a-crust" is packed with three kinds of meat and a simply fantastic flavor. It's a must-have food at our house during football season.

Edgar Peavy *Oxnard, California*

- **2 packages (6½ ounces each) pizza crust mix**
- **1 tablespoon olive oil**
- **1½ teaspoons garlic powder, divided**
- **¼ pound ground beef**
- **½ teaspoon onion powder**
- **⅔ cup spaghetti sauce**
- **1 package (3½ ounces) sliced pepperoni**
- **6 ounces Canadian bacon, quartered**
- **¼ cup sliced fresh mushrooms**
- **2 tablespoons sliced ripe olives**
- **2 cups (8 ounces) shredded part-skim mozzarella cheese**

1 Prepare pizza dough according to package directions. With floured hands, press dough onto a greased 14-in. pizza pan. Bake at 425° for 7-9 minutes or until lightly browned. Combine oil and 1 teaspoon garlic powder; brush over crust edges.

2 In a large skillet over medium heat, cook beef with onion powder and remaining garlic powder until no longer pink; drain.

3 Spread spaghetti sauce over crust to within 1 in. of edges. Top with beef mixture, pepperoni, Canadian bacon, mushrooms, olives and mozzarella cheese.

4 Bake at 425° for 10-15 minutes or until cheese is melted and crust is golden brown.

Orzo-Stuffed Peppers

PREP: 30 MIN. • BAKE: 15 MIN. • YIELD: 4 SERVINGS

Packed with tender orzo and savory Italian sausage, these stuffed peppers make a fun, fast-to-fix meal. Use more or less red pepper to adjust the level of heat.

Kelly Evans *Kalamazoo, Michigan*

- **4 large green peppers**
- **1 cup uncooked orzo pasta**
- **1 pound bulk Italian sausage**
- **½ cup chopped red onion**
- **2 teaspoons minced garlic**
- **2 cups marinara or spaghetti sauce**
- **1 medium tomato, chopped**
- **¼ cup minced fresh basil or 1 tablespoon dried basil**
- **2 teaspoons dried rosemary, crushed**
- **1 teaspoon crushed red pepper flakes**
- **¼ cup shredded part-skim mozzarella cheese**
- **2 tablespoons grated Parmesan cheese**

1 Cut tops off peppers and remove seeds. In a large Dutch oven, cook peppers in boiling water for 3-5 minutes. Drain and rinse in cold water; set aside.

2 Cook orzo according to package directions. Meanwhile, in a large skillet, cook the sausage and onion over medium heat until meat is no longer pink. Add garlic; cook 1 minute longer.

3 Drain meat and orzo; stir orzo into meat mixture. Add the marinara sauce, tomato, basil, rosemary and pepper flakes. Spoon into peppers.

4 Place in a greased 11-in. x 7-in. baking dish. Cover and bake at 350° for 10 minutes. Uncover; sprinkle with cheeses. Bake 5 minutes longer or until cheese is melted. Serve immediately.

5 Casserole can be covered and frozen prior to baking. Freeze for up to 3 months.

TO USE FROZEN CASSEROLE: Thaw in the refrigerator overnight. Remove from the refrigerator 30 minutes before baking. Bake, covered, according to directions.

Ham and Cheese Loaf

PREP: 15 MIN. • BAKE: 30 MIN. • YIELD: 6 SERVINGS

Convenient refrigerated dough is the foundation for this golden loaf stuffed with ham and cheese. I created the recipe by experimenting with a few simple ingredients my family loves. It makes a delicious hot sandwich in no time.

Gloria Lindell *Welcome, Minnesota*

- **1 tube (13.8 ounces) refrigerated pizza crust**
- **10 slices deli ham**
- **¼ cup sliced green onions**
- **1 cup (4 ounces) shredded part-skim mozzarella cheese**
- **1 cup (4 ounces) shredded cheddar cheese**
- **4 slices provolone cheese**
- **1 tablespoon butter, melted**

1 Unroll dough onto a greased baking sheet; top with the ham, onions and cheeses. Roll up tightly jelly-roll style, starting with a long side; pinch seam to seal and tuck ends under. Brush with butter.

2 Bake at 350° for 30-35 minutes or until golden brown. Let stand for 5 minutes; cut into 1-in. slices. If desired, cool loaf on a wire rack; wrap in foil and freeze for up to 3 months.

TO USE FROZEN LOAF: Thaw at room temperature for 2 hours. Unwrap and place on a greased baking sheet. Bake at 350° for 15-20 minutes or until heated through. Let stand for 5 minutes; cut into 1-in. slices.

Grilled Whiskey Chops 

PREP/TOTAL TIME: 25 MIN. • YIELD: 4 SERVINGS

It's almost guaranteed to see these savory chops on the menu at summertime gatherings. The molasses butter nicely contrasts with the whiskey and peppercorn taste.

Kelly Melling *Frankton, Indiana*

- **¼ cup butter, softened**
- **1 tablespoon molasses**
- **½ teaspoon ground cinnamon**
- **½ teaspoon lemon juice**
- **3 tablespoons coarsely ground pepper**
- **⅓ cup whiskey**
- **½ teaspoon salt**
- **4 bone-in pork loin chops (¾ inch thick)**

1 In a small bowl, combine the butter, molasses, cinnamon and lemon juice; chill until serving.

2 Place pepper in a shallow bowl. In another shallow bowl, combine the whiskey and salt. Dip chops in whiskey mixture, then pepper.

3 Moisten a paper towel with cooking oil; using long-handled tongs, lightly coat the grill rack. Grill chops, covered, over medium heat or broil 4 in. from the heat for 4-5 minutes on each side or until a thermometer reads 160°. Serve with molasses butter.

FROZEN LEMON JUICE

>> Keep fresh lemon juice on hand—it's such an easy way to add refreshing flavor to many recipes. After juicing the lemons, freeze the juice in ice cube trays. Then simply defrost them and use in poultry recipes, lemon desserts, iced or hot teas and many other dishes.

Sweet & Sour Sausage

PREP/TOTAL TIME: 20 MIN. • YIELD: 4 SERVINGS

Get dinner on the table in no time with this yummy twist on sweet and sour using smoked sausage. We always keep Polish sausage in the freezer specifically for this busy-night favorite.

Carol Matthews *Lima, New York*

- **1 can (20 ounces) pineapple chunks**
- **½ cup apricot preserves**
- **2 teaspoons cornstarch**
- **1 tablespoon cider vinegar**
- **1 tablespoon soy sauce**
- **½ teaspoon ground ginger**
- **1 pound smoked Polish sausage, cut into ½-inch slices**
- **1 large onion, cut into 1-inch pieces**
- **1 medium green pepper, cut into 1-inch pieces**
- **1 tablespoon canola oil**

Hot cooked rice

1 Drain pineapple, reserving ¼ cup juice; set pineapple aside. In a bowl, combine the preserves, cornstarch, vinegar, soy sauce, ginger and reserved juice.

2 In a large skillet, saute the sausage, onion and pepper in oil until vegetables are tender. Add sauce mixture and pineapple. Bring to a boil; cook and stir for 2 minutes or until thickened. Serve with rice.

Creamy Spinach Sausage Pasta

30 min.

PREP: 15 MIN. • BAKE: 45 MIN.
YIELD: 5 SERVINGS

So rich and creamy, this pasta dish is the definition of comfort food! For time-saving convenience, I like to assemble it in the evening, then bake it the next day.

Susie Sizemore *Collinsville, Virginia*

- **3 cups uncooked rigatoni or large tube pasta**
- **1 pound bulk Italian sausage**
- **1 cup finely chopped onion**
- **1 can (14½ ounces) Italian diced tomatoes, undrained**
- **1 package (10 ounces) frozen creamed spinach, thawed**
- **1 package (8 ounces) cream cheese, softened**
- **2 cups (8 ounces) shredded part-skim mozzarella cheese, divided**

1 Cook pasta according to package directions. Meanwhile, in a Dutch oven, cook sausage and onion over medium heat until sausage is no longer pink; drain. Stir in the tomatoes, spinach, cream cheese and 1 cup mozzarella cheese. Transfer to a greased 11-in. x 7-in. baking dish.

2 Cover and bake at 350° for 35 minutes. Uncover; sprinkle with remaining cheese. Bake 10 minutes longer or until cheese is melted.

WINNERS
CIRCLE

poultry

Most families will agree—chicken and turkey take the prize when it comes to mass appeal and versatile preparation. Winners for everyday meals and special occasions, the pleasing poultry favorites featured here show off plenty of home-cooked flavor.

HERB-ROASTED TURKEY, 144

Chicken Enchilada Casserole

PREP: 30 MIN. • BAKE: 30 MIN. • YIELD: 6 SERVINGS

Look no further for a family-friendly recipe that offers a new take on classic enchiladas. If you like yours with a little extra "oomph," sprinkle some seeded, freshly chopped jalapenos and cilantro on top.

Amy Johnson *New Braunfels, Texas*

- **1 large onion, chopped**
- **1 medium green pepper, chopped**
- **1 teaspoon butter**
- **3 cups shredded cooked chicken breast**
- **2 cans (4 ounces each) chopped green chilies**
- **¼ cup all-purpose flour**
- **1½ to 2 teaspoons ground coriander**
- **2½ cups reduced-sodium chicken broth**
- **1 cup (8 ounces) reduced-fat sour cream**
- **1 cup (4 ounces) reduced-fat Monterey Jack or reduced-fat Mexican cheese blend, divided**
- **12 corn tortillas (6 inches), warmed**

1 In a small skillet, saute onion and green pepper in butter until tender. In a large bowl, combine the chicken, green chilies and onion mixture.

2 In a small saucepan, combine flour and coriander. Add broth; stir until smooth. Cook and stir over medium heat until mixture comes to a boil. Cook and stir 1-2 minutes longer or until thickened. Remove from the heat; stir in sour cream and ½ cup cheese. Stir ¾ cup sauce into chicken mixture.

3 Place ⅓ cup chicken mixture down the center of each tortilla. Roll up and place seam side down in a 13-in. x 9-in. baking dish coated with cooking spray. Pour remaining sauce over top; sprinkle with remaining cheese. Bake, uncovered, at 350° for 30-35 minutes or until heated through.

Green Bean Chicken Casserole

PREP: 15 MIN. • BAKE: 25 MIN. • YIELD: 2 CASSEROLES (4-6 SERVINGS EACH)

My husband, who claims to be strictly a meat-and-potatoes man, asked for seconds the first time I threw together this comforting all-in-one meal. My daughter and several guests raved about it, too.

DeLissa Mingee *Warr Acres, Oklahoma*

- **1 package (6 ounces) long grain and wild rice mix**
- **4 cups cubed cooked chicken**
- **1¾ cups frozen french-style green beans**
- **1 can (10¾ ounces) condensed cream of mushroom soup, undiluted**
- **1 can (10¾ ounces) condensed cream of broccoli soup, undiluted**
- **1 can (4 ounces) mushroom stems and pieces, drained**
- **⅔ cup chopped onion**
- **⅔ cup chopped green pepper**
- **1 envelope onion soup mix**
- **¾ cup shredded Colby cheese**

ADDITIONAL INGREDIENT (FOR EACH CASSEROLE):

- **⅔ cup french-fried onions**

1 Prepare wild rice according to package directions. Stir in the chicken, beans, soups, mushrooms, onion, green pepper and soup mix. Spoon into two greased 1½-qt. baking dishes. Sprinkle with cheese.

2 Cover and freeze one casserole for up to 3 months. Cover and bake the second casserole at 350° for 25-30 minutes or until heated through. Uncover and sprinkle with french-fried onions; bake 5 minutes longer or until onions are golden.

TO USE FROZEN CASSEROLE: Completely thaw in the refrigerator. Remove from the refrigerator 30 minutes before baking. Cover and bake at 350° for 60-65 minutes or until heated through. Uncover and sprinkle with french-fried onions; bake 5 minutes longer.

Lemony Spinach-Stuffed Chicken Breasts

PREP: 30 MIN. • COOK: 20 MIN.
YIELD: 4 SERVINGS

Easy preparation and visual appeal are the reasons this dish is my "go-to" recipe when company is coming over. I usually serve this dish with couscous, rice or garlic mashed potatoes along with a vegetable saute or tossed salad.

Pam Nelson *Beaverton, Oregon*

- **½ cup chopped sweet onion**
- **3 teaspoons olive oil, divided**
- **6½ cups fresh baby spinach, chopped**
- **1 garlic clove, minced**
- **1 tablespoon balsamic vinegar**
- **¼ cup crumbled feta cheese**
- **½ teaspoon grated lemon peel**
- **¼ teaspoon salt**
- **¼ teaspoon pepper**
- **4 boneless skinless chicken breast halves (6 ounces each)**

1 In a large skillet, cook onion in 2 teaspoons oil over medium heat for 15-20 minutes or until onion is golden brown, stirring frequently. Add the spinach, garlic and vinegar; cook 1 minute longer. Remove from the heat; cool for 5 minutes. Stir in the cheese, lemon peel, salt and pepper.

2 Flatten chicken to ¼-in. thickness. Spread spinach mixture over chicken. Roll up and secure with toothpicks.

3 In a large skillet over medium heat, cook chicken in remaining oil for 8-10 minutes on each side or until chicken juices run clear. Discard toothpicks.

Bruschetta Chicken

PREP: 10 MIN. • BAKE: 30 MIN.
YIELD: 4 SERVINGS

My husband and I enjoy serving this tasty chicken to company as well as family. I found the recipe years ago and have made this dish many times. It usually prompts recipe requests.

Carolin Cattoi-Demkiw *Lethbridge, Alberta*

- **½ cup all-purpose flour**
- **½ cup egg substitute**
- **4 boneless skinless chicken breast halves (4 ounces each)**
- **¼ cup grated Parmesan cheese**
- **¼ cup dry bread crumbs**
- **1 tablespoon butter, melted**
- **2 large tomatoes, seeded and chopped**
- **3 tablespoons minced fresh basil**
- **2 garlic cloves, minced**
- **1 tablespoon olive oil**
- **½ teaspoon salt**
- **¼ teaspoon pepper**

1 Place flour and egg in separate shallow bowls. Dip chicken in flour, then in egg; place in a greased 13-in. x 9-in. baking dish. Combine the cheese, bread crumbs and butter; sprinkle over chicken.

2 Loosely cover baking dish with foil. Bake at 375° for 20 minutes. Uncover; bake 5-10 minutes longer or until a thermometer reads 170°.

3 Meanwhile, in a small bowl, combine the remaining ingredients. Spoon over the chicken. Return to the oven for 3-5 minutes or until tomato mixture is heated through.

Chicken 'n' Dressing Casserole

PREP: 1 HOUR • BAKE: 35 MIN. • YIELD: 8 SERVINGS

This casserole is a real favorite in our area and in my family, too. It's a great way to use leftover chicken or turkey, and so easy that even beginner cooks will have success making it.

Billie Blanton *Kingsport, Tennessee*

- **4 cups cubed cooked chicken**
- **2 tablespoons all-purpose flour**
- **½ cup chicken broth**
- **½ cup milk**

Salt and pepper to taste

DRESSING:

- **2 celery ribs, chopped**
- **1 small onion, finely chopped**
- **1 tablespoon butter**
- **1 teaspoon rubbed sage**
- **½ teaspoon poultry seasoning**
- **¼ teaspoon salt**
- **⅛ teaspoon pepper**
- **2 cups unseasoned stuffing cubes, crushed**
- **2 cups coarsely crumbled corn bread**
- **½ cup chicken broth**
- **1 egg, beaten**

GRAVY:

- **¼ cup butter**
- **6 tablespoons all-purpose flour**
- **2 cups chicken broth**
- **½ cup milk**

1 Place chicken in a greased 2-qt. baking dish; set aside. In a small saucepan, combine the flour, broth and milk until smooth. Bring to a boil; cook and stir for 2 minutes. Season with salt and pepper. Spoon over chicken.

2 In a large skillet, saute celery and onion in butter until tender. Stir in seasonings. Remove from the heat; add the stuffing cubes, corn bread, broth and egg. Mix well. Spoon over chicken mixture. Cover and bake at 350° for 35-40 minutes or until a thermometer inserted near the center reads 160°.

3 For gravy, melt butter in a small saucepan. Stir in flour until smooth; gradually add broth and milk. Bring to a boil; cook and stir for 2 minutes or until thickened. Serve with chicken and dressing.

Chipotle Chicken Fajitas

PREP: 30 MIN. + MARINATING • GRILL: 10 MIN.
YIELD: 5 SERVINGS

I've had this recipe for three years, and my husband and I just love it. Be careful with the chipotle peppers, as they can be very hot. I changed it a little to fit our taste. You may want to adjust the amount to your preference.

Melissa Thomeczek *Hannibal, Missouri*

- **1 bottle (12 ounces) chili sauce**
- **¼ cup lime juice**
- **4 chipotle peppers in adobo sauce**
- **1 pound boneless skinless chicken breasts, cut into strips**
- **½ cup cider vinegar**
- **⅓ cup packed brown sugar**
- **⅓ cup molasses**
- **4 medium green peppers, cut into 1-inch pieces**
- **1 large onion, cut into 1-inch pieces**
- **1 tablespoon olive oil**
- **⅛ teaspoon salt**
- **⅛ teaspoon pepper**
- **10 flour tortillas (8 inches)**
- **1½ cups chopped tomatoes**
- **1 cup (4 ounces) shredded Mexican cheese blend**

1 Place the chili sauce, lime juice and chipotle peppers in a food processor; cover and process until blended. Transfer ½ cup to a large resealable plastic bag; add chicken. Seal bag and turn to coat; refrigerate for 1-4 hours.

2 Pour remaining marinade into a small bowl; add the vinegar, brown sugar and molasses. Cover and refrigerate.

3 On six metal or soaked wooden skewers, alternately thread chicken and vegetables. Brush with oil; sprinkle with salt and pepper. Grill, covered, over medium heat for 10-16 minutes or until a thermometer reads 170°, turning occasionally.

4 Unskewer chicken and vegetables into a large bowl; add ½ cup chipotle-molasses mixture and toss to coat. Keep warm.

5 Grill tortillas, uncovered, over medium heat for 45-55 seconds on each side or until warmed. Top with chicken mixture, tomatoes, cheese and remaining chipotle-molasses mixture.

Chicken Cordon Bleu Calzones

PREP: 40 MIN. • BAKE: 15 MIN. • YIELD: 4 SERVINGS

I'm a fan of chicken Cordon Bleu and beef Wellington, so I created a recipe that blends the best of both dishes.

Kathy Gounaud *Warwick, Rhode Island*

- **4 boneless skinless chicken breasts (4 ounces each)**
- **1 cup sliced fresh mushrooms**
- **½ medium onion, chopped**
- **2 tablespoons butter**
- **3 tablespoons cornstarch**
- **1¼ cups 2% milk**
- **1 tablespoon minced fresh basil or 1 teaspoon dried basil**
- **1 teaspoon salt**
- **¼ teaspoon pepper**
- **1 package (17.3 ounces) frozen puff pastry, thawed**
- **8 thin slices deli ham**
- **4 slices provolone cheese**

Additional milk, optional

1 Place chicken in a greased 2-qt. baking dish; cover with water. Cover and bake at 350° for 30 minutes or until a thermometer reads 170°.

2 Meanwhile, in a small skillet, saute mushrooms and onion in butter until tender. Combine cornstarch and milk until smooth; stir into skillet. Add seasonings. Bring to a boil; cook and stir for 2 minutes or until thickened.

3 Drain chicken. Cut pastry sheets in half widthwise. On one side of each half, place a chicken breast, ¼ cup mushroom mixture, two ham slices and one cheese slice. Fold pastry over filling and seal edges.

4 Place on a greased baking sheet. Brush tops with milk if desired. Bake at 400° for 15-20 minutes or until puffed and golden.

Chicken Penne Casserole

PREP: 35 MIN. • BAKE: 45 MIN. • YIELD: 4 SERVINGS

I could make this casserole every week or two and my family would never tire of it. I like that I can clean my kitchen and then relax while it bakes. It won't disappoint!

Carmen Vanosch *Vernon, British Columbia*

- **1 pound boneless skinless chicken thighs, cut into 1-inch pieces**
- **½ cup each chopped onion, green pepper and sweet red pepper**
- **1 teaspoon each dried basil, oregano and parsley flakes**
- **½ teaspoon salt**
- **½ teaspoon crushed red pepper flakes**
- **1 tablespoon canola oil**
- **3 garlic cloves, minced**
- **1½ cups uncooked penne pasta**
- **1 can (14½ ounces) diced tomatoes, undrained**
- **3 tablespoons tomato paste**
- **¾ cup chicken broth**
- **2 cups (8 ounces) shredded part-skim mozzarella cheese**
- **½ cup grated Romano cheese**

1 In a large saucepan, saute the chicken, onion, peppers and seasonings in oil until chicken is no longer pink. Add garlic; cook 1 minute longer.

2 Cook pasta according to package directions. Meanwhile, process tomatoes and tomato paste in a blender; add to chicken mixture. Stir in broth. Bring to a boil. Reduce heat; cover and simmer for 10-15 minutes or until slightly thickened.

3 Drain pasta; toss with chicken mixture. Spoon half of the mixture into a greased 2-qt. baking dish. Sprinkle with half of the cheeses. Repeat layers.

4 Cover and bake at 350° for 30 minutes. Uncover; bake 15-20 minutes longer or until heated through.

Curry Chicken Tenderloin with Sweet Potatoes

PREP: 15 MIN. • COOK: 25 MIN. • YIELD: 3 SERVINGS

The luscious, fragrant sauce is reason enough to make this deliciously different dish. I suggest serving it to people who are unfamiliar with curry—it'll win them over with just one bite!

Gloria Bradley *Naperville, Illinois*

- **¾ pound chicken tenderloins, cut into 1-inch cubes**
- **1 small green pepper, cut into thin strips**
- **2 shallots, thinly sliced**
- **2 teaspoons minced fresh gingerroot**
- **1 teaspoon curry powder**
- **1 garlic clove, minced**
- **1 tablespoon canola oil**
- **1⅓ cups chicken broth**
- **1 tablespoon lime juice**
- **½ teaspoon sugar**
- **¼ teaspoon crushed red pepper flakes**
- **1 medium sweet potato, peeled and cut into 1-inch pieces**
- **¾ cup light coconut milk**

Chopped peanuts and flaked coconut, optional

Hot cooked rice, optional

1 In a large skillet, saute the chicken, green pepper, shallots, ginger, curry and garlic in oil until chicken is no longer pink.

2 Stir in the broth, lime juice, sugar and pepper flakes. Bring to a boil. Reduce heat; simmer, uncovered, for 10 minutes or until thickened.

3 Add sweet potato and coconut milk; bring to a boil. Reduce heat; cover and simmer for 8-10 minutes or until potato is tender. If desired, sprinkle with peanuts and coconut, and serve with rice.

Honey-Brined Turkey Breast

PREP: 50 MIN. + CHILLING • BAKE: 1¾ HOURS
YIELD: 8 SERVINGS

Here's a traditional turkey breast with a sweet and spicy zest. Moist and savory, it also makes great leftovers.

Deirdre Dee Cox *Milwaukee, Wisconsin*

- **2 quarts apple cider or juice**
- **½ cup kosher salt**
- **⅓ cup honey**
- **2 tablespoons Dijon mustard**
- **1½ teaspoons crushed red pepper flakes**
- **1 fresh rosemary sprig**
- **2 large oven roasting bags**
- **1 bone-in turkey breast (4 to 5 pounds)**
- **1 tablespoon olive oil**

1 In a Dutch oven, bring the first five ingredients to a boil. Cook and stir until salt and honey are dissolved. Stir in rosemary. Remove from the heat; cool to room temperature. Refrigerate until chilled.

2 Place a large oven roasting bag inside a second roasting bag; add turkey breast. Carefully pour brine into bag. Squeeze out as much air as possible; seal bags and turn to coat. Place in a roasting pan. Refrigerate for 8 hours or overnight, turning occasionally.

3 Line the bottom of a large shallow roasting pan with foil. Drain turkey and discard brine; place on a rack in prepared pan. Pat dry. Bake, uncovered, at 325° for 30 minutes. Brush with oil. Bake 1½ to 2 hours longer or until a thermometer reads 170°. (Cover loosely with foil if turkey browns too quickly.) Cover and let stand for 15 minutes before carving.

EDITOR'S NOTE: This recipe was tested with Morton brand kosher salt. It is best not to use a prebasted turkey breast for this recipe. However, if you do, omit the salt in the recipe.

Turkey Cordon Bleu with Alfredo Sauce

PREP: 30 MIN. • BAKE: 20 MIN. • YIELD: 8 SERVINGS

For our annual Kentucky Derby party I wanted to create a twist on a traditional Kentucky Hot Brown sandwich. The turkey is tender and flavorful, full of smoky ham and melted cheese, but the crispy bacon really sets the dish apart.

Sandy Komisarek *Swanton, Ohio*

- **8 slices part-skim mozzarella cheese**
- **8 thin slices deli honey ham**
- **8 turkey breast cutlets**
- **2 cups panko (Japanese) bread crumbs**
- **2 eggs, lightly beaten**
- **½ cup all-purpose flour**
- **½ teaspoon salt**
- **¼ teaspoon pepper**
- **¼ cup canola oil**
- **1 jar (15 ounces) Alfredo sauce, warmed**
- **8 bacon strips, cooked and crumbled**
- **¼ cup grated Parmesan cheese**

1 Place one slice mozzarella cheese and ham on each cutlet. Roll up each from a short side and secure with toothpicks.

2 Place bread crumbs and eggs in separate shallow bowls. In another shallow bowl, combine the flour, salt and pepper. Dip turkey in the flour mixture, eggs, then bread crumbs.

3 In a large skillet, brown turkey in oil in batches. Place in a greased 13-in. x 9-in. baking dish. Bake, uncovered, at 350° for 20-25 minutes or until turkey juices run clear. Discard toothpicks.

4 Spoon the Alfredo sauce over turkey. Sprinkle with crumbled bacon and grated Parmesan cheese.

Grilled Rosemary Chicken

PREP: 15 MIN. + MARINATING • GRILL: 10 MIN. • YIELD: 6 SERVINGS

This moist, tender chicken has a touch of rosemary flavor. It's so easy to throw together, which makes it a great dish when time is limited. I always prepare extra pieces of chicken so that we can use it later in the week—it's splendid the first day grilled, but also makes fantastic chicken salad.

Holly Jackson *Calera, Alabama*

- **2/3 cup ranch salad dressing**
- **3 tablespoons olive oil**
- **3 tablespoons Worcestershire sauce**
- **2 tablespoons dried rosemary, crushed**
- **2 teaspoons dried basil**
- **2 teaspoons white wine vinegar**
- **2 teaspoons lemon juice**
- **1 1/4 teaspoons dried oregano**
- **1 1/4 teaspoons honey**
- **1/2 teaspoon salt**
- **1/4 teaspoon pepper**
- **6 boneless skinless chicken breast halves (5 ounces each)**

1 In a large resealable plastic bag, combine first 11 ingredients. Flatten chicken to 1/2-in. thickness; add to bag. Seal and turn to coat. Refrigerate for 8 hours or overnight.

2 Drain chicken and discard marinade. Moisten a paper towel with cooking oil; using long-handled tongs, lightly coat the grill rack. Grill chicken, covered, over medium heat or broil 4 in. from the heat for 4-7 minutes on each side or until a thermometer reads 170°.

Jalapeno Chicken Pizza

30 min.

PREP/TOTAL TIME: 25 MIN. • YIELD: 12 PIECES

Jalapeno is a yummy way to kick up ordinary pizza. A prebaked crust makes this quick and easy recipe a hit on busy weeknights.

Linda Ewankowich *Raleigh, North Carolina*

- **2 plum tomatoes, quartered**
- **1/3 cup fresh cilantro leaves**
- **1 tablespoon tomato paste**
- **1 teaspoon chopped chipotle peppers in adobo sauce**
- **1 garlic clove, peeled and quartered**
- **1/2 teaspoon salt**
- **1 prebaked 12-inch thin pizza crust**
- **2 cups shredded cooked chicken breast**
- **3/4 cup shredded reduced-fat Monterey Jack cheese or Mexican cheese blend**
- **2 jalapeno peppers, seeded and sliced into rings**

1 Place the first six ingredients in a food processor; cover and process until blended. Place the crust on an ungreased 12-in. pizza pan; spread with tomato mixture. Top with chicken, cheese and jalapenos.

2 Bake at 450° for 10-12 minutes or until heated through and cheese is melted.

EDITOR'S NOTE: Wear disposable gloves when cutting hot peppers; the oils can burn skin. Avoid touching your face.

Creamy Chicken Casserole

PREP: 20 MIN. • BAKE: 25 MIN.
YIELD: 2 SERVINGS

French onion dip lends a tangy accent to this cheesy rice bake. Short prep time means you can eat a scrumptious dinner without spending hours in the kitchen.

Jaky Broussard *Greensboro, Alabama*

- **⅔ cup uncooked instant rice**
- **¼ cup chopped onion**
- **2 teaspoons butter**
- **½ cup 4% cottage cheese**
- **⅓ cup French onion dip**
- **3 tablespoons sour cream**
- **¼ teaspoon salt**
- **Dash white pepper**
- **½ cup cubed cooked chicken**
- **½ cup shredded cheddar cheese**
- **2 tablespoons chopped green chilies**

1 Cook rice according to package directions. Meanwhile, in a small skillet, saute onion in butter until tender; set aside. In a small bowl, combine the cottage cheese, onion dip, sour cream, salt and pepper. Stir in rice and onion.

2 Spread half of the rice mixture into a 3-cup baking dish coated with cooking spray. Layer with chicken, ¼ cup cheddar cheese and green chilies. Top with remaining rice mixture; sprinkle with remaining cheese.

3 Bake, uncovered, at 350° for 25-30 minutes or until bubbly.

Turkey Potpie

PREP: 20 MIN. • BAKE: 40 MIN. • YIELD: 6 SERVINGS

My family raves over this comforting dish with its flaky homemade crust and saucy meat and veggie filling. Sometimes I cook a bird specifically with this potpie in mind, when we just can't wait for leftovers to make it!

Marie Elaine Basinger *Connellsville, Pennsylvania*

- **1 medium onion, chopped**
- **⅓ cup butter**
- **½ cup all-purpose flour**
- **1 teaspoon salt**
- **¼ teaspoon pepper**
- **1¾ cups chicken broth**
- **⅔ cup milk**
- **2 cups cubed cooked turkey**
- **1 cup (4 ounces) shredded cheddar cheese**
- **2 cups frozen peas and carrots**

PASTRY:

- **2 cups all-purpose flour**
- **2 teaspoons celery seed**
- **1 teaspoon salt**
- **⅔ cup plus 2 tablespoons shortening**
- **4 to 5 tablespoons cold water**
- **Milk, optional**

1 In a saucepan, saute onion in butter. Stir in the flour, salt and pepper until blended. Gradually add broth and milk. Bring to a boil; cook and stir for 2 minutes or until thickened. Add the turkey, cheese and vegetables; cook until the cheese is melted. Set aside and keep warm.

2 For the crust, combine flour, celery seed and salt in a bowl. Cut in shortening until mixture resembles coarse crumbs. Add enough water until dough forms a ball.

3 Divide dough in half. Line a 9-in. pie plate with bottom pastry; trim even with edge of plate. Pour hot turkey filling into crust. Roll out remaining pastry to fit top of pie; place over the filling. Trim, seal and flute edges. Cut slits in pastry. Brush tops with milk if desired.

4 Bake at 375° for 40-45 minutes or until crust is golden brown.

Sunday Chicken Stew

PREP: 30 MIN. • COOK: 6½ HOURS
YIELD: 6 SERVINGS

It wouldn't be Sunday without the addition of this homestyle stew. I brown the chicken and assemble everything in the slow cooker before heading out.

Diane Halferty *Corpus Christi, Texas*

- **½ cup all-purpose flour**
- **1 teaspoon salt**
- **½ teaspoon white pepper**
- **1 broiler/fryer chicken (3 pounds), cut up and skin removed**
- **2 tablespoons canola oil**
- **3 cups chicken broth**
- **6 large carrots, cut into 1-inch pieces**
- **2 celery ribs, cut into ½-inch pieces**
- **1 large sweet onion, thinly sliced**
- **1 teaspoon dried rosemary, crushed**
- **1½ cups frozen peas**

DUMPLINGS:

- **1 cup all-purpose flour**
- **2 teaspoons baking powder**
- **½ teaspoon salt**
- **½ teaspoon dried rosemary, crushed**
- **1 egg, lightly beaten**
- **½ cup 2% milk**

1 In a large resealable plastic bag, combine the flour, salt and pepper; add chicken, a few pieces at a time, and shake to coat. In a large skillet, brown chicken in oil; remove and keep warm. Gradually add broth to the skillet; bring to a boil.

2 In a 5-qt. slow cooker, layer the carrots, celery and onion; sprinkle with rosemary. Add the chicken and hot broth. Cover and cook on low for 6-8 hours or until chicken is tender, vegetables are tender and stew is bubbling.

3 Remove chicken; when cool enough to handle, remove meat from the bones and discard bones. Cut meat into bite-size pieces and return to the slow cooker. Stir in peas.

4 For dumplings, in a small bowl, combine the flour, baking powder, salt and rosemary. Combine the egg and milk; stir into dry ingredients. Drop by heaping teaspoonfuls onto simmering chicken mixture.

5 Cover and cook on high for 25-30 minutes or until a toothpick inserted in a dumpling comes out clean (do not lift the cover while simmering).

Herb-Roasted Turkey

PREP: 10 MIN. • BAKE: 4 HOURS
YIELD: 12-14 SERVINGS

Our guests comment on how moist and flavorful this elegant entree is. Rubbed with garden-fresh herbs, the turkey has such a wonderful aroma when it's roasting that it lures everyone into the kitchen.

Becky Goldsmith *Eden Prairie, Minnesota*

- **1 turkey (14 pounds)**
- **1 tablespoon salt**
- **1 teaspoon pepper**
- **18 sprigs fresh thyme, divided**
- **4 medium onions, sliced**
- **4 celery ribs, sliced**
- **2 medium carrots, sliced**
- **3 bay leaves**
- **1 tablespoon peppercorns**
- **½ cup butter, melted**
- **1 teaspoon minced fresh sage or ½ teaspoon rubbed sage**
- **1 teaspoon minced fresh thyme or ½ teaspoon dried thyme**
- **1 teaspoon minced chives**

1 Rub the surface of the turkey and sprinkle cavity with salt and pepper. Place 12 sprigs of thyme in cavity.

2 In a large heavy roasting pan, place onions, celery, carrots, bay leaves, peppercorns and remaining thyme sprigs. Place the turkey, breast side up, over vegetables. Drizzle butter over turkey and sprinkle with minced herbs.

3 Cover loosely with foil. Bake at 325° for 2½ hours. Remove foil; bake 1½ to 2 hours longer or until a thermometer reads 180°, basting every 20 minutes.

4 Cover and let stand for 20 minutes before carving. Discard bay leaves and peppercorns; thicken pan drippings for gravy if desired.

Thai Chicken Lettuce Wraps

PREP: 35 MIN. • YIELD: 6 SERVINGS

My recipe is so flavorful and fresh tasting, you'd think it came from a restaurant. The teachers and staff at my school love it because it's fun to put together.

Laureen Pittman *Riverside, California*

- **¼ cup rice vinegar**
- **2 tablespoons lime juice**
- **2 tablespoons reduced-fat mayonnaise**
- **2 tablespoons reduced-fat creamy peanut butter**
- **1 tablespoon brown sugar**
- **1 tablespoon reduced-sodium soy sauce**
- **2 teaspoons minced fresh gingerroot**
- **1 teaspoon sesame oil**
- **1 teaspoon Thai chili sauce**
- **1 garlic clove, chopped**
- **3 tablespoons canola oil**
- **½ cup minced fresh cilantro**

CHICKEN SALAD:

- **2 cups cubed cooked chicken breast**
- **1 small sweet red pepper, diced**
- **½ cup chopped green onions**
- **½ cup shredded carrot**
- **½ cup unsalted dry roasted peanuts, chopped, divided**
- **6 Bibb or Boston lettuce leaves**

1 In a blender, combine the first 10 ingredients. While processing, gradually add oil in a steady stream; stir in cilantro. Set aside.

2 In a large bowl, combine the chicken, red pepper, onions, carrot and ¼ cup peanuts. Add dressing and toss to coat. Divide among lettuce leaves; sprinkle with remaining peanuts. Fold lettuce over filling.

Savory Oven-Fried Chicken

PREP: 20 MIN. + MARINATING • BAKE: 50 MIN.
YIELD: 4 SERVINGS

You won't believe how moist this chicken is. It has a nicely seasoned crumb crust that bakes up to a golden color. It's tasty, healthy and easy.

Ranee Bullard *Evans, Georgia*

- **½ cup buttermilk**
- **1 tablespoon Dijon mustard**
- **2 garlic cloves, minced**
- **1 teaspoon hot pepper sauce**
- **4 bone-in chicken breast halves (12 ounces each), skin removed**
- **½ cup whole wheat flour**
- **1½ teaspoons paprika**
- **1 teaspoon baking powder**
- **1 teaspoon dried thyme**
- **¼ teaspoon salt**
- **¼ teaspoon pepper**
- **Cooking spray**

1 In a large resealable plastic bag, combine the buttermilk, mustard, garlic and pepper sauce. Add the chicken; seal bag and turn to coat. Refrigerate for 8 hours or overnight. Drain and discard marinade.

2 In another large resealable plastic bag, combine the flour, paprika, baking powder, thyme, salt and pepper. Add chicken, one piece at a time, and shake to coat.

3 Place chicken bone side down on a rack in a shallow baking pan. Spritz chicken with cooking spray. Bake, uncovered, at 425° for 50-60 minutes or until a thermometer reads 170°.

Moroccan Chicken

PREP: 20 MIN. • COOK: 6 HOURS • YIELD: 4 SERVINGS

Herbs and spices really work their magic on plain chicken in this dish, and the dried fruit adds an exotic touch.

Kathy Morgan *Ridgefield, Washington*

- **4 medium carrots, sliced**
- **2 large onions, halved and sliced**
- **1 broiler/fryer chicken (3 to 4 pounds), cut up, skin removed**
- **½ teaspoon salt**
- **½ cup chopped dried apricots**
- **½ cup raisins**
- **2 tablespoons all-purpose flour**
- **1 can (14½ ounces) reduced-sodium chicken broth**
- **¼ cup tomato paste**
- **2 tablespoons lemon juice**
- **2 garlic cloves, minced**
- **1½ teaspoons ground ginger**
- **1½ teaspoons ground cumin**
- **1 teaspoon ground cinnamon**
- **¾ teaspoon pepper**

Hot cooked couscous

1 Place carrots and onions in a greased 5-qt. slow cooker. Sprinkle chicken with salt; add to slow cooker. Top with apricots and raisins. In a small bowl, combine flour and broth until smooth; whisk in the tomato paste, lemon juice, garlic, ginger, cumin, cinnamon and pepper. Pour over chicken.

2 Cover and cook on low for 6 to 7 hours or until chicken is tender. Serve with couscous.

Spicy Coconut Chicken Strips

PREP: 25 MIN. • COOK: 5 MIN./BATCH
YIELD: 4 SERVINGS (⅔ CUP SAUCE)

My family has always enjoyed Thai food, but we really love chicken curry. Since we have a young son, I wanted to make something that he would eat. His favorite food is chicken strips, so I started making the strips with some curry flavor. Now my family likes these even more than my chicken curry.

Daniel Fox *Queen Creek, Arizona*

- **2 eggs**
- **½ cup coconut milk**
- **2 tablespoons red curry paste**
- **1 tablespoon cornstarch**
- **1 cup flaked coconut**
- **1 cup all-purpose flour**
- **4 teaspoons chili powder**
- **12 chicken tenderloins**

Oil for deep-fat frying

PEANUT DIPPING SAUCE:

- **¼ cup chunky peanut butter**
- **¼ cup coconut milk**
- **3 tablespoons 2% milk**
- **4½ teaspoons reduced-sodium soy sauce**
- **3 garlic cloves, minced**
- **1 tablespoon minced fresh cilantro**
- **1 tablespoon brown sugar**
- **1 tablespoon lime juice**

1 In a shallow bowl, whisk the eggs, coconut milk, curry paste and cornstarch until smooth. In another shallow bowl, combine the coconut, flour and chili powder. Dip chicken in egg mixture, then coat with coconut mixture.

2 In an electric skillet or deep fryer, heat oil to 375°. Fry chicken, a few at a time, for 2-3 minutes on each side or until golden brown. Drain on paper towels.

3 In a microwave-safe bowl, combine sauce ingredients. Cover and microwave on high for 45 seconds or until heated through, stirring once. Serve with chicken.

Spicy Apricot Chicken Thighs

PREP: 30 MIN. • BAKE: 35 MIN. • YIELD: 6 SERVINGS

Chicken thighs are inexpensive and make a great dinner for a large group. The apricot glaze gives the meat a tempting gloss and the few minutes in the broiler crisp the skin to perfection. Leftovers are great the next day, too! Just turn oven on 375° and heat chicken for 10-15 minutes.

Marcy Gallinger *Deer Park, Washington*

- **3 tablespoons minced fresh rosemary or 1 tablespoon dried rosemary, crushed**
- **2 tablespoons brown sugar**
- **2 teaspoons salt**
- **2 teaspoons pepper**
- **1 teaspoon crushed red pepper flakes**
- **12 bone-in chicken thighs (about 5 pounds)**

SAUCE:

- **1 jar (12 ounces) apricot preserves**
- **¼ cup rice vinegar**
- **1 tablespoon honey**
- **2 teaspoons minced fresh rosemary or ½ teaspoon dried rosemary, crushed**

1 In a small bowl, combine the first five ingredients; rub over chicken. Place chicken, skin side up, on a rack in a shallow roasting pan. Bake at 375° for 35-40 minutes or until a thermometer reads 180°.

2 Meanwhile, in a small saucepan, combine sauce ingredients; bring to a boil over medium-high heat, stirring frequently. Reduce heat; simmer, uncovered, for 5 minutes, stirring occasionally.

3 Turn chicken. Spoon some sauce over chicken. Broil 4-6 in. from the heat for 3-5 minutes or until browned. Turn chicken again; baste with sauce. Broil for 2-3 minutes longer or until browned. Serve with remaining sauce.

Penne Gorgonzola with Chicken

30 min.

PREP/TOTAL TIME: 30 MIN. • YIELD: 8 SERVINGS

This rich, creamy pasta dish is a snap to throw together for a weeknight meal but special enough for company. You can substitute another cheese for the Gorgonzola if you like.

George Schroeder *Port Murray, New Jersey*

- **1 package (16 ounces) penne pasta**
- **1 pound boneless skinless chicken breasts, cut into ½-inch pieces**
- **1 tablespoon olive oil**
- **1 large garlic clove, minced**
- **¼ cup white wine**
- **1 cup heavy whipping cream**
- **¼ cup chicken broth**
- **2 cups (8 ounces) crumbled Gorgonzola cheese**
- **6 to 8 fresh sage leaves, thinly sliced**

Salt and pepper to taste

Grated Parmigiano-Reggiano cheese and minced fresh parsley

1 Cook pasta according to package directions. Meanwhile, in a large skillet over medium heat, brown chicken in oil on all sides. Add garlic; cook 1 minute longer. Add wine, stirring to loosen browned bits from pan.

2 Add cream and broth; cook until sauce is slightly thickened and chicken is no longer pink. Stir in the Gorgonzola cheese, sage, salt and pepper; cook just until cheese is melted.

3 Drain pasta; toss with sauce. Sprinkle with Parmigiano-Reggiano cheese and parsley.

Grilled Chicken with Peaches

PREP: 15 MIN. • GRILL: 20 MIN.
YIELD: 8 SERVINGS

My grandmother gave me this recipe, which I lightened up. Now my grandchildren ask for this meal when they come over. The peaches are delicious hot off the grill.

Linda McCluskey *Cullman, Alabama*

- **1 cup 100% peach spreadable fruit**
- **2 tablespoons olive oil**
- **4 teaspoons reduced-sodium soy sauce**
- **1 tablespoon ground mustard**
- **1 garlic clove, minced**
- **½ teaspoon salt**
- **¼ teaspoon pepper**
- **¼ teaspoon cayenne pepper**
- **8 boneless skinless chicken breast halves (4 ounces each)**
- **8 medium ripe peaches, halved and pitted**

1 In a small bowl, combine the first eight ingredients; set aside. Using long-handled tongs, moisten a paper towel with cooking oil and lightly coat the grill rack.

2 Grill chicken, covered, over medium heat for 5-7 minutes on each side or until a thermometer reads 170°, basting occasionally with some of the reserved glaze. Transfer to a serving platter; keep warm.

3 Grill peaches cut side down for 8-10 minutes or until tender, turning and basting every 2 minutes with remaining glaze. Serve with chicken.

Turkey Enchiladas

PREP: 40 MIN. • BAKE: 40 MIN. • YIELD: 8 SERVINGS

My family likes these enchiladas so much, they request a turkey dinner several times a year just so I'll make this dish with the leftovers. I usually double the recipe—they're that popular!

Beverly Matthews *Pasco, Washington*

- **3 cups cubed cooked turkey**
- **1 cup chicken broth**
- **1 cup cooked long grain rice**
- **2 plum tomatoes, chopped**
- **1 medium onion, chopped**
- **½ cup canned chopped green chilies**
- **½ cup sour cream**
- **¼ cup sliced ripe or green olives with pimientos**
- **¼ cup minced fresh cilantro**
- **1 teaspoon ground cumin**
- **8 flour tortillas (10 inches)**
- **1 can (28 ounces) green enchilada sauce, divided**
- **2 cups (8 ounces) shredded Mexican cheese blend, divided**

1 In a large saucepan, combine the first 10 ingredients. Bring to a boil. Reduce heat; simmer, uncovered, for 20 minutes. Remove from the heat.

2 Place ½ cup turkey mixture down the center of each tortilla; top each with 1 teaspoon enchilada sauce and 1 tablespoon cheese. Roll up and place seam side down in a greased 13-in. x 9-in. baking dish. Pour remaining enchilada sauce over top; sprinkle with remaining cheese.

3 Cover and bake at 350° for 30 minutes. Uncover; bake 8-10 minutes longer or until bubbly.

BBQ Chicken Pizzas

PREP: 30 MIN. + RISING • GRILL: 5 MIN.
YIELD: 4 INDIVIDUAL PIZZAS

This is so much fun to do with company on a summer night. Each person can adjust the ingredients as he or she sees fit. The dough is easy to work with and grilling it gives the crust deliciously different flavor.

Cara Langer *Overland Park, Kansas*

- **2 packages (¼ ounce each) active dry yeast**
- **1 cup warm water (110° to 115°)**
- **¼ cup whole wheat flour**
- **3 tablespoons olive oil**
- **1 tablespoon honey**
- **1 teaspoon salt**
- **2¼ to 2¾ cups all-purpose flour**

TOPPINGS:

- **¾ pound boneless skinless chicken breasts, cut into ½-inch pieces**
- **½ medium red onion, thinly sliced and separated into rings**
- **2 tablespoons olive oil, divided**
- **3 garlic cloves, minced**
- **1 cup barbecue sauce**
- **2 cups (8 ounces) shredded smoked Gouda cheese**
- **1 cup (4 ounces) shredded Asiago cheese**
- **½ cup pickled pepper rings**

Minced fresh basil leaves, optional

1 In a large bowl, dissolve yeast in warm water. Add the whole wheat flour, oil, honey, salt and 1½ cups flour. Beat until smooth. Stir in enough remaining flour to form a soft dough.

2 Turn onto a floured surface; knead until smooth and elastic, about 6-8 minutes. Place in a greased bowl, turning once to grease the top. Cover and let rise in a warm place until doubled, about 1 hour.

3 Punch dough down. On a lightly floured surface, divide dough into four portions. Roll each into a 10-in. circle; build up edges slightly. Cover and let rest for 10 minutes.

4 Meanwhile, in a large skillet, saute chicken and onion in 1 tablespoon oil until chicken is no longer pink. Add garlic; cook 1 minute longer. Stir in barbecue sauce; heat through. Remove from the heat and set aside.

5 Moisten a paper towel with cooking oil; using long-handled tongs, lightly coat the grill rack. Brush both sides of dough with remaining oil. Grill dough, covered, over medium heat for 1-2 minutes or until the crust is lightly browned. Remove from the grill.

6 Layer the grilled side of each pizza with the chicken mixture, cheeses and pepper rings. Return pizzas to grill.

7 Cover and cook for 4-5 minutes or until crust is lightly browned and cheese is melted, rotating pizzas halfway through cooking to ensure an evenly browned crust. Sprinkle with basil if desired.

Chicken Cutlets with Citrus Cherry Sauce

30 min.

PREP/TOTAL TIME: 30 MIN. • YIELD: 4 SERVINGS

You'll love the sweet-tart tanginess of this restaurant-quality chicken dish. Served with a salad, this is a meal to remember. The recipe is also good using pork cutlets and dried cranberries instead of chicken and cherries.

Charlene Chambers *Ormond Beach, Florida*

- **4 boneless skinless chicken breast halves (6 ounces each)**
- **½ teaspoon salt**
- **¼ teaspoon pepper**
- **¼ cup all-purpose flour**
- **½ cup ruby red grapefruit juice**
- **½ cup orange juice**
- **⅓ cup dried cherries**
- **2 teaspoons Dijon mustard**
- **1 tablespoon butter**
- **1 tablespoon canola oil**

1 Flatten chicken breasts to ½-in. thickness; sprinkle with salt and pepper. Place flour in a large resealable plastic bag. Add the chicken, a few pieces at a time, and shake to coat; set aside.

2 In a small saucepan, combine the juices, cherries and mustard. Bring to a boil; cook until liquid is reduced to ½ cup.

3 In a large skillet over medium heat, cook chicken in butter and oil for 5-7 minutes on each side or until juices run clear. Serve with sauce.

FLATTENING CHICKEN

>> Place boneless chicken breasts between two pieces of waxed paper or plastic wrap or in a resealable plastic bag. Starting in the center and working out to the edges, pound lightly with the flat side of a meat mallet until the chicken is even in thickness.

Slow 'n' Easy Barbecued Chicken

PREP: 20 MIN. • COOK: 3 HOURS • YIELD: 4 SERVINGS

I rely on this yummy recipe often during the summer and fall when I know I'm going to be out working in the yard all day. I just pair it with a side vegetable and salad, and supper is served! It's also delicious with pork or beef and easy to double for a crowd.

Dreama Hughes *London, Kentucky*

- **¼ cup water**
- **3 tablespoons brown sugar**
- **3 tablespoons white vinegar**
- **3 tablespoons ketchup**
- **2 tablespoons butter**
- **2 tablespoons Worcestershire sauce**
- **1 tablespoon lemon juice**
- **1 teaspoon salt**
- **1 teaspoon paprika**
- **1 teaspoon ground mustard**
- **½ teaspoon cayenne pepper**
- **1 broiler/fryer chicken (2½ to 3 pounds), cut up and skin removed**
- **4 teaspoons cornstarch**
- **1 tablespoon cold water**

1 In a small saucepan, combine the first 11 ingredients. Bring to a boil. Reduce heat; simmer, uncovered, for 5 minutes. Remove from the heat.

2 Place the chicken in a 3-qt. slow cooker. Top with sauce. Cover and cook on low for 3-4 hours or until chicken juices run clear.

3 Remove chicken to a serving platter; keep warm. Skim fat from cooking juices; transfer to a small saucepan. Bring liquid to a boil.

4 Combine cornstarch and water until smooth. Gradually stir into the pan. Bring to a boil; cook and stir for 2 minutes or until thickened. Spoon some of the sauce over chicken and serve the remaining sauce on the side.

Chicken with Cranberry-Balsamic Sauce

PREP: 20 MIN. • BAKE: 15 MIN.
YIELD: 4 SERVINGS

Here's a quick and delicious way to make ordinary chicken breasts elegant. The fruity sauce also livens up roasted pork and turkey.

Susan Cortesi *Northbrook, Illinois*

- **4 boneless skinless chicken breast halves (6 ounces each)**
- **1¼ teaspoons salt, divided**
- **½ teaspoon pepper**
- **1 tablespoon olive oil**
- **1 cup cranberry juice**
- **⅓ cup balsamic vinegar**
- **¼ cup whole-berry cranberry sauce**
- **2 tablespoons finely chopped shallot**
- **3 tablespoons butter**

1 Sprinkle chicken with 1 teaspoon salt and the pepper. In a large skillet, brown chicken in oil on both sides. Transfer to a greased 13-in. x 9-in. baking pan. Bake at 425° for 12-15 minutes or until a thermometer reads 170°.

2 Add the cranberry juice, vinegar, cranberry sauce and shallot to the skillet, stirring to loosen browned bits from pan. Bring to a boil; cook until liquid is reduced to about ½ cup. Stir in butter and remaining salt until butter is melted. Serve with chicken.

WINNERS CIRCLE

seafood

Enjoy the catch of the day—be it fish or shellfish—in dozens of tempting dishes that will please the entire family. Shrimp tossed with pasta, golden crab cakes, restaurant-style fish tacos and flame-kissed salmon are just some of the succulent and flavorful entrees waiting to grace your table.

SALMON SPIRALS WITH CUCUMBER SAUCE, 162

Sesame Salmon with Wasabi Mayo

PREP: 15 MIN. • BAKE: 20 MIN. • YIELD: 6 SERVINGS

While I adore sushi, it's not something I'd make at home. I created this recipe to mimic its wonderful flavor.

Carolyn Ketchum *Wakefield, Massachusetts*

- **2 tablespoons butter, melted**
- **3 tablespoons sesame oil, divided**
- **1 salmon fillet (2 pounds)**
- **¼ teaspoon salt**
- **¼ teaspoon pepper**
- **⅓ cup mayonnaise**
- **1½ teaspoons lemon juice**
- **1 teaspoon prepared wasabi**
- **4 green onions, chopped**
- **2 tablespoons sesame seeds, toasted**

1 Drizzle butter and 2 tablespoons oil into a 13-in. x 9-in. baking dish; tilt to coat bottom. Place salmon in dish; brush with remaining oil and sprinkle with salt and pepper.

2 Bake, uncovered, at 425° for 18-22 minutes or until fish flakes easily with a fork. Meanwhile, combine the mayonnaise, lemon juice and wasabi. Sprinkle salmon with onions and sesame seeds. Serve with sauce.

WASABI

>> This Japanese version of horseradish is bright green in color and has a sharp, pungent and fiery-hot flavor. It is traditionally used as a condiment with sushi and sashimi. Today, many Western sauces, mustards and other condiments are seasoned with wasabi. Wasabi powder and paste are also available in the Asian food section of the grocery store.

Mixed Paella 

PREP/TOTAL TIME: 30 MIN. • YIELD: 6 SERVINGS

Packed with chicken, shrimp, rice, tomatoes, peas and stuffed olives, this vibrant meal is quick and filling. It will take the chill off any cool evening.

Libby Walp *Chicago, Illinois*

- **1¼ pounds boneless skinless chicken breasts, thinly sliced**
- **2 tablespoons olive oil**
- **1 medium onion, chopped**
- **2 garlic cloves, minced**
- **2¼ cups chicken broth**
- **1 cup uncooked long grain rice**
- **1 teaspoon dried oregano**
- **½ teaspoon ground turmeric**
- **½ teaspoon paprika**
- **¼ teaspoon salt**
- **¼ to ½ teaspoon pepper**
- **1 pound cooked medium shrimp, peeled and deveined**
- **1 can (14½ ounces) diced tomatoes, undrained**
- **¾ cup frozen peas, thawed**
- **½ cup sliced pimiento-stuffed olives**

1 In a large skillet, saute chicken in oil until no longer pink. Remove and keep warm. In the same skillet, saute onion until tender. Add garlic; cook 1 minute longer. Stir in the broth, rice and seasonings. Bring to a boil. Reduce heat; cover and simmer for 15-18 minutes or until rice is tender.

2 Stir in the shrimp, tomatoes, peas, olives and chicken; cover and cook for 3-4 minutes or until heated through.

Skillet Sea Scallops 30 min.

PREP/TOTAL TIME: 25 MIN.
YIELD: 3-4 SERVINGS

You'll want to slip this recipe into the front of your "last-minute guests" file. Pasta and mixed greens nicely complement the tender, citrusy shellfish.

Margaret E. Lowenberg *Kingman, Arizona*

- **½ cup dry bread crumbs**
- **½ teaspoon salt**
- **1 pound sea scallops**
- **2 tablespoons butter**
- **1 tablespoon olive oil**
- **¼ cup white wine or reduced-sodium chicken broth**
- **2 tablespoons lemon juice**
- **1 teaspoon minced fresh parsley**
- **1 garlic clove, minced**

1 In a large resealable plastic bag, combine bread crumbs and salt. Add scallops, a few at a time, and shake to coat.

2 In a large skillet over medium-high heat, brown scallops in butter and oil for 1½ to 2 minutes on each side or until firm and opaque. Remove and keep warm. Add the wine, lemon juice, parsley and garlic to the skillet; bring to a boil. Pour over scallops. Serve immediately.

Creamy Pesto Shrimp Linguine

30 min.

PREP/TOTAL TIME: 30 MIN.
YIELD: 4 SERVINGS

This is a fantastic dish for impressing friends. They never suspect how easy it is to make. The pesto cream sauce makes it even more delectable than a typical Alfredo sauce.

Jessica Kempton *Logan, Utah*

- **8 ounces linguine**
- **1 pound uncooked large shrimp, peeled and deveined**
- **¼ cup butter, cubed**
- **2 cups heavy whipping cream**
- **1 cup grated Parmesan cheese**
- **⅓ cup prepared pesto**
- **¼ teaspoon pepper**

1 Cook linguine according to package directions.

2 Meanwhile, in a large skillet, saute shrimp in butter until shrimp turn pink. Remove and set aside. Add cream to the pan; bring to a gentle boil. Reduce heat; cook, uncovered, for 4-6 minutes or until slightly thickened, stirring occasionally.

3 Stir in the cheese, pesto and pepper until smooth. Return shrimp to the pan; heat through. Drain linguine; serve with sauce.

Pineapple Pico Tuna Steaks

PREP: 10 MIN. + MARINATING • GRILL: 10 MIN. • YIELD: 4 SERVINGS

Bursting with flavor from a quick-and-easy marinade, these tuna steaks are topped with pico de gallo made from pineapple, tomato, lime juice and a nice kick of jalapeno.

Sally Sibthorpe *Shelby Township, Michigan*

- **½ cup tequila**
- **3 tablespoons brown sugar**
- **2 tablespoons lime juice**
- **1 tablespoon chili powder**
- **1 tablespoon olive oil**
- **1 teaspoon salt**
- **4 tuna steaks (6 ounces each)**

PICO DE GALLO:

- **1 cup chopped fresh pineapple**
- **1 plum tomato, finely chopped**
- **⅓ cup finely chopped onion**
- **¼ cup minced fresh cilantro**
- **2 tablespoons minced seeded jalapeno pepper**
- **2 tablespoons lime juice**
- **1 tablespoon olive oil**
- **2 teaspoons grated lime peel**
- **½ teaspoon salt**

1 In a large resealable plastic bag, combine the first six ingredients. Add the tuna; seal bag and turn to coat. Refrigerate for 30 minutes. Meanwhile, in a small bowl, combine pico de gallo ingredients. Cover and refrigerate until serving.

2 Drain and discard marinade. Using long-handled tongs, moisten a paper towel with cooking oil and lightly coat the grill rack. For medium-rare, grill tuna, covered, over high heat or broil 3-4 in. from the heat for 3-4 minutes on each side or until slightly pink in the center. Serve with pico de gallo.

EDITOR'S NOTE: Wear disposable gloves when cutting hot peppers; the oils can burn skin. Avoid touching your face.

Seafood Pasta Alfredo

PREP/TOTAL TIME: 30 MIN. • YIELD: 6 SERVINGS

My husband loves seafood, and I created this recipe one night with a little of this and a little of that. Luckily, I wrote it down because he asks for this dish often.

Rebekah Beyer *Sabetha, Kansas*

- **8 ounces uncooked linguine**
- **1 small zucchini, quartered and sliced**
- **1 cup julienned carrots**
- **1 small onion, chopped**
- **1 tablespoon olive oil**
- **1 garlic clove, minced**
- **Dash crushed red pepper flakes**
- **1 cup heavy whipping cream**
- **½ cup grated Parmesan cheese**
- **2 tablespoons butter**
- **½ teaspoon salt**
- **⅛ teaspoon pepper**
- **1 pound cooked medium shrimp, peeled and deveined**
- **2 plum tomatoes, chopped**
- **1 can (6 ounces) crab, drained**
- **4 ounces imitation crabmeat, chopped**
- **3 green onions, sliced**

1 Cook linguine according to package directions. Meanwhile, in a large skillet, saute the zucchini, carrots and onion in oil until crisp-tender. Add garlic and pepper flakes; cook 1 minute longer. Stir in the cream, cheese, butter, salt and pepper.

2 Bring to a gentle boil; cook for 1-2 minutes or until slightly thickened. Add the shrimp, tomatoes, crab, imitation crabmeat and green onions. Drain linguine; toss with shrimp mixture.

Seafood Medley with Linguine

PREP: 35 MIN. • COOK: 5 MIN. • YIELD: 8 SERVINGS

Who can resist a savory blend of seafood and pasta? Teeming with scallops, shrimp and tomatoes, my linguine dish is nutritious and rich in flavor.

Charlene Chambers *Ormond Beach, Florida*

- **1 large onion, chopped**
- **2 tablespoons butter**
- **1 tablespoon olive oil**
- **3 garlic cloves, minced**
- **1 cup white wine or chicken broth**
- **1 can (28 ounces) diced fire-roasted tomatoes**
- **1 tablespoon minced fresh rosemary or 1 teaspoon dried rosemary, crushed**
- **1 teaspoon sugar**
- **1 teaspoon minced fresh oregano or ¼ teaspoon dried oregano**
- **¼ teaspoon salt**
- **¼ teaspoon pepper**
- **1 package (16 ounces) linguine**
- **1 pound sea scallops**
- **9 ounces uncooked large shrimp, peeled and deveined**
- **2 tablespoons minced fresh parsley**

Shredded Parmesan cheese, optional

1 In a large skillet, saute onion in butter and oil until tender. Add garlic; cook 1 minute longer. Add wine. Bring to a boil; cook until liquid is reduced to ½ cup. Add the tomatoes, rosemary, sugar, oregano, salt and pepper. Bring to a boil over medium heat. Reduce heat; simmer, uncovered, for 15 minutes.

2 Meanwhile, cook linguine according to package directions. Add scallops and shrimp to tomato mixture; cook for 4-5 minutes or until shrimp turn pink and scallops are opaque. Stir in parsley.

3 Drain linguine. Serve seafood mixture with linguine; garnish with cheese if desired.

Mango Shrimp Pitas

PREP: 15 MIN. + MARINATING • GRILL: 10 MIN. • YIELD: 4 SERVINGS

Mango, ginger and curry combine with a splash of lime juice to coat this juicy grilled shrimp. Stuffed in pitas, the shrimp combo makes for an easy-to-hold, fabulous entree! You could also serve on a bed of rice for a less casual presentation.

Beverly Oferrall *Linkwood, Maryland*

- **½ cup mango chutney**
- **3 tablespoons lime juice**
- **1 teaspoon grated fresh gingerroot**
- **½ teaspoon curry powder**
- **1 pound uncooked large shrimp, peeled and deveined**
- **2 pita breads (6 inches), halved**
- **8 Bibb or Boston lettuce leaves**
- **1 large tomato, thinly sliced**

1 In a small bowl, combine the chutney, lime juice, ginger and curry. Pour ½ cup marinade into a large resealable plastic bag; add the shrimp. Seal bag and turn to coat; refrigerate for at least 15 minutes. Cover and refrigerate remaining marinade.

2 Drain shrimp and discard marinade. Thread shrimp onto four metal or soaked wooden skewers. Moisten a paper towel with cooking oil; using long-handled tongs, lightly coat the grill rack.

3 Grill shrimp, covered, over medium heat or broil 4 in. from the heat for 6-8 minutes or until shrimp turn pink, turning frequently.

4 Fill pita halves with lettuce, tomato and shrimp; spoon reserved chutney mixture over filling.

WINNERS CIRCLE

Southwestern Scallops

30 min.

PREP/TOTAL TIME: 20 MIN.
YIELD: 4 SERVINGS

My saucy sea scallops are popular at dinner parties, and they're in my collection of easy weekday meals. The seasoning gives the sweet shellfish a pleasant kick.

Maggie Fontenot *The Woodlands, Texas*

- **2 teaspoons chili powder**
- **½ teaspoon ground cumin**
- **¼ teaspoon salt**
- **⅛ teaspoon pepper**
- **1 pound sea scallops (about 12)**
- **2 tablespoons butter, divided**
- **½ cup white wine or chicken broth**

1 In a small bowl, combine the chili powder, cumin, salt and pepper. Pat scallops dry with paper towels. Rub seasoning mixture over scallops.

2 In a large heavy skillet over medium heat, melt 1 tablespoon butter. Cook scallops for 2 minutes on each side or until opaque and golden brown. Remove from the skillet; keep warm.

3 Add wine to skillet, stirring to loosen any browned bits from pan. Bring to a boil; cook until liquid is reduced by half. Stir in remaining butter until melted. Serve with scallops.

Peking Shrimp

30 min.

PREP/TOTAL TIME: 25 MIN. • YIELD: 4 SERVINGS

In the summer, we spend as much time as possible at our vacation home in a beach town. I prepare lots of seafood because it's so fresh and readily available there, but this main dish is a year-round favorite.

Janet Edwards *Beaverton, Oregon*

- **1 tablespoon cornstarch**
- **¼ cup cold water**
- **¼ cup corn syrup**
- **2 tablespoons reduced-sodium soy sauce**
- **2 tablespoons sherry or chicken broth**
- **1 garlic clove, minced**
- **¼ teaspoon ground ginger**
- **1 small green pepper, cut into 1-inch pieces**
- **2 tablespoons canola oil**
- **1 pound uncooked medium shrimp, peeled and deveined**
- **1 medium tomato, cut into wedges**

Hot cooked rice, optional

1 In a small bowl, combine cornstarch and water until smooth. Stir in the corn syrup, soy sauce, sherry, garlic and ginger; set aside.

2 In a nonstick skillet or wok, stir-fry green pepper in oil for 3 minutes. Add shrimp; stir-fry 3 minutes longer or until shrimp turn pink.

3 Stir cornstarch mixture and add to the pan. Bring to a boil; cook and stir for 2 minutes or until thickened. Add tomato; heat through. Serve with rice if desired.

Scallops with Citrus Glaze

30 min.

PREP/TOTAL TIME: 20 MIN. • YIELD: 4 SERVINGS

These scallops are especially scrumptious when served on steamed rice with a green salad on the side.

Patricia Nieh *Portola Valley, California*

- **12 sea scallops (about 1½ pounds)**
- **½ teaspoon pepper**
- **¼ teaspoon salt**
- **2 tablespoons olive oil, divided**
- **4 garlic cloves, minced**
- **½ cup orange juice**
- **¼ cup lemon juice**
- **1 tablespoon reduced-sodium soy sauce**
- **½ teaspoon grated orange peel**

1 Sprinkle scallops with pepper and salt. In a large skillet, saute scallops in 1 tablespoon oil until firm and opaque. Remove and keep warm.

2 In the same skillet, cook garlic in remaining oil for 1 minute. Add the juices, soy sauce and orange peel. Bring to a boil; cook and stir for 5 minutes or until thickened. Serve with scallops.

Halibut with Orange Salsa

PREP: 25 MIN. + MARINATING • BAKE: 15 MIN.
YIELD: 4 SERVINGS

Crispy orange halibut is topped with a homemade salsa featuring tomatoes, orange, kalamata olives and basil for a company-worthy dish that'll bring raves.

Gloria Bradley *Naperville, Illinois*

- **1 cup orange juice**
- **1¼ teaspoons Caribbean jerk seasoning, divided**
- **4 halibut fillets (6 ounces each)**
- **½ cup panko (Japanese) bread crumbs**
- **2 teaspoons grated orange peel**
- **½ teaspoon salt**

SALSA:

- **2 plum tomatoes, seeded and chopped**
- **1 large navel orange, peeled, sectioned and chopped**
- **¼ cup pitted Greek olives, chopped**
- **2 tablespoons minced fresh basil**
- **1 tablespoon olive oil**
- **1 garlic clove, minced**
- **⅛ teaspoon salt**
- **⅛ teaspoon pepper**

1 In a large resealable plastic bag, combine orange juice and 1 teaspoon jerk seasoning. Add the halibut; seal bag and turn to coat. Set aside for 15 minutes.

2 Meanwhile, in a shallow bowl, combine the bread crumbs, orange peel, salt and remaining jerk seasoning. Drain and discard marinade. Coat halibut with bread crumb mixture. Place on a greased baking sheet.

3 Bake at 400° for 15-20 minutes or until fish flakes easily with a fork. Broil 4-6 in. from the heat for 3-4 minutes or until lightly browned.

4 In a small bowl, combine the salsa ingredients. Serve with halibut.

Feta Shrimp Tacos

PREP/TOTAL TIME: 30 MIN. • YIELD: 4 SERVINGS

A unique combination of taco seasoning and feta cheese works remarkably well in these refreshing tacos. It's a good thing you get two per serving, because you won't want to stop at one!

Athena Russell *Florence, South Carolina*

- **2 cups shredded red cabbage**
- **¼ cup finely chopped sweet onion**
- **1 banana pepper, finely chopped**
- **¼ cup Miracle Whip Light**
- **1 tablespoon cider vinegar**
- **1 tablespoon stone-ground mustard**
- **¼ teaspoon pepper**
- **1 pound uncooked medium shrimp, peeled and deveined**
- **1 tablespoon reduced-sodium taco seasoning**
- **1 tablespoon olive oil**
- **8 whole wheat tortillas (8 inches)**
- **¾ cup crumbled feta cheese**

Sliced avocado, optional

1 In a small bowl, combine the cabbage, onion and banana pepper. In another small bowl, whisk the Miracle Whip, vinegar, mustard and pepper. Pour over cabbage mixture and toss to coat. Chill until serving.

2 Sprinkle shrimp with taco seasoning. In a large nonstick skillet, saute shrimp in oil for 3-4 minutes or until shrimp turn pink. Place shrimp on tortillas; top with cheese, coleslaw and avocado if desired.

Spicy Chorizo & Shrimp Rice

30 min.

PREP/TOTAL TIME: 30 MIN.
YIELD: 4 SERVINGS

Looking for an easy one-skillet meal for dinner tonight? This dish has a fresh Southwestern flavor your family will warm up to!

Cheryl Perry *Hertford, North Carolina*

- **½ pound uncooked chorizo or bulk spicy pork sausage**
- **4 tomatillos, husks removed, chopped**
- **1 cup uncooked long grain rice**
- **¼ cup chopped onion**
- **¼ cup chopped celery leaves**
- **¼ cup chopped carrot**
- **½ teaspoon garlic powder**
- **¼ teaspoon pepper**
- **2 cups chicken broth**
- **½ pound uncooked medium shrimp, peeled and deveined**
- **¼ cup crumbled queso fresco or diced part-skim mozzarella cheese**
- **2 teaspoons minced fresh cilantro**

1 Crumble chorizo into a large skillet; add tomatillos. Cook over medium heat for 6-8 minutes or until meat is fully cooked. Add the rice, onion, celery leaves, carrot, garlic powder and pepper; cook and stir for 2 minutes.

2 Add broth; bring to a boil. Reduce heat; cover and simmer for 10 minutes. Stir in shrimp; cover and cook 5 minutes longer or until shrimp turn pink and rice is tender. Sprinkle with cheese and cilantro.

Salmon Spirals with Cucumber Sauce

PREP: 20 MIN. + MARINATING • GRILL: 10 MIN.
YIELD: 4 SKEWERS (1⅓ CUPS SAUCE)

When you serve this entree, it'll be hard to tell which impresses your guests more: the delicious taste or the classy presentation.

Rosalind Pope *Greensboro, North Carolina*

- **1 salmon fillet (1 pound)**
- **8 fresh dill sprigs**
- **¼ cup lime juice**
- **1 tablespoon olive oil**
- **2 teaspoons Dijon mustard**

SAUCE:

- **1 cup (8 ounces) fat-free plain yogurt**
- **¼ cup fat-free mayonnaise**
- **2 tablespoons finely chopped seeded peeled cucumber**
- **2 tablespoons snipped fresh dill**
- **1 tablespoon lemon juice**

1 Remove skin from fillet and discard. Cut fillet lengthwise into four strips. Place two dill sprigs on each strip; roll up. Thread salmon onto four metal or soaked wooden skewers.

2 In a large resealable plastic bag, combine the lime juice, oil and mustard; add salmon. Seal bag and turn to coat; refrigerate for 30 minutes, turning occasionally.

3 Drain and discard marinade. Using long-handled tongs, moisten a paper towel with cooking oil and lightly coat the grill rack. Grill salmon, covered, over high heat or broil 3-4 in. from the heat for 4-5 minutes on each side or until fish flakes easily with a fork.

4 Meanwhile, in a small bowl, combine the sauce ingredients. Serve with salmon.

Spicy Shrimp Pizza

PREP: 30 MIN. • BAKE: 10 MIN. • YIELD: 6 SLICES

The sophisticated blend of seasonings, shrimp and a splash of white wine will make this awesome pizza a favorite with your friends. This recipe is special enough for company, but quick enough for weeknights, too.

Debra Udden *Colorado Springs, Colorado*

- **1 pound uncooked medium shrimp, peeled and deveined**
- **½ to ¾ teaspoon crushed red pepper flakes**
- **2 tablespoons olive oil**
- **1 medium onion, chopped**
- **5 garlic cloves, minced**
- **12 cherry tomatoes, halved**
- **1 can (15 ounces) crushed tomatoes, undrained**
- **1 cup white wine or chicken broth**
- **½ teaspoon dried oregano**
- **⅛ teaspoon pepper**
- **3 tablespoons minced fresh parsley**
- **1 prebaked 12-inch thin pizza crust**
- **1 cup (4 ounces) shredded Italian cheese blend**
- **1 cup (4 ounces) shredded Parmesan or Parmigiano-Reggiano cheese**

1 In a large skillet over medium heat, cook shrimp and pepper flakes in oil for 2-3 minutes or until shrimp turn pink. Remove and keep warm.

2 In the same skillet, saute onion until tender. Add garlic; cook 1 minute longer.

3 Add the cherry tomatoes, crushed tomatoes, wine, oregano and pepper. Bring to a boil; cook until liquid is reduced, stirring occasionally. Add shrimp and parsley; heat through.

4 Place crust on an ungreased pizza pan. Spread shrimp mixture over crust to within ½ in. of edges; sprinkle with cheeses.

5 Bake at 450° for 8-10 minutes or until cheese is melted and edges are lightly browned.

Crab Cake-Stuffed Portobellos

PREP/TOTAL TIME: 30 MIN. • YIELD: 6 SERVINGS

Served as an appetizer or a light main dish, these stuffed mushrooms are pretty and delicious. Canned crabmeat becomes absolutely elegant.

Jennifer Coduto *Kent, Ohio*

- **6 large portobello mushrooms**
- **¾ cup finely chopped sweet onion**
- **2 tablespoons olive oil, divided**
- **1 package (8 ounces) cream cheese, softened**
- **1 egg**
- **½ cup seasoned bread crumbs**
- **½ cup plus 1 teaspoon grated Parmesan cheese, divided**
- **1 teaspoon seafood seasoning**
- **2 cans (6½ ounces each) lump crabmeat, drained**
- **¼ teaspoon paprika**

1 Remove stems from mushrooms (discard or save for another use); set caps aside. In a small skillet, saute onion in 1 tablespoon oil until tender. In a small bowl, combine the cream cheese, egg, bread crumbs, ½ cup cheese and seafood seasoning. Gently stir in crab and onion.

2 Spoon ½ cup crab mixture into each mushroom cap; drizzle with remaining oil. Sprinkle with paprika and remaining cheese. Place in a greased 15-in. x 10-in. x 1-in. baking pan.

3 Bake, uncovered, at 400° for 15-20 minutes or until mushrooms are tender.

FROZEN SWEET ONIONS

>> For longer storage, sweet onions can be frozen. Chop and place in a 15-in. x 10-in. x 1-in. pan in the freezer. When they're frozen, place in freezer bags or containers and freeze for up to 1 year. Frozen chopped onions are best used in recipes such as soups, sauces and casseroles.

Mediterranean Shrimp Couscous

PREP: 20 MIN. • COOK: 25 MIN. • YIELD: 6 SERVINGS

It makes me feel good to know this is a low-fat, flavorful recipe my family loves! Elegant and light, this dish's flavors work really well together.

Heather Carroll *Colorado Springs, Colorado*

- **1½ pounds uncooked medium shrimp, peeled and deveined**
- **1 tablespoon chopped shallot**
- **2 garlic cloves, minced**
- **3 tablespoons olive oil, divided**
- **1 cup chopped zucchini**
- **½ cup white wine or reduced-sodium chicken broth**
- **¼ cup chopped sun-dried tomatoes (not packed in oil)**
- **2 tablespoons capers, drained**
- **3 cups fresh baby spinach**
- **1½ cups reduced-sodium chicken broth**
- **1½ cups uncooked couscous**
- **2 tablespoons lemon juice**
- **2 tablespoons balsamic vinegar**
- **½ cup crumbled feta cheese, divided**
- **½ teaspoon dried oregano**
- **¼ teaspoon salt**
- **¼ teaspoon pepper**

1 In a large skillet, saute the shrimp, shallot and garlic in 1 tablespoon oil until shrimp turn pink. Remove and keep warm.

2 In the same skillet, cook and stir the zucchini, wine, tomatoes and capers until zucchini is tender. Add spinach; cook just until wilted. Add broth and bring to a boil. Stir in couscous.

3 Cover and remove from the heat; let stand for 5 minutes or until liquid is absorbed. Fluff with a fork.

4 Whisk the lemon juice, vinegar and remaining oil; add to the pan. Stir in ¼ cup cheese, the seasonings and reserved shrimp mixture; cook and stir over low heat until heated through. Sprinkle with remaining cheese.

WINNERS CIRCLE

Shrimp & Macaroni Casserole

PREP: 20 MIN. • BAKE: 20 MIN.
YIELD: 3 SERVINGS

Mac and cheese goes upscale in this deliciously cheesy variation. The shrimp gives a unique twist to this popular standard.

Michael Cohen *Los Angeles, California*

- **1 cup uncooked elbow macaroni**
- **1 egg**
- **¼ cup half-and-half cream**
- **2 tablespoons butter, melted**
- **½ cup grated Parmesan cheese**
- **¾ cup shredded part-skim mozzarella cheese, divided**
- **1 garlic clove, minced**
- **¼ teaspoon salt**
- **⅛ teaspoon pepper**
- **¼ pound uncooked medium shrimp, peeled, deveined and chopped**
- **¾ cup chopped fresh spinach**

1 Cook macaroni according to package directions. Meanwhile, in a small bowl, combine the egg, cream and butter; set aside. Drain macaroni. Add the Parmesan cheese, ½ cup mozzarella cheese, garlic, salt, pepper and reserved egg mixture; toss to coat. Stir in shrimp and spinach.

2 Transfer to a 1-qt. baking dish coated with cooking spray. Sprinkle with remaining mozzarella cheese. Bake, uncovered, at 350° for 20-25 minutes or until shrimp turn pink and cheese is melted.

Chipotle Salmon with Strawberry Mango Salsa 

PREP/TOTAL TIME: 25 MIN. • YIELD: 4 SERVINGS

I've made this recipe several times for family dinners and have always received compliments. Even the kids like this sweet berry salsa with the spicy, savory salmon.

Naylet LaRochelle *Miami, Florida*

- **2 tablespoons brown sugar**
- **3 garlic cloves, minced**
- **2 teaspoons finely chopped chipotle peppers in adobo sauce**
- **¼ teaspoon salt**
- **4 salmon fillets (6 ounces each)**

SALSA:

- **2 cups chopped fresh strawberries**
- **⅔ cup chopped peeled mango**
- **⅓ cup chopped red onion**
- **2 tablespoons lime juice**
- **1 tablespoon minced fresh cilantro**
- **1 tablespoon minced fresh mint**
- **2 teaspoons olive oil**

1 In a small bowl, combine the brown sugar, garlic, chipotle peppers and salt; rub over salmon.

2 Moisten a paper towel with cooking oil; using long-handled tongs, lightly coat the grill rack. Place salmon skin side down on grill rack. Grill salmon, covered, over high heat or broil 3-4 in. from the heat for 5-10 minutes or until the fish flakes easily with a fork.

3 In a small bowl, combine the salsa ingredients; serve with salmon.

BBQ Shrimp Quesadillas

**PREP: 30 MIN. + MARINATING • COOK: 5 MIN.
YIELD: 4 SERVINGS**

My husband loves corn, shrimp and anything with barbecue sauce. One night, when I was low on groceries, ideas and time, I went to the cupboards and garden and this recipe was born.

Christine Parsons *Bountiful, Utah*

- **2 tablespoons lime juice**
- **2 teaspoons olive oil**
- **1½ teaspoons grated lime peel**
- **¼ teaspoon salt**
- **¼ teaspoon pepper**
- **¾ pound uncooked medium shrimp, peeled and deveined**
- **2 medium ears sweet corn, husks removed**
- **2 medium zucchini, chopped**
- **4 green onions, thinly sliced**
- **2 tablespoons barbecue sauce**
- **2 cups (8 ounces) shredded Monterey Jack cheese**
- **8 flour tortillas (8 inches)**

Salsa and additional barbecue sauce

1 In a large resealable plastic bag, combine the lime juice, oil, lime peel, salt and pepper. Add the shrimp; seal bag and turn to coat. Refrigerate for 15 minutes.

2 Meanwhile, remove corn from cobs. Drain and discard marinade from shrimp. Chop shrimp and set aside. In a large nonstick skillet coated with cooking spray, saute the zucchini, corn and onions until crisp-tender. Add shrimp; saute 2-3 minutes longer or until shrimp turn pink. Remove from the heat; stir in barbecue sauce.

3 Sprinkle cheese over half of the tortillas. Spoon shrimp mixture over cheese. Top with remaining tortillas. Cook on a griddle coated with cooking spray over low heat for 1-2 minutes on each side or until cheese is melted. Serve with salsa and additional barbecue sauce.

Crab Toast

PREP: 20 MIN. • BAKE: 20 MIN. • YIELD: 6 SERVINGS

When you're in the mood for casual dining, try this oven-baked, open-faced sandwich that's crunchy, creamy and delightfully rich. You could serve it as an appetizer by cutting thinner slices.

Teri Rasey *Cadillac, Michigan*

- **1 loaf (16 ounces) French bread**
- **¼ cup butter, cubed**
- **4 plum tomatoes, peeled and finely chopped, divided**
- **1 jalapeno pepper, seeded and chopped**
- **2 garlic cloves, minced**
- **2 teaspoons minced fresh cilantro**
- **2 packages (8 ounces each) imitation crabmeat**
- **¾ cup ricotta cheese**
- **½ cup sour cream**
- **2 cups (8 ounces) shredded Italian cheese blend, divided**

1 Cut bread in half horizontally; hollow out top and bottom, leaving 1-in. shells. Crumble removed bread; set aside.

2 In a large skillet, melt butter over medium heat; add half of the tomatoes. Add the jalapeno, garlic and cilantro; cook and stir for 4 minutes. Remove from the heat.

3 In a large bowl, combine the crab, ricotta and sour cream. Stir in the tomato mixture, reserved bread crumbs and 1 cup cheese blend. Spoon into bread shells. Place on an ungreased baking sheet. Bake at 375° for 15 minutes. Top with remaining cheese blend and tomatoes. Bake 5-7 minutes longer or until cheese is melted.

EDITOR'S NOTE: Wear disposable gloves when cutting hot peppers; the oils can burn skin. Avoid touching your face.

Fruity Halibut Steaks

30 min.

PREP/TOTAL TIME: 30 MIN. • YIELD: 6 SERVINGS

My friends and family rave about this recipe whenever I serve it. I make the salsa about four hours early so the flavors can blend.

Patricia Nieh *Portola Valley, California*

- **1 cup chopped fresh pineapple**
- **1 cup chopped peeled mango**
- **⅔ cup chopped sweet red pepper**
- **1 medium tomato, seeded and chopped**
- **⅓ cup chopped seeded peeled cucumber**
- **¼ cup minced fresh cilantro**
- **2 tablespoons chopped seeded jalapeno pepper**
- **2 tablespoons lime juice**
- **6 halibut steaks (8 ounces each)**
- **2 tablespoons olive oil**
- **½ teaspoon salt**
- **½ teaspoon pepper**

1 In a small bowl, combine the first eight ingredients; chill until serving.

2 Brush halibut with oil; sprinkle with salt and pepper. Moisten a paper towel with cooking oil; using long-handled tongs, lightly coat the grill rack. Grill halibut, covered, over high heat or broil 3-4 in. from the heat for 3-5 minutes on each side or until fish flakes easily with a fork. Serve with salsa.

EDITOR'S NOTE: Wear disposable gloves when cutting hot peppers; the oils can burn skin. Avoid touching your face.

Southwestern Shrimp with Salsa

PREP: 45 MIN. • GRILL: 10 MIN. • YIELD: 4 SERVINGS

I prefer grilling in the summer because you don't need to turn on the stove and heat up the house. If you want to get fancy, serve this in a chilled martini glass for a beautiful presentation. The rice and shrimp can be cooked a day ahead and refrigerated until serving.

Lindsay Matuszak *Reno, Nevada*

- **2 tablespoons olive oil**
- **1 tablespoon chili powder**
- **1 teaspoon garlic salt**
- **1 teaspoon ground coriander**
- **1 teaspoon dried oregano**
- **½ teaspoon ground cumin**
- **½ teaspoon pepper**
- **20 uncooked jumbo shrimp, peeled and deveined**
- **1 cup uncooked saffron rice**

AVOCADO-CORN SALSA:

- **1 medium ripe avocado, peeled and cubed**
- **2 to 3 tablespoons lime juice**
- **1½ cups frozen corn, thawed**
- **1 medium tomato, peeled, seeded and chopped**
- **2 jalapeno peppers, seeded and minced**
- **¼ cup minced fresh cilantro**
- **1 green onion, chopped**
- **⅛ teaspoon salt**
- **⅛ teaspoon pepper**

1 In a large resealable plastic bag, combine the first seven ingredients. Add the shrimp; seal and turn to coat. Refrigerate for 30 minutes. Meanwhile, cook rice according to package directions.

2 In a small bowl, combine avocado and lime juice; toss to coat. Add the remaining ingredients; gently stir to combine.

3 Drain shrimp and discard marinade. Thread shrimp onto metal or soaked wooden skewers. Moisten a paper towel with cooking oil; using long-handled tongs, lightly coat the grill rack.

4 Grill shrimp, covered, over medium heat or broil 4 in. from the heat for 6-9 minutes or until shrimp turn pink, turning once. Serve with rice and salsa.

EDITOR'S NOTE: Wear disposable gloves when cutting hot peppers; the oils can burn skin. Avoid touching your face.

Scallop Mac & Cheese

PREP: 35 MIN. • BAKE: 15 MIN. • YIELD: 5 SERVINGS

Who knew scallops could transform macaroni and cheese into an upscale specialty? It's such a simple alternative to traditional comfort food.

Laurie Lufkin *Essex, Massachusetts*

- **2 cups uncooked medium pasta shells**
- **½ cup butter, divided**
- **1 cup French bread baguette crumbs**
- **1 pound bay scallops**
- **1 cup sliced fresh mushrooms**
- **1 small onion, chopped**
- **3 tablespoons all-purpose flour**
- **¾ teaspoon dried thyme**
- **¼ teaspoon salt**
- **⅛ teaspoon pepper**
- **2 cups whole milk**
- **½ cup white wine or chicken broth**
- **2 tablespoons sherry or chicken broth**
- **1 cup (4 ounces) shredded Swiss cheese**
- **1 cup (4 ounces) shredded sharp cheddar cheese**

1 Cook pasta according to package directions. Meanwhile, in a small skillet, melt 4 tablespoons butter. Add bread crumbs; cook and stir until lightly toasted. Set aside.

2 In a large skillet over medium heat, melt 2 tablespoons butter. Add scallops; cook and stir for 2 minutes or until firm and opaque. Remove and keep warm. Melt remaining butter in the pan; add mushrooms and onion. Cook and stir until tender. Stir in the flour, thyme, salt and pepper until blended.

3 Gradually add the milk, wine and sherry. Bring to a boil; cook and stir for 1-2 minutes or until thickened. Stir in cheeses until melted. Drain pasta; stir pasta and scallops into sauce.

4 Divide among five 10 oz. ramekins or custard cups. Sprinkle with bread crumbs. Place ramekins on a baking sheet. Bake, uncovered, at 350° for 15-20 minutes or until heated through. Spoon onto plates if desired.

30 min.

Southwest Fish Tacos

PREP/TOTAL TIME: 20 MIN.
YIELD: 4 SERVINGS

These fish tacos are an adaptation of a dish I was served in Bermuda. With such little prep work involved, they're a quick choice for dinner

Jennifer Reid *Farmington, Maine*

- **1½ pounds sole fillets, cut into 1-inch strips**
- **1 tablespoon taco seasoning**
- **¼ cup butter, cubed**
- **1 package (10 ounces) angel hair coleslaw mix**
- **½ cup minced fresh cilantro**
- **½ cup reduced-fat mayonnaise**
- **1 tablespoon lime juice**
- **1 teaspoon sugar**
- **¼ teaspoon salt**
- **¼ teaspoon pepper**
- **8 taco shells, warmed**
- **8 lime wedges**

1 Sprinkle fish with taco seasoning. In a large skillet over medium heat, cook fish in butter for 3-4 minutes on each side or until fish flakes easily with a fork.

2 Meanwhile, in a small bowl, combine the coleslaw, cilantro, mayonnaise, lime juice, sugar, salt and pepper.

3 Place fish in taco shells. Top with coleslaw mixture; serve with lime wedges.

WINNERS CIRCLE

meatless

It's another Meatless Monday and you've run through your entire repertoire of family-approved meals. Never fear—just page through this mouthwatering selection of veggie-laden and cheese-filled options sure to satisfy even the heartiest appetites.

MEDITERRANEAN PIZZA, 179

Weeknight Pasta Supper

PREP: 20 MIN. • COOK: 20 MIN. • YIELD: 4 SERVINGS

After a long day teaching, I want something that is healthy but also quick to prepare, and this pasta dish fits my needs.

Cathy Rau *Newport, Oregon*

- **3 cups uncooked bow tie pasta**
- **10 ounces lean ground turkey**
- **8 ounces sliced baby portobello mushrooms**
- **2 garlic cloves, minced**
- **2 teaspoons olive oil**
- **1 can (14½ ounces) fire-roasted diced tomatoes, undrained**
- **¼ cup dry red wine or chicken broth**
- **5 pitted Greek olives, chopped**
- **1 teaspoon dried basil**
- **1 teaspoon dried oregano**
- **1 teaspoon dried parsley flakes**
- **½ teaspoon salt**
- **⅛ teaspoon coarsely ground pepper**
- **2 cups fresh baby spinach, chopped**
- **1 tablespoon grated Parmesan cheese**

1 Cook pasta according to package directions. Drain.

2 Meanwhile, in a large nonstick skillet, cook turkey until no longer pink; drain. Remove turkey; set aside and keep warm.

3 In the same skillet, cook mushrooms and garlic in oil until tender. Stir in the tomatoes, wine, olives, seasonings and turkey. Bring to a boil. Reduce heat; simmer, uncovered, for 10 minutes.

4 Stir pasta into turkey mixture. Stir in spinach; cook 1-2 minutes longer or until the spinach is wilted. Sprinkle with Parmesan cheese.

PORTOBELLOS

>> With their large size and meaty texture, portobello mushrooms are well suited for grilling or broiling. Their meaty texture makes them popular as vegetarian burgers and in other vegetarian recipes. Baby portobello mushrooms are also known as cremini mushrooms. They can be used instead of white mushrooms for a flavor boost.

Black Bean Cakes with Mole Salsa

PREP/TOTAL TIME: 30 MIN. • YIELD: 6 SERVINGS (1¼ CUPS SALSA)

Homemade salsa adds zip to these mouthwatering bean cakes. Serve on a bun for a scrumptious veggie burger!

Roxanne Chan *Albany, California*

- **1 can (15 ounces) black beans, rinsed and drained**
- **1 egg, beaten**
- **1 cup shredded zucchini**
- **½ cup dry bread crumbs**
- **¼ cup shredded Mexican cheese blend**
- **2 tablespoons chili powder**
- **¼ teaspoon salt**
- **¼ teaspoon baking powder**
- **¼ teaspoon ground cumin**
- **2 tablespoons olive oil**

SALSA:

- **2 medium tomatoes, chopped**
- **1 small green pepper, chopped**
- **3 tablespoons grated chocolate**
- **1 green onion, thinly sliced**
- **2 tablespoons minced fresh cilantro**
- **1 tablespoon lime juice**
- **1 to 2 teaspoons minced chipotle pepper in adobo sauce**
- **1 teaspoon honey**

1 In a small bowl, mash beans. Add the egg, zucchini, bread crumbs, cheese, chili powder, salt, baking powder and cumin; mix well. Shape into six patties; brush both sides with oil. Place on a baking sheet.

2 Broil 3-4 in. from the heat for 3-4 minutes on each side or until a thermometer reads 160°.

3 Meanwhile, in a small bowl, combine the salsa ingredients. Serve with black bean cakes.

Eggplant Parmesan

PREP: 40 MIN. • COOK: 25 MIN.
YIELD: 8 SERVINGS

Baking the eggplant instead of frying it makes my version of the popular Italian dish much healthier! The prep time is a little longer than some other recipes, but the robust flavors and rustic elegance are well worth it.

Laci Hooten *McKinney, Texas*

- **3 eggs, beaten**
- **2½ cups panko (Japanese) bread crumbs**
- **3 medium eggplant, cut into ¼-inch slices**
- **2 jars (4½ ounces each) sliced mushrooms, drained**
- **½ tsp dried basil**
- **⅛ teaspoon dried oregano**
- **2 cups (8 ounces) shredded part-skim mozzarella cheese**
- **½ cup grated Parmesan cheese**
- **1 jar (28 ounces) spaghetti sauce**

1 Place eggs and bread crumbs in separate shallow bowls. Dip eggplant in eggs, then coat with crumbs. Place on baking sheets coated with cooking spray. Bake at 350° for 15-20 minutes or until tender and golden brown, turning once.

2 In a small bowl, combine the mushrooms, basil and oregano. In another small bowl, combine mozzarella and Parmesan cheeses.

3 Spread ½ cup spaghetti sauce in a 13-in. x 9-in. baking dish coated with cooking spray. Layer with a third of the mushroom mixture, a third of the eggplant, ¾ cup sauce and a third of the cheese mixture. Repeat layers twice.

4 Bake, uncovered, at 350° for 25-30 minutes or until heated through and cheese is melted.

Asian Vegetable Pasta

30 min.

PREP/TOTAL TIME: 20 MIN.
YIELD: 5 SERVINGS

A little peanut butter and a sprinkling of peanuts give this dish plenty of flavor. While red pepper flakes offer a little kick, brown sugar balances it out with a hint of sweetness.

Mitzi Sentiff *Annapolis, Maryland*

- **4 quarts water**
- **1 pound fresh asparagus, trimmed and cut into 1-inch pieces**
- **8 ounces uncooked angel hair pasta**
- **¾ cup julienned carrots**
- **⅓ cup reduced-fat creamy peanut butter**
- **3 tablespoons rice vinegar**
- **3 tablespoons reduced-sodium soy sauce**
- **2 tablespoons brown sugar**
- **½ teaspoon crushed red pepper flakes**
- **¼ cup unsalted peanuts, chopped**

1 In a Dutch oven, bring the water to a boil. Add asparagus and pasta; cook for 3 minutes. Stir in carrots; cook for 1 minute or until pasta is tender. Drain and keep warm.

2 In a small saucepan, combine the peanut butter, vinegar, soy sauce, brown sugar and pepper flakes. Bring to a boil over medium heat, stirring constantly. Pour over pasta mixture; toss to coat. Sprinkle with peanuts.

Risotto-Stuffed Portobellos

PREP: 45 MIN. • BAKE: 20 MIN. • YIELD: 4 SERVINGS

I invented this dish one night when I was having last-minute dinner guests. I ran to a local farm stand for some amazing produce and created this using fresh portobellos and leftover risotto. My friends still ask for the recipe!

Rian Macdonald *Powder Springs, Georgia*

- **1 can (14½ ounces) reduced-sodium chicken or vegetable broth**
- **1 cup water**
- **2 celery ribs, finely chopped**
- **2 medium carrots, finely chopped**
- **1 large onion, finely chopped**
- **1 tablespoon olive oil**
- **1 cup uncooked arborio rice**
- **½ cup chopped shallots**
- **1 garlic clove, minced**
- **1 cup dry white wine or additional broth**
- **½ cup grated Parmesan cheese**
- **4 green onions, finely chopped**
- **4 large portobello mushrooms (4 to 4½ inches), stems removed**

Cooking spray

- **¼ teaspoon salt**
- **⅛ teaspoon pepper**
- **¼ cup shredded part-skim mozzarella cheese**

1 In a small saucepan, heat broth and water and keep warm. In a large nonstick skillet coated with cooking spray, saute the celery, carrots and onion in oil until crisp-tender. Add the rice, shallots and garlic; cook and stir for 2-3 minutes. Reduce heat; stir in wine. Cook and stir until all of the liquid is absorbed.

2 Add heated broth mixture, ½ cup at a time, stirring constantly. Allow the liquid to absorb between additions. Cook just until risotto is creamy and rice is almost tender. (Cooking time is about 20 minutes.) Remove from the heat; add Parmesan cheese and green onions. Stir until cheese is melted.

3 Spritz mushrooms with cooking spray; sprinkle with salt and pepper. Fill each with 1 cup risotto mixture and sprinkle with mozzarella cheese. Place in a 13-in. x 9-in. baking dish coated with cooking spray.

4 Bake, uncovered, at 350° for 20-25 minutes or until mushrooms are tender and cheese is melted.

Roasted Eggplant Lasagna

PREP: 50 MIN. • BAKE: 30 MIN. + STANDING
YIELD: 8 SERVINGS

With a vegetarian on my guest list, I was inspired to make this lasagna for a party. While watching the cheese bubbling and smelling the veggies roasting, I couldn't wait for the party to start!

Margaret Welder *Madrid, Iowa*

- **1 small eggplant**
- **2 small zucchini**
- **5 plum tomatoes, seeded**
- **1 large sweet red pepper**
- **1 large onion, cut into small wedges**
- **¼ cup olive oil**
- **3 tablespoons minced fresh basil, *divided***
- **3 garlic cloves, minced**
- **¾ teaspoon salt, *divided***
- **½ teaspoon pepper, *divided***
- **⅔ cup pitted Greek olives, chopped**
- **¼ cup butter, cubed**
- **¼ cup all-purpose flour**
- **2¾ cups milk**
- **1 bay leaf**
- **⅛ teaspoon ground nutmeg**
- **5 tablespoons grated Parmesan cheese, *divided***
- **2 tablespoons shredded Asiago cheese**
- **¾ cup shredded part-skim mozzarella cheese**
- **6 no-cook lasagna noodles**

1 Cut eggplant, zucchini, tomatoes and red pepper into 1-in. pieces; place in a large bowl. Add onion, oil, 2 tablespoons basil, garlic, ½ teaspoon salt and ¼ teaspoon pepper; toss. Transfer to two greased 15-in. x 10-in. x 1-in. baking pans. Bake at 450° for 20-25 minutes or until crisp-tender. Stir in olives.

2 In a large saucepan, melt butter; stir in flour until smooth. Gradually stir in milk. Add bay leaf and nutmeg. Bring to a boil; cook and stir for 2 minutes or until thickened. Remove from heat. Stir in 3 tablespoons Parmesan, Asiago and remaining basil, salt and pepper. Discard bay leaf.

3 Spread a fourth of the sauce in a greased 11-in. x 7-in. baking dish. Top with 2⅓ cups vegetables, ¼ cup mozzarella and three noodles. Repeat layers. Top with a fourth of the sauce, remaining vegetables, mozzarella, sauce and Parmesan. Cover and bake at 375° for 30-40 minutes or until bubbly. Let stand 15 minutes before serving.

Butternut Squash Enchiladas

PREP: 1¼ HOURS • BAKE: 25 MIN. • YIELD: 8 SERVINGS

When you want to go meatless for a meal, try this satisfying take on a southwestern favorite. It's a tasty way to enjoy butternut squash.

Rachel Erdstein *Ann Arbor, Michigan*

- **1 medium butternut squash (3½ to 4 pounds)**
- **1 medium sweet red pepper, chopped**
- **½ cup chopped onion**
- **1 garlic clove, minced**
- **1 teaspoon canola oil**
- **1 teaspoon ground cumin**
- **½ teaspoon chili powder**
- **½ teaspoon pepper**
- **¼ teaspoon salt**
- **1 package (12 ounces) frozen vegetarian meat crumbles, thawed**
- **1 can (10 ounces) enchilada sauce, divided**
- **8 flour tortillas (8 inches), warmed**
- **1 cup (4 ounces) shredded reduced-fat Mexican cheese blend, divided**

1 Cut squash in half; discard seeds. Place squash cut side down in a 15-in. x 10-in. x 1-in. baking pan coated with cooking spray. Bake at 350° for 55-65 minutes or until tender. Cool slightly; scoop out pulp and set aside.

2 In a large nonstick skillet coated with cooking spray, cook the red pepper, onion and garlic in oil until tender. Stir in the cumin, chili powder, pepper and salt; cook 1 minute longer. Stir in crumbles and reserved squash; heat through.

3 Spread ¼ cup enchilada sauce in a 13-in. x 9-in. baking dish coated with cooking spray. Place about ¾ cup squash mixture down the center of each tortilla; top with 1 tablespoon cheese. Roll up and place seam side down in prepared dish. Pour remaining enchilada sauce over the top; sprinkle with remaining cheese.

4 Bake, uncovered, at 350° for 25-35 minutes or until heated through.

EDITOR'S NOTE: Vegetarian meat crumbles are a nutritious protein source made from soy. Look for them in the natural foods freezer section.

Black Bean Veggie Burritos

PREP: 30 MIN. • BAKE: 25 MIN. • YIELD: 8 SERVINGS

Sweet potatoes give these baked burritos a unique twist. Packed with tender veggies, cheese and spices, they'll make a mouthwatering dinner any night.

Carissa Sumner *Alexandria, Virginia*

- **1 large sweet potato, peeled and cut into ½-inch cubes**
- **1 medium onion, finely chopped**
- **1 tablespoon water**
- **1 can (15 ounces) black beans, rinsed and drained**
- **1 cup frozen corn**
- **1 medium green pepper, chopped**
- **2 tablespoons lemon juice**
- **3 garlic cloves, minced**
- **1 tablespoon chili powder**
- **2 teaspoons dried oregano**
- **1 teaspoon ground cumin**
- **8 whole wheat tortillas (8 inches), warmed**
- **2 cups (8 ounces) shredded Monterey Jack cheese**
- **½ cup fat-free plain yogurt**
- **½ cup salsa**

1 In a large microwave-safe bowl, combine the sweet potato, onion and water. Cover and microwave on high for 4-5 minutes or until potato is almost tender. Stir in the beans, corn, green pepper, lemon juice, garlic and seasonings.

2 Spoon a heaping ½ cup filling off center on each tortilla. Sprinkle with ¼ cup cheese. Fold sides and ends over filling and roll up.

3 Place seam side down in a 13-in. x 9-in. baking dish coated with cooking spray. Cover and bake at 350° for 25-30 minutes or until heated through. Serve with yogurt and salsa.

Three-Cheese Spirals

PREP: 15 MIN. • BAKE: 30 MIN.
YIELD: 8 SERVINGS

Sour cream and three kinds of cheese create the creamy coating for this tasty twist on macaroni and cheese. It calls for only six ingredients and can be served as an entree or a side dish.

Deb Collette *Holland, Ohio*

- **1 package (16 ounces) spiral pasta**
- **1 egg**
- **1½ cups (12 ounces) sour cream**
- **1½ cups (12 ounces) 4% cottage cheese**
- **1 pound process cheese (Velveeta), cubed**
- **2 cups (8 ounces) shredded cheddar cheese**

1 Cook pasta according to package directions. Meanwhile, in a blender, combine the egg, sour cream and cottage cheese; cover and process until smooth. Transfer to a large bowl; add process and cheddar cheeses. Drain pasta; stir into cheese mixture until evenly coated.

2 Transfer to a greased shallow 3-qt. baking dish. Bake, uncovered, at 350° for 15 minutes; stir. Bake 15-20 minutes longer or until bubbly and edges begin to brown.

Fresh Tomato Pasta Toss 

PREP/TOTAL TIME: 30 MIN. • YIELD: 8 SERVINGS

Dipping whole tomatoes into boiling water makes them easier to peel for this garden-fresh recipe. Parmesan or Romano cheese makes a great topper.

Cheryl Travagliante *Cleveland, Ohio*

- **3 pounds ripe fresh tomatoes**
- **1 package (16 ounces) uncooked penne pasta**
- **2 garlic cloves, minced**
- **1 tablespoon canola oil**
- **1 tablespoon minced fresh parsley or 1 teaspoon dried parsley flakes**
- **1 tablespoon minced fresh basil or 1 teaspoon dried basil**
- **2 teaspoons minced fresh oregano or ¾ teaspoon dried oregano**
- **1 teaspoon salt**
- **¼ teaspoon sugar**
- **⅛ teaspoon pepper**
- **¼ cup heavy whipping cream**
- **¼ cup shredded Parmesan or Romano cheese**

1 To remove skin from tomatoes, fill a large saucepan with water and bring to a boil. Place tomatoes, one at a time, in boiling water for 30 seconds. Immediately plunge into ice water. Peel skins with a sharp paring knife and discard. Chop pulp; set aside.

2 Cook pasta according to package directions. In a large skillet, cook garlic in oil over medium heat for 1 minute or until tender. Add the parsley, basil, oregano, salt, sugar, pepper and reserved tomato pulp. Bring to a boil; reduce heat. Add cream; heat through.

3 Drain pasta and transfer to a serving bowl. Pour tomato sauce over pasta; toss to coat. Sprinkle with cheese.

Overnight Spinach Manicotti

PREP: 10 MIN. + CHILLING • BAKE: 40 MIN. • YIELD: 7 SERVINGS

A friend gave me an awesome recipe for manicotti, and I set out to make it a little healthier. When we have company, my husband asks me to serve this. Even our young son loves it!

Tonya Fitzgerald *West Monroe, Louisiana*

- **1 carton (15 ounces) reduced-fat ricotta cheese**
- **1 package (10 ounces) frozen chopped spinach, thawed and squeezed dry**
- **1½ cups (6 ounces) shredded part-skim mozzarella cheese, divided**
- **½ cup grated Parmesan cheese, divided**
- **2 egg whites**
- **2 teaspoons minced fresh parsley**
- **½ teaspoon salt**
- **½ teaspoon onion powder**
- **½ teaspoon pepper**
- **¼ teaspoon garlic powder**
- **4½ cups meatless spaghetti sauce**
- **¾ cup water**
- **1 package (8 ounces) manicotti shells**

1 In a large bowl, combine the ricotta cheese, spinach, 1 cup mozzarella cheese, ¼ cup Parmesan cheese, egg whites, parsley, salt, onion powder, pepper and garlic powder. Combine spaghetti sauce and water; spread 1 cup in an ungreased 13-in. x 9-in. baking dish. Stuff uncooked manicotti shells with ricotta mixture; arrange over sauce. Top with remaining sauce. Cover and refrigerate overnight.

2 Remove from the refrigerator 30 minutes before baking. Sprinkle with remaining mozzarella and Parmesan cheeses. Bake, uncovered, at 350° for 40-45 minutes or until heated through.

Artichoke & Spinach Enchiladas

PREP: 30 MIN. • BAKE: 20 MIN. • YIELD: 8 SERVINGS

Surprise your gang with these delightful vegetarian enchiladas. The mushroom, artichoke and spinach filling is so hearty and flavorful, you'll never miss the meat!

Joan Kollars *Norfolk, Nebraska*

- **3 tablespoons butter**
- **3 tablespoons all-purpose flour**
- **1 can (14½ ounces) vegetable broth**
- **1 can (8 ounces) tomato sauce**
- **1½ teaspoons chili powder**
- **¾ teaspoon ground cumin**

ENCHILADAS:

- **1 large onion, chopped**
- **3 garlic cloves, minced**
- **2 tablespoons olive oil**
- **½ pound medium fresh mushrooms, quartered**
- **1 can (14 ounces) water-packed artichoke hearts, rinsed, drained and chopped**
- **1 package (10 ounces) frozen chopped spinach, thawed and squeezed dry**
- **1 carton (15 ounces) ricotta cheese**
- **1 cup (8 ounces) sour cream**
- **2 cups (8 ounces) shredded Monterey Jack cheese, divided**
- **8 whole wheat tortillas (8 inches), warmed**

1 In a small saucepan, melt butter. Stir in flour until smooth; gradually add broth. Bring to a boil; cook and stir for 2 minutes or until thickened. Stir in the tomato sauce, chili powder and cumin. Simmer, uncovered, for 6-8 minutes or until slightly thickened. Spread ¾ cup sauce into a greased 13-in. x 9-in. baking dish. Set aside remaining sauce.

2 In a large skillet, saute onion and garlic in oil until tender. Stir in mushrooms; cook 3 minutes longer. Add artichokes and spinach; cook for 4-5 minutes longer. Remove from the heat; stir in the ricotta cheese, sour cream and 1 cup Monterey Jack cheese.

3 Place ⅔ cup mushroom mixture down the center of each tortilla. Roll up and place seam side down in prepared dish. Pour reserved sauce over the top; sprinkle with remaining cheese.

4 Bake, uncovered, at 375° for 20-25 minutes or until heated through.

Mediterranean Pizza

PREP/TOTAL TIME: 20 MIN. • YIELD: 12 PIECES

Every year my sisters and I have a "Sister's Day," which includes a special lunch. This fast and easy pizza is one of our favorites. Serve with a garden salad for a light and nutritious meal.

Deborah Prevost *Barnet, Vermont*

- **1 prebaked 12-inch thin whole wheat pizza crust**
- **3 tablespoons prepared pesto**
- **2 medium tomatoes, thinly sliced**
- **¾ cup water-packed artichoke hearts, rinsed, drained and chopped**
- **½ cup crumbled reduced-fat feta cheese**
- **¼ cup sliced ripe olives**

1 Place the crust on an ungreased 12-in. pizza pan; spread with pesto. Top with tomatoes, artichokes, cheese and olives.

2 Bake at 450° for 10-12 minutes or until heated through.

Creamy Baked Macaroni

PREP: 20 MIN. • BAKE: 25 MIN.
YIELD: 4-6 SERVINGS

Gouda cheese gives this old-fashioned macaroni casserole a tasty twist. It bakes up nice and creamy with just a hint of zip from the hot sauce. It's comfort food at its yummiest.

Heather Eplett *Mossley, Ontario*

- **1⅔ cups uncooked elbow macaroni**
- **1 can (10¾ ounces) condensed cream of chicken soup, undiluted**
- **1 cup milk**
- **1 tablespoon minced chives**
- **½ teaspoon ground mustard**
- **¼ teaspoon hot pepper sauce**
- **1½ cups (6 ounces) Gouda or cheddar cheese (½-inch cubes)**
- **2 tablespoons dry bread crumbs**
- **1 tablespoon butter, melted**

1 Cook macaroni according to package directions; drain. In a large bowl, combine the soup, milk, chives, mustard and hot pepper sauce. Stir in macaroni and cheese.

2 Spoon into a greased shallow 2-qt. baking dish. Combine bread crumbs and butter; sprinkle over the top. Bake, uncovered, at 400° for 25-30 minutes or until heated through and bubbly.

Fiery Stuffed Poblanos

PREP: 50 MIN. + STANDING • BAKE: 20 MIN. • YIELD: 8 SERVINGS

I love Southwest-inspired cuisine, but since it's often laden with fatty meat and cheese, I tend to steer clear. As a dietitian, I try to come up with healthy twists on recipes. That's how my stuffed chili pepper dish was born.

Amber Massey *Fort Worth, Texas*

- **8 poblano peppers**
- **1 can (15 ounces) black beans, rinsed and drained**
- **1 medium zucchini, chopped**
- **1 small red onion, chopped**
- **4 garlic cloves, minced**
- **1 can (15¼ ounces) whole kernel corn, drained**
- **1 can (14½ ounces) fire-roasted diced tomatoes, undrained**
- **1 cup cooked brown rice**
- **1 tablespoon ground cumin**
- **1 to 1½ teaspoons ground ancho chili pepper**
- **¼ teaspoon salt**
- **¼ teaspoon pepper**
- **1 cup (4 ounces) shredded reduced-fat Mexican cheese blend, divided**
- **3 green onions, chopped**
- **½ cup reduced-fat sour cream**

1 Broil peppers 3 in. from the heat until skins blister, about 5 minutes. With tongs, rotate peppers a quarter turn. Broil and rotate until all sides are blistered and blackened. Immediately place peppers in a large bowl; cover and let stand for 20 minutes.

2 Meanwhile, in a small bowl, coarsely mash beans; set aside. In a large nonstick skillet coated with cooking spray, cook and stir zucchini and onion until tender. Add garlic; cook 1 minute longer. Add the corn, tomatoes, rice, seasonings and beans. Remove from the heat; stir in ½ cup cheese. Set aside.

3 Peel off and discard charred skins from poblanos. Cut a lengthwise slit down each pepper, leaving the stem intact; remove membranes and seeds. Fill each pepper with ⅔ cup filling.

4 Place peppers in a 13-in. x 9-in. baking dish coated with cooking spray. Bake, uncovered, at 375° for 18-22 minutes or until heated through, sprinkling with green onions and remaining cheese during last 5 minutes of baking. Garnish with sour cream.

Savory Pumpkin Ravioli

PREP: 2 HOURS • COOK: 10 MIN. • YIELD: 6 SERVINGS

My recipe may sound complicated, but if you follow the steps, it's really simple. The result will be pure pumpkin heaven. I like to sprinkle the ravioli with Parmesan as well. You can also add salt and pepper to the rich sage sauce, to taste.

Christopher Presutti *Jacksonville, Florida*

- **2½ to 3 cups all-purpose flour**
- **5 eggs**
- **1 tablespoon olive oil**

FILLING:

- **1 small pie pumpkin (about 2¼ pounds), peeled and cut into 1-inch cubes**
- **4 teaspoons chopped shallot**
- **⅓ cup butter, cubed**
- **2 teaspoons minced fresh sage**
- **¾ teaspoon minced fresh thyme**
- **¼ teaspoon salt**
- **¼ teaspoon pepper**
- **⅔ cup heavy whipping cream**
- **1 small bay leaf**
- **1 egg, lightly beaten**

SAUCE:

- **1 cup heavy whipping cream**
- **3 tablespoons butter**
- **2 teaspoons minced fresh sage**

1 Place 2½ cups flour in a large bowl; make a well in the center. Beat eggs and oil; pour into well. Stir together, forming a ball. Turn onto a floured surface; knead until smooth and elastic, about 8-10 minutes, adding remaining flour if necessary to keep dough from sticking. Cover and let rest for 30 minutes.

2 Meanwhile, in a large skillet, saute pumpkin and shallot in butter until tender. Add the sage, thyme, salt and pepper. Transfer to a food processor; cover and process until blended. Return to the pan; stir in cream and bay leaf. Bring to a boil, stirring constantly. Reduce heat; simmer, uncovered, for 15-20 minutes or until thickened. Discard bay leaf.

3 Divide pasta dough into fourths; roll one portion to 1/16-in. thickness. (Keep remaining dough covered until ready to use.) Working quickly, place rounded teaspoonfuls of filling 1 in. apart over half of pasta sheet. Brush around filling with egg. Fold sheet over; press down to seal. Cut into squares with a pastry wheel. Repeat with remaining dough and filling.

4 Bring a stock pot of salted water to a boil. Add ravioli. Reduce heat to a gentle simmer; cook for 1-2 minutes or until ravioli float to the top and are tender. Drain and keep warm.

5 In a small saucepan, bring cream to a boil; cook, uncovered, until reduced by half. Stir in butter and sage. Serve with ravioli.

EDITOR'S NOTE: If pumpkin is not available, use butternut squash.

Roasted Vegetable Quesadillas

PREP: 40 MIN. • COOK: 5 MIN./BATCH
YIELD: 8 SERVINGS

I am always looking for recipes that will encourage kids to eat vegetables, and this one has been a huge success. You can also use other vegetables, such as mushrooms, eggplant, asparagus and broccoli. Just remember to roast your vegetables before making the quesadillas.

Kathy Carlan *Canton, Georgia*

- **2 medium red potatoes, quartered and sliced**
- **1 medium zucchini, quartered and sliced**
- **1 medium sweet red pepper, sliced**
- **1 small onion, chopped**
- **2 tablespoons olive oil**
- **1 garlic clove, minced**
- **½ teaspoon salt**
- **½ teaspoon dried oregano**
- **¼ teaspoon pepper**
- **1 cup (4 ounces) shredded part-skim mozzarella cheese**
- **1 cup (4 ounces) shredded reduced-fat cheddar cheese**
- **8 whole wheat tortillas (8 inches)**

1 In a large bowl, combine the first nine ingredients. Transfer to a 15-in. x 10-in. x 1-in. baking pan. Bake at 425° for 24-28 minutes or until potatoes are tender.

2 In a small bowl, combine cheeses. Place tortillas on a griddle coated with cooking spray. Spread ⅓ cup vegetable mixture over half of each tortilla. Sprinkle with ¼ cup cheese. Fold over and cook over low heat for 1-2 minutes on each side or until cheese is melted.

CHEDDAR TIP

>> Select sharp cheddar when using packaged shredded cheese if you'd like to have a bolder flavor. If you will be shredding cheese at home from bulk cheddar, you can choose from mild, medium, sharp and extra sharp.

Grilled Veggie Pizza

PREP: 30 MIN. • BAKE: 10 MIN. • YIELD: 6 SERVINGS

Excess summer bounty is perfect for this delightfully simple pizza. Grilling the veggies first brings out their sizzling flavors. Try sprinkling olives or pine nuts before adding the cheese.

Susan Marshall *Colorado Springs, Colorado*

- **8 small fresh mushrooms, halved**
- **1 small zucchini, cut into ¼-inch slices**
- **1 small sweet yellow pepper, sliced**
- **1 small sweet red pepper, sliced**
- **1 small onion, sliced**
- **1 tablespoon white wine vinegar**
- **1 tablespoon water**
- **4 teaspoons olive oil, divided**
- **2 teaspoons minced fresh basil or ½ teaspoon dried basil**
- **¼ teaspoon salt**
- **¼ teaspoon pepper**
- **1 prebaked 12-inch thin whole wheat pizza crust**
- **1 can (8 ounces) pizza sauce**
- **2 small tomatoes, chopped**
- **2 cups (8 ounces) shredded part-skim mozzarella cheese**

1 In a large bowl, combine the mushrooms, zucchini, peppers, onion, vinegar, water, 3 teaspoons oil and seasonings. Transfer to a grill wok or basket. Grill, covered, over medium heat for 8-10 minutes or until tender, stirring once.

2 Prepare grill for indirect heat. Brush crust with remaining oil; spread with pizza sauce. Top with grilled vegetables, tomatoes and cheese. Grill, covered, over indirect medium heat for 10-12 minutes or until edges are lightly browned and cheese is melted. Rotate pizza halfway through cooking to ensure evenly browned crust.

EDITOR'S NOTE: If you do not have a grill wok or basket, use a disposable foil pan. Poke holes in the bottom of the pan with a meat fork to allow liquid to drain.

Spinach Artichoke Pizza

PREP: 40 MIN. • BAKE: 20 MIN. + RISING
YIELD: 6 SERVINGS

I was experimenting with spinach artichoke pizzas when I came up with this rich treat.

Martha Muellenberg *Vermillion, South Dakota*

- **1 package (¼ ounce) active dry yeast**
- **¾ cup warm water (110° to 115°)**
- **½ teaspoon sugar**
- **4 teaspoons olive oil**
- **¾ teaspoon salt**
- **1¾ to 2 cups all-purpose flour**

TOPPINGS:

- **1 cup Alfredo sauce**
- **3 cups fresh baby spinach**
- **1 cup (4 ounces) shredded part-skim mozzarella cheese**
- **¾ cup crumbled feta cheese**
- **½ cup shredded Parmesan cheese**
- **¾ cup water-packed artichoke hearts, rinsed, drained and chopped**
- **½ teaspoon dried oregano**

1 In a large bowl, dissolve yeast in warm water; stir in sugar. Let stand for 5-10 minutes. Add oil, salt and 1 cup flour. Beat until smooth. Stir in enough remaining flour to form a soft dough.

2 Turn onto a floured surface; knead until smooth and elastic, about 6-8 minutes. Place in a greased bowl, turning once to grease the top. Cover and let rise in a warm place until doubled, about 1 hour.

3 Grease a 15-in. x 10-in. x 1-in. baking pan. Punch down dough. Roll out to fit prepared pan.

4 Spread with Alfredo sauce. Layer with the spinach and cheeses. Sprinkle with artichokes and dried oregano. Bake at 400° for 18-22 minutes or until crust is lightly browned.

Loaded Mexican Pizza 

PREP/TOTAL TIME: 30 MIN. • YIELD: 6 SLICES

My husband is a picky eater, but because this healthy pizza is loaded with flavor he actually looks forward to it. Leftovers are no problem—it tastes better the next day.

Mary Barker *Knoxville, Tennessee*

- **1 can (15 ounces) black beans, rinsed and drained**
- **1 medium red onion, chopped**
- **1 small sweet yellow pepper, chopped**
- **3 teaspoons chili powder**
- **¾ teaspoon ground cumin**
- **3 medium tomatoes, chopped**
- **1 jalapeno pepper, seeded and finely chopped**
- **1 garlic clove, minced**
- **1 prebaked 12-inch thin pizza crust**
- **2 cups chopped fresh spinach**
- **2 tablespoons minced fresh cilantro**

Hot pepper sauce to taste

- **½ cup shredded reduced-fat cheddar cheese**
- **½ cup shredded pepper jack cheese**

1 In a small bowl, mash black beans. Stir in the onion, yellow pepper, chili powder and cumin. In another bowl, combine the tomatoes, jalapeno and garlic.

2 Place crust on an ungreased 12-in. pizza pan; spread with bean mixture. Top with tomato mixture and spinach. Sprinkle with cilantro, pepper sauce and cheeses.

3 Bake at 400° for 12-15 minutes or until cheese is melted.

EDITOR'S NOTE: Wear disposable gloves when cutting hot peppers; the oils can burn skin. Avoid touching your face.

Four-Cheese Baked Penne

PREP: 30 MIN. + COOLING • BAKE: 20 MIN. • YIELD: 6 SERVINGS

For a meal that is hearty, comforting and delicious, look no further. My family-pleasing pasta dish has it all.

Scarlett Elrod *Newnan, Georgia*

- **4 cups uncooked whole wheat penne pasta**
- **1 medium onion, chopped**
- **2 teaspoons olive oil**
- **4 garlic cloves, minced**
- **1 can (15 ounces) crushed tomatoes**
- **1 can (8 ounces) tomato sauce**
- **3 tablespoons minced fresh parsley or 1 tablespoon dried parsley flakes**
- **1 teaspoon dried oregano**
- **1 teaspoon dried rosemary, crushed**
- **½ teaspoon crushed red pepper flakes**
- **¼ teaspoon pepper**
- **1½ cups (12 ounces) 2% cottage cheese**
- **1¼ cups (5 ounces) shredded part-skim mozzarella cheese, divided**
- **1 cup part-skim ricotta cheese**
- **¼ cup grated Parmesan cheese**

1 Cook penne according to package directions.

2 Meanwhile, in a large skillet, saute onion in oil until tender. Add garlic; cook 1 minute longer. Stir in the tomatoes, tomato sauce, parsley, oregano, rosemary, pepper flakes and pepper. Bring to a boil. Remove from the heat; cool for 15 minutes.

3 Drain penne; add to sauce. Stir in the cottage cheese, ½ cup mozzarella and all of the ricotta. Transfer to a 13-in. x 9-in. baking dish coated with cooking spray. Top with Parmesan cheese and remaining mozzarella.

4 Bake, uncovered, at 400° for 20-25 minutes or until bubbly.

Zucchini Ricotta Bake

PREP: 15 MIN. • BAKE: 1 HOUR + STANDING
YIELD: 12 SERVINGS

I have made this lasagna-like zucchini casserole frequently over the years and shared the recipe with many people. Best of all, it's a little bit lighter than other layered casseroles, making it a great choice for anyone trying to eat right.

Eleanor Hauserman *Huntsville, Alabama*

- **2 pounds zucchini**
- **1 carton (15 ounces) reduced-fat ricotta cheese**
- **½ cup egg substitute**
- **¼ cup dry bread crumbs, *divided***
- **5 tablespoons grated Parmesan cheese, *divided***
- **1 tablespoon minced fresh parsley**
- **¼ teaspoon dried oregano**
- **¼ teaspoon dried basil**
- **⅛ teaspoon pepper**
- **1 jar (28 ounces) reduced-sodium meatless spaghetti sauce**
- **1½ cups (6 ounces) shredded reduced-fat mozzarella cheese**

5 Cut zucchini lengthwise into ¼-in. slices. Place in a basket over 1 in. of boiling water. Cover and steam for 5-6 minutes or until just tender. Drain; pat dry.

6 In a large bowl, combine ricotta, egg substitute, 3 tablespoons bread crumbs, 3 tablespoons Parmesan, parsley, oregano, basil and pepper; set aside.

7 Spread a third of the spaghetti sauce in a 13-in. x 9-in. baking dish coated with cooking spray. Sprinkle with 2 tablespoons bread crumbs. Cover with half of the zucchini, ricotta mixture and mozzarella. Repeat layers of sauce, zucchini, ricotta mixture and mozzarella. Cover with remaining sauce.

8 Combine remaining crumbs and Parmesan; sprinkle over top. Cover and bake at 350° for 45 minutes. Uncover; bake 15 minutes longer. Let stand 15 minutes before cutting.

Pasta with Eggplant Sauce

PREP: 35 MIN. • COOK: 15 MIN. • YIELD: 6 SERVINGS

A thick, chunky sauce makes this pasta favorite simply splendid. I like to have it with a glass of red wine, crusty Italian bread and a tossed garden salad.

Jean Lawrence *Rochester, New York*

- **1 large eggplant, cut into 1-inch cubes**
- **½ cup finely chopped onion**
- **2 tablespoons minced fresh parsley**
- **1 garlic clove, chopped**
- **¼ cup olive oil**
- **1 can (14½ ounces) Italian stewed tomatoes, cut up**
- **½ cup dry red wine or chicken broth**
- **1 can (6 ounces) Italian tomato paste**
- **1 can (4½ ounces) sliced mushrooms, drained**
- **1 teaspoon sugar**
- **1 teaspoon dried oregano**
- **½ teaspoon salt**
- **¾ pound thin spaghetti**

Grated Parmesan cheese

1 In a Dutch oven, saute the eggplant, onion, parsley and garlic in oil until tender.

2 Stir in the tomatoes, wine, tomato paste, mushrooms, sugar, oregano and salt. Bring to a boil. Reduce heat; simmer, uncovered, for 10-15 minutes or until thickened, stirring occasionally.

3 Meanwhile, cook pasta according to package directions. Drain pasta. Serve with sauce. Sprinkle with cheese.

Tuscan Portobello Stew

PREP: 20 MIN. • COOK: 20 MIN. • YIELD: 4 SERVINGS

My heart-healthy, one-skillet meal is quick and easy to prepare yet elegant enough for company. I'm a teacher, and my vegetarian co-workers and students alike enjoy this stew when I serve it at school potlucks.

Jane Siemon *Viroqua, Wisconsin*

- **2 large portobello mushrooms, coarsely chopped**
- **1 medium onion, chopped**
- **3 garlic cloves, minced**
- **2 tablespoons olive oil**
- **½ cup white wine or vegetable broth**
- **1 can (28 ounces) diced tomatoes, undrained**
- **2 cups chopped fresh kale**
- **1 bay leaf**
- **1 teaspoon dried thyme**
- **½ teaspoon dried basil**
- **½ teaspoon dried rosemary, crushed**
- **¼ teaspoon salt**
- **¼ teaspoon pepper**
- **2 cans (15 ounces each) white kidney or cannellini beans, rinsed and drained**

1 In a large skillet, saute the mushrooms, onion and garlic in oil until tender. Add the wine. Bring to a boil; cook until liquid is reduced by half. Stir in the tomatoes, kale and seasonings. Bring to a boil. Reduce heat; cover and simmer for 8-10 minutes.

2 Add beans; heat through. Discard bay leaf.

WHITE KIDNEY BEANS

>> Cannellini beans are large white kidney beans and are generally available dry and canned. Some canned products will list both cannellini beans and large white kidney beans on the label. If you can't find them in your area, feel free to substitute navy beans or great northern beans.

Vegetarian Stuffed Peppers

PREP: 30 MIN. • COOK: 3½ HOURS • YIELD: 6 SERVINGS

These filling and flavorful peppers are an updated version of my mom's stuffed peppers, which were a favorite when I was growing up in upstate New York. Whenever I make them, I'm reminded of home.

Melissa Mccabe *Long Beach, California*

- **6 large sweet peppers**
- **2 cups cooked brown rice**
- **3 small tomatoes, chopped**
- **1 cup frozen corn, thawed**
- **1 small sweet onion, chopped**
- **⅓ cup canned red beans, rinsed and drained**
- **⅓ cup canned black beans, rinsed and drained**
- **¾ cup cubed Monterey Jack cheese**
- **1 can (4¼ ounces) chopped ripe olives**
- **4 fresh basil leaves, thinly sliced**
- **3 garlic cloves, minced**
- **1 teaspoon salt**
- **½ teaspoon pepper**
- **¾ cup meatless spaghetti sauce**
- **½ cup water**
- **4 tablespoons grated Parmesan cheese, divided**

1 Cut tops off peppers and remove seeds; set aside. In a large bowl, combine the rice, tomatoes, corn, onion and beans. Stir in the Monterey Jack cheese, olives, basil, garlic, salt and pepper. Spoon into peppers.

2 Combine spaghetti sauce and water; pour half into an oval 5-qt. slow cooker. Add the stuffed peppers. Top with remaining sauce. Sprinkle with 2 tablespoons Parmesan cheese.

3 Cover and cook on low for 3½ to 4 hours or until peppers are tender and filling is heated through. Sprinkle with remaining Parmesan cheese.

BAKED VEGETARIAN STUFFED PEPPERS: Fill peppers as directed. Spoon half of the sauce mixture into an ungreased 3-qt. baking dish. Add the peppers; top with remaining sauce mixture. Sprinkle with cheese as directed. Cover and bake at 350° for 30-35 minutes or until peppers are tender and filling is heated through.

Rich 'n' Cheesy Macaroni

PREP: 30 MIN. • BAKE: 30 MIN.
YIELD: 6-8 SERVINGS

Three different cheeses blend wonderfully in this easy-to-prepare, oven-baked casserole.

Gwen Miller *Rolling Hills, Alberta*

- **2½ cups uncooked elbow macaroni**
- **6 tablespoons butter, divided**
- **¼ cup all-purpose flour**
- **1 teaspoon salt**
- **1 teaspoon sugar**
- **2 cups milk**
- **8 ounces process cheese (Velveeta), cubed**
- **1⅓ cups 4% cottage cheese**
- **⅔ cup sour cream**
- **2 cups (8 ounces) shredded sharp cheddar cheese**
- **1½ cups soft bread crumbs**

1 Cook macaroni according to package directions; drain. Place in a greased 2½-qt. baking dish. In a saucepan, melt 4 tablespoons butter. Stir in the flour, salt and sugar until smooth. Gradually stir in milk. Bring to a boil; cook and stir for 2 minutes or until thickened.

2 Reduce heat; stir in process cheese until melted. Stir in cottage cheese and sour cream. Pour over macaroni. Sprinkle with cheddar cheese. Melt remaining butter and toss with bread crumbs; sprinkle over top.

3 Bake, uncovered, at 350° for 30 minutes or until golden brown.

WINNERS
CIRCLE

quick breads

True to their name, quick breads are a speedy way to brighten up any day. Bring smiles to your friends and family—in a flash—with the berry-studded muffins, tender loaves and streusel-topped delights featured here, all just begging to be baked.

GET UP & GO MUFFINS, 193

Irish Soda Bread

PREP: 20 MIN. • BAKE: 50 MIN. + COOLING
YIELD: 1 LOAF (16 SLICES)

My husband's family is Irish. Wanting to impress my future mother-in-law, I baked this bread and took it along with me when I met her the first time. Needless to say, it worked!

Padmini Roy-Dixon *Columbus, Ohio*

- **¾ cup raisins**
- **1 cup boiling water**
- **2 cups all-purpose flour**
- **1 cup whole wheat flour**
- **⅓ cup sugar**
- **3 teaspoons baking powder**
- **1 teaspoon baking soda**
- **1 teaspoon salt**
- **1 egg**
- **2 cups buttermilk**
- **¼ cup butter, melted**

1 Place raisins in a small bowl. Cover with boiling water; let stand for 5 minutes. Drain and pat dry.

2 In a large bowl, combine the flours, sugar, baking powder, baking soda and salt. In a small bowl, whisk the egg, buttermilk and butter. Stir into dry ingredients just until moistened. Fold in raisins.

3 Transfer to a 9-in. x 5-in. loaf pan coated with cooking spray. Bake at 350° for 50-60 minutes or until a toothpick inserted near the center comes out clean. Cool for 10 minutes before removing from pan to a wire rack.

IRISH SODA BREAD STORY

>> This classic quick bread from Ireland is so named because it uses baking soda for leavening. Legend has it that the X is cut into the top of the bread before baking to ward off evil spirits.

Garlic Asiago Bread

PREP: 30 MIN. + RISING • BAKE: 20 MIN. + COOLING
YIELD: 2 LOAVES (10 WEDGES EACH)

My friends and family rave about this recipe. It has chunks of cheese and a fabulous garlic taste. We have bread sales at our school as a fundraiser and this is always one of the top sellers.

Charlotte Thomas *Pollock Pines, California*

- **1 package (1/4 ounce) active dry yeast**
- **1 1/4 cups warm water (110° to 115°)**
- **2 tablespoons plus 2 teaspoons olive oil**
- **7 garlic cloves, minced**
- **1 tablespoon sugar**
- **2 teaspoons salt**
- **1 1/2 teaspoons white vinegar**
- **3 to 3 1/4 cups bread flour**
- **1 cup cubed Asiago cheese**

EGG WASH:

- **1 egg**
- **1 tablespoon water**

1 In a large bowl, dissolve yeast in warm water. Add the oil, garlic, sugar, salt, vinegar and 2 cups flour. Beat until smooth. Stir in enough remaining flour to form a firm dough. Stir in cheese.

2 Turn onto a floured surface; knead until smooth and elastic, about 6-8 minutes. Place in a greased bowl, turning once to grease the top. Cover and let rise in a warm place until doubled, about 1 hour.

3 Punch dough down; divide in half. Shape into 5-in.-round loaves. Place on lightly greased baking sheets. Cover and let rise in a warm place until doubled, about 30 minutes.

4 For egg wash, in a small bowl, combine egg and water. Brush over loaves. Bake at 375° for 20-25 minutes or until golden brown. Cool on wire racks.

Brown Sugar Oat Muffins

30 min.

PREP/TOTAL TIME: 30 MIN. • YIELD: 1 DOZEN

With Kansas being one of the top wheat-producing states, it seems only fitting to share a recipe containing whole wheat flour. These are great muffins to have for breakfast or as a late night snack with a cup of hot cocoa.

Regina Stock *Topeka, Kansas*

- **1 cup old-fashioned oats**
- **1 cup whole wheat flour**
- **3/4 cup packed brown sugar**
- **1/2 cup all-purpose flour**
- **2 teaspoons baking powder**
- **1/2 teaspoon salt**
- **2 eggs**
- **3/4 cup 2% milk**
- **1/4 cup canola oil**
- **1 teaspoon vanilla extract**

1 In a small bowl, combine the first six ingredients. In another small bowl, beat the eggs, milk, oil and vanilla. Stir into the dry ingredients just until moistened.

2 Fill greased or paper-lined muffin cups two-thirds full. Bake at 400° for 15-17 minutes or until a toothpick inserted near the center comes out clean. Cool for 5 minutes before removing from pan to a wire rack. Serve warm.

Coffee Lover's Coffee Cake

PREP: 25 MIN. • BAKE: 25 MIN. • YIELD: 9 SERVINGS

I had this cake at a friend's brunch and she graciously shared the recipe. People request it from me because it's so tasty and always a hit.

Gale Lalmond *Deering, New Hampshire*

- **⅓ cup sugar**
- **4½ teaspoons instant coffee granules**
- **1½ teaspoons ground cinnamon**

BATTER:

- **3 tablespoons butter, softened**
- **½ cup sugar**
- **1 egg**
- **1 teaspoon vanilla extract**
- **1½ cups all-purpose flour**
- **1 teaspoon baking powder**
- **½ teaspoon baking soda**
- **⅛ teaspoon salt**
- **1 cup (8 ounces) plain yogurt**
- **2 tablespoons chopped walnuts or pecans**

1 In a small bowl, combine the sugar, coffee granules and cinnamon; set aside. In a large bowl, beat butter and sugar until crumbly, about 2 minutes. Beat in egg and vanilla. Combine the flour, baking powder, baking soda and salt; add to butter mixture alternately with yogurt, beating just until combined.

2 Spread half of the batter evenly into a 9-in. square baking pan coated with cooking spray; sprinkle with half of the reserved sugar mixture. Repeat layers; cut through batter with a knife to swirl. Sprinkle with nuts.

3 Bake at 350° for 25-30 minutes or until a toothpick inserted near the center comes out clean. Cool for 5 minutes on a wire rack. Serve warm.

Apricot & White Chocolate Coffee Cake

PREP: 15 MIN. • BAKE: 20 MIN.
YIELD: 12 SERVINGS

Here's a luscious make-and-take recipe for those holiday brunches you're invited to. It couldn't be simpler or quicker to prepare, and you can vary the preserves to any flavor you have on hand.

Holly Bauer *West Bend, Wisconsin*

- **2 cups biscuit/baking mix**
- **2 tablespoons sugar**
- **1 egg**
- **⅔ cup 2% milk**
- **2 tablespoons canola oil**
- **½ cup white baking chips**
- **½ cup apricot preserves**

TOPPING:

- **⅓ cup biscuit/baking mix**
- **⅓ cup sugar**
- **2 tablespoons cold butter**

1 In a large bowl, combine the biscuit mix and sugar. Whisk the egg, milk and oil; stir into dry ingredients just until moistened. Fold in chips. Pour into a greased 9-in. round baking pan.

2 Drop preserves by teaspoonfuls over batter. Cut through batter with a knife to swirl the preserves.

3 For topping, combine biscuit mix and sugar in small bowl; cut in butter until crumbly. Sprinkle over batter.

4 Bake at 400° for 20-25 minutes or until golden brown. Serve warm.

Get Up & Go Muffins

PREP: 25 MIN. • BAKE: 20 MIN. • YIELD: 1½ DOZEN

I created this recipe by trial and error. I've only had one outstanding bran muffin at a restaurant, and wanted to come up with an awesome one to make myself. These are moist, healthy and full of grains and fruits.

Nancy Rens *Prescott, Arizona*

- **1½ cups bran flakes**
- **⅓ cup boiling water**
- **1 cup whole wheat flour**
- **1 cup all-purpose flour**
- **¾ cup packed brown sugar**
- **⅓ cup quick-cooking oats**
- **¾ teaspoon baking powder**
- **½ teaspoon baking soda**
- **½ teaspoon salt**
- **1 cup buttermilk**
- **½ cup unsweetened applesauce**
- **1 egg, beaten**
- **2 tablespoons molasses**
- **¾ cup fresh or frozen blueberries**
- **¾ cup pitted dried plums, coarsely chopped**
- **¼ cup slivered almonds**
- **2 tablespoons honey**

1 Place bran flakes and water in a small bowl. Cover and set aside.

2 In a large bowl, combine the flours, brown sugar, oats, baking powder, baking soda and salt.

3 In a small bowl, combine the buttermilk, applesauce, egg, molasses and bran mixture. Stir into dry ingredients just until moistened. Fold in the blueberries, plums and almonds. Fill greased muffin cups three-fourths full. Drizzle with honey.

4 Bake at 375° for 18-20 minutes or until a toothpick inserted near the center comes out clean. Cool for 5 minutes before removing from pans to wire racks. Serve warm.

EDITOR'S NOTE: If using frozen blueberries, use without thawing to avoid discoloring the batter.

Chocolate Ribbon Banana Loaf

PREP: 20 MIN. • BAKE: 40 MIN. + COOLING
YIELD: 1 LOAF (12 SLICES)

My loaf is a combination of three of my favorite foods: bananas, chocolate and peanut butter. I try to make other quick breads but this one is always requested.

Sharon Giljum *Arlington, Virginia*

- **¼ cup butter, softened**
- **1 cup sugar**
- **2 eggs**
- **1 cup mashed ripe bananas (about 2 medium)**
- **⅓ cup fat-free plain yogurt**
- **1 teaspoon vanilla extract**
- **1½ cups all-purpose flour**
- **½ cup whole wheat pastry flour**
- **¾ teaspoon baking soda**
- **½ teaspoon salt**
- **½ teaspoon ground cinnamon**
- **½ cup peanut butter chips**
- **½ cup semisweet chocolate chips, melted**

1 In a large bowl, beat butter and sugar until crumbly. Add eggs, one at a time, beating well after each addition. Beat in the bananas, yogurt and vanilla. Combine the flours, baking soda, salt and cinnamon; gradually add to butter mixture just until moistened. Fold in peanut butter chips.

2 Remove 1 cup batter to a small bowl; stir in chocolate until well blended. Pour half of the remaining plain batter into a 9-in. x 5-in. loaf pan coated with cooking spray; top with half of the chocolate batter. Repeat layers. Cut through batter with a knife to swirl.

3 Bake at 350° for 40-50 minutes or until a toothpick inserted near the center comes out clean. Cool for 10 minutes before removing from pan to a wire rack.

Cinnamon Roll Coffee Cake

PREP: 20 MIN. • BAKE: 25 MIN. + STANDING
YIELD: 12 SERVINGS

Sunday mornings are extra special with this fresh-from-the-oven treat on the table, especially when you have company. Guests will never guess how easy it is to whip up.

Teresa Maag *Leipsic, Ohio*

- **1 tube (17½ ounces) large refrigerated cinnamon rolls with cream cheese icing**
- **2 packages (8 ounces each) cream cheese, softened**
- **3 eggs**
- **½ cup sugar**
- **1 teaspoon vanilla extract**
- **½ cup chopped pecans**
- **¼ cup all-purpose flour**
- **¼ cup quick-cooking oats**
- **¼ cup packed brown sugar**
- **1 teaspoon ground cinnamon**
- **3 tablespoons butter, melted**

Whipped cream and additional ground cinnamon, optional

1 Unroll the tube of cinnamon rolls into one long rectangle. Press onto the bottom of a greased 13-in. x 9-in. baking dish; seal perforations. Set aside icing packet from cinnamon rolls.

2 In a large bowl, beat the cream cheese, eggs, sugar and vanilla until smooth. Pour over crust. In a small bowl, combine the pecans, flour, oats, brown sugar and cinnamon; stir in butter. Sprinkle over cream cheese layer.

3 Bake at 350° for 25-30 minutes or until a toothpick inserted near the center comes out clean. Drizzle with contents of icing packet; let stand for 15 minutes before serving. If desired, serve with a dollop of whipped cream sprinkled with additional cinnamon.

Rhubarb Coffee Cake with Caramel Sauce

PREP: 20 MIN. • BAKE: 35 MIN. + COOLING
YIELD: 18 SERVINGS (1⅔ CUPS SAUCE)

When I was growing up, I couldn't wait for the rhubarb to ripen so Mom could bake this luscious coffee cake. Now the recipe is part of my own collection.

Angie Fehr *Ottosen, Iowa*

- **½ cup shortening**
- **1½ cups sugar**
- **1 egg**
- **2 cups all-purpose flour**
- **1 teaspoon baking soda**
- **1 cup buttermilk**
- **1½ cups finely chopped fresh or frozen rhubarb**

TOPPING:

- **½ cup packed brown sugar**
- **¼ cup all-purpose flour**
- **1 teaspoon ground cinnamon**
- **3 tablespoons cold butter**

SAUCE:

- **½ cup butter, cubed**
- **1 cup packed brown sugar**
- **½ cup heavy whipping cream**

1 In a large bowl, cream shortening and sugar until light and fluffy. Add egg; beat well. Combine flour and baking soda; add to creamed mixture alternately with buttermilk. Fold in rhubarb. Transfer to a greased 13-in. x 9-in. baking pan.

2 For topping, in a small bowl, combine the brown sugar, flour and cinnamon; cut in butter until crumbly. Sprinkle over batter.

3 Bake at 350° for 35-40 minutes or until a toothpick inserted near the center comes out clean. Cool for 10 minutes before serving.

4 For sauce, in a small saucepan, melt butter. Stir in brown sugar and cream; bring to a boil. Reduce heat; simmer for 3 to 4 minutes or until slightly thickened. Serve with warm coffee cake.

Cocoa Macaroon Muffins

PREP: 15 MIN. • BAKE: 20 MIN. • YIELD: 1 DOZEN

A longtime favorite that I've modified over the years, this recipe is as wonderful at brunch as it is for dessert. I love chocolate in any form, and these muffins pair it with coconut for a yummy result.

Carol Wilson *Rio Rancho, New Mexico*

- **2 cups all-purpose flour**
- **½ cup sugar**
- **3 tablespoons baking cocoa**
- **3 teaspoons baking powder**
- **1 teaspoon salt**
- **1 cup milk**
- **1 egg**
- **⅓ cup canola oil**
- **1¼ cups flaked coconut, divided**
- **¼ cup sweetened condensed milk**
- **¼ teaspoon almond extract**

1 In a large bowl, combine the flour, sugar, cocoa, baking powder and salt. Combine the milk, egg and oil. Stir into dry ingredients just until moistened.

2 Spoon 2 tablespoonfuls into 12 greased or paper-lined muffin cups. Combine 1 cup coconut, condensed milk and extract; place 2 teaspoonfuls in the center of each cup (do not spread). Top with remaining batter; sprinkle with remaining coconut.

3 Bake at 400° for 20-22 minutes or until a toothpick inserted near the center comes out clean. Cool for 5 minutes before removing from pan to a wire rack. Serve warm.

Blueberry Cornmeal Muffins

PREP: 20 MIN. • BAKE: 20 MIN. • YIELD: 1 DOZEN

When I bring treats to the staff at the school where I work, I try to keep many of them healthy. The cornmeal adds an interesting texture to this guilt-free treat.

Elizabeth Bergeron *Denver, Colorado*

- **1 cup yellow cornmeal**
- **½ cup all-purpose flour**
- **½ cup whole wheat flour**
- **½ cup plus 1½ teaspoons sugar, divided**
- **4 teaspoons baking powder**
- **½ teaspoon salt**
- **2 eggs**
- **¾ cup fat-free milk**
- **¼ cup canola oil**
- **1 teaspoon vanilla extract**
- **2 cups fresh or frozen blueberries**

1 In a small bowl, combine the cornmeal, flours, ½ cup sugar, baking powder and salt. In another bowl, combine the eggs, milk, oil and vanilla. Stir into dry ingredients just until moistened. Fold in blueberries.

2 Fill greased muffin cups three-fourths full; sprinkle with remaining sugar. Bake at 350° for 18-22 minutes or until a toothpick inserted into muffin comes out clean. Cool for 5 minutes before removing from pan to a wire rack. Serve warm.

EDITOR'S NOTE: If using frozen blueberries, use without thawing to avoid discoloring the batter.

TYPES OF CORNMEAL

>> Cornmeal can be either white, yellow or blue depending on which strain of corn is used. Traditionally, white cornmeal is more popular in the South and yellow is preferred in the North. Blue cornmeal can be found in specialty stores. All three types can be used interchangeably in recipes.

Fruit-Nut Pumpkin Bread

PREP: 30 MIN. • BAKE: 1 HOUR + COOLING
YIELD: 2 LOAVES (12 SLICES EACH) AND 1 CUP SPREAD

Our family dinners wouldn't be complete without this easy and versatile loaf. I bake a variety to suit everyone: one plain, one with just nuts, one with raisins and dried cranberries, and one with everything.

Priscilla Gilbert *Indian Harbour Beach, Florida*

- **2⅔ cups sugar**
- **1 can (15 ounces) solid-pack pumpkin**
- **1 cup canola oil**
- **4 eggs**
- **1 teaspoon vanilla extract**
- **3½ cups all-purpose flour**
- **1½ teaspoons ground cinnamon**
- **1 teaspoon salt**
- **1 teaspoon baking soda**
- **¼ teaspoon ground cloves**
- **1½ cups coarsely chopped walnuts**
- **⅔ cup golden raisins**
- **⅔ cup raisins**
- **⅔ cup dried cranberries**

CRANBERRY CREAM CHEESE SPREAD:

- **½ cup dried cranberries**
- **1½ cups boiling water**
- **1 package (8 ounces) cream cheese, softened**
- **⅓ cup chopped walnuts**

1 In a large bowl, beat the sugar, pumpkin, oil, eggs and vanilla until well blended. Combine the flour, cinnamon, salt, baking soda and cloves; gradually beat into pumpkin mixture until blended. Fold in the walnuts, raisins and cranberries.

2 Transfer to two greased 9-in. x 5-in. loaf pans. Bake at 350° for 60-70 minutes or until a toothpick inserted near the center comes out clean. Cool for 10 minutes before removing from pans to wire racks.

3 For spread, place cranberries in a small bowl; add boiling water. Let stand for 5 minutes; drain. In a small bowl, beat cream cheese until smooth. Beat in cranberries and walnuts until blended. Serve with bread.

Cowboy Corn Bread

PREP: 15 MIN. • BAKE: 25 MIN.
YIELD: 12 SERVINGS

My corn bread is richer and sweeter than others I've tried. It's especially luscious alongside ham and beans.

Karen Ann Bland *Gove, Kansas*

- **2 cups biscuit/baking mix**
- **1 cup yellow cornmeal**
- **¾ cup sugar**
- **½ teaspoon baking soda**
- **½ teaspoon salt**
- **2 eggs**
- **1 cup butter, melted**
- **1 cup half-and-half cream**

1 In a large bowl, combine the first five ingredients. In another bowl, combine the eggs, butter and cream; stir into the dry ingredients just until moistened. Spread into a greased 13-in. x 9-in. baking pan.

2 Bake at 350° for 25-30 minutes or until a toothpick inserted near the center comes out clean. Serve warm.

Lemon Yogurt Bread

PREP: 15 MIN. • BAKE: 45 MIN. + COOLING
YIELD: 1 LOAF (12 SLICES)

If you love pound cake, you'll devour this luscious loaf. Its mild lemon flavor and cake-like texture make it the perfect choice for brunch or a midafternoon snack.

Suzy Horvath *Gladstone, Oregon*

- **1½ cups all-purpose flour**
- **¾ cup sugar**
- **½ teaspoon salt**
- **½ teaspoon baking soda**
- **¼ teaspoon baking powder**
- **1 egg**
- **1 cup (8 ounces) lemon yogurt**
- **⅓ cup canola oil**
- **1 tablespoon lemon juice**

1 In a large bowl, combine the flour, sugar, salt, baking soda and baking powder. In another bowl, combine the egg, yogurt, oil and lemon juice. Stir into dry ingredients just until moistened.

2 Pour into an 8-in. x 4-in. loaf pan coated with cooking spray. Bake at 325° for 45-50 minutes or until a toothpick inserted near the center comes out clean. Cool for 10 minutes before removing from pan to a wire rack.

Cherry Cream Cheese Coffee Cake

PREP: 25 MIN. • BAKE: 50 MIN. + COOLING • YIELD: 8-10 SERVINGS

You'll like the texture of this tender coffee cake. The sour cream pairs well with the cherries, and the crunchy almonds make a nice accent. But watch out—the sweet streusel topping makes it hard to eat only one slice.

Linda Guiles *Belvidere, New Jersey*

- **2¼ cups all-purpose flour**
- **¾ cup sugar**
- **¾ cup cold butter, cubed**
- **½ teaspoon baking powder**
- **½ teaspoon baking soda**
- **½ teaspoon salt**
- **1 egg, lightly beaten**
- **¾ cup sour cream**
- **1 teaspoon almond extract**

FILLING:

- **1 package (8 ounces) cream cheese, softened**
- **¼ cup sugar**
- **1 egg, lightly beaten**
- **1 can (21 ounces) cherry pie filling**
- **½ cup slivered almonds**

1 In a bowl, combine flour and sugar. Cut in butter until crumbly. Reserve ¾ cup crumb mixture. Add the baking powder, baking soda and salt to remaining crumb mixture. Stir in the egg, sour cream and almond extract until blended. Press onto the bottom and 1 in. up the sides of an ungreased 9-in. springform pan with removable bottom.

2 For filling, in a large bowl, beat cream cheese and sugar for 1 minute. Add egg; beat just until combined. Spread over crust. Carefully top with pie filling. Sprinkle with almonds and reserved crumb mixture.

3 Bake at 350° for 50-60 minutes or until center is set. Cool on a wire rack. Carefully run a knife around edge of pan to loosen; remove sides of pan. Store in the refrigerator.

APPLE CREAM CHEESE COFFEE CAKE: Substitute apple pie filling for the cherry filling and ½ cup chopped pecans or walnuts for the almonds.

BLUEBERRY CREAM CHEESE COFFEE CAKE: Substitute blueberry pie filling for the cherry filling.

Raspberry Streusel Coffee Cake

PREP: 25 MIN. + COOLING • BAKE: 40 MIN.
YIELD: 12-16 SERVINGS

One of my mother's friends used to bring this over on holidays, and it never lasted long. With the tangy raspberry filling, tender cake and crunchy topping, it's become a favorite at our house.

Amy Mitchell *Sabetha, Kansas*

- **3½ cups unsweetened raspberries**
- **1 cup water**
- **2 tablespoons lemon juice**
- **1¼ cups sugar**
- **⅓ cup cornstarch**

BATTER:

- **3 cups all-purpose flour**
- **1 cup sugar**
- **1 teaspoon baking powder**
- **1 teaspoon baking soda**
- **1 cup cold butter, cubed**
- **2 eggs, lightly beaten**
- **1 cup (8 ounces) sour cream**
- **1 teaspoon vanilla extract**

TOPPING:

- **½ cup all-purpose flour**
- **½ cup sugar**
- **¼ cup butter, softened**
- **½ cup chopped pecans**

GLAZE:

- **½ cup confectioners' sugar**
- **2 teaspoons 2% milk**
- **½ teaspoon vanilla extract**

1 In a large saucepan, cook raspberries and water over medium heat for 5 minutes. Add lemon juice. Combine sugar and cornstarch; stir into fruit mixture. Bring to a boil; cook and stir for 2 minutes or until thickened. Cool.

2 In a large bowl, combine the flour, sugar, baking powder and baking soda. Cut in butter until mixture resembles coarse crumbs. Stir in eggs, sour cream and vanilla (batter will be stiff).

3 Spread half into a greased 13-in. x 9-in. baking dish. Spread raspberry filling over batter; spoon remaining batter over filling. Combine topping ingredients; sprinkle over top.

4 Bake at 350° for 40-45 minutes or until golden brown. Combine the glaze ingredients; drizzle over warm cake.

Streusel Fruit Bread

PREP: 20 MIN. • BAKE: 40 MIN. + COOLING
YIELD: 1 MINI LOAF (6 SLICES)

This recipe has been handed down through the years in my family, but I scaled it down. The result is a delightful bread chock-full of dried fruits and nuts.

Robert Logan *Clayton, California*

- **3/4 cup all-purpose flour**
- **1/3 cup sugar**
- **3/4 teaspoon ground cinnamon**
- **1/4 teaspoon salt**
- **1/4 teaspoon baking soda**
- **1 egg**
- **1/3 cup mashed ripe banana**
- **2 tablespoons canola oil**
- **2 tablespoons light corn syrup**
- **3/4 teaspoon vanilla extract**
- **1/4 cup chopped pecans**
- **2 tablespoons dried cranberries**
- **2 tablespoons chopped dried apricots**

TOPPING:

- **2 tablespoons brown sugar**
- **1 tablespoon all-purpose flour**
- **1 1/2 teaspoons cold butter**

1 In a small bowl, combine the flour, sugar, cinnamon, salt and baking soda; set aside. In another bowl, beat the egg, banana, oil, corn syrup and vanilla. Stir into dry ingredients just until moistened. Fold in the pecans, cranberries and apricots.

2 Pour into a 5 3/4-in. x 3-in. x 2-in. loaf pan coated with cooking spray. For topping, combine brown sugar and flour in a small bowl. Cut in butter until crumbly. Sprinkle over batter.

3 Bake at 325° for 40-45 minutes or until a toothpick inserted near the center comes out clean. Cool for 10 minutes before removing from pan to a wire rack.

Peanut Butter Banana Bread

PREP: 25 MIN. • BAKE: 45 MIN. + COOLING
YIELD: 2 LOAVES (12 SLICES EACH)

My family literally comes running when they smell this bread baking. A thick chocolate layer and crumbly topping make the special loaf simply scrumptious!

Sherry Lee *Columbus, Ohio*

TOPPING:

- **½ cup all-purpose flour**
- **½ cup packed brown sugar**
- **¼ cup creamy peanut butter**
- **½ teaspoon ground cinnamon**

BATTER:

- **½ cup butter, softened**
- **1 package (8 ounces) cream cheese, softened**
- **1¼ cups sugar**
- **2 eggs**
- **1 cup mashed ripe bananas**
- **1 teaspoon vanilla extract**
- **2¼ cups all-purpose flour**
- **1½ teaspoons baking powder**
- **½ teaspoon baking soda**
- **1 teaspoon ground cinnamon**
- **1½ cups semisweet chocolate chips**

1 In a small bowl, stir the flour, brown sugar, peanut butter and cinnamon until crumbly; set aside.

2 In a large bowl, cream the butter, cream cheese and sugar until light and fluffy. Add eggs, one at a time, beating well after each addition. Beat in bananas and vanilla. Combine the flour, baking powder, baking soda and cinnamon; stir into creamed mixture just until moistened.

3 Divide half of the batter between two greased 8-in. x 4-in. loaf pans; sprinkle with half of the topping. Top with chocolate chips. Repeat layers of batter and topping.

4 Bake at 350° for 45-55 minutes or until a toothpick inserted near the center comes out clean. Cool for 10 minutes before removing from pans to wire racks.

EDITOR'S NOTE: Reduced-fat peanut butter is not recommended for this recipe.

Rosemary Cheddar Muffins

30 min.

PREP/TOTAL TIME: 25 MIN. • YIELD: 1 DOZEN

My 96-year-old stepmother gave me this recipe many years ago. We have enjoyed these luscious biscuit-like muffins ever since. They're so cheesy and tender, you might not even need butter!

Bonnie Stallings *Martinsburg, West Virginia*

- **2 cups self-rising flour**
- **½ cup shredded sharp cheddar cheese**
- **1 tablespoon minced fresh rosemary or 1 teaspoon dried rosemary, crushed**
- **1¼ cups 2% milk**
- **3 tablespoons mayonnaise**

1 In a large bowl, combine the flour, cheese and rosemary. In another bowl, combine milk and mayonnaise; stir into dry ingredients just until moistened. Spoon into 12 greased muffin cups.

2 Bake at 400° for 8-10 minutes or until lightly browned and toothpick inserted into muffin comes out clean. Cool for 5 minutes before removing from pan to a wire rack. Serve warm.

Peppery Cheese Bread

PREP: 15 MIN. • BAKE: 45 MIN. + COOLING
YIELD: 1 LOAF (16 SLICES)

When the warm, moist bread hits your palate, it's just heavenly! This never lasts long in our house; it's my daughter's favorite savory quick bread.

Sharon Boren *Salem, Oregon*

- **2½ cups all-purpose flour**
- **1 tablespoon sugar**
- **1½ teaspoons coarsely ground pepper**
- **1 teaspoon baking powder**
- **¾ teaspoon salt**
- **½ teaspoon baking soda**
- **2 eggs**
- **1 cup (8 ounces) reduced-fat plain yogurt**
- **½ cup canola oil**
- **¼ cup 2% milk**
- **1 tablespoon spicy brown mustard**
- **1 cup (4 ounces) shredded cheddar cheese**
- **2 green onions, thinly sliced**

1 In a large bowl, combine the first six ingredients. In a small bowl, whisk the eggs, yogurt, oil, milk and mustard. Stir into dry ingredients just until moistened. Fold in cheese and onions.

2 Transfer to a greased 9-in. x 5-in. loaf pan. Bake at 350° for 45-55 minutes or until a toothpick inserted near the center comes out clean. Cool for 10 minutes before removing from pan to a wire rack.

Orange Nut Bread & Cream Cheese Spread

PREP: 40 MIN. • BAKE: 35 MIN. + COOLING
YIELD: 3 MINI LOAVES (6 SLICES EACH) AND 1 CUP SPREAD

This delectable sweet bread was my mother's favorite. Every bite gives you a burst of orange and the crunch of chopped walnuts.

Karen Sue Garback-Pristera *Albany, New York*

- **⅓ cup butter, softened**
- **⅔ cup sugar**
- **2 eggs**
- **½ teaspoon orange extract**
- **½ teaspoon vanilla extract**
- **2 cups all-purpose flour**
- **1 teaspoon baking powder**
- **½ teaspoon salt**
- **¼ teaspoon baking soda**
- **1 cup orange juice**
- **1 cup chopped walnuts**

SPREAD:

- **1 package (8 ounces) cream cheese, softened**
- **2 tablespoons orange juice**
- **1 tablespoon confectioners' sugar**
- **1 teaspoon grated orange peel**

1 In a large bowl, cream butter and sugar until light and fluffy. Add eggs, one at a time, beating well after each addition. Beat in extracts.

2 Combine the flour, baking powder, salt and baking soda; add to creamed mixture alternately with orange juice. Fold in walnuts.

3 Transfer to three greased 5¾-in. x 3-in. x 2-in. loaf pans. Bake at 350° for 35-40 minutes or until a toothpick inserted near the center comes out clean. Cool for 10 minutes before removing from pans to wire racks.

4 In a small bowl, beat the cream cheese, orange juice, confectioners' sugar and peel until well blended. Chill until serving. Serve with bread.

Cranberry Banana Bread

PREP: 25 MIN. • BAKE: 50 MIN. + COOLING
YIELD: 1 LOAF (12 SLICES)

Studded with cranberries and nuts, these moist golden loaves make wonderful breakfast treats and gifts for grateful friends. I experimented for years, and this recipe is now near perfection!

Eva Rider *Montgomery, Alabama*

- **⅓ cup shortening**
- **⅔ cup sugar**
- **2 eggs**
- **1 cup mashed ripe bananas (about 2 medium)**
- **1½ cups all-purpose flour**
- **⅓ cup cinnamon graham cracker crumbs (about 2 whole crackers)**
- **1½ teaspoons baking powder**
- **½ teaspoon baking soda**
- **½ teaspoon salt**
- **½ cup chopped walnuts or pecans**
- **½ cup dried cranberries**

1 In a large bowl, cream shortening and sugar until light and fluffy. Add eggs, one at a time, beating well after each addition. Stir in bananas. Combine the flour, cracker crumbs, baking powder, baking soda and salt; gradually add to creamed mixture and mix well. Fold in walnuts and cranberries. Pour into a greased 8-in. x 4-in. loaf pan.

2 Bake at 350° for 50-55 minutes or until a toothpick inserted near the center comes out clean. Cool for 10 minutes before removing from pan to a wire rack.

Swirl Cinnamon Bread

PREP: 25 MIN. • BAKE: 45 MIN. + COOLING
YIELD: 1 LOAF (12 SLICES)

If you like cinnamon, you'll love this quick bread! It's crusty on top, soft and moist inside—and one of my very most-requested recipes. I always make extra loaves for the holidays and give them to family and friends.

Meryl Sheppard *Greensboro, North Carolina*

- **2 cups all-purpose flour**
- **¾ cup sugar**
- **½ teaspoon baking soda**
- **½ teaspoon plus 1½ teaspoons ground cinnamon, divided**
- **¼ teaspoon salt**
- **1 egg**
- **1 cup (8 ounces) reduced-fat plain yogurt**
- **¼ cup canola oil**
- **1 teaspoon vanilla extract**
- **¼ cup packed brown sugar**

1 In a large bowl, combine the flour, sugar, baking soda, ½ teaspoon cinnamon and salt. In a small bowl, whisk the egg, yogurt, oil and vanilla. Stir into dry ingredients just until moistened. In a small bowl, combine brown sugar and remaining cinnamon.

2 Spoon a third of the batter into an 8-in. x 4-in. loaf pan coated with cooking spray. Top with a third of the brown sugar mixture. Repeat layers twice. Cut through batter with a knife to swirl the brown sugar mixture.

3 Bake at 350° for 45-55 minutes or until a toothpick inserted near the center comes out clean. Cool for 10 minutes before removing from pan to a wire rack.

Pina Colada Zucchini Bread

PREP: 25 MIN. • BAKE: 45 MIN. + COOLING • YIELD: 3 LOAVES (12 SLICES EACH)

At my husband's request, I entered this recipe at the Pennsylvania Farm Show and won first place! I think you'll love the cakelike texture and tropical flavors.

Sharon Rydbom *Tipton, Pennsylvania*

- **4 cups all-purpose flour**
- **3 cups sugar**
- **2 teaspoons baking powder**
- **1½ teaspoons salt**
- **1 teaspoon baking soda**
- **4 eggs**
- **1½ cups canola oil**
- **1 teaspoon each coconut, rum and vanilla extracts**
- **3 cups shredded zucchini**
- **1 cup canned crushed pineapple, drained**
- **½ cup chopped walnuts or chopped pecans**

1 Line the bottoms of three greased and floured 8-in. x 4-in. loaf pans with waxed paper and grease the paper; set aside.

2 In a large bowl, combine the flour, sugar, baking powder, salt and baking soda. In another bowl, whisk the eggs, oil and extracts. Stir into dry ingredients just until moistened. Fold in the zucchini, pineapple and walnuts.

3 Transfer to prepared pans. Bake at 350° for 45-55 minutes or until a toothpick inserted near the center comes out clean. Cool for 10 minutes before removing from pans to wire racks. Gently remove waxed paper.

Pull-Apart Caramel Coffee Cake

PREP: 10 MIN. • BAKE: 25 MIN.
YIELD: 12 SERVINGS

The first time I made this delightful breakfast treat for a brunch party, it was a huge hit. Now I get requests every time family or friends do anything around the breakfast hour! I always keep the four simple ingredients on hand.

Jaime Keeling *Keizer, Oregon*

- **2 tubes (12 ounces each) refrigerated flaky buttermilk biscuits**
- **1 cup packed brown sugar**
- **½ cup heavy whipping cream**
- **1 teaspoon ground cinnamon**

1 Cut each biscuit into four pieces; arrange evenly in a 10-in. fluted tube pan coated with cooking spray. Combine the brown sugar, cream and cinnamon; pour over biscuits.

2 Bake at 350° for 25-30 minutes or until golden brown. Cool for 5 minutes before inverting onto a serving platter.

Triple-Chocolate Quick Bread

PREP: 20 MIN. • BAKE: 35 MIN. + COOLING
YIELD: 4 MINI LOAVES

Some argue this decadent loaf is more like dessert than a quick bread. I suppose it's easy to taste why. Chocolate chips dot the batter, while melted chips form the glaze. Each slice is divine.

Karen Grimes *Stephens City, Virginia*

- **1½ cups miniature semisweet chocolate chips, divided**
- **½ cup butter, softened**
- **⅔ cup packed brown sugar**
- **2 eggs**
- **1½ cups unsweetened applesauce**
- **2 teaspoons vanilla extract**
- **2½ cups all-purpose flour**
- **1 teaspoon baking powder**
- **1 teaspoon baking soda**
- **1 teaspoon salt**

GLAZE:

- **½ cup miniature semisweet chocolate chips**
- **1 tablespoon butter**
- **2 to 3 tablespoons half-and-half cream**
- **½ cup confectioners' sugar**
- **¼ teaspoon vanilla extract**

Pinch salt

1 In a microwave-safe bowl, melt 1 cup chocolate chips; set aside to cool. In a large bowl, cream butter and brown sugar until light and fluffy.

2 Add eggs and cooled chocolate; mix well. Add applesauce and vanilla; set aside. Combine the flour, baking powder, baking soda and salt; add to creamed mixture and mix well. Stir in the remaining chocolate chips.

3 Spoon into four greased 5¾-in. x 3-in. x 2-in. loaf pans. Bake at 350° for 35-40 minutes or until a toothpick inserted near the center comes out clean. Cool for 10 minutes before removing to wire racks.

4 For glaze, melt chocolate chips and butter in a small heavy saucepan; stir in cream. Remove from the heat; stir in confectioners' sugar, vanilla and salt. Drizzle over warm breads. Cool completely.

Southwestern Corn Bread

PREP: 20 MIN. • BAKE: 25 MIN.
YIELD: 15 SERVINGS (½ CUP BUTTER)

I put a wonderful twist on my Grandma's classic corn bread. The teachers at my kids' school thought it was sensational. Any extra of the flavored butter can be kept in the refrigerator for about a week, and used in other great recipes or on seeded toast.

Elizabeth Charpiot *Santa Rosa, California*

- **2 cups all-purpose flour**
- **2 cups yellow cornmeal**
- **½ cup sugar**
- **4 teaspoons baking powder**
- **1 teaspoon baking soda**
- **1 teaspoon salt**
- **1 teaspoon dried minced garlic**
- **1 teaspoon dried minced onion**
- **1 teaspoon paprika**
- **1 teaspoon chili powder**
- **2 cups buttermilk**
- **½ cup canola oil**
- **2 eggs**
- **1 jar (7 ounces) roasted sweet red peppers, drained, patted dry and chopped**
- **1 cup frozen corn, thawed**
- **¼ cup minced chives**

CHILI HONEY-LIME BUTTER:

- **½ cup butter, softened**
- **1 tablespoon lime juice**
- **1 tablespoon honey**
- **1 teaspoon chili powder**
- **1 teaspoon grated lime peel**

1 In a large bowl, combine the first 10 ingredients. In a small bowl, whisk the buttermilk, oil and eggs. Stir into dry ingredients just until moistened. Fold in the red peppers, corn and chives.

2 Transfer to a greased 13-in. x 9-in. baking dish. Bake at 400° for 23-28 minutes or until a toothpick inserted near the center comes out clean. Remove to a wire rack.

3 In a small bowl, combine the butter, lime juice, honey, chili powder and lime peel. Serve with warm corn bread.

Sour Cream Loaves

PREP: 15 MIN. • BAKE: 40 MIN. + COOLING
YIELD: 2 MINI LOAVES (6 SLICES EACH)

Cinnamon and nutmeg lend just the right amount of flavor to these moist mini loaves. Sometimes I use the batter to make muffins instead.

Joyce Lemkuil *Branson, Missouri*

- **⅔ cup butter, softened**
- **⅔ cup plus 1 tablespoon sugar, divided**
- **1 egg**
- **½ teaspoon vanilla extract**
- **1½ cups all-purpose flour**
- **½ teaspoon baking soda**
- **½ teaspoon salt**
- **½ teaspoon ground nutmeg**
- **½ teaspoon ground cinnamon, divided**
- **½ cup sour cream**

1 In a large bowl, cream butter and ⅔ cup sugar until light and fluffy. Beat in egg and vanilla. Combine the flour, baking soda, salt, nutmeg and ¼ teaspoon cinnamon; gradually add to creamed mixture alternately with sour cream.

2 Pour into two 5¾-in. x 3-in. x 2-in. loaf pans coated with cooking spray. Combine remaining sugar and cinnamon; sprinkle over batter.

3 Bake at 350° for 40-45 minutes or until a toothpick inserted near the center comes out clean. Cool for 10 minutes before removing from pans to a wire rack.

Zucchini Banana Bread

PREP: 15 MIN. • BAKE: 40 MIN. + COOLING
YIELD: 3 MINI LOAVES (6 SLICES EACH)

I got this recipe from a friend at work and now it's one of my favorites. It makes three small loaves and they freeze very well.

Donna Hall *Wolfforth, Texas*

- **1½ cups all-purpose flour**
- **1 cup sugar**
- **1 teaspoon ground cinnamon**
- **½ teaspoon baking powder**
- **½ teaspoon baking soda**
- **½ teaspoon salt**
- **1 egg**
- **1 cup mashed ripe bananas**
- **½ cup canola oil**
- **½ teaspoon banana extract**
- **½ teaspoon vanilla extract**
- **1 cup shredded zucchini**
- **½ cup chopped walnuts**

1 In a large bowl, combine the first six ingredients. In a small bowl, beat the egg, bananas, oil and extracts. Stir into dry ingredients just until moistened. Fold in zucchini and walnuts.

2 Transfer to three 5¾-in. x 3-in. x 2-in. loaf pans coated with cooking spray. Bake at 325° for 40-45 minutes or until a toothpick inserted near the center comes out clean. Cool for 10 minutes before removing from pans to wire racks.

WINNERS
CIRCLE

yeast breads

You "knead" not worry about whether this delightful assortment of loaves, sweet rolls, croissants and more will satisfy your craving for freshly baked bread. Each is a proven ribbon winner, destined to turn your kitchen into your favorite corner bakery.

RASPBERRY-CREAM CHEESE LADDER LOAVES, 215

Cinnamon Bagels with Crunchy Topping

PREP: 40 MIN. + RISING • BAKE: 15 MIN.
YIELD: 1 DOZEN

Once you get the hang of it, you won't believe how simple it is to make these bakery-quality bagels right in your kitchen.

Kristen Streepey *Geneva, Illinois*

- **2 teaspoons active dry yeast**
- **1½ cups warm water (110° to 115°)**
- **¼ cup packed brown sugar, divided**
- **3 teaspoons ground cinnamon**
- **1½ teaspoons salt**
- **2¾ to 3¼ cups all-purpose flour**

TOPPING:

- **¼ cup sugar**
- **¼ cup packed brown sugar**
- **3 teaspoons ground cinnamon**

1 In a large bowl, dissolve yeast in warm water. Add 3 tablespoons brown sugar, cinnamon and salt; mix well. Stir in enough flour to form a soft dough.

2 Turn onto a lightly floured surface; knead until smooth and elastic, about 6-8 minutes. Place in a bowl coated with cooking spray, turning once to coat the top. Cover and let rise in a warm place until doubled, about 1 hour.

3 Punch dough down. Shape into 12 balls. Push thumb through centers to form a 1½-in. hole. Stretch and shape dough to form an even ring. Place on a floured surface. Cover and let rest for 10 minutes.

4 Fill a Dutch oven two-thirds full with water and remaining brown sugar; bring to a boil. Drop bagels, two at a time, into boiling water. Cook for 45 seconds; turn and cook 45 seconds longer. Remove with a slotted spoon; drain well on paper towels.

5 Combine topping ingredients; sprinkle over bagels. Place 2 in. apart on baking sheets coated with cooking spray. Bake at 400° for 15-20 minutes or until golden brown. Remove to wire racks to cool.

Black Raspberry Bubble Ring

PREP: 35 MIN. + RISING • BAKE: 25 MIN. • YIELD: 1 LOAF

I first made this pretty bread years ago for a 4-H project. It helped me win Grand Champion for my county and took me to the Ohio State Fair. It takes some time to make, but I pull out this recipe any time I want a breakfast or dessert that will really impress my family and friends.

Kila Frank *Reedsville, Ohio*

- **1 package (¼ ounce) active dry yeast**
- **¼ cup warm water (110° to 115°)**
- **1 cup warm milk (110° to 115°)**
- **¼ cup plus 2 tablespoons sugar, divided**
- **½ cup butter, melted, divided**
- **1 egg**
- **1 teaspoon salt**
- **4 cups all-purpose flour**
- **1 jar (10 ounces) seedless black raspberry preserves**

SYRUP:

- **⅓ cup corn syrup**
- **2 tablespoons butter, melted**
- **¼ teaspoon vanilla extract**

1 In a large bowl, dissolve yeast in warm water. Add the milk, ¼ cup sugar, ¼ cup butter, egg, salt and 3½ cups flour. Beat until smooth. Stir in enough remaining flour to form a soft dough.

2 Turn onto a floured surface; knead until smooth and elastic, about 6-8 minutes. Place in a greased bowl, turning once to grease top. Cover and let rise in a warm place until doubled, about 1¼ hours.

3 Punch dough down. Turn onto a lightly floured surface; divide into 32 pieces. Flatten each into a 3-in. disk. Place about 1 teaspoon of preserves on the center of each piece; bring edges together and seal.

4 Place 16 dough balls in a greased 10-in. fluted tube pan. Brush with half of the remaining butter; sprinkle with 1 tablespoon sugar. Top with remaining balls, butter and sugar. Cover and let rise until doubled, about 35 minutes.

5 Bake at 350° for 25-30 minutes or until golden brown. Combine syrup ingredients; pour over warm bread. Cool for 5 minutes before inverting onto a serving plate.

Pumpernickel Caraway Bread

PREP: 10 MIN. • BAKE: 3-4 HOURS
YIELD: 1 LOAF (1 POUND)

Molasses and caraway seeds are the secret to making this hearty loaf moist and flavorful.

Lorraine Darocha *Berkshire, Massachusetts*

- **¾ cup water (70° to 80°)**
- **2 tablespoons molasses**
- **4½ teaspoons butter**
- **1 teaspoon salt**
- **1 cup bread flour**
- **⅔ cup rye flour**
- **⅓ cup whole wheat flour**
- **2 tablespoons cornmeal**
- **5 teaspoons baking cocoa**
- **4½ teaspoons sugar**
- **3 teaspoons nonfat dry milk powder**
- **1 teaspoon caraway seeds**
- **¼ teaspoon instant coffee granules**
- **1½ teaspoons active dry yeast**

1 In bread machine pan, place all ingredients in order suggested by manufacturer. Select basic bread setting. Choose crust color and loaf size if available.

2 Bake according to bread machine directions (check dough after 5 minutes of mixing; add 1 to 2 tablespoons of water or flour if needed).

Christmas Morning Croissants

PREP: 50 MIN. + CHILLING + RISING
BAKE: 20 MIN. • YIELD: 32 ROLLS

Growing up in France, we often enjoyed buttery croissants for breakfast. I've tried to re-create the experience for my family with this recipe.

Tish Stevenson *Grand Rapids, Michigan*

- **2 packages (¼ ounce each) active dry yeast**
- **1 cup warm water (110° to 115°)**
- **1¼ cups cold butter, divided**
- **5 cups all-purpose flour, divided**
- **⅓ cup sugar**
- **1½ teaspoons salt**
- **¾ cup evaporated milk**
- **2 eggs**
- **1 tablespoon water**

1 In a large bowl, dissolve yeast in warm water; let stand for 5 minutes. Melt ¼ cup butter; set aside. Combine 1 cup flour, sugar and salt; add to yeast mixture. Add the milk, 1 egg and melted butter; beat until smooth.

2 Place remaining flour in a large bowl; cut in remaining butter until crumbly. Add yeast mixture; mix well. Do not knead. Cover and refrigerate overnight.

3 Punch dough down. Turn onto a lightly floured surface; knead about six times. Divide dough into four pieces. Roll each piece into a 16-in. circle; cut each circle into eight wedges. Roll up wedges from the wide ends and place point side down 3 in. apart on ungreased baking sheets. Curve ends to form crescents. Cover and let rise in a warm place for 1 hour.

4 Beat water and remaining egg; brush over rolls. Bake at 325° for 20-25 minutes or until lightly browned. Serve warm.

Cheddar-Chili Bread Twists

PREP: 30 MIN. + RISING • BAKE: 15 MIN. • YIELD: 2 DOZEN

Green chilies are abundant here in New Mexico, so I'm always looking for ways to cook with them. These twists are often requested by my family.

Carol Whitfield *Mentmore, New Mexico*

- **1¼ cups buttermilk**
- **2 cups (8 ounces) shredded cheddar cheese**
- **2 tablespoons sugar**
- **1 package (¼ ounce) active dry yeast**
- **¼ cup warm water (110° to 115°)**
- **2 eggs**
- **½ teaspoon salt**
- **5¼ to 5¾ cups all-purpose flour**

TOPPING:

- **1½ cups (6 ounces) shredded cheddar cheese**
- **1 can (4 ounces) chopped green chilies, drained**

Grated Parmesan cheese

1 In a large saucepan, heat the buttermilk and cheese over low heat, stirring until cheese is melted (mixture will appear curdled). Cool to 110° to 115°. In a large bowl, dissolve sugar and yeast in warm water. Add the buttermilk mixture, eggs, salt and 3 cups flour. Beat until smooth. Stir in enough remaining flour to form a soft dough.

2 Turn onto a floured surface; knead until smooth and elastic, about 6-8 minutes. Place in a greased bowl, turning once to grease top. Cover and let rise in a warm place until doubled, about 1 hour. Meanwhile, for topping, combine cheddar cheese and chilies; set aside.

3 Punch dough down; turn onto a lightly floured surface and divide in half. Roll each portion into an 18-in. x 12-in. rectangle. Spray one half with cooking spray. Top with cheese mixture and remaining dough.

4 Cut into twelve 1½-in. strips. Cut each strip in half and twist. Place 1 in. apart on greased foil-lined baking sheets. Sprinkle with Parmesan cheese.

5 Bake at 375° for 15-20 minutes or until lightly browned. Remove to wire racks. Serve warm. Refrigerate any leftovers.

Spinach Pinwheel Rolls

PREP: 30 MIN. + RISING • BAKE: 30 MIN.
YIELD: 20 ROLLS

Whether eaten warm or cold, these rolls are always a hit. The spinach and cream cheese filling sets them apart.

Maryalice Wood *Langley, British Columbia*

- **4 to 5 cups all-purpose flour, divided**
- **1 tablespoon sugar**
- **3 teaspoons active dry yeast**
- **1 teaspoon grated lemon peel**
- **1½ teaspoons salt, divided**
- **¾ cup water**
- **¾ cup plus 2 tablespoons fat-free milk, divided**
- **1 tablespoon canola oil**
- **4 teaspoons lemon juice, divided**
- **1 package (10 ounces) fresh spinach, trimmed and torn**
- **4 ounces reduced-fat cream cheese**
- **2 tablespoons reduced-fat mayonnaise**
- **1 teaspoon salt-free lemon-pepper seasoning**
- **3 tablespoons cornmeal**

1 In a large bowl, combine 2 cups flour, sugar, yeast, lemon peel and 1 teaspoon salt. In a small saucepan, heat water, ¾ cup milk, oil and 3 teaspoons lemon juice to 120°-130°. Add to dry ingredients; beat just until moistened. Stir in enough remaining flour to form a soft dough (dough will be sticky).

2 Turn onto a lightly floured surface; knead until smooth and elastic, about 6-8 minutes. Place in a bowl coated with cooking spray, turning once to coat the top. Cover and let rise until doubled, about 1 hour.

3 Place spinach in a steamer basket; place in a large saucepan over 1 in. of water. Bring to a boil; cover and steam until wilted. Drain. Combine the cream cheese, mayonnaise, lemon-pepper and remaining lemon juice and salt. Stir in spinach; cool.

4 Punch dough down. Roll into a 24-in. x 14-in. rectangle. Spread filling to within ½ in. of edges. Roll up jelly-roll style, starting with a long side; pinch seam to seal. Cut into 20 slices. Coat baking pans with cooking spray and sprinkle with cornmeal. Place rolls, cut side up, on prepared pans. Cover and let rise until doubled, about 30 minutes.

5 Brush remaining milk over rolls. Bake at 325° for 30-35 minutes or until golden brown. Remove from pans to wire racks.

Rosemary Orange Bread

PREP: 20 MIN. + RISING • BAKE: 45 MIN. + COOLING
YIELD: 1 LOAF

Rosemary is the perfect herb to pair with homemade bread. When it is subtly combined with orange, the end result is divine!

Deidre Fallavollita *Vienna, Virginia*

- **1 package (1/4 ounce) active dry yeast**
- **3/4 cup warm water (110° to 115°)**
- **3/4 cup orange juice**
- **2 tablespoons honey**
- **1 tablespoon vegetable oil**
- **1 tablespoon minced fresh rosemary or 1 teaspoon dried rosemary, crushed**
- **2 teaspoons salt**
- **1 teaspoon grated orange peel**
- **3 3/4 to 4 1/2 cups all-purpose flour**
- **1 egg white**

Additional fresh rosemary and whole peppercorns, optional

1 In a large bowl, dissolve yeast in warm water. Add orange juice, honey, oil, rosemary, salt, orange peel and 2 cups flour; beat until smooth. Stir in enough remaining flour to form a soft dough.

2 Turn onto a floured surface; knead until smooth and elastic, about 6-8 minutes. Place in a greased bowl, turning once to grease top. Cover and let rise in a warm place until doubled, about 1 hour.

3 Punch dough down. Roll into a 15-in. x 1-in. rectangle. Starting at the short end, roll up jelly-roll style. Pinch edges to seal and shape into an oval. Place with seam side down on a greased baking sheet. Cover and let rise until nearly doubled, about 30 minutes.

4 Bake at 375° for 20 minutes. Whisk egg white; brush over loaf. Place small sprigs of rosemary and peppercorns on top if desired. Bake 25 minutes longer or until browned. Remove from pan to wire rack to cool.

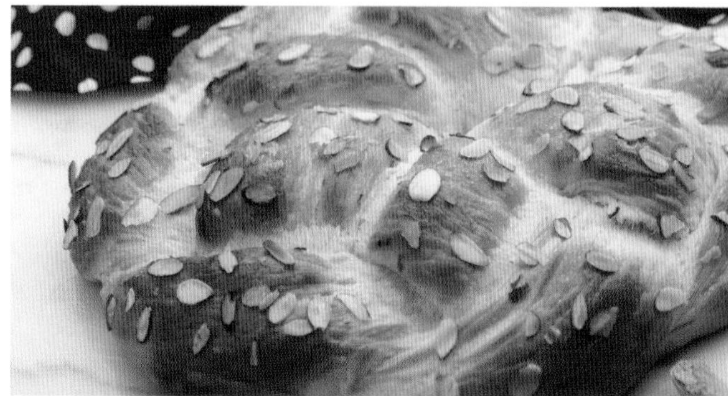

Delightful Holiday Bread

PREP: 40 MIN. + RISING • BAKE: 30 MIN.
YIELD: 1 LOAF (24 SLICES)

The first time I made this braided bread for Christmas, everyone loved it. In fact, when my sister-in-law came for a visit the following July, she asked me to teach her how to make it.

Cheri Neustifter *Sturtevant, Wisconsin*

- **2 packages (1/4 ounce each) active dry yeast**
- **1 3/4 cups warm water (110° to 115°)**
- **2 eggs**
- **3 tablespoons sugar**
- **2 tablespoons almond extract**
- **2 tablespoons canola oil**
- **1 1/2 teaspoons salt**
- **5 3/4 to 6 1/4 cups all-purpose flour**

TOPPING:

- **1 egg**
- **1 tablespoon water**
- **5 teaspoons sugar**
- **3 tablespoons sliced almonds**

1 In a large bowl, dissolve yeast in warm water. Add the eggs, sugar, extract, oil, salt and 4 cups flour; beat until smooth. Stir in enough remaining flour to form a soft dough (dough will be sticky).

2 Turn onto a lightly floured surface; knead until smooth and elastic, about 6-8 minutes. Place in a large bowl coated with cooking spray; turn once to coat top. Cover and let rise until doubled, about 1 hour.

3 Punch dough down; turn onto a lightly floured surface. Divide into thirds; shape each portion into a 20-in. rope. Place ropes on a large baking sheet coated with cooking spray; braid. Pinch ends together, forming a round loaf. Cover and let rise until doubled, about 40 minutes.

4 Beat egg and water; brush over loaf. Sprinkle with sugar and almonds. Bake at 350° for 30-35 minutes or until golden brown. Remove to a wire rack.

Raspberry-Cream Cheese Ladder Loaves

PREP: 45 MIN. + RISING • BAKE: 15 MIN. + COOLING
YIELD: 2 LOAVES (8 SLICES EACH)

Created by my dear friend Debbie, this is a delicious way to start your day. The bread may be sprinkled with granulated sugar before baking if desired.

Char Ouellette *Colton, Oregon*

- **3¾ to 4¼ cups all-purpose flour, divided**
- **¼ cup sugar**
- **1 package (¼ ounce) quick-rise yeast**
- **1¼ teaspoons salt**
- **1 teaspoon baking powder**
- **½ cup buttermilk**
- **½ cup sour cream**
- **¼ cup butter, cubed**
- **¼ cup water**
- **1 egg**
- **½ teaspoon almond extract**

FILLING:

- **1 package (8 ounces) cream cheese, softened**
- **¼ cup sugar**
- **3 tablespoons all-purpose flour**
- **1 egg yolk**
- **⅓ cup seedless raspberry jam**

1 In a large bowl, combine 2 cups flour, sugar, yeast, salt and baking powder. In a small saucepan, heat the buttermilk, sour cream, butter and water to 120°-130°; add to dry ingredients. Beat on medium speed for 2 minutes. Add the egg, extract and ½ cup flour; beat 2 minutes longer. Stir in enough remaining flour to form a soft dough.

2 Turn dough onto a floured surface; knead until smooth and elastic, about 6-8 minutes. Cover and let rest for 10 minutes.

3 Meanwhile, in a small bowl, beat the cream cheese, sugar, flour and egg yolk until smooth; set aside.

4 Divide dough in half. Roll each piece into a 12-in. x 10-in. rectangle; place on greased baking sheets. Spread cheese mixture down the center of each rectangle. Stir jam; spoon over cheese mixture.

5 On each long side, cut ¾-in.-wide strips about 2½ in. into center. Starting at one end, fold alternating strips at an angle across filling; pinch ends to seal. Cover and let rise until doubled, about 1 hour.

6 Bake at 350° for 15-19 minutes or until golden brown. Cool on wire racks. Store leftovers in refrigerator.

Tomato & Brie Focaccia

PREP: 20 MIN. + RISING • BAKE: 25 MIN. • YIELD: 12 SERVINGS

Combine tender yeast bread with creamy melted Brie cheese and tomatoes, and you've got an appetizer that guests will line up for. The focaccia can also make an ideal side for salad or soup.

Laurie Figone *Petaluma, California*

- **2½ to 3 cups all-purpose flour**
- **2 packages (¼ ounce each) quick-rise yeast**
- **1 teaspoon sugar**
- **1 teaspoon salt**
- **1 cup water**
- **¼ cup plus 1 tablespoon olive oil, divided**
- **1 can (14½ ounces) diced tomatoes, drained**
- **2 garlic cloves, minced**
- **1 teaspoon Italian seasoning**
- **6 ounces Brie cheese, cut into ½-inch cubes**

1 In a large bowl, combine 2 cups flour, yeast, sugar and salt. In a small saucepan, heat the water and ¼ cup oil to 120°-130°. Add to dry ingredients; beat just until moistened. Stir in enough remaining flour to form a soft dough.

2 Turn onto a floured surface; knead until smooth and elastic, about 6-8 minutes. Place in a greased bowl, turning once to grease the top. Cover and let rise for 20 minutes.

3 Punch dough down. Press into a greased 13-in. x 9-in. baking pan. Cover and let rest for 10 minutes.

4 In a small bowl, combine the tomatoes, garlic, Italian seasoning and remaining oil. Spread over dough; top with cheese. Bake at 375° for 25-30 minutes or until golden brown and cheese is melted. Place pan on a wire rack.

Tomato & Olive Bread

PREP: 30 MIN. + RISING • BAKE: 15 MIN. + COOLING
YIELD: 1 MINI LOAF (6 SLICES)

Here is the perfect sidekick for spaghetti and meatballs or a good steak. Pesto and ripe olives give the loaf a distinctive flavor that prompts recipe requests.

Ann Baker *Texarkana, Texas*

- **1⅛ teaspoons active dry yeast**
- **¼ cup warm water (110° to 115°)**
- **1 tablespoon grated Parmesan cheese**
- **1 tablespoon chopped ripe olives**
- **1 tablespoon olive oil**
- **1 tablespoon sun-dried tomato pesto**
- **1 tablespoon egg white**
- **2¼ teaspoons sugar**
- **⅛ teaspoon salt**
- **1 to 1¼ cups all-purpose flour**

1 In a small bowl, dissolve yeast in warm water. Add the cheese, olives, oil, pesto, egg white, sugar, salt and ¾ cup flour. Beat until smooth. Stir in enough remaining flour to form a soft dough.

2 Turn onto a lightly floured surface; knead until smooth and elastic, about 6-8 minutes. Place in a bowl coated with cooking spray, turning once to coat the top. Cover and let rise in a warm place until doubled, about 1 hour.

3 Punch dough down; shape into a loaf. Place in a 5¾-in. x 3-in. x 2-in. loaf pan coated with cooking spray. Cover and let rise until doubled, about 20 minutes.

4 Bake at 350° for 15-20 minutes or until golden brown. Remove from pan to a wire rack to cool.

MEASURING YEAST

>> Envelopes of yeast generally weigh 1/4 ounce each and measure approximately 2¼ teaspoons. If your recipe calls for less yeast, just measure the amount called for from an individual packet, then fold the packet closed and store remaining yeast in the fridge for next time.

Vanilla Cinnamon Rolls

PREP: 30 MIN. + RISING • BAKE: 20 MIN. • YIELD: 32 ROLLS

This is the best recipe I have found for cinnamon rolls. They're so tender with a delightful vanilla flavor and yummy frosting.

Linda Martin *Warsaw, Indiana*

- **2 cups cold milk**
- **1 package (3.4 ounces) instant vanilla pudding mix**
- **2 packages (¼ ounce each) active dry yeast**
- **½ cup warm water (110° to 115°)**
- **½ cup plus 2 tablespoons butter, melted, divided**
- **2 eggs**
- **2 tablespoons sugar**
- **1 teaspoon salt**
- **6 cups all-purpose flour**
- **½ cup packed brown sugar**
- **1 teaspoon ground cinnamon**

FROSTING:

- **1 cup packed brown sugar**
- **½ cup heavy whipping cream**
- **½ cup butter, cubed**
- **2 cups confectioners' sugar**

1 In a large bowl, whisk milk and pudding mix for 2 minutes. Let stand for 2 minutes or until soft set; set aside.

2 In a large bowl, dissolve yeast in warm water. Add ½ cup butter, eggs, sugar, salt and 2 cups flour. Beat on medium speed for 3 minutes. Add pudding; beat until smooth. Stir in enough remaining flour to form a soft dough (dough will be sticky).

3 Turn onto a floured surface; knead until smooth and elastic, about 6-8 minutes. Place in a greased bowl, turning once to grease top. Cover and let rise in a warm place until doubled, about 1 hour.

4 Punch dough down. Turn onto a floured surface; divide in half. Roll each portion into an 18-in. x 11-in. rectangle; brush with remaining butter. Combine brown sugar and cinnamon; sprinkle over dough to within ½ in. of edges.

5 Roll up jelly-roll style, starting with a long side; pinch seams to seal. Cut each roll into 16 slices. Place cut side down in two greased 13-in. x 9-in. baking dishes. Cover and let rise until doubled, about 30 minutes.

6 Bake at 350° for 20-25 minutes or until golden brown. Meanwhile, in a large saucepan, combine the brown sugar, cream and butter. Bring to a boil; cook and stir for 2 minutes. Remove from the heat. Beat in confectioners' sugar with a hand mixer until creamy. Frost warm rolls. Serve warm.

Pepper Asiago Loaf

PREP: 10 MIN. • BAKE: 3-4 HOURS
YIELD: 1 LOAF (16 SLICES)

With its golden crust and tender interior, this high, rustic-looking white bread is a great addition to any main course.

Lois Kinneberg *Phoenix, Arizona*

- **1 cup water (70° to 80°)**
- **1 egg**
- **1 tablespoon butter, melted**
- **½ cup nonfat dry milk powder**
- **½ cup shredded Asiago cheese**
- **4½ teaspoons chopped green onion**
- **1 tablespoon sugar**
- **1¼ teaspoons salt**
- **½ teaspoon coarsely ground pepper**
- **3 cups bread flour**
- **2¼ teaspoons active dry yeast**

1 In bread machine pan, place all ingredients in order suggested by manufacturer. Select basic bread setting. Choose crust color and loaf size if available.

2 Bake according to bread machine directions (check the dough after 5 minutes of mixing; add 1 to 2 tablespoons of water or flour if needed).

EDITOR'S NOTE: We recommend you do not use a bread machine's time-delay feature for this recipe.

Honey Wheat Breadsticks

**PREP: 30 MIN. + RISING • BAKE: 10 MIN.
YIELD: 16 BREADSTICKS**

Not only are these breadsticks delicious, but they come together very easily. Whole wheat flour and a little honey help give them a wholesome taste and keep them on the healthy side.

Ted Van Schoick *Jersey Shore, Pennsylvania*

- **1⅓ cups water (70° to 80°)**
- **3 tablespoons honey**
- **2 tablespoons canola oil**
- **1½ teaspoons salt**
- **2 cups bread flour**
- **2 cups whole wheat flour**
- **3 teaspoons active dry yeast**

1 In bread machine pan, place all ingredients in order suggested by manufacturer. Select dough setting (check dough after 5 minutes of mixing; add 1 to 2 tablespoons of water or flour if needed.

2 When cycle is completed, turn dough onto a lightly floured surface. Divide into 16 portions; shape each into a ball. Roll each into an 8-in. rope. Place 2 in. apart on greased baking sheets.

3 Cover and let rise in a warm place until doubled, about 30 minutes. Bake at 375° for 10-12 minutes or until golden brown. Remove to wire racks.

Cran-Apple Tea Ring

PREP: 45 MIN. + RISING • BAKE: 20 MIN. + COOLING • YIELD: 16 SERVINGS

A comforting combination of cranberries, apples and walnuts makes this tea ring a lovely addition to brunch or weekend morning. Invite friends and family over to enjoy a few slices over coffee.

Nellie Grimes *Jacksonville, Texas*

- **1 package (¼ ounce) active dry yeast**
- **¼ cup warm water (110° to 115°)**
- **½ cup warm fat-free milk (110° to 115°)**
- **1 egg**
- **2 tablespoons butter, softened**
- **1 tablespoon grated orange peel**
- **1 teaspoon salt**
- **3 tablespoons plus ½ cup sugar, divided**
- **2¾ to 3¼ cups all-purpose flour**
- **1 cup thinly sliced peeled apple**
- **1 cup dried cranberries**
- **½ cup chopped walnuts, toasted**
- **1½ teaspoons ground cinnamon**
- **1 egg white**
- **1 tablespoon water**
- **½ cup confectioners' sugar**
- **1 tablespoon orange juice**

1 In a large bowl, dissolve yeast in warm water. Add milk, egg, butter, orange peel, salt, 3 tablespoons sugar and 1 cup flour; beat until smooth. Stir in enough remaining flour to form a soft dough.

2 Turn onto a floured surface; knead until smooth and elastic, about 6-8 minutes. Place in a bowl coated with cooking spray; turn once to coat top. Cover and let rise in a warm place for 1 hour.

3 In a bowl, toss the apple, cranberries, walnuts, cinnamon and remaining sugar; set aside. Punch dough down; turn onto a lightly floured surface. Roll into a 20-in. x 10-in. rectangle. Combine egg white and water; chill 3 tablespoons. Brush remaining mixture over dough. Spoon fruit mixture to within 1 in. of edges. Roll up tightly jelly-roll style, starting with a long side; seal ends.

4 Place seam side down in a 15-in. x 10-in. x 1-in. baking pan coated with cooking spray; pinch ends to form a ring. With scissors, cut from outside edge two-thirds of the way toward center of ring at 1-in. intervals. Separate strips slightly; twist so filling shows. Cover and let rise until doubled, about 40 minutes.

5 Brush with reserved egg white mixture. Bake at 375° for 20-25 minutes or until golden brown (cover with foil during the last 10 minutes). Remove to a wire rack to cool. Combine confectioners' sugar and orange juice; drizzle over ring.

Hungarian Nut Rolls

PREP: 40 MIN. + RISING • BAKE: 30 MIN. + COOLING
YIELD: 4 LOAVES (12 SLICES EACH)

It isn't officially Christmas until I've made this treasured recipe from my husband's grandmother.

Donna Bardocz *Howell, Michigan*

- **2 packages (¼ ounce each) active dry yeast**
- **½ cup warm 2% milk (110° to 115°)**
- **¼ cup plus 2 tablespoons sugar**
- **¾ teaspoon salt**
- **1 cup butter, softened**
- **1 cup (8 ounces) sour cream**
- **3 eggs, lightly beaten**
- **6 to 6½ cups all-purpose flour**

FILLING:

- **1¼ cups sugar**
- **½ cup butter, cubed**
- **1 egg**
- **½ teaspoon ground cinnamon**
- **4½ cups ground walnuts**
- **1 large apple, peeled and grated**

ICING:

- **2 cups confectioners' sugar**
- **2 to 3 tablespoons 2% milk**

1 In a large bowl, dissolve yeast in warm milk. Add sugar, salt, butter, sour cream, eggs and 3 cups flour. Beat on medium speed for 3 minutes. Beat until smooth. Stir in enough remaining flour to form a soft dough (dough will be sticky). Turn onto a floured surface; knead until smooth and elastic, about 6-8 minutes. Place in a greased bowl, turning once to grease top. Cover and let rise in a warm place until doubled, about 1 hour.

2 Meanwhile, in a large saucepan, combine the sugar, butter, egg and cinnamon. Cook and stir over medium heat until mixture reaches 160° or is thick enough to coat the back of a metal spoon. Remove from the heat; gently stir in walnuts and apple. Cool completely.

3 Punch dough down. Turn onto a lightly floured surface; divide into four portions. Roll each into a 12-in. x 10-in. rectangle. Spread filling to within ½ in. of edges. Roll up jelly-roll style, starting with a long side; pinch seams to seal. Place seam side down on greased baking sheets. Cover and let rise until doubled, about 30 minutes.

4 Bake at 350° for 30-40 minutes or until lightly browned. Remove from pans to wire racks to cool. Meanwhile, in a small bowl, combine confectioner's sugar and enough milk to achieve desired consistency; drizzle over warm loaves.

Soft Italian Breadsticks

PREP: 25 MIN. + RISING • BAKE: 15 MIN.
YIELD: 2 DOZEN

Use the dough-only cycle on your bread machine to prepare these melt-in-your-mouth favorites. The soft, chewy breadsticks are irresistible when brushed with butter and sprinkled with Parmesan cheese. They're the perfect accompaniment to soups or Italian entrees.

Christy Eichelberger *Jesup, Iowa*

- **1 cup water (70° to 80°)**
- **3 tablespoons butter, softened**
- **1½ teaspoons salt**
- **3 cups bread flour**
- **2 tablespoons sugar**
- **1 teaspoon Italian seasoning**
- **1 teaspoon garlic powder**
- **2¼ teaspoons active dry yeast**

TOPPING:

- **1 tablespoon butter, melted**
- **1 tablespoon grated Parmesan cheese**

1 In bread machine pan, place the water, butter, salt, flour, sugar, Italian seasoning, garlic powder and yeast in order suggested by manufacturer. Select dough setting (check dough after 5 minutes of mixing; add 1 to 2 tablespoons of water or flour if needed).

2 When cycle is completed, turn dough onto a lightly floured surface; divide in half. Cut each portion into 12 pieces; roll each into a 4-in. to 6-in. rope. Place 2 in. apart on greased baking sheets. Cover and let rise in a warm place until doubled, about 20 minutes.

3 Bake at 350° for 15-18 minutes or until golden brown. Immediately brush with butter; sprinkle with Parmesan cheese. Serve warm.

Hearty Sweet Potato Braids

PREP: 45 MIN. + RISING • BAKE: 30 MIN. • YIELD: 2 LOAVES (12 SLICES EACH)

We make these delicious and nutritious loaves during the holidays. Thyme gives the pretty braids a lovely flavor. For a change, I will use safflower oil in this recipe.

Suzanne Kesel *Cohocton, New York*

- **1 package (¼ ounce) active dry yeast**
- **¼ cup warm water (110° to 115°)**
- **1½ cups mashed sweet potatoes, room temperature**
- **1 cup warm fat-free milk (110° to 115°)**
- **¼ cup canola oil**
- **3 tablespoons honey**
- **1 cup all-purpose flour**
- **½ cup yellow cornmeal**
- **2 teaspoons salt**
- **1 teaspoon dried thyme**
- **2¾ to 3¼ cups whole wheat flour**
- **1 tablespoon cold fat-free milk**

1 In a large bowl, dissolve yeast in warm water. Add the sweet potatoes, milk, oil, honey, all-purpose flour, cornmeal, salt, thyme and 2 cups whole wheat flour; beat until smooth. Stir in enough remaining whole wheat flour to form a firm dough.

2 Turn onto a lightly floured surface. Knead until smooth and elastic, about 6-8 minutes. Place in a bowl coated with cooking spray; turn once to coat top. Cover and let rise in a warm place until doubled, about 1 hour.

3 Punch dough down; divide into six equal portions. Shape each into a 20-in. rope. Place three ropes on a baking sheet coated with cooking spray; braid. Pinch ends to seal and tuck under. Repeat with remaining ropes. Cover and let rise in a warm place until doubled, about 35 minutes.

4 Brush loaves with cold milk. Bake at 350° for 30-35 minutes or until golden brown. Remove to wire racks.

Frosted Cinnamon Rolls

PREP: 35 MIN. + RISING • BAKE: 20 MIN.
YIELD: 21 ROLLS

My pretty cinnamon rolls are absolutely marvelous and taste just like the ones sold at the mall. Topped with a sweet cream cheese frosting, they're best served warm with steaming cups of coffee.

Velma Horton *LaGrange, California*

- **1 cup warm milk (70° to 80°)**
- **¼ cup water (70° to 80°)**
- **¼ cup butter, softened**
- **1 egg**
- **1 teaspoon salt**
- **4 cups bread flour**
- **¼ cup instant vanilla pudding mix**
- **1 tablespoon sugar**
- **1 tablespoon active dry yeast**

FILLING:

- **¼ cup butter, softened**
- **1 cup packed brown sugar**
- **2 teaspoons ground cinnamon**

FROSTING:

- **4 ounces cream cheese, softened**
- **¼ cup butter, softened**
- **1½ cups confectioners' sugar**
- **1½ teaspoons milk**
- **½ teaspoon vanilla extract**

1 In bread machine pan, place first nine ingredients in order suggested by the manufacturer. Select dough setting (check dough after 5 minutes of mixing; add 1 to 2 tablespoons water or flour if needed).

2 When cycle is completed, turn dough onto lightly floured surface. Roll into a 17-in. x 10-in. rectangle. Spread with butter; sprinkle with brown sugar and cinnamon. Roll up, jelly-roll style, starting from a long side; pinch seam to seal. Cut into 21 slices.

3 Place 12 slices, cut side down, in a greased 13-in. x 9-in. baking pan and nine slices in a 9-in. square pan. Cover; let rise in a warm place until doubled, about 45 minutes.

4 Bake at 350° for 20-25 minutes or until golden brown. Cool for 10 minutes before removing from pans to wire racks to cool. In a large bowl, beat frosting ingredients until smooth. Frost warm rolls. Store in refrigerator.

EDITOR'S NOTE: We recommend you do not use a bread machine's time-delay feature for this recipe.

Streusel Pumpkin Sweet Rolls

PREP: 45 MIN. + RISING • BAKE: 20 MIN.
YIELD: 2 DOZEN

My sons love anything that tastes like pumpkin, including these yummy rolls. I can't think of an easier way to get vitamin A into them!

Julie Fehr *Martensville, Saskatchewan*

- **1 package (¼ ounce) active dry yeast**
- **1¼ cups warm 2% milk (110° to 115°)**
- **1 cup solid-pack pumpkin**
- **½ cup sugar**
- **½ cup butter, melted**
- **1 teaspoon salt**
- **4¾ to 5¾ cups all-purpose flour**

STREUSEL:

- **1½ cups all-purpose flour**
- **1 cup packed brown sugar**
- **1 teaspoon ground cinnamon**
- **½ teaspoon ground allspice**
- **¾ cup cold butter, cubed**

GLAZE:

- **1 cup confectioners' sugar**
- **½ teaspoon vanilla extract**
- **1 to 2 tablespoons 2% milk**

1 In a large bowl, dissolve yeast in warm milk. Add the pumpkin, sugar, butter, salt and 4¾ cups flour. Beat until smooth. Stir in enough remaining flour to form a soft dough (dough will be sticky).

2 Turn onto a floured surface; knead until smooth and elastic, about 6-8 minutes. Place in a greased bowl, turning once to grease top. Cover and let rise in a warm place until doubled, about 1 hour.

3 Punch dough down; divide in half. Roll each portion into a 12-in. x 10-in. rectangle. Combine the flour, brown sugar, cinnamon and allspice; cut in butter until crumbly. Set aside 1 cup.

4 Sprinkle remaining streusel over dough to within ½ in. of edges; press down lightly. Roll up jelly-roll style, starting with a long side; pinch seams to seal.

5 Cut each roll into 12 slices. Place cut side down in two greased 13-in. x 9-in. baking pans. Sprinkle with reserved streusel. Cover and let rise until doubled, about 30 minutes.

6 Bake at 375° for 20-25 minutes or until golden brown. Meanwhile, combine the confectioners' sugar, vanilla and enough milk to achieve desired consistency; drizzle over rolls. Serve warm.

Garlic Cheese Breadsticks

PREP: 45 MIN. + RISING • BAKE: 10 MIN. • YIELD: 32 BREADSTICKS

Breadsticks complement so many dishes. I like to pair these chewy bites with Italian dishes, salads and soups. When I use bread flour instead of all-purpose flour, the texture is even lighter.

Ann Volner *Maryville, Missouri*

- **1 package (¼ ounce) active dry yeast**
- **1½ cups warm water (110° to 115°)**
- **½ cup warm 2% milk (110° to 115°)**
- **3 tablespoons sugar**
- **3 tablespoons butter, melted**
- **1½ teaspoons salt**
- **½ teaspoon baking soda**
- **4½ to 5½ cups all-purpose flour**

TOPPING:

- **½ cup butter, melted**
- **1 cup grated Parmesan cheese**
- **4½ teaspoons Italian seasoning**
- **1 teaspoon garlic powder**

1 In a large bowl, dissolve yeast in warm water and milk. Add the sugar, butter, salt, baking soda and 3 cups flour. Beat until smooth. Stir in enough remaining flour to form a firm dough.

1 Turn onto a floured surface; knead until smooth and elastic, about 6-8 minutes. Place in a greased bowl, turning once to grease the top. Cover and let rise in a warm place until doubled, about 1 hour.

2 Turn onto a lightly floured surface; cover and let rest for 10 minutes. Divide into 32 pieces. Shape each into a 4½-in. rope.

3 Place melted butter in a shallow bowl. Place cheese in a separate shallow bowl. Dip ropes in butter then coat with cheese. Place 3 in. apart on lightly greased baking sheets. Combine Italian seasoning and garlic powder; sprinkle over breadsticks. Cover and let rise until doubled, about 30 minutes.

4 Bake at 375° for 10-15 minutes or until golden brown. Remove to wire racks. Serve warm.

Multigrain Bread

PREP: 10 MIN. • BAKE: 3-4 HOURS
YIELD: 1 LOAF (2 POUNDS)

It's hard to get a good whole-grain bread where I live, so my bread machine comes in very handy when making this hearty loaf. I adapted it from an old recipe, and I've been enjoying it ever since.

Michele MacKinlay *Madoc, Ontario*

- **1 cup water (70° to 80°)**
- **2 tablespoons canola oil**
- **2 egg yolks**
- **¼ cup molasses**
- **1 teaspoon salt**
- **1½ cups bread flour**
- **1 cup whole wheat flour**
- **½ cup rye flour**
- **½ cup nonfat dry milk powder**
- **¼ cup quick-cooking oats**
- **¼ cup toasted wheat germ**
- **¼ cup cornmeal**
- **2¼ teaspoons active dry yeast**

1 In bread machine pan, place all ingredients in order suggested by the manufacturer. Select basic bread setting. Choose crust color and loaf size if available.

2 Bake according to bread machine directions (check dough after 5 minutes of mixing; add 1 to 2 tablespoons water or flour if needed).

EDITOR'S NOTE: We recommend you do not use a bread machine's time-delay feature for this recipe.

WINNERS
CIRCLE

cookies & candies

"C" is for cookie...and candies! Enjoy the very best of both worlds with this outstanding selection of sweet treats. Luscious fudge, decadent bonbons, chewy cookies and other heavenly delights are ready to satisfy even the biggest sweet tooth.

CINNAMON CHOCOLATE MINTIES, 231

Pecan Toffee Fudge

PREP: 20 MIN. + CHILLING • YIELD: 2½ POUNDS

This quick fudge is popular wherever it shows up. People love the creaminess and toffee bits. And it's so easy, even young children can help make it with a little supervision.

Diane Willey *Bozman, Maryland*

- **1 teaspoon butter**
- **1 package (8 ounces) cream cheese, softened**
- **3¾ cups confectioners' sugar**
- **6 ounces unsweetened chocolate, melted and cooled**
- **¼ teaspoon almond extract**

Dash salt

- **¼ cup coarsely chopped pecans**
- **¼ cup English toffee bits**

1 Line a 9-in. square pan with foil and grease the foil with butter; set aside. In a large bowl, beat cream cheese until fluffy. Gradually beat in confectioners' sugar. Beat in the melted chocolate, extract and salt until smooth. Stir in pecans and toffee bits.

2 Spread into prepared pan. Cover and refrigerate overnight or until firm. Using foil, lift fudge out of pan. Gently peel off foil; cut fudge into 1-in. squares. Store in an airtight container in the refrigerator.

CHOCOLATE LOVER'S TREAT

>> Here's a tip for all you die-hard chocolate lovers. Dip bite-size pieces of your favorite homemade fudge into a melted chocolate of your choice. Place on waxed paper until set and enjoy!

Chocolate Pretzel Cookies

PREP: 30 MIN. + CHILLING • BAKE: 5 MIN./BATCH + COOLING • YIELD: 4 DOZEN

These pretzel-shaped, buttery chocolate cookies are covered in a rich mocha glaze and drizzled with white chocolate. My family goes wild over their chocolaty crunch.

Priscilla Anderson *Salt Lake City, Utah*

- **½ cup butter, softened**
- **⅔ cup sugar**
- **1 egg**
- **2 ounces unsweetened chocolate, melted and cooled**
- **2 teaspoons vanilla extract**
- **1¾ cups all-purpose flour**
- **½ teaspoon salt**

MOCHA GLAZE:

- **1 cup (6 ounces) semisweet chocolate chips**
- **1 teaspoon shortening**
- **1 teaspoon light corn syrup**
- **1 cup confectioners' sugar**
- **4 to 5 tablespoons strong brewed coffee**
- **2 ounces white baking chocolate**

1 In a large bowl, cream butter and sugar until light and fluffy. Add the egg, chocolate and vanilla; mix well. Combine flour and salt; gradually add to creamed mixture and mix well. Cover and refrigerate for 1 hour or until firm.

2 Divide dough into fourths; form each portion into a 6-in. roll. Cut each roll into ½-in. slices; roll each into a 9-in. rope. Place ropes on greased baking sheets; form into pretzel shapes and space 2 in. apart. Bake at 400° for 5-7 minutes or until firm. Cool 1 minute before removing to wire racks to cool completely.

3 For glaze, in a microwave-safe bowl, melt the chocolate chips, shortening and corn syrup; stir until smooth. Stir in confectioners' sugar and enough coffee to make a smooth glaze.

4 Dip pretzels; allow excess to drip off. Place on waxed paper until set. Melt white chocolate. Drizzle with white chocolate; allow excess to drip off. Let stand until chocolate is completely set. Store in an airtight container.

Lime-in-the-Coconut Almond Bark

PREP: 10 MIN. • COOK: 5 MIN.+ CHILLING
YIELD: ABOUT 1 POUND

I love the combination of flavors in this tropical treat! It takes mere minutes to make. If you need something for a school or church bake sale, this will get you out of the kitchen in a flash.

Julie Beckwith *Crete, Illinois*

- **1 package (10 to 12 ounces) white baking chips**
- **4 teaspoons shortening**
- **2 to 4 drops green food coloring, optional**
- **½ cup flaked coconut, toasted**
- **½ cup chopped almonds, toasted**
- **4 teaspoons grated lime peel**

1 Line a 9-in. square baking pan with foil; set aside. In a microwave, melt chips and shortening; stir until smooth. Stir in food coloring if desired. Stir in the coconut, almonds and lime peel. Spread into prepared pan. Chill for 10-15 minutes or until firm.

2 Break into small pieces. Store in an airtight container at room temperature.

Raspberry-Almond Thumbprint Cookies

PREP: 40 MIN. + CHILLING • BAKE: 15 MIN./BATCH + COOLING • YIELD: 3½ DOZEN

People always comment on these crisp, buttery thumbprints, which deliver a hint of almond flavor, a touch of sweetness from the raspberry jam and a light drizzle of almond glaze.

Lana White *Roy, Washington*

- **1 cup butter, softened**
- **⅔ cup sugar**
- **½ teaspoon almond extract**
- **2 cups all-purpose flour**
- **½ cup seedless raspberry jam**

GLAZE:

- **⅓ cup confectioners' sugar**
- **½ teaspoon almond extract**
- **1 teaspoon water**

1 In a large bowl, cream butter, sugar and extract until light and fluffy. Add flour and mix well. Chill for 1 hour.

2 Roll into 1-in. balls. Place 2 in. apart on greased baking sheets. Using the end of a wooden spoon handle, make an indentation in the center of each; fill with ¼ teaspoon jam. Bake at 350° for 13-16 minutes or until the edges are lightly browned. Remove to wire racks to cool completely.

3 For glaze, in a small bowl, combine the confectioners' sugar, extract and water. Drizzle over cookies.

German Chocolate Thumbprints

PREP: 45 MIN. • BAKE: 10 MIN./BATCH + COOLING • YIELD: 4 DOZEN

At the holidays, I place these sweet bites in red or gold foil candy cups or on a red or gold foil doily for a festive presentation.

Donna Marie Ryan *Topsfield, Massachusetts*

- **½ cup semisweet chocolate chips**
- **1 tablespoon shortening**
- **½ cup butter, softened**
- **¾ cup sugar**
- **1 egg**
- **1 tablespoon strong brewed coffee**
- **1 teaspoon vanilla extract**
- **2 cups all-purpose flour**
- **1 tablespoon baking cocoa**
- **1 teaspoon baking powder**
- **¼ teaspoon salt**

FILLING:

- **¾ cup flaked coconut, toasted**
- **¾ cup chopped pecans, toasted**
- **1 teaspoon vanilla extract**
- **4 to 6 tablespoons sweetened condensed milk**

DRIZZLE:

- **½ cup semisweet chocolate chips**
- **1 tablespoon shortening**

1 In a microwave, melt chips and shortening; stir until smooth. Set aside. In a large bowl, cream butter and sugar until light and fluffy. Beat in the egg, coffee, vanilla and melted chocolate mixture. Combine the flour, cocoa, baking powder and salt; gradually add to creamed mixture and mix well.

2 Roll into 1-in. balls. Place 2 in. apart on greased baking sheets. Using the end of a wooden spoon handle, make an indentation in the center of each ball. Bake at 350° for 6-8 minutes or until firm. Remove to wire racks to cool completely.

3 Meanwhile, for filling, in a small bowl, combine the coconut, pecans and vanilla. Stir in enough milk to form a stiff mixture. Fill each cookie with a rounded teaspoonful of mixture. Melt chips with shortening; stir until smooth. Drizzle over cookies. Store in an airtight container.

Italian Rainbow Cookies

PREP: 35 MIN. • BAKE: 10 MIN./BATCH + CHILLING
YIELD: 11 DOZEN

My family has made these classic Italian cookies for generations, and this homemade version is so much better than the bakery variety. They are always a special treat during the holidays or any time of year!

Cindy Casazza *Hopewell, New Jersey*

- **4 eggs**
- **1 cup sugar**
- **3½ ounces almond paste, cut into small pieces**
- **1 cup all-purpose flour**
- **1 cup butter, melted and cooled**
- **½ teaspoon salt**
- **½ teaspoon almond extract**
- **6 to 8 drops red food coloring**
- **6 to 8 drops green food coloring**
- **¼ cup seedless raspberry jam**

GLAZE:

- **1 cup (6 ounces) semisweet chocolate chips**
- **1 teaspoon shortening**

1 In a large bowl, beat eggs and sugar for 2 to 3 minutes or until thick and lemon-colored. Gradually add almond paste; mix well. Gradually add the flour, butter, salt and extract.

2 Divide batter into thirds. Tint one portion red and one portion green; leave remaining portion plain. Spread one portion into each of three well-greased 11-in. x 7-in. baking dishes.

3 Bake at 375° for 7-11 minutes or until a toothpick inserted near the center comes out clean and edges begin to brown. Cool for 10 minutes before removing from pans to wire racks to cool completely.

4 Place red layer on waxed paper; spread with 2 tablespoons jam. Top with plain layer and remaining jam. Add green layer; press down gently.

5 For glaze, in a microwave, melt chocolate chips and shortening; stir until smooth. Spread half over green layer. Refrigerate for 20 minutes or until set. Turn over; spread remaining glaze over red layer. Refrigerate for 20 minutes or until set.

6 With a sharp knife, trim edges. Cut rectangle lengthwise into fourths. Cut each portion into ¼-in. slices.

Peanut Butter Oatmeal-Chip Cookies

PREP: 25 MIN. • BAKE: 10 MIN./BATCH
YIELD: 11 DOZEN

This is my husband's favorite, my students' favorite, my colleagues' favorite and frankly, it's my favorite, too It's just plain yummy, and the large yield makes it perfect for bake sales.

Dana Chew *Okemah, Oklahoma*

- **2½ cups butter, softened**
- **2 cups sugar**
- **2 cups packed brown sugar**
- **½ cup creamy peanut butter**
- **4 eggs**
- **2 teaspoons vanilla extract**
- **6 cups all-purpose flour**
- **2 teaspoons salt**
- **2 teaspoons baking soda**
- **½ teaspoon baking powder**
- **1 package (12 ounces) semisweet chocolate chips**
- **1 package (11 ounces) peanut butter and milk chocolate chips**
- **1 cup quick-cooking oats**

1 In a large bowl, cream the butter, sugars and peanut butter until light and fluffy. Beat in eggs and vanilla. Combine the flour, salt, baking soda and baking powder; gradually add to creamed mixture and mix well.

2 Stir in the chips and oats. Drop by rounded tablespoonfuls 2 in. apart onto ungreased baking sheets. Bake at 375° for 9-12 minutes or until golden brown.

3 Cool for 2 minutes before removing from pans to wire racks. Store in an airtight container.

Cinnamon Chocolate Minties

PREP: 45 MIN. • BAKE: 10 MIN./BATCH + COOLING • YIELD: ABOUT 4 DOZEN

These cookies are also great with white chocolate instead of semisweet. For a simple topping, you can also use powdered sugar with peppermint candies.

Barbara Estabrook *Rhinelander, Wisconsin*

- **½ cup butter, softened**
- **½ cup sugar**
- **½ cup packed brown sugar**
- **1 egg**
- **1 teaspoon vanilla extract**
- **1½ cups all-purpose flour**
- **⅓ cup baking cocoa**
- **1 teaspoon ground cinnamon**
- **¼ teaspoon baking soda**
- **⅓ cup coarsely crushed soft peppermint candies**
- **⅓ cup dark chocolate chips**

DRIZZLE:

- **½ cup semisweet chocolate chips**
- **½ teaspoon canola oil**
- **2 teaspoons finely crushed soft peppermint candies**

1 In a small bowl, cream butter and sugars until light and fluffy. Beat in egg and vanilla. Combine the flour, cocoa, cinnamon and baking soda; gradually add to creamed mixture and mix well. Fold in candies and dark chocolate chips.

2 Shape into 1-in. balls; place 1 in. apart on greased baking sheets. Flatten slightly. Bake at 350° for 6-8 minutes or until set. Remove to wire racks to cool completely.

3 In a small bowl, melt semisweet chips with oil; stir until smooth. Drizzle over cookies. Sprinkle with candies. Let stand until set. Store in an airtight container.

EDITOR'S NOTE: This recipe was tested with Bob's Sweet Stripes peppermint candies.

Sweet & Salty Candy

PREP: 15 MIN. • BAKE: 10 MIN. + COOLING
YIELD: ABOUT 1½ POUNDS

I've been making this candy for the past few years and serving it at teacher appreciation lunches and bake sales. It never fails to win praise from anyone who tries it. For bake sales, I break the candy up and package it in little cellophane bags from the craft store.

Anna Ginsberg *Austin, Texas*

- **2 cups miniature pretzels, coarsely crushed**
- **½ cup corn chips, coarsely crushed**
- **½ cup salted peanuts**
- **½ cup butter, cubed**
- **½ cup packed brown sugar**
- **1½ cups semisweet chocolate chips**

1 Line a 13-in. x 9-in. baking pan with foil and grease the foil; set aside. In a large bowl, combine the pretzels, corn chips and peanuts.

2 In a small saucepan, melt butter. Stir in brown sugar until melted. Bring to a boil, stirring frequently. Boil for 1 minute, stirring twice. Pour over pretzel mixture; toss to coat. Transfer to prepared pan.

3 Bake at 350° for 7 minutes. Sprinkle with chocolate chips. Bake 1-2 minutes longer or until chips are softened. Spread over top. Cool on a wire rack for 1 hour. Break into pieces. Store in an airtight container.

Hint-of-Berry Bonbons

PREP: 1½ HOURS + CHILLING • YIELD: ABOUT 4½ DOZEN

You'll have a hard time eating just one of these heavenly sweets. Inside the rich milk chocolate coating is a fudgy center with a hint of strawberry. Their white chocolate drizzle makes these bonbons even more special.

Brenda Hoffman *Stanton, Michigan*

- **1 package (8 ounces) cream cheese, softened**
- **1 cup milk chocolate chips, melted and cooled**
- **¾ cup crushed vanilla wafers (about 25 wafers)**
- **¼ cup strawberry preserves**
- **15 ounces milk chocolate candy coating, chopped**
- **2 ounces white baking chocolate**

1 In a large bowl, beat cream cheese until fluffy. Beat in melted chocolate chips. Stir in wafer crumbs and preserves. Cover and refrigerate for 2 hours or until easy to handle.

2 Divide mixture in half. Return one portion to refrigerator. Shape remaining mixture into 1-in. balls. Place on a waxed paper-lined pan; refrigerate. Repeat with remaining mixture.

3 In a microwave, melt milk chocolate coating; stir until smooth. Dip balls in coating; allow excess to drip off. Place on waxed paper-lined baking sheets. Refrigerate until set.

4 Melt white chocolate; stir until smooth. Transfer to a heavy-duty resealable plastic bag; cut a small hole in a corner of bag. Decorate candies with white chocolate. Store in an airtight container in the refrigerator.

Iced Cinnamon Chip Cookies

PREP: 30 MIN. • BAKE: 10 MIN./BATCH + COOLING
YIELD: ABOUT 3½ DOZEN

I take these cookies to family gatherings and socials and give them as gifts to friends. The cinnamon flavor and soft frosting make them special. My mom helped me bake my first batch of cookies when I was 8!

Katie Jean Boyd *Roachdale, Indiana*

- **1 cup butter, softened**
- **¾ cup sugar**
- **¾ cup packed brown sugar**
- **2 eggs**
- **1 teaspoon vanilla extract**
- **3 cups all-purpose flour**
- **1 teaspoon baking soda**
- **1 teaspoon salt**
- **1 package (10 ounces) cinnamon baking chips**

ICING:

- **¼ cup butter, melted**
- **¼ cup shortening**
- **1¼ cups confectioners' sugar**
- **1 tablespoon milk**
- **¾ teaspoon vanilla extract**

1 In a large bowl, cream butter and sugars until light and fluffy. Beat in eggs and vanilla. Combine the flour, baking soda and salt; gradually add to creamed mixture and mix well. Fold in cinnamon chips.

2 Drop by rounded tablespoonfuls 2 in. apart onto ungreased baking sheets. Bake at 350° for 10-12 minutes or until golden brown. Remove to wire racks to cool.

3 In a small bowl, combine icing ingredients; beat on high speed for 1-2 minutes or until fluffy. Spread over cooled cookies.

Almost a Candy Bar

PREP: 15 MIN. • BAKE: 15 MIN. + CHILLING • YIELD: 3 DOZEN

Candy bars and marshmallows are my favorite sweets, so this recipe was a cinch to invent. I've yet to find anyone who doesn't enjoy it! With all the different layers and flavors, the bars are sure to please just about everyone.

Barb Wyman *Hankinson, North Dakota*

- **1 tube (16½ ounces) refrigerated chocolate chip cookie dough**
- **4 nutty s'mores trail mix bars (1.23 ounces each), chopped**
- **1 package (10 to 11 ounces) butterscotch chips**
- **2½ cups miniature marshmallows**
- **1 cup chopped walnuts**
- **1½ cups miniature pretzels**
- **1 package (10 ounces) peanut butter chips**
- **¾ cup light corn syrup**
- **¼ cup butter, cubed**
- **1 package (11½ ounces) milk chocolate chips**

1 Let dough stand at room temperature for 5-10 minutes to soften. In a large bowl, combine dough and trail mix bars. Press into an ungreased 13-in. x 9-in. baking pan. Bake, uncovered, at 350° for 10-12 minutes or until golden brown.

2 Sprinkle with butterscotch chips and marshmallows. Bake 3-4 minutes longer or until marshmallows begin to brown. Sprinkle with walnuts; arrange pretzels over the top. In a small saucepan, melt the peanut butter chips, corn syrup and butter; spoon over bars.

3 In a microwave, melt chocolate chips; stir until smooth. Spread or drizzle over bars. Refrigerate for 1 hour or until firm before cutting.

Hawaiian Turtle Cups

PREP: 20 MIN. + CHILLING • YIELD: 1 DOZEN

Because my mother-in-law loves macadamia nuts and my daughter prefers white chocolate to milk chocolate, I came up with this fun twist on classic turtle candy. Now a family favorite, it goes together in minutes for great gifts, too!

Larisa Sarver *LaSalle, Illinois*

- **1½ cups white baking chips**
- **½ cup macadamia nuts, chopped**
- **18 caramels**
- **2 teaspoons heavy whipping cream**
- **12 dried pineapple pieces, chopped**

1 In a microwave, melt chips; stir until smooth. Pour a teaspoonful each into 12 greased miniature muffin cups; set aside remaining melted chips. Sprinkle the center of each muffin cup with nuts.

2 In a microwave, melt caramels and cream; stir until smooth. Pour over nuts. Reheat reserved chips if necessary; pour over caramel mixture. Top each with pineapple.

3 Chill for 30 minutes or until set. Carefully run a knife around the edge of each muffin cup to loosen candy.

Peppermint Meltaways

PREP: 30 MIN. • BAKE: 10 MIN./BATCH + COOLING • YIELD: 3½ DOZEN

Turn to this minty gem when you need a festive-looking addition to your cookie platter. I often cover a plate of these meltaways with red or green plastic wrap and a bright holiday bow in one corner. And yes, they really do melt in your mouth!

Denise Wheeler *Newaygo, Michigan*

- **1 cup butter, softened**
- **½ cup confectioners' sugar**
- **½ teaspoon peppermint extract**
- **1¼ cups all-purpose flour**
- **½ cup cornstarch**

FROSTING:

- **2 tablespoons butter, softened**
- **1½ cups confectioners' sugar**
- **2 tablespoons 2% milk**
- **¼ teaspoon peppermint extract**
- **2 to 3 drops red food coloring, optional**
- **½ cup crushed peppermint candies**

1 In a small bowl, cream butter and confectioners' sugar until light and fluffy. Beat in extract. Combine flour and cornstarch; gradually add to creamed mixture and mix well.

2 Shape into 1-in. balls. Place 2 in. apart on ungreased baking sheets. Bake at 350° for 10-12 minutes or until bottoms are lightly browned. Remove to wire racks to cool.

3 In a small bowl, beat butter until fluffy. Add the confectioners' sugar, milk, extract and food coloring if desired; beat until smooth. Spread over cooled cookies; sprinkle with crushed candies. Store in an airtight container.

Macadamia-Coconut Candy Clusters

PREP: 25 MIN. + STANDING • YIELD: 3½ DOZEN

Great for bake sales, teacher gifts or candy platters, these white chocolate confections are a nice change from milk or dark chocolate.

Lori Bondurant *Paducah, Kentucky*

- **1 package (10 to 12 ounces) white baking chips**
- **2 teaspoons shortening**
- **1 cup flaked coconut, toasted**
- **½ cup crisp rice cereal**
- **½ cup chopped macadamia nuts, toasted**

1 In a microwave, melt baking chips and shortening; stir until smooth. Add the coconut, cereal and nuts.

2 Drop by teaspoonfuls onto waxed paper; let stand until set. Store in an airtight container at room temperature.

Watermelon Slice Cookies

PREP: 25 MIN. + CHILLING • BAKE: 10 MIN./BATCH
YIELD: ABOUT 3 DOZEN

When I made these rich butter cookies for a community event, one neighbor thought they were so attractive that she kept one in her freezer for the longest time so she could show it to friends and relatives.

Sue Ann Benham *Valparaiso, Indiana*

- **¾ cup butter, softened**
- **¾ cup sugar**
- **1 egg**
- **½ teaspoon almond extract**
- **2 cups all-purpose flour**
- **¼ teaspoon baking powder**
- **⅛ teaspoon salt**

Red and green gel food coloring

- **⅓ cup raisins**
- **1 teaspoon sesame seeds**

1 In a large bowl, cream butter and sugar until light and fluffy. Beat in egg and extract. Combine the flour, baking powder and salt; gradually add to creamed mixture and mix well. Set aside 1 cup of dough.

2 Tint remaining dough red; shape into a 3½-in.-long log. Wrap in plastic wrap. Tint ⅓ cup of the reserved dough green; wrap in plastic wrap. Wrap remaining plain dough. Refrigerate for 2 hours or until firm.

3 On a lightly floured surface, roll plain dough into a 8½-in. x 3½-in. rectangle. Place red dough log on the end of a short side of the rectangle; roll up.

4 Roll green dough into a 10-in. x 3½-in. rectangle. Place red and white log on the end of a short side of green dough; roll up. Wrap in plastic wrap; refrigerate overnight.

5 Unwrap and cut into 3/16-in. slices (just less than ¼ in.). Place 2 in. apart on ungreased baking sheets. Cut raisins into small pieces. Lightly press raisin bits and sesame seeds into red dough to resemble watermelon seeds.

6 Bake at 350° for 9-11 minutes or until firm. Immediately cut cookies in half. Remove to wire racks to cool.

Chunky Fruit 'n' Nut Fudge

PREP: 30 MIN. + STANDING • YIELD: 6¾ POUNDS

Variations on fudge are endless, but this recipe is my favorite. Besides five types of chips, it includes everything from dried fruit to nuts. Every bite is packed with flavor and crunch.

Allene Bary-Cooper *Wichita Falls, Texas*

- **1 package (11 ounces) dried cherries**
- **1 cup dried cranberries**
- **1½ teaspoons plus ¾ cup butter, softened, divided**
- **1 can (14 ounces) sweetened condensed milk**
- **1 package (12 ounces) miniature semisweet chocolate chips**
- **1 package (11½ ounces) milk chocolate chips**
- **1 package (10 to 11 ounces) butterscotch chips**
- **1 package (10 ounces) peanut butter chips**
- **3 tablespoons heavy whipping cream**
- **1 jar (7 ounces) marshmallow creme**
- **½ teaspoon almond or rum extract**
- **1½ cups unsalted cashew halves**
- **1 package (11½ ounces) semisweet chocolate chunks**

1 In a large bowl, combine cherries and cranberries. Add enough warm water to cover; set aside. Line a 15-in. x 10-in. x 1-in. pan with foil and grease the foil with 1½ teaspoons butter; set aside.

2 In a large heavy saucepan, melt remaining butter. Stir in the milk, chips and whipping cream. Cook and stir over low heat for 15-20 minutes or until chips are melted and mixture is smooth and blended (mixture will first appear separated, but continue stirring until fully blended). Remove from the heat; stir in marshmallow creme and extract.

3 Drain cherries and cranberries; pat dry with paper towels. Stir the fruit, cashews and chocolate chunks into chocolate mixture. Spread into prepared pan. Let stand at room temperature until set.

4 Using foil, lift fudge out of pan. Discard foil; cut fudge into 1-in. squares.

Coconut Almond Bombs

PREP: 50 MIN. + CHILLING • BAKE: 15 MIN./BATCH • YIELD: 3½ DOZEN

These are beautiful for holiday parties. They're a big hit each time! To make them extra-special, use a new small paintbrush to lightly dust the almonds with a gold luster.

Deb Holbrook *Abington, Massachusetts*

- **1 package (7 ounces) almond paste**
- **2 cups confectioners' sugar**
- **1 package (14 ounces) flaked coconut**
- **3 egg whites**
- **1 teaspoon vanilla extract**
- **1 carton (8 ounces) Mascarpone cheese**
- **2 pounds white candy coating, chopped**
- **⅔ cup sliced almonds**

Gold pearl dust

1 Place almond paste in a food processor; cover and process until finely chopped. Transfer to a large bowl; add confectioners' sugar and coconut. Beat until mixture resembles coarse crumbs. In a small bowl, beat egg whites and vanilla until stiff peaks form; fold into coconut mixture.

2 Drop by tablespoonfuls 2 in. apart onto parchment paper-lined baking sheets. Bake at 325° for 14-18 minutes or until lightly browned. Remove to wire racks to cool.

3 Spread about 1 teaspoon cheese over each cookie; refrigerate for 20 minutes or until cheese is firm.

4 In a microwave, melt candy coating; stir until smooth. Dip cookies in coating; allow excess to drip off. Place on waxed paper; sprinkle with almonds. Let stand until set. Brush pearl dust over almonds. Refrigerate in an airtight container.

EDITOR'S NOTE: Pearl dust is available from Wilton Industries. Call 800-794-5866 or visit wilton.com.

Trail Mix Clusters

PREP: 25 MIN. + CHILLING • YIELD: 4 DOZEN

Although they look and taste like they came from an expensive chocolate shop, my nutty, chocolaty snacks couldn't be more guilt-free. The dried fruit and nuts are heart-healthy and full of fiber. Bet you can't eat just one!

Alina Niemi *Honolulu, Hawaii*

- **2 cups (12 ounces) semisweet chocolate chips**
- **½ cup unsalted sunflower kernels**
- **½ cup salted pumpkin seeds or pepitas**
- **½ cup coarsely chopped cashews**
- **½ cup coarsely chopped pecans**
- **¼ cup flaked coconut**
- **¼ cup finely chopped dried apricots**
- **¼ cup dried cranberries**
- **¼ cup dried cherries or blueberries**

1 In a microwave-safe bowl, melt chocolate chips; stir until smooth. Stir in the remaining ingredients.

2 Drop by tablespoonfuls onto waxed paper-lined baking sheets. Refrigerate until firm. Store in the refrigerator.

Chocolate Malt Ball Cookies

PREP: 30 MIN. • BAKE: 10 MIN./BATCH + COOLING
YIELD: 2½ DOZEN

I like malt ball candies, so I decided to create a cookie that captured that fantastic flavor. These chewy cookies have just the right balance of chocolate and malt, but you can vary the amount of malt powder to make the taste stronger or milder.

Lynne Weddell *Vacaville, California*

- **1 cup butter, softened**
- **1 cup packed brown sugar**
- **1 egg**
- **1¼ cups old-fashioned oats**
- **1 cup all-purpose flour**
- **½ cup whole wheat flour**
- **¼ cup malted milk powder**
- **1½ teaspoons baking powder**
- **¼ teaspoon salt**
- **2 cups coarsely chopped malted milk balls**

1 In a large bowl, cream butter and brown sugar until light and fluffy. Beat in egg. Combine the oats, flours, malted milk powder, baking powder and salt; gradually add to creamed mixture and mix well. Stir in malted milk balls.

2 Drop by heaping tablespoonfuls 3 in. apart onto ungreased baking sheets. Bake at 350° for 10-14 minutes or until set and edges begin to brown. Cool for 2 minutes before removing from pans to wire racks.

Lemon Stars

PREP: 35 MIN. + CHILLING • BAKE: 10 MIN./BATCH + COOLING
YIELD: 9 DOZEN

These cookies have a citrus zing and a light, crunchy texture. The star theme makes them ideal for the Christmas season.

Jacqueline Hill *Norwalk, Ohio*

- **½ cup butter-flavored shortening**
- **1 cup sugar**
- **1 egg**
- **1½ teaspoons lemon extract**
- **½ cup sour cream**
- **1 teaspoon grated lemon peel**
- **2¾ cups all-purpose flour**
- **½ teaspoon baking soda**
- **½ teaspoon salt**

FROSTING:

- **1½ cups confectioners' sugar**
- **6 tablespoons butter**
- **¾ teaspoon lemon extract**
- **3 drops yellow food coloring, optional**
- **3 to 4 tablespoons 2% milk**

Yellow colored sugar, optional

1 In a large bowl, cream shortening and sugar until light and fluffy. Beat in egg and extract. Stir in sour cream and peel. Combine the flour, baking soda and salt; gradually add to creamed mixture and mix well. Divide dough into three balls; cover and refrigerate for 3 hours or until easy to handle.

2 Remove one portion of dough from the refrigerator at a time. On a lightly floured surface, roll out dough to ¼-in. thickness. Cut with a floured 2-in. star cookie cutter. Place 1 in. apart on ungreased baking sheets.

3 Bake at 375° for 6-8 minutes or until edges are lightly browned. Remove to wire racks to cool.

4 For frosting, in a small bowl, combine the confectioners' sugar, butter, extract, food coloring if desired and enough milk to achieve spreading consistency. Frost cookies; sprinkle with colored sugar if desired.

Peter Peter Pumpkin Whoopies

PREP: 35 MIN. + COOLING • BAKE: 10 MIN./BATCH
YIELD: 10 WHOOPIE PIES

When fall rolls around and it's time for a bake sale, this is the recipe I turn to. The whoopie pies are a great fall bake sale favorite. The cream cheese filling is perked up with cinnamon and nutmeg. It is perfect with the cakelike outside.

Dawn Conte *Sicklerville, New Jersey*

- **1 package (18¼ ounces) spice cake mix**
- **1¼ cups canned pumpkin**
- **2 eggs**
- **½ cup 2% milk**
- **⅓ cup butter, softened**

FILLING:

- **2 packages (3 ounces each) cream cheese, softened**
- **½ cup marshmallow creme**
- **⅓ cup butter, softened**
- **1½ cups confectioners' sugar**
- **¾ teaspoon vanilla extract**
- **½ teaspoon ground cinnamon**
- **⅛ teaspoon ground nutmeg**

1 In a large bowl, combine the first five ingredients; beat until well blended. Drop by ¼ cupfuls 3 in. apart onto lightly greased baking sheets. Bake at 375° for 7-10 minutes or until set and edges are lightly browned. Remove to wire racks to cool completely.

2 For filling, in a small bowl, beat the cream cheese, marshmallow creme and butter. Beat in the remaining ingredients. Spread on the bottoms of half of the cookies; top with remaining cookies. Store in the refrigerator.

Peanut Butter Turtle Candies

PREP: 30 MIN. + CHILLING • YIELD: 2 DOZEN

Every year at the holidays, these candy turtles are a huge hit with family, friends and co-workers. I get lots of requests for more and have even been told not to bother with a holiday visit if I don't bring my turtles—talk about a compliment! They're also good with dark chocolate and salted pecans.

Misty Schwotzer *Groveport, Ohio*

- **72 pecan halves (about 1¾ cups)**
- **¼ cup peanut butter**
- **2 tablespoons butter, softened**
- **½ cup confectioners' sugar**
- **5 ounces milk chocolate candy coating, coarsely chopped**
- **2 teaspoons shortening**

1 On waxed paper-lined pans, arrange pecan halves in clusters of three.

2 In a small bowl, beat peanut butter and butter until blended; gradually beat in confectioners' sugar. In a microwave, melt candy coating and shortening; stir until smooth.

3 Spoon ¼ teaspoon melted chocolate into the center of each pecan cluster. Place teaspoonfuls of peanut butter mixture into the center of each cluster; press down slightly. Spoon remaining melted chocolate over tops. Chill for 10 minutes or until set. Store in an airtight container in the refrigerator.

Double-Drizzle Pecan Cookies

PREP: 25 MIN. • BAKE: 10 MIN./BATCH + COOLING
YIELD: ABOUT 3½ DOZEN

My chewy toasted pecan treats are a must with my cookie munchers every holiday. Using caramel and chocolate drizzle makes them doubly delicious and so pretty on the plate.

Paula Marchesi *Lenhartsville, Pennsylvania*

- **½ cup butter, softened**
- **1½ cups packed brown sugar**
- **1 egg**
- **1 teaspoon vanilla extract**
- **1½ cups all-purpose flour**
- **1½ teaspoons baking powder**
- **¼ teaspoon salt**
- **1¼ cups chopped pecans, toasted**

CARAMEL DRIZZLE:

- **½ cup packed brown sugar**
- **¼ cup heavy whipping cream**
- **½ cup confectioners' sugar**

CHOCOLATE DRIZZLE:

- **1 ounce semisweet chocolate**
- **1 tablespoon butter**

1 In a large bowl, cream butter and brown sugar until light and fluffy. Beat in egg and vanilla. Combine the flour, baking powder and salt; gradually add to creamed mixture and mix well.

2 Shape dough into 1-in. balls; roll in pecans. Place 2 in. apart on ungreased baking sheets; flatten slightly. Bake at 350° for 8-10 minutes or until lightly browned. Cool for 2 minutes before removing to wire racks to cool completely.

3 In a small saucepan, bring brown sugar and cream to a boil. Remove from the heat; whisk in confectioners' sugar. Immediately drizzle over cookies.

4 In a microwave, melt chocolate and butter; stir until smooth. Drizzle over cookies. Let stand until set. Store in an airtight container.

Browned-Butter Sandwich Spritz

PREP: 50 MIN. + CHILLING • BAKE: 10 MIN./BATCH + COOLING
YIELD: ABOUT 3 DOZEN

A heavenly sweet maple filling makes these scrumptious spritz cookies a little different. You can count on them to come out buttery and tender. They're almost too pretty to eat.

Deirdre Dee Cox *Milwaukee, Wisconsin*

- **1 cup plus 2 tablespoons butter, cubed**
- **1¼ cups confectioners' sugar, divided**
- **1 egg**
- **1 egg yolk**
- **2 teaspoons vanilla extract**
- **2¼ cups all-purpose flour**
- **½ teaspoon salt**
- **½ cup maple syrup**

1 In a small heavy saucepan, cook and stir butter over medium heat for 8-10 minutes or until golden brown. Transfer to a small bowl; refrigerate until firm, about 1 hour.

2 Set aside 2 tablespoons browned butter for filling. In a large bowl, beat ½ cup confectioners' sugar and remaining browned butter until smooth. Beat in the egg, yolk and vanilla. Combine flour and salt; gradually add to creamed mixture and mix well.

3 Using a cookie press fitted with the disk of your choice, press dough 2 in. apart onto parchment paper-lined baking sheets. Bake at 375° for 8-9 minutes or until set (do not brown). Remove to wire racks to cool.

4 In a small heavy saucepan, bring syrup to a boil. Cool slightly. Whisk in remaining confectioners' sugar until smooth. Beat reserved browned butter until light and fluffy. Beat in syrup mixture until smooth.

5 Turn over half the cookies and spread 1 teaspoon of filling on them. Top with the remaining cookies.

Cran-Orange Oatmeal Cookies

PREP: 20 MIN. • BAKE: 15 MIN./BATCH
YIELD: 4 DOZEN

Dried cranberries, coconut and orange make this crisp, chewy oatmeal cookie a real standout.

Ellen Woodham-Johnson *Matteson, Illinois*

- **1 cup butter, softened**
- **1 cup packed brown sugar**
- **½ cup sugar**
- **1 egg**
- **1 tablespoon grated orange peel**
- **1½ teaspoons orange extract**
- **1¾ cups all-purpose flour**
- **1 teaspoon baking powder**
- **¼ teaspoon baking soda**
- **2 cups old-fashioned oats**
- **1 cup dried cranberries**
- **1 cup flaked coconut**

1 In a large bowl, cream butter and sugars until light and fluffy. Beat in the egg, orange peel and extract.

2 Combine the flour, baking powder and baking soda; gradually add to creamed mixture and mix well. Stir in the oats, cranberries and coconut. Shape into 1-in. balls; place 2 in. apart on ungreased baking sheets.

3 Bake at 375° for 11-13 minutes or until bottoms are browned. Remove to wire racks. Store in airtight container.

WINNERS
CIRCLE

cakes & cheesecakes

Homemade cakes and impressive cheesecakes have such a way of making celebrations memorable. And when those decadent treats are also ribbon-awarded recipes, they're guaranteed to make the occasion extra special. So break out the pans and mixers and bake some happiness.

PEANUT BUTTER CHEESECAKE, 247

Eggnog Cranberry Cheesecake

PREP: 30 MIN. + COOLING • BAKE: 1 HOUR + CHILLING
YIELD: 12 SERVINGS

My lovely cheesecake, which uses cranberries and eggnog, is a perfect Christmas dessert. Just be sure to remind folks to save room.

Nancy Zimmerman *Cape May Court House, New Jersey*

- **1 cup sugar**
- **2 tablespoons cornstarch**
- **1 cup cranberry juice**
- **1½ cups fresh or frozen cranberries**

CRUST:

- **1 cup graham cracker crumbs (about 16 squares)**
- **3 tablespoons sugar**
- **3 tablespoons butter, melted**

FILLING:

- **4 packages (8 ounces each) cream cheese, softened**
- **1 cup sugar**
- **3 tablespoons all-purpose flour**
- **4 eggs, lightly beaten**
- **1 cup eggnog**
- **1 tablespoon vanilla extract**

1 In a large saucepan, combine sugar and cornstarch. Stir in cranberry juice until smooth. Add cranberries. Bring to a boil over medium heat; cook and stir for 2 minutes or until thickened. Remove from the heat; set aside.

2 In a small bowl, combine cracker crumbs and sugar; stir in butter. Press onto the bottom of a greased 9-in. springform pan. Place pan on a baking sheet. Bake at 325° for 10 minutes. Cool on a wire rack.

3 In a large bowl, beat cream cheese and sugar until smooth. Add flour and beat well. Add eggs, beat on low just until combined. Add eggnog and vanilla; beat just until blended. Pour two-thirds of the filling over crust. Top with half of the cranberry mixture (cover and refrigerate remaining cranberry mixture). Carefully spoon remaining filling on top. Return pan to baking sheet.

4 Bake at 325° for 60-70 minutes or until center is almost set. Cool on a wire rack for 10 minutes. Carefully run a knife around edge of pan to loosen; cool 1 hour longer. Refrigerate overnight. Remove sides of pan. Spoon remaining cranberry mixture over cheesecake. Refrigerate leftovers.

EDITOR'S NOTE: This recipe was tested with commercially prepared eggnog.

Lemon-Rosemary Layer Cake

PREP: 20 MIN. • BAKE: 25 MIN. + COOLING • YIELD: 16 SERVINGS

Tall and impressive, this unique dessert is a treat for the senses with flecks of lemon peel and fresh rosemary. Just wait till you taste it!

Mary Fraser *Surprise, Arizona*

- **1 cup plus 2 tablespoons butter, softened**
- **2½ cups sugar**
- **4 eggs**
- **1 egg yolk**
- **4 cups all-purpose flour**
- **3 teaspoons baking powder**
- **1½ teaspoons salt**
- **¼ teaspoon plus ⅛ teaspoon baking soda**
- **1½ cups (12 ounces) sour cream**
- **6 tablespoons lemon juice**
- **3 teaspoons grated lemon peel**
- **3 teaspoons minced fresh rosemary**

FROSTING:

- **2 packages (8 ounces each) cream cheese, softened**
- **8¼ cups confectioners' sugar**
- **3 teaspoons grated lemon peel**
- **2¼ teaspoons lemon juice**

1 In a large bowl, cream butter and sugar until light and fluffy. Add eggs and yolk, one at a time, beating well after each addition. Combine the flour, baking powder, salt and baking soda; add to the creamed mixture alternately with sour cream, beating well after each addition. Beat in the lemon juice, peel and rosemary.

2 Transfer to three greased and floured 9-in. round baking pans. Bake at 350° for 25-30 minutes or until edges begin to brown. Cool for 10 minutes before removing cake from pans to wire racks to cool completely.

3 For frosting, in a large bowl, beat cream cheese until fluffy. Add the confectioners' sugar, lemon peel and juice; beat until smooth.

4 Spread frosting between layers and over top and sides of cake. Refrigerate the leftovers.

Chunky Apple Cake

PREP: 20 MIN. • BAKE: 40 MIN. + COOLING • YIELD: 12-14 SERVINGS

For a cake full of old-fashioned comfort and flavor, turn to this family favorite.

Debi Benson *Bakersfield, California*

- **½ cup butter, softened**
- **2 cups sugar**
- **½ teaspoon vanilla extract**
- **2 eggs**
- **2 cups all-purpose flour**
- **1½ teaspoons ground cinnamon**
- **1 teaspoon ground nutmeg**
- **½ teaspoon salt**
- **½ teaspoon baking soda**
- **6 cups chopped peeled tart apples**

BUTTERSCOTCH SAUCE:

- **½ cup packed brown sugar**
- **¼ cup butter, cubed**
- **½ cup heavy whipping cream**

1 In a large bowl, cream butter, sugar and vanilla. Add eggs, one at a time, beating well after each addition. Combine flour, cinnamon, nutmeg, salt and baking soda; gradually add to creamed mixture and mix well. Stir in apples until well combined Spread into a greased 13-in. x 9-in. baking dish. Bake at 350° for 40-45 minutes or until top is lightly browned and springs back when lightly touched. Cool for 30 minutes before serving.

2 Meanwhile, in a small saucepan, combine brown sugar and butter. Cook over medium heat until butter is melted. Gradually add cream. Bring to a slow boil over medium heat, stirring constantly. Remove from the heat. Serve with cake.

French Toast Cupcakes

PREP: 25 MIN. • BAKE: 20 MIN. + COOLING • YIELD: 1½ DOZEN

Baking is like therapy to me. Whenever I feel down or stressed, I know I can go into the kitchen and whip up a batch of these delicious cupcakes. This delicious combination tastes like Sunday brunch in cupcake form.

Jenny Weaver *Glendale, Arizona*

- **½ cup butter, softened**
- **1½ cups sugar**
- **2 eggs**
- **2 teaspoons vanilla extract**
- **2 cups all-purpose flour**
- **2 teaspoons ground cinnamon**
- **½ teaspoon baking powder**
- **½ teaspoon baking soda**
- **¼ teaspoon salt**
- **¼ teaspoon ground nutmeg**
- **1⅓ cups buttermilk**

MAPLE BUTTERCREAM FROSTING:

- **½ cup butter, softened**
- **¼ cup shortening**
- **½ cup maple syrup**
- **Dash salt**
- **2½ cups confectioners' sugar**
- **6 bacon strips, cooked and crumbled, optional**

1 In a large bowl, cream butter and sugar until light and fluffy. Add eggs, one at a time, beating well after each addition. Beat in vanilla. Combine the flour, cinnamon, baking powder, baking soda, salt and nutmeg; add to the creamed mixture alternately with buttermilk, beating well after each addition.

2 Fill paper-lined muffin cups two-thirds full. Bake at 350° for 17-22 minutes or until a toothpick inserted near the center comes out clean. Cool for 10 minutes before removing from pans to wire racks to cool completely.

3 For frosting, in a small bowl, beat butter and shortening until fluffy. Beat in maple syrup and salt. Add confectioners' sugar; beat until smooth. Frost cupcakes. Sprinkle with bacon if desired.

Mint Brownie Cupcakes

PREP: 25 MIN. + COOLING • BAKE: 15 MIN. + CHILLING
YIELD: 10 CUPCAKES

Are they brownies or are they cupcakes? There's no wrong answer to this question, I tell my first-grade students. I found the recipe when I began teaching more than 20 years ago. My husband and children like this treat, too.

Carol Maertz *Spruce Grove, Alberta*

- **½ cup mint chocolate chips**
- **½ cup butter, cubed**
- **½ cup sugar**
- **2 eggs**
- **½ cup all-purpose flour**

TOPPING:

- **2 cups miniature marshmallows**
- **⅓ cup 2% milk**
- **½ teaspoon peppermint extract**
- **Green or red food coloring, optional**
- **¾ cup heavy whipping cream, whipped**
- **Additional chocolate chips, optional**

1 In a large microwave-safe bowl, melt chips and butter; stir until smooth. Cool slightly; stir in sugar and eggs. Gradually stir flour into chocolate mixture until smooth.

2 Fill paper-lined muffin cups two-thirds full. Bake at 350° for 15-20 minutes or until a toothpick inserted near the center comes out clean. Remove from pan to a wire rack to cool.

3 In a large saucepan, cook and stir marshmallows and milk over low heat until smooth. Remove from the heat; stir in extract and food coloring if desired.

4 Transfer to a bowl; refrigerate for 15 minutes or until cooled. Fold in whipped cream. Spread over cupcakes. Refrigerate for at least 1 hour. Sprinkle with additional chocolate chips if desired. Store in the refrigerator.

EDITOR'S NOTE: If mint chocolate chips are not available, place

2 cups (12 ounces) semisweet chocolate chips and ¼ teaspoon peppermint extract in a plastic bag; seal and toss to coat. Allow chips to stand for 24-48 hours.

Peanut Butter Cheesecake

PREP: 20 MIN. + COOLING • BAKE: 55 MIN. + CHILLING
YIELD: 12-14 SERVINGS

The first time I served this cheesecake, my friends went wild over it. They were surprised when I told them the crust is made of pretzels. The pairing of sweet and salty, and creamy and crunchy, plus peanut butter and chocolate is incredible!

Lois Brooks *Newark, Delaware*

- **1½ cups crushed pretzels**
- **⅓ cup butter, melted**

FILLING:

- **5 packages (8 ounces each) cream cheese, softened**
- **1½ cups sugar**
- **¾ cup creamy peanut butter**
- **2 teaspoons vanilla extract**
- **3 eggs, lightly beaten**
- **1 cup peanut butter chips**
- **1 cup (6 ounces) semisweet chocolate chips**

TOPPING:

- **1 cup (8 ounces) sour cream**
- **3 tablespoons creamy peanut butter**
- **½ cup sugar**
- **½ cup finely chopped unsalted peanuts**

1 In a small bowl, combine pretzels and butter. Press onto the bottom and 1 in. up the sides of a greased 10-in. springform pan. Place pan on a baking sheet. Bake at 350° for 5 minutes. Cool on a wire rack.

2 In a large bowl, beat cream cheese and sugar until smooth. Add peanut butter and vanilla; mix well. Add eggs; beat on low just until combined. Stir in chips. Pour over the crust. Return pan to baking sheet.

3 Bake at 350° for 50-55 minutes or until center is almost set. Remove from the oven; let stand for 15 minutes (leave oven on).

4 For topping, in a small bowl, combine the sour cream, peanut butter and sugar; spread over filling. Sprinkle with nuts. Bake 5 minutes longer.

5 Cool on a wire rack for 10 minutes. Carefully run a knife around the edge of the pan to loosen; cool 1 hour longer. Refrigerate overnight. Remove sides of pan. Refrigerate leftovers.

Lime Cheesecake

PREP: 30 MIN. + CHILLING • YIELD: 12 SERVINGS

Being from the Sunshine State, I love any recipe containing citrus. This one, featuring lime, is quick to mix up and disappears almost as fast. Substitute orange juice, zest and slices for the lime for a great variation.

Robin Spires *Tampa, Florida*

- **3 cups graham cracker crumbs**
- **⅔ cup sugar**
- **⅔ cup butter, melted**

FILLING:

- **2 envelopes unflavored gelatin**
- **1 cup lime juice**
- **¼ cup cold water**
- **1½ cups sugar**
- **5 eggs, lightly beaten**
- **2 teaspoons grated lime peel**
- **2 packages (8 ounces each) cream cheese, softened**
- **½ cup butter, softened**
- **½ cup heavy whipping cream**

1 In a large bowl, combine the graham cracker crumbs, sugar and butter. Press onto the bottom and 2 in. up the sides of a greased 9-in. springform pan. Cover and refrigerate for at least 30 minutes.

2 In a small saucepan, sprinkle gelatin over lime juice and cold water; let stand for 1 minute. Stir in the sugar, eggs and lime peel. Cook and stir over medium heat until mixture reaches 160°. Remove from the heat.

3 In a large bowl, beat cream cheese and butter until fluffy. Gradually beat in gelatin mixture. Cover and refrigerate for 45 minutes or until partially set, stirring occasionally.

4 In a small bowl, beat cream until stiff peaks form; fold into lime mixture. Spoon into crust. Cover and refrigerate for 3-4 hours or until set. Just before serving, remove sides of pan. Refrigerate leftovers.

PERFECT CHEESECAKE

>> To prevent cracks in a baked cheesecake, avoid overbeating after adding the eggs—beat on low just until blended and don't overbake.

Chocolate Ganache Peanut Butter Cupcakes

PREP: 55 MIN. • BAKE: 20 MIN. + COOLING
YIELD: 2 DOZEN

To make these decadent gems, I blended two popular flavors: peanut butter and chocolate. As soon as I took the first bite of these cupcakes, I knew I had created something divine! Most people who try them say they are the best thing they've ever eaten, which definitely makes them worth the time and effort.

Ronda Schabes *Vicksburg, Michigan*

- **2 cups sugar**
- **1¾ cups all-purpose flour**
- **¾ cup baking cocoa**
- **½ teaspoon salt**
- **½ teaspoon baking soda**
- **½ teaspoon baking powder**
- **1 cup buttermilk**
- **1 cup strong brewed coffee, room temperature**
- **½ cup canola oil**
- **2 eggs**
- **1 teaspoon vanilla extract**

FILLING:

- **½ cup creamy peanut butter**
- **3 tablespoons unsalted butter, softened**
- **1 cup confectioners' sugar**
- **2 to 4 tablespoons 2% milk**

GANACHE:

- **2 cups (12 ounces) semisweet chocolate chips**
- **½ cup heavy whipping cream**

PEANUT BUTTER FROSTING:

- **1 cup packed brown sugar**
- **4 egg whites**
- **¼ teaspoon salt**
- **¼ teaspoon cream of tartar**
- **1 teaspoon vanilla extract**
- **2 cups unsalted butter, softened**
- **⅓ cup creamy peanut butter**

1 In a large bowl, combine the first six ingredients. Whisk the buttermilk, coffee, oil, eggs and vanilla until blended; add to the dry ingredients until combined. (Batter will be very thin.) Fill paper-lined muffin cups two-thirds full.

2 Bake at 350° for 18-20 minutes or until a toothpick inserted near the center comes out clean. Cool for 10 minutes before removing from pans to wire racks to cool.

3 In a small bowl, cream the peanut butter, butter, confectioners' sugar and enough milk to achieve piping consistency. Cut a small hole in the corner of a pastry or plastic bag; insert a small round tip. Fill with peanut butter filling. Insert tip into the top center of each cupcake; pipe about 1 tablespoon filling into each.

4 Place chocolate chips in a small bowl. In a small saucepan, bring cream just to a boil. Pour over chocolate; whisk until smooth. Dip the top of each cupcake into ganache; place on wire racks to set.

5 In a large heavy saucepan, combine the brown sugar, egg whites, salt and cream of tartar over low heat. With a hand mixer, beat on low speed for 1 minute. Continue beating on low over low heat until frosting reaches 160°, about 8-10 minutes. Pour into a large bowl; add vanilla. Beat on high until stiff peaks form, about 5 minutes.

6 Add butter, 1 tablespoon at a time, beating well after each addition. If mixture begins to look curdled, place frosting bowl in another bowl filled with hot water for a few seconds. Continue adding butter and beating until smooth. Beat in peanut butter for 1-2 minutes or until smooth.

7 Place frosting in a pastry or plastic bag with large star tip; pipe onto each cupcake. Store in an airtight container in the refrigerator. Let stand at room temperature before serving.

Hot Fudge Cake

PREP: 20 MIN. • COOK: 4 HOURS
YIELD: 8 SERVINGS

A cake baked in a slow cooker may seem unusual, but the smiles seen around the table will prove how tasty it is. Sometimes, for a change of pace, I substitute butterscotch chips for chocolate.

Marleen Adkins *Placentia, California*

- **1¾ cups packed brown sugar, divided**
- **1 cup all-purpose flour**
- **6 tablespoons baking cocoa, divided**
- **2 teaspoons baking powder**
- **½ teaspoon salt**
- **½ cup 2% milk**
- **2 tablespoons butter, melted**
- **½ teaspoon vanilla extract**
- **1½ cups semisweet chocolate chips**
- **1¾ cups boiling water**
- **Vanilla ice cream**

1 In a small bowl, combine 1 cup brown sugar, flour, 3 tablespoons cocoa, baking powder and salt. In another bowl, combine the milk, butter and vanilla; stir into dry ingredients just until combined. Spread evenly in a 3-qt. slow cooker coated with cooking spray. Sprinkle with chocolate chips.

2 In another small bowl, combine the remaining brown sugar and cocoa; stir in boiling water. Pour over batter (do not stir). Cover and cook on high for 4 to 4½ hours or until a toothpick inserted near the center of the cake comes out clean. Serve warm with ice cream.

EDITOR'S NOTE: This recipe does not use eggs.

Red Velvet Cheesecake

PREP: 30 MIN. • BAKE: 1 HOUR + CHILLING • YIELD: 16 SERVINGS

Festive and oh-so-good, this cheesecake will become a fixture on your Christmas dessert menu. The red velvet filling is spiked with cocoa, topped with cream cheese frosting, and baked in a chocolate cookie crumb crust.

Karen Dively *Chapin, South Carolina*

- **17 chocolate cream-filled chocolate sandwich cookies, crushed**
- **¼ cup butter, melted**
- **1 tablespoon sugar**

FILLING:

- **3 packages (8 ounces each) cream cheese, softened**
- **1½ cups sugar**
- **1 cup (8 ounces) sour cream**
- **½ cup buttermilk**
- **3 tablespoons baking cocoa**
- **2 teaspoons vanilla extract**
- **4 eggs, lightly beaten**
- **1 bottle (1 ounce) red food coloring**

FROSTING:

- **1 package (3 ounces) cream cheese, softened**
- **¼ cup butter, softened**
- **2 cups confectioners' sugar**
- **1 teaspoon vanilla extract**

1 Place a greased 9-in. springform pan on a double thickness of heavy-duty foil (about 18 in. square). Securely wrap foil around pan.

2 In a small bowl, combine the cookie crumbs, butter and sugar. Press onto the bottom of prepared pan.

3 In a large bowl, beat cream cheese and sugar until smooth. Beat in the sour cream, buttermilk, cocoa and vanilla. Add eggs; beat on low speed just until combined. Stir in food coloring. Pour over crust. Place springform pan in a large baking pan; add 1 in. of hot water to larger pan.

4 Bake at 325° for 60-70 minutes or until center is just set and top appears dull. Remove springform pan from water bath. Cool on a wire rack for 10 minutes. Carefully run a knife around edge of pan to loosen; cool 1 hour longer. Refrigerate overnight. Remove sides of pan.

5 For frosting, in a small bowl, beat cream cheese and butter until fluffy. Add confectioners' sugar and vanilla; beat until smooth. Frost top of cheesecake. Refrigerate until serving.

Neapolitan Cheesecake

PREP: 45 MIN. • BAKE: 65 MIN. + CHILLING
YIELD: 12 SERVINGS

As a child, I loved Neapolitan ice cream. I thought it would be fun to create a cheesecake with the same flavors. This smooth, creamy layered beauty is the result. Each layer is just rich with flavor.

Sue Gronholz *Beaver Dam, Wisconsin*

- **1 cup cream-filled chocolate sandwich cookie crumbs**
- **3 tablespoons sugar**
- **3 tablespoons butter, melted**

FILLING:

- **4 packages (8 ounces *each*) cream cheese, softened**
- **1⅓ cups sugar**
- **2 tablespoons all-purpose flour**
- **2 tablespoons heavy whipping cream**
- **1 teaspoon vanilla extract**
- **½ teaspoon almond extract**
- **4 eggs, lightly beaten**
- **¾ cup semisweet chocolate chips**
- **1 cup fresh strawberries, hulled**
- **1 to 2 drops red food coloring, optional**
- **¼ cup seedless strawberry jam, warmed**

Sliced fresh strawberries and sweetened whipped cream

1 Place a greased 9-in. springform pan on a double thickness of heavy-duty foil (about 18 in. square). Securely wrap foil around pan.

2 In a small bowl, combine the cookie crumbs, sugar and butter. Press onto the bottom of pan; set aside.

3 In a large bowl, beat cream cheese and sugar until smooth. Beat in the flour, cream and extracts. Add eggs; beat on low speed just until combined. Divide batter into thirds.

4 In a microwave, melt chocolate chips; cool to room temperature. Stir melted chocolate into one portion of batter; pour over crust. In a food processor, puree strawberries. Add pureed strawberries and food coloring if desired to another portion; gently spread over chocolate layer. Place springform pan in a large baking pan; add 1 in. of hot water to larger pan.

5 Bake at 325° for 40 minutes or until center is just set and top appears dull. Gently spread remaining batter over top. Bake for 25-30 minutes or until top appears dull. Remove springform pan from water bath. Cool on a wire rack for 10 minutes. Carefully run a knife around edge of pan to loosen; cool 1 hour longer. Refrigerate overnight.

6 Remove sides of pan. Drizzle jam over cheesecake; garnish with strawberries and whipped cream.

Coconut Pecan Cupcakes

PREP: 50 MIN. • BAKE: 20 MIN. + COOLING
YIELD: 2 DOZEN

Pecan lovers have lots to cheer about with these flavorful cupcakes. I created the recipe for a dear friend who loved Italian cream cake but didn't want a whole cake. The cupcakes have a wonderful aroma and fabulous flavor.

Tina Harrison *Prairieville, Louisiana*

- **5 eggs, separated**
- **½ cup butter, softened**
- **½ cup shortening**
- **2 cups sugar**
- **¾ teaspoon vanilla extract**
- **¼ teaspoon almond extract**
- **1½ cups all-purpose flour**
- **¼ cup cornstarch**
- **½ teaspoon baking soda**
- **½ teaspoon salt**
- **1 cup buttermilk**
- **2 cups flaked coconut**
- **1 cup finely chopped pecans**

FROSTING:

- **1 package (8 ounces) cream cheese, softened**
- **¼ cup butter, softened**
- **½ teaspoon vanilla extract**
- **¼ teaspoon almond extract**
- **3¾ cups confectioners' sugar**
- **¾ cup chopped pecans**

1 Let eggs stand at room temperature for 30 minutes. In a large bowl, cream the butter, shortening and sugar until light and fluffy. Add egg yolks, one at a time, beating well after each addition. Stir in extracts. Combine the flour, cornstarch, baking soda and salt; add to the creamed mixture alternately with buttermilk, beating well after each addition.

2 In a small bowl, beat egg whites on high speed until stiff peaks form. Fold into batter. Stir in coconut and pecans.

3 Fill paper-lined muffin cups three-fourths full. Bake at 350° for 20-25 minutes or until a toothpick inserted near the center comes out clean. Cool 10 minutes; remove from pans to wire racks to cool completely.

4 In a large bowl, combine frosting ingredients until smooth; frost cupcakes. Store in the refrigerator.

Best Maple-Cranberry Cheesecake

PREP: 30 MIN. • BAKE: 1¼ HOURS + CHILLING
YIELD: 16 SERVINGS (2 CUPS COMPOTE)

This maple cheesecake recipe may look intimidating, but it's not. If you make one holiday dessert, this is the one to showcase.

Tonya Burkhard *Davis, Illinois*

- **2 cups graham cracker crumbs**
- **⅓ cup butter, melted**
- **3 tablespoons sugar**
- **½ teaspoon ground cinnamon**

FILLING:

- **1½ cups maple syrup**
- **3 packages (8 ounces each) cream cheese, softened**
- **½ cup packed brown sugar**
- **⅔ cup sour cream**
- **3 tablespoons all-purpose flour**
- **2 teaspoons vanilla extract**
- **¼ teaspoon salt**
- **4 eggs, lightly beaten**

COMPOTE:

- **2 cups fresh or frozen cranberries, thawed**
- **⅔ cup dried cranberries**
- **1 cup maple syrup**
- **½ cup packed brown sugar**

1 Place a greased 9-in. springform pan on a double thickness of heavy-duty foil (about 18 in. square). Securely wrap foil around pan.

2 Combine the cracker crumbs, butter, sugar and cinnamon; press onto the bottom and 1½ in. up the sides of prepared pan. Place pan on a baking sheet. Bake at 375° for 8-10 minutes or until set. Cool on a wire rack. Reduce heat to 325°.

3 Meanwhile, place maple syrup in a small saucepan. Bring to a boil; cook until syrup is reduced to about 1 cup. Cool to room temperature; set aside.

4 In a large bowl, beat cream cheese and brown sugar until smooth. Beat in the sour cream, flour, vanilla, salt and cooled syrup. Add eggs; beat on low speed just until combined. Pour into crust. Place springform pan in a large baking pan; add 1 in. of hot water to larger pan.

5 Bake at 325° for 1¼ to 1½ hours or until center is just set and top appears dull. Remove springform pan from water bath. Cool on a wire rack for 10 minutes. Carefully run a knife around edge of pan to loosen; cool 1 hour longer. Refrigerate overnight. Remove sides of pan.

6 In a large saucepan, combine the cranberries, syrup and brown sugar. Cook over medium heat until the berries pop, about 10 minutes. Serve warm with cheesecake.

Strawberry Jam Cake

PREP: 35 MIN. • BAKE: 25 MIN. + COOLING
YIELD: 12 SERVINGS

When I need a cake for a special occasion, this is my go-to recipe because everyone is crazy about it. Every year I make it for a cake raffle we have at work for Relay for Life. It has raised a lot of money for a very good cause.

Tammy Urbina *Warner Robins, Georgia*

- **1 cup butter, softened**
- **1¾ cups sugar**
- **5 egg whites**
- **2 cups pureed strawberries**
- **½ cup sour cream**
- **1 teaspoon strawberry extract**
- **3 cups cake flour**
- **2½ teaspoons baking powder**
- **¼ teaspoon baking soda**
- **¼ teaspoon salt**

FROSTING:

- **1 package (8 ounces) cream cheese, softened**
- **¼ cup butter, softened**
- **3¼ cups confectioners' sugar**
- **¼ cup pureed strawberries**
- **½ teaspoon strawberry extract**
- **1 cup seedless strawberry jam, divided**

Sliced fresh strawberries, optional

1 Grease and flour three 9-in. round baking pans; set aside.

2 In a large bowl, cream butter and sugar until light and fluffy. Add egg whites, one at a time, beating well after each addition. Beat in the strawberries, sour cream and extract. Combine the flour, baking powder, baking soda and salt; add to the creamed mixture. Transfer batter to prepared pans.

3 Bake at 350° for 22-26 minutes or until a toothpick inserted near the center comes out clean. Cool for 10 minutes before removing from pans to wire racks to cool completely.

4 For frosting, in a large bowl, beat cream cheese and butter until fluffy. Add the confectioners' sugar, strawberries and extract; beat until smooth.

5 Place bottom cake layer on a serving plate; top with ½ cup jam and ½ cup frosting. Repeat layers. Top with remaining cake layer. Spread remaining frosting over top and sides of cake. Garnish with sliced strawberries if desired.

Peppermint Cheesecake

PREP: 40 MIN. • BAKE: 1¼ HOURS + CHILLING
YIELD: 16 SERVINGS

People are thrilled when they see me coming with this rich, smooth and refreshing cheesecake. It's always a crowd-pleaser. Not only does it look sensational, it tastes scrumptious.

Carrie Price *Ottawa, Illinois*

- **2½ cups cream-filled chocolate sandwich cookie crumbs**
- **⅓ cup butter, melted**
- **5 packages (8 ounces each) cream cheese, softened**
- **1 cup sugar**
- **1 cup (8 ounces) sour cream**
- **3 tablespoons all-purpose flour**
- **3 teaspoons vanilla extract**
- **1 teaspoon peppermint extract**
- **3 eggs, lightly beaten**
- **1 package (10 ounces) Andes creme de menthe baking chips or 2 packages (4.67 ounces each) mint Andes candies, chopped**

TOPPING:

- **1 package (8 ounces) cream cheese, softened**
- **⅓ cup sugar**
- **1 carton (12 ounces) frozen whipped topping, thawed**

Miniature candy canes, optional

1 Place a greased 9-in. springform pan on a double thickness of heavy-duty foil (about 18 in. square). Securely wrap foil around pan.

2 In a small bowl, combine cookie crumbs and butter. Press onto the bottom and 1 in. up the sides of prepared pan. Place pan on a baking sheet. Bake at 325° for 12-14 minutes or until set. Cool on a wire rack.

3 In a large bowl, beat cream cheese and sugar until smooth. Beat in the sour cream, flour and extracts. Add eggs; beat on low speed just until combined. Fold in chips. Pour into crust. (Pan will be full.) Place springform pan in a large baking pan; add 1 in. of hot water to larger pan.

4 Bake at 325° for 1¼ to 1½ hours or until center is just set and top appears dull. Remove springform pan from water bath. Cool on a wire rack for 10 minutes. Carefully run a knife around edge of pan to loosen; cool 1 hour longer. Refrigerate overnight. Remove sides of pan.

5 For topping, in a large bowl, beat cream cheese and sugar until smooth. Stir whipped topping into mixture, one-fourth at a time. Spread or pipe onto cheesecake. Garnish with miniature candy canes if desired.

Raspberry Almond Cheesecake

PREP: 45 MIN. • BAKE: 65 MIN. + CHILLING
YIELD: 14 SERVINGS

My son requests this cheesecake for his birthday cake every year, and our school auction committee asks me to make it for their annual auction. It's definitely one of the best cheesecakes I make

Diane Schumann *Fredonia, Wisconsin*

- **2 cups vanilla wafers (about 60 wafers)**
- **½ cup butter, melted**
- **¼ cup sugar**

FILLING:

- **4 packages (8 ounces each) cream cheese, softened**
- **1¼ cups sugar**
- **1 tablespoon Triple Sec**
- **1 teaspoon almond extract**
- **⅛ teaspoon salt**
- **4 eggs, lightly beaten**
- **⅓ cup seedless raspberry spreadable fruit**
- **½ teaspoon raspberry extract**

TOPPING:

- **2 cups (16 ounces) sour cream**
- **¼ cup sugar**
- **½ teaspoon almond extract**

1 Place a greased 10-in. springform pan on a double thickness of heavy-duty foil (about 18 in. square). Securely wrap foil around pan. In a small bowl, combine the wafer crumbs, butter and sugar. Press onto the bottom and 1 in. up the sides of prepared pan.

2 In a large bowl, beat cream cheese and sugar until smooth. Beat in the Triple Sec, extract and salt. Add eggs; beat on low speed just until combined.

3 Remove 1 cup batter to a small bowl; stir in spreadable fruit and extract until well blended. Pour plain batter over crust. Drop raspberry batter by tablespoons over plain batter; spread evenly. Place springform pan in a large baking pan; add 1 in. of hot water to larger pan.

4 Bake at 325° for 50-60 minutes or until almost set and top appears dull. Remove springform pan from water bath. Let stand for 5 minutes.

5 For topping, combine all the ingredients; spread over top of cheesecake. Bake 5 minutes longer. Cool on a wire rack for 10 minutes. Carefully run a knife around edge of pan to loosen; cool 1 hour longer. Refrigerate overnight. Remove sides of pan.

Blueberry Bounty Cake

PREP: 20 MIN. • BAKE: 45 MIN. + COOLING
YIELD: 12 SERVINGS (1 CUP SAUCE)

Everyone loves this moist, golden cake bursting with blueberries and drizzled with fruity sauce. You'll have a hard time deciding whether to serve it for dessert, breakfast or brunch.

Alice Tesch *Watertown, Wisconsin*

- **1½ cups butter, softened**
- **1¾ cups sugar**
- **4 eggs**
- **1 tablespoon grated lemon peel**
- **2 teaspoons vanilla extract**
- **3 cups cake flour**
- **2½ teaspoons baking powder**
- **¼ teaspoon salt**
- **1 cup lemonade**
- **1½ cups fresh or frozen blueberries**

BLUEBERRY SAUCE:

- **2 teaspoons cornstarch**
- **¼ cup sugar**
- **¼ cup water**
- **1 cup fresh or frozen blueberries, thawed**

1 In a large bowl, cream butter and sugar until light and fluffy. Add eggs, one at a time, beating well after each addition. Beat in lemon peel and vanilla.

2 Combine the flour, baking powder and salt; add to creamed mixture alternately with lemonade, beating well after each addition. Fold in blueberries.

3 Pour into a greased and floured 10-in. fluted tube pan. Bake at 350° for 45-50 minutes or until a toothpick inserted near the center comes out clean. Cool for 20 minutes before removing from pan to a wire rack to cool completely.

4 In a small saucepan, combine cornstarch and sugar. Stir in water until smooth. Add blueberries; bring to a boil over medium heat, stirring constantly. Cook and stir 1 minute longer or until thickened. Serve warm with cake.

EDITOR'S NOTE: If using frozen blueberries, use without thawing to avoid discoloring the batter.

White Chocolate-Coconut Layer Cake

PREP: 25 MIN. • BAKE: 35 MIN. + COOLING
YIELD: 12 SERVINGS

This cake is special to me because I took a recipe I had been making for years and added my own touches. I incorporated fresh peaches and macadamia nuts to the batter. I also switched from dark to white chocolate. My family gave the results a thumbs-up.

Darl Collins *Marklevile, Indiana*

- **8 ounces white baking chocolate, chopped**
- **¾ cup butter, softened**
- **1½ cups sugar**
- **⅛ teaspoon salt**
- **4 eggs**
- **1 teaspoon coconut extract**
- **2½ cups cake flour**
- **6 teaspoons baking powder**
- **1¼ cups 2% milk**
- **1 cup frozen unsweetened sliced peaches, thawed and finely chopped**
- **½ cup macadamia nuts, chopped, toasted**

FROSTING:

- **6 ounces white baking chocolate, chopped**
- **¼ cup heavy whipping cream**
- **1 cup butter, softened**
- **½ teaspoon coconut extract**
- **4 cups confectioners' sugar**
- **1 cup flaked coconut, toasted**
- **¼ cup macadamia nuts, chopped, toasted**

1 Line three 8-in. round baking pans with parchment paper; coat paper with cooking spray and set aside. In a small bowl, melt chocolate; set aside.

2 In a large bowl, cream butter, sugar and salt until light and fluffy. Add eggs, one at a time, beating well after each addition. Beat in extract. In a small bowl, sift flour and baking powder; add to the creamed mixture alternately with milk, beating well after each addition.

3 Pat peaches dry with paper towels. Fold in the peaches, chocolate and macadamia nuts. Divide among prepared pans.

4 Bake at 350° for 35-40 minutes or until a toothpick inserted near the center comes out clean. Cool for 15 minutes before removing from pans to wire racks to cool completely.

5 For frosting, in a microwave, melt chocolate with cream; cool to room temperature. In a large bowl, cream butter and extract until light and fluffy; add cooled chocolate mixture. Gradually beat in confectioners' sugar. Spread between layers and over top and sides of cake. Sprinkle with coconut and macadamia nuts.

Chocolate Banana Cream Cake

PREP: 30 MIN. • BAKE: 20 MIN. + COOLING
YIELD: 12 SERVINGS

My inspiration for this cake came from my desire to create a dessert combining my father's love for cake, my mother's love for chocolate and my love for bananas. It's divine!

Susie Pattison *Dublin, Ohio*

- **½ cup butter, softened**
- **1¼ cups sugar**
- **2 eggs, separated**
- **1½ cups mashed ripe bananas (about 3 medium)**
- **¼ cup sour cream**
- **2 teaspoons vanilla extract**
- **1½ cups all-purpose flour**
- **1 teaspoon baking soda**
- **¼ teaspoon salt**

FILLING/FROSTING:

- **1½ cups cold 2% milk**
- **1 package (3.4 ounces) instant banana cream pudding mix**
- **1 can (16 ounces) chocolate frosting**
- **2 medium firm bananas, sliced**
- **3 tablespoons lemon juice**

1 In a large bowl, cream butter and sugar until light and fluffy. Beat in egg yolks. Beat in the bananas, sour cream and vanilla. Combine the flour, baking soda and salt; add to the creamed mixture and mix well.

2 In a small bowl, beat egg whites until stiff peaks form. Fold into batter. Transfer to two greased and floured 9-in. round baking pans. Bake at 350° for 20-25 minutes or until a toothpick inserted near the center comes out clean. Cool for 10 minutes before removing from pans to wire racks to cool completely.

3 For filling, in a small bowl, whisk milk and pudding mix for 2 minutes. Let stand for 2 minutes or until soft-set. Cover and refrigerate until chilled.

4 In a small bowl, beat frosting until light and fluffy. Place bananas in a small bowl; toss with lemon juice.

5 Place one cake layer on a serving plate; spread with 3 tablespoons frosting. Stir pudding; spread half over the frosting. Top with half of the bananas and the remaining cake layer. Repeat frosting, filling and banana layers. Frost sides and decorate top edge of cake with remaining frosting. Store in the refrigerator.

Give Me S'more Cake

PREP: 50 MIN. • BAKE: 20 MIN. + COOLING
YIELD: 12 SERVINGS

Bring a yummy campfire favorite to your table minus the sticky marshmallow fingers. Kids and kids at heart will love this new take on the time-honored treat.

Katie Lemery *Cuddebackville, New York*

- **½ cup shortening**
- **¼ cup butter, softened**
- **1 cup sugar**
- **3 eggs**
- **1 teaspoon vanilla extract**
- **2¾ cups graham cracker crumbs**
- **3 teaspoons baking powder**
- **1 can (12 ounces) evaporated milk**

MARSHMALLOW FROSTING:

- **4 egg whites**
- **1 cup sugar**
- **½ teaspoon cream of tartar**
- **1½ teaspoons vanilla extract**
- **1½ cups miniature semisweet chocolate chips, divided**

1 Line two 9-in. round baking pans with waxed paper and grease the paper; set aside. In a large bowl, cream the shortening, butter and sugar until light and fluffy. Add eggs, one at a time, beating well after each addition. Beat in vanilla. Combine cracker crumbs and baking powder; add to the creamed mixture alternately with milk, beating well after each addition.

2 Transfer to prepared pans. Bake at 350° for 18-22 minutes or until a toothpick inserted near the center comes out clean. Cool for 10 minutes before removing from pans to wire racks to cool completely.

3 In a large heavy saucepan, combine the egg whites, sugar and cream of tartar over low heat. With a hand mixer, beat on low speed for 1 minute. Continue beating on low over low heat until frosting reaches 160°, about 8-10 minutes. Pour into a large bowl; add vanilla. Beat on high until stiff peaks form, about 7 minutes.

4 Place a cake layer on a serving plate; spread with ⅔ cup frosting and sprinkle with half of chips. Top with remaining cake layer. Frost top and sides of cake; sprinkle with remaining chips.

Apple Cakes with Lemon Sauce

PREP: 15 MIN. • BAKE: 30 MIN. • YIELD: 2 SERVINGS

Perfect for dessert or brunch, these rich apple mini cakes are irresistible, especially with a cup of coffee. I make them often when I have fresh apples from our small orchard.

Mary Shivers *Ada, Oklahoma*

- **2 tablespoons shortening**
- **¼ cup sugar**
- **1 egg white**
- **½ cup all-purpose flour**
- **¼ teaspoon baking soda**
- **¼ teaspoon ground cinnamon**
- **⅛ teaspoon salt**
- **⅛ teaspoon ground nutmeg**
- **1 cup shredded peeled apple**
- **¼ cup chopped pecans**

LEMON SAUCE:

- **2 tablespoons plus 2 teaspoons sugar**
- **1 teaspoon cornstarch**
- **¼ cup cold water**
- **1½ teaspoons lemon juice**
- **1½ teaspoons butter**

1 In a small bowl, beat shortening and sugar until crumbly, about 2 minutes. Beat in egg white until combined. Combine the flour, baking soda, cinnamon, salt and nutmeg; add to shortening mixture just until combined. Fold in apple and pecans (batter will be thick).

2 Divide between two 8-oz. ramekins or custard cups coated with cooking spray. Bake at 325° for 28-30 minutes or until a toothpick comes out clean.

3 In a small microwave-safe bowl, combine the sugar, cornstarch and water until smooth. Microwave, uncovered, on high for 2-3 minutes or until thickened, stirring every 30 seconds. Stir in lemon juice and butter until blended. Spoon over warm cakes.

EDITOR'S NOTE: This recipe was tested in a 1,100-watt microwave.

WINNERS
CIRCLE

pies

Flaky crusts, crumbly toppings and a variety of fillings make this collection of pies perfectly praiseworthy. From sweet berries and crunchy nuts to smooth ice cream and rich custard, the tempting variety featured here will win you over. So cut yourself a generous slice and indulge in a dessert experience unlike any other.

CHOCOLATE-AMARETTO MOUSSE PIE, 278

French Apple Tart

PREP: 20 MIN. + CHILLING • BAKE: 40 MIN. + CHILLING
YIELD: 12 SERVINGS

I used to prepare this eye-catching tart with my grandmother. It has a buttery, tender crust that's topped with glossy glazed apple slices.

Esteban Vazquez *Encino, California*

- **2 cups all-purpose flour**
- **¾ cup cold unsalted butter, cubed**
- **1 tablespoon sugar**
- **¼ teaspoon salt**
- **6 tablespoons ice water**

TOPPING:

- **4 medium tart apples, peeled and sliced**
- **½ cup sugar**
- **¼ cup cold unsalted butter, cubed**
- **¼ cup apricot preserves**
- **1 tablespoon apple brandy or water**

1 In a food processor, combine the flour, butter, sugar and salt; cover and pulse until mixture resembles coarse crumbs. While processing, gradually add water in a steady stream until dough forms a ball. Wrap in plastic. Refrigerate for 1 hour or until easy to handle.

2 Roll out pastry to a 14-in. x 10-in. rectangle; transfer pastry to a parchment paper-lined baking sheet. Beginning at one corner of the pastry, arrange overlapping apple slices diagonally to opposite corner. Repeat rows. Sprinkle with sugar; dot with butter.

3 Bake at 400° for 40-45 minutes or until golden brown and apples are tender. In a small microwave-safe bowl, combine preserves and brandy; microwave on high for 30 seconds or until blended. Brush over warm tart. Serve warm or at room temperature.

KITCHEN GLOSSARY

>> "Pulsing" means processing in a food processor or a blender using short bursts of power. This is accomplished by quickly turning the machine on and off.

Mom's Cheese Pie

PREP: 20 MIN. • BAKE: 45 MIN. + COOLING • YIELD: 4 SERVINGS

My mother brought this Old World recipe with her from the Ukraine. A sprinkling of cinnamon enhances the pie's subtly sweet flavor.

Anne Kulick *Phillipsburg, New Jersey*

- **2 eggs**
- **1 sheet refrigerated pie pastry**
- **1 teaspoon ground cinnamon, divided**
- **1¾ cups ricotta cheese**
- **4 ounces cream cheese, softened**
- **3 tablespoons confectioners' sugar**
- **1½ teaspoons cornstarch**
- **½ teaspoon vanilla extract**
- **½ teaspoon salt**

1 Separate one egg. In a small bowl, lightly beat egg white; set aside. In another small bowl, combine egg and egg yolk; set aside.

2 On a lightly floured surface, unroll pastry; cut in half. Roll out one half of pastry into an 8-in. circle. Transfer to a 7-in. pie plate; trim pastry even with edge. Brush with egg white; sprinkle with ½ teaspoon cinnamon.

3 In a large bowl, combine the cheeses, confectioners' sugar, cornstarch, vanilla, salt and egg mixture. Pour into prepared pastry.

4 Roll out remaining pastry to fit top of pie. Place over filling. Trim, seal and flute edges. Cut slits in pastry. Brush remaining egg white over pastry; sprinkle with remaining cinnamon.

5 Bake at 350° for 45-50 minutes or until a knife inserted near the center comes out clean. Cool completely on wire rack. Refrigerate leftovers

Caramel Banana Ice Cream Pie

PREP: 20 MIN. + FREEZING • YIELD: 8 SERVINGS

With six ingredients and a prepared graham cracker crust, this pie is easy to make and luscious, too. Guests will enjoy the symphony of caramel, banana and toffee bits.

April Timboe *Siloam Springs, Arkansas*

- **¼ cup plus 1 tablespoon caramel ice cream topping, divided**
- **1 graham cracker crust (9 inches)**
- **1 cup cold 2% milk**
- **2 packages (3.4 ounces each) instant banana cream pudding mix**
- **1 quart vanilla ice cream, softened**
- **1¾ cups whipped topping**
- **1 English toffee candy bar (1.4 ounces), chopped**

1 Spread ¼ cup caramel topping into crust. In a large bowl, beat milk and pudding mix on low speed for 2 minutes. Add ice cream; mix well.

2 Spoon into prepared crust. Top with whipped topping. Drizzle with remaining caramel topping; sprinkle with chopped candy bar. Cover and freeze for 2 hours or until firm. Remove from the freezer 15 minutes before serving.

CARAMEL-CHOCOLATE ICE CREAM PIE: Substitute chocolate pudding for banana pudding.

TRIPLE-CHOCOLATE ICE CREAM PIE: Substitute chocolate ice cream topping for the caramel topping, chocolate pudding for the banana pudding and chocolate ice cream for the vanilla.

Chocolate Shoofly Pie

PREP: 20 MIN. • BAKE: 45 MIN. + COOLING
YIELD: 6-8 SERVINGS

If you like traditional shoofly pie, the chocolate version is even better! I sometimes serve it with vanilla ice cream, but it's just as good on its own.

Gwen Brounce Widdowson
Fleetwood, Pennsylvania

Pastry for single-crust pie (9 inches)
- **½ cup semisweet chocolate chips**
- **1½ cups all-purpose flour**
- **½ cup packed brown sugar**
- **3 tablespoons butter-flavored shortening**
- **1 teaspoon baking soda**
- **1½ cups water**
- **1 egg, lightly beaten**
- **1 cup molasses**

1 Line a 9-in. deep-dish pie plate with pastry. Trim to ½ in. beyond edge of plate; flute edges. Sprinkle chocolate chips into shell; set aside.

2 In a large bowl, combine flour and brown sugar; cut in shortening until crumbly. Set aside 1 cup for topping. Add the baking soda, water, egg and molasses to remaining crumb mixture and mix well. Pour over chips. Sprinkle with reserved crumb mixture.

3 Bake at 350° for 45-55 minutes or until a knife inserted near the center comes out clean. Cool on a wire rack for 20 minutes before cutting. Serve warm.

Mocha Chip Pie

PREP: 35 MIN. + CHILLING • YIELD: 8 SERVINGS

My mocha pie is chocolaty from top to bottom. The only thing hard about making it is waiting for it to set. Your friends and family will want to dig right in.

Sheila Watson *Stettler, Alberta*

- **1½ cups chocolate wafer crumbs**
- **¼ cup butter, softened**
- **1 envelope unflavored gelatin**
- **½ cup milk**
- **½ cup plus 1 tablespoon sugar, divided**
- **½ cup strong brewed coffee**
- **¼ cup water**
- **¼ teaspoon salt**
- **2 ounces unsweetened chocolate, melted and cooled**
- **1 teaspoon vanilla extract**
- **2 cups heavy whipping cream, divided**

Toasted sliced almonds, optional

1 In a small bowl, combine wafer crumbs and butter. Press onto the bottom and up the sides of a greased 9-in. pie plate. Bake at 375° for 5-7 minutes or until lightly browned. Cool on a wire rack.

2 In a small saucepan, sprinkle gelatin over milk; let stand for 1 minute. Cook and stir over low heat until gelatin is completely dissolved. Add ½ cup sugar, coffee, water and salt; cook and stir for 5 minutes or until sugar is dissolved. Remove from the heat; stir in melted chocolate and vanilla. Transfer to a large bowl; cover and refrigerate until slightly thickened, stirring occasionally.

3 In a small bowl, beat 1 cup cream until stiff peaks form; fold into chocolate mixture. Spread evenly into crust. Refrigerate for 4 hours or until set.

4 Just before serving, in a small bowl, beat remaining cream until it begins to thicken. Add remaining sugar; beat until stiff peaks form. Pipe over pie. Garnish with almonds if desired. Refrigerate leftovers.

Berry-Apple-Rhubarb Pie

PREP: 30 MIN. + CHILLING • BAKE: 65 MIN. + COOLING
YIELD: 8 SERVINGS

I make this family favorite every year using only fresh berries, apples and rhubarb I grow myself.

Michael Powers *New Baltimore, Virginia*

- **2⅔ cups all-purpose flour**
- **1 teaspoon salt**
- **1 cup butter-flavored shortening**
- **6 to 8 tablespoons cold water**

FILLING:

- **2 cups thinly sliced peeled tart apples**
- **1 tablespoon lemon juice**
- **1 teaspoon vanilla extract**
- **1 cup halved fresh strawberries**
- **1 cup fresh blueberries**
- **1 cup fresh raspberries**
- **1 cup fresh blackberries**
- **1 cup sliced fresh or frozen rhubarb**
- **⅓ cup all-purpose flour**
- **1 teaspoon ground allspice**
- **1 teaspoon ground cinnamon**
- **1½ cups plus 1 teaspoon sugar, divided**
- **2 tablespoons butter**
- **1 tablespoon 2% milk**

1 In a large bowl, combine flour and salt; cut in shortening until crumbly. Gradually add water, tossing with a fork until dough forms a ball. Divide dough in half so that one portion is slightly larger than the other; wrap each in plastic wrap. Refrigerate for 30 minutes or until easy to handle.

2 On a lightly floured surface, roll out larger portion of dough to fit a 9-in. deep-dish pie plate. Transfer to pie plate.

3 In a large bowl, toss apples with lemon juice and vanilla; add berries and rhubarb. Combine the flour, allspice, cinnamon and 1½ cups sugar; add to apple mixture and toss gently to coat. Spoon into crust; dot with butter.

4 Roll out remaining pastry; make a lattice crust. Trim, seal and flute edges. Brush milk over lattice top. Sprinkle with remaining sugar.

5 Bake at 400° for 15 minutes. Reduce heat to 350°; bake 50-60 minutes longer or until crust is golden brown and filling is bubbly. Cover edges with foil during the last 15 minutes to prevent overbrowning if necessary. Cool on a wire rack.

EDITOR'S NOTE: If using frozen rhubarb, measure rhubarb while still frozen, then thaw completely. Drain in a colander, but do not press liquid out.

Dreamy S'more Pie

PREP: 10 MIN. + CHILLING • BROIL: 5 MIN. • YIELD: 8 SERVINGS

I love desserts and was looking for a way to use hazelnut spread when I came up with this recipe. I wanted something that could be prepped quickly, and this is wonderful!

Karen Bowlden *Boise, Idaho*

- **1 package (8 ounces) cream cheese, softened**
- **1¼ cups heavy whipping cream**
- **1 jar (13 ounces) Nutella**
- **1 graham cracker crust (9 inches)**
- **3 cups miniature marshmallows**

1 In a large bowl, beat cream cheese and cream until thickened. Add Nutella; beat just until combined. Spoon into crust. Cover and refrigerate for at least 3 hours.

2 Just before serving, top with marshmallows; press gently into filling. Broil 6 in. from the heat for 1-2 minutes or until marshmallows are golden brown.

Apple-Cranberry Tart

PREP: 30 MIN. • BAKE: 40 MIN. + COOLING
YIELD: 14 SERVINGS

A treat for all tastes, this one's sweet, tart and nutty all rolled into one. Make it during the holidays, for birthdays and whenever you crave something fabulous and fruity.

Sonya Labbe *West Hollywood, California*

- **1⅔ cups all-purpose flour**
- **⅔ cup sugar**
- **⅓ cup finely chopped walnuts**
- **⅔ cup cold butter**

FILLING:

- **3 medium tart apples, peeled and thinly sliced**
- **½ cup sugar**
- **2 tablespoons cornstarch**
- **1 teaspoon ground cinnamon**
- **¼ teaspoon ground nutmeg**
- **2 cups fresh or frozen cranberries**

STREUSEL:

- **½ cup all-purpose flour**
- **½ cup packed brown sugar**
- **1 teaspoon grated orange peel**
- **¼ cup cold butter**
- **⅓ cup chopped walnuts**

1 In a small bowl, combine the flour, sugar and walnuts; cut in butter until crumbly. Press onto the bottom and up the sides of an ungreased 11-in. fluted tart pan with removable bottom.

2 In a large bowl, combine the apples, sugar, cornstarch, cinnamon and nutmeg. Gently stir in cranberries. Transfer to crust.

3 Bake at 425° for 25 minutes. In a small bowl, combine the flour, brown sugar and orange peel. Cut in butter until crumbly. Stir in walnuts. Sprinkle over filling. Bake 15-20 minutes longer or until filling is bubbly and topping is golden brown. Cool on a wire rack.

Brandy Pear Pie

PREP: 1 HOUR 20 MIN. • BAKE: 50 MIN. + COOLING
YIELD: 8 SERVINGS

I tapped into my French heritage for this recipe by incorporating Calvados, an apple brandy from the Normandy region of France. The sweet filling is balanced out by a buttery crust, making for an indulgent treat.

Nicole Jackson *Beverly, Massachusetts*

- **2½ cups all-purpose flour**
- **½ teaspoon salt**
- **1 cup cold butter**
- **½ cup ice water**

FILLING:

- **1 cup raisins**
- **½ cup apple brandy**
- **½ cup sugar**
- **¼ cup all-purpose flour**
- **½ teaspoon ground cinnamon**
- **¼ teaspoon salt**
- **¼ teaspoon ground nutmeg**
- **4 cups cubed peeled fresh pears**
- **2 tablespoons lemon juice**
- **2 tablespoons butter**

1 In a large bowl, combine flour and salt; cut in butter until crumbly. Gradually add water, tossing with a fork until a ball forms. Divide dough in half so that one portion is slightly larger than the other; wrap each in plastic wrap. Refrigerate for at least 1 hour or until easy to handle.

2 Meanwhile, in a small saucepan over low heat, cook raisins in brandy for 13-15 minutes or until raisins are plump. Strain, reserving liquid. Set raisins aside.

3 In a large bowl, combine the sugar, flour, cinnamon, salt and nutmeg. Add the pears, lemon juice, reserved raisins and ½ teaspoon of reserved liquid.

4 On a lightly floured surface, roll out larger portion of dough to fit a 9-in. pie plate. Transfer pastry to pie plate. Trim pastry even with edges. Add pear filling; dot with butter.

5 Roll out remaining pastry to fit top of pie. Place over filling. Trim, seal and flute edges. Cut slits in pastry. Cover edges loosely with foil.

6 Bake at 400° for 45-55 minutes or until bubbly. Cool on a wire rack for at least 30 minutes.

Orange & Blackberry Panther Tart

PREP: 25 MIN. • BAKE: 35 MIN. + COOLING
YIELD: 10 SERVINGS

I took this wonderful tart to school for a potluck that we had during homecoming. I work with fourth-graders and we typically eat at staggered times, starting with kindergarten and working our way up to fourth grade. By the time I got to eat lunch, my tart was gone but there was a nice note left telling me how good it was.

Dianna Wara *Washington, Illinois*

- **1 sheet refrigerated pie pastry**
- **1 package (8 ounces) cream cheese, softened**
- **3 tablespoons confectioners' sugar**
- **2 tablespoons orange marmalade**
- **3 cups fresh blackberries**
- **½ cup macadamia nuts, finely chopped**
- **3 tablespoons sugar**
- **1 tablespoon all-purpose flour**
- **1 tablespoon butter, melted**
- **½ cup white baking chips**
- **½ teaspoon shortening**
- **¼ teaspoon apple pie spice**

1 On a lightly floured surface, roll dough into a 12-in. circle. Transfer to a parchment paper-lined baking sheet.

2 In a small bowl, combine the cream cheese, confectioners' sugar and marmalade. Spread over the pastry to within 1¼ in. of edges. Top with blackberries to within 1 in. of cream cheese edge. Fold up edges of pastry over filling, leaving center uncovered.

3 In a small bowl, combine the nuts, sugar, flour and butter; sprinkle over blackberries. Bake at 400° for 35-40 minutes or until crust is golden and filling is bubbly. Using the parchment paper, slide tart onto a wire rack to cool.

4 In a microwave, melt baking chips and shortening; stir until smooth. Stir in apple pie spice. Drizzle over tart.

Cherry Cream Pie

PREP: 40 MIN. + CHILLING • YIELD: 6-8 SERVINGS

A favorite vacation spot in Wisconsin, Door County (in the "thumb" of the state), is known for its abundance of cherry orchards, and that's where this recipe originated. We think it's a delectable dessert, with a nutty crumb crust, real whipped cream and, of course, cherry pie filling.

Carol Wencka *Greenfield, Wisconsin*

CRUST:

- **1 cup all-purpose flour**
- **1 cup finely chopped walnuts**
- **½ cup butter, softened**
- **¼ cup packed brown sugar**

FILLING:

- **1 package (8 ounces) cream cheese, softened**
- **1 cup confectioners' sugar**
- **¼ teaspoon almond extract**
- **½ cup heavy whipping cream, whipped**
- **1 can (21 ounces) cherry pie filling**

1 In a small bowl, combine the flour, walnuts, butter and brown sugar. Transfer to a 13-in. x 9-in. baking pan. Bake at 375° for 15 minutes, stirring once. Set aside 1 cup of crumbs. While warm, press the remaining crumbs into a greased 9-in. pie plate, firmly pressing onto the bottom and up the sides. Chill for 30 minutes.

2 In a small bowl, beat the cream cheese, confectioners' sugar and almond extract until smooth. Spread over bottom of crust. Gently fold whipped cream into the pie filling; spread over cream cheese layer. Sprinkle with reserved crumbs. Chill for at least 4 hours before serving.

Eggnog Cranberry Pie

PREP: 40 MIN. + CHILLING
YIELD: 6-8 SERVINGS

Here's an elegant pie that says "holiday" in every bite. The tart cranberries contrast nicely with the rich gelatin-thickened eggnog.

Ruth White *Bedford, Ohio*

- **½ cup sugar**
- **1 tablespoon cornstarch**
- **6 tablespoons cold water, divided**
- **2 cups fresh or frozen cranberries**
- **1 pastry shell (9 inches), baked**
- **1 tablespoon unflavored gelatin**
- **1¾ cups eggnog**
- **2 tablespoons rum or 1 teaspoon rum extract**
- **½ cup heavy whipping cream, whipped**
- **⅛ teaspoon ground nutmeg**

1 In a large saucepan, combine the sugar, cornstarch and 2 tablespoons water until smooth; stir in cranberries. Cook over medium heat for 5 minutes or until thickened, stirring occasionally. Cool for 15 minutes. Pour into pastry shell; set aside.

2 In a small saucepan, sprinkle gelatin over remaining water; let stand for 5 minutes. Cook and stir over low heat until gelatin is dissolved. Gradually stir in eggnog and rum.

3 Refrigerate for 5 minutes or until slightly thickened, stirring occasionally. Fold in whipped cream; pour over cranberry layer. Refrigerate for 2 hours or until set. Sprinkle with nutmeg.

EDITOR'S NOTE: This recipe was tested with commercially prepared eggnog.

Raspberry Cream Pie

PREP: 30 MIN. + CHILLING • YIELD: 8 SERVINGS

This recipe is delicious with either fresh-picked or frozen raspberries. That means you can make it year-round. One bite of raspberry pie will instantly turn winter to summer.

Julie Price *Nashville, Tennessee*

- **1½ cups crushed vanilla wafers (about 45 wafers)**
- **⅓ cup chopped pecans**
- **¼ cup butter, melted**

FILLING:

- **1 package (8 ounces) cream cheese, softened**
- **⅔ cup confectioners' sugar**
- **2 tablespoons orange liqueur**
- **1 teaspoon vanilla extract**
- **1 cup heavy whipping cream, whipped**

TOPPING:

- **1 cup sugar**
- **3 tablespoons cornstarch**
- **3 tablespoons water**
- **2½ cups fresh or frozen raspberries, divided**

1 Combine the wafer crumbs, pecans and butter. Press onto the bottom and up the sides of a greased 9-in. pie plate.

2 In a large bowl, beat the cream cheese, confectioners' sugar, liqueur and vanilla until light and fluffy. Fold in whipped cream. Spread into crust. Chill until serving.

3 In a small saucepan, combine sugar and cornstarch; stir in water and 1½ cups raspberries. Bring to a boil; cook and stir for 2 minutes or until thickened. Transfer to a bowl; refrigerate until chilled.

4 Spread topping over filling. Garnish with remaining berries.

Fresh Blueberry Pie

PREP: 20 MIN. + CHILLING
YIELD: 6-8 SERVINGS

We live in blueberry country, and this pie is a perfect way to showcase the luscious berries. A neighbor made this pie for us when we had a death in the family several years ago, and she shared the recipe, too. Our whole family enjoys it.

R. Ricks *Kalamazoo, Michigan*

- **¾ cup sugar**
- **3 tablespoons cornstarch**
- **⅛ teaspoon salt**
- **¼ cup water**
- **4 cups fresh blueberries, divided**
- **1 graham cracker crust (9 inches)**

Whipped cream

1 In a large saucepan, combine the sugar, cornstarch and salt. Gradually add water, stirring until smooth. Stir in 2 cups of blueberries. Bring to a boil; cook and stir for 1-2 minutes or until thickened. Remove from the heat; cool to room temperature.

2 Spoon remaining blueberries into the crust; top with cooled blueberry mixture. Cover and refrigerate for 1-2 hours or until chilled. Serve with whipped cream.

Lemon Curd Chiffon Pie

PREP: 30 MIN. • BAKE: 10 MIN. + CHILLING
YIELD: 8 SERVINGS

A real showstopper, this pie is very refreshing and tart. I get frequent requests from my gang to make it. Normally I am a chocolate lover, but this pie makes me forget about chocolate in one bite.

Callie Palen-Lowrie *Louisville, Colorado*

- **9 whole graham crackers, broken into large pieces**
- **½ cup chopped pecans**
- **3 tablespoons sugar**
- **¼ teaspoon vanilla extract**
- **⅛ teaspoon salt**
- **5 tablespoons butter, melted**

FILLING:

- **1½ cups heavy whipping cream**
- **3 tablespoons sugar**
- **3 teaspoons vanilla extract**
- **1 jar (11 ounces) lemon curd**
- **1 package (8 ounces) cream cheese, softened**
- **1 tablespoon grated lemon peel**
- **1½ teaspoons unflavored gelatin**
- **⅓ cup lemon juice**
- **1 tablespoon limoncello**

BERRY SAUCE:

- **½ pint fresh raspberries**
- **½ pint fresh blueberries**
- **½ pint fresh strawberries**
- **¼ cup sugar**
- **1 tablespoon seedless raspberry jam**
- **1 tablespoon lemon juice**
- **1 tablespoon raspberry liqueur**

1 Place the graham crackers, pecans, sugar, vanilla and salt in a food processor; cover and pulse until mixture resembles fine crumbs. Add the butter; process until blended.

2 Press crumb mixture onto the bottom and up the sides of a greased 9-in. deep-dish pie plate. Bake at 350° for 10-12 minutes or until light golden brown. Cool completely on a wire rack.

3 In a small bowl, combine the cream, sugar and vanilla. Beat until stiff peaks form; set aside. In a large bowl, beat the lemon curd, cream cheese and lemon peel until blended; set aside.

4 Sprinkle gelatin over lemon juice; let stand for 1 minute. Microwave on high for 20 seconds. Stir and let stand for 1 minute or until gelatin is completely dissolved. Stir in limoncello. Gradually beat into lemon curd mixture until well blended. Fold in whipped cream; pour into the crust. Refrigerate for 3 hours or until set.

5 In a small saucepan over medium heat, combine the berries, sugar and jam. Cook and stir for 3-5 minutes or until fruit is softened. In a blender, cover and process berry mixture for 1-2 minutes or until blended. Strain, reserving juice. Discard seeds.

6 Return juice to the saucepan; cook for 15-18 minutes or until reduced to desired consistency, stirring occasionally. Stir in lemon juice and raspberry liqueur. Chill for 1 hour. Garnish servings with sauce.

Elegant Fresh Berry Tart

PREP: 45 MIN. + CHILLING • BAKE: 10 MIN. + COOLING
YIELD: 16 SERVINGS

My elegant tart was my first original creation. If other fresh fruits are used for the topping, simply adjust the syrup flavor to match.

Denise Nakamoto *Elk Grove, California*

- **½ cup butter, softened**
- **⅓ cup sugar**
- **½ teaspoon grated orange peel**
- **¼ teaspoon orange extract**
- **⅛ teaspoon vanilla extract**
- **1 cup all-purpose flour**

FILLING:

- **1 package (8 ounces) cream cheese, softened**
- **¼ cup sugar**
- **½ teaspoon lemon juice**

SYRUP:

- **½ cup water**
- **1 tablespoon sugar**
- **1 tablespoon red raspberry or strawberry preserves**
- **¼ teaspoon lemon juice**

TOPPING:

- **1 pound fresh strawberries, sliced**
- **1 cup fresh raspberries**
- **2 medium kiwifruit, peeled and sliced**
- **½ cup fresh blueberries**

1 In a small bowl, cream butter and sugar until light and fluffy. Add the orange peel and extracts. Gradually add flour until mixture forms a ball. Press into a greased 11-in. fluted tart pan with a removable bottom. Bake at 375° for 10-12 minutes or until golden brown. Cool on a wire rack.

2 For filling, in a small bowl, beat the cream cheese, sugar and lemon juice until smooth. Spread over crust. Cover and refrigerate for 30 minutes or until set.

3 Meanwhile, in a small saucepan, bring the water, sugar, preserves and lemon juice to a boil. Reduce heat; simmer, uncovered, for 10 minutes. Set aside to cool.

4 Arrange the strawberries, raspberries, kiwi and blueberries over filling. Brush with sugar mixture. Cover and refrigerate for at least 1 hour before serving.

Triple-Berry Crumb Pie

PREP: 25 MIN. • BAKE: 55 MIN. + COOLING • YIELD: 8 SERVINGS

Berries and hazelnuts are plentiful here in the Pacific Northwest, so ingredients for this treat are often at my fingertips. I like to freeze a couple of pies so we can enjoy sweet slices in winter.

Katherine Barrett *Bellevue, Washington*

- **1½ cups all-purpose flour**
- **1½ cups ground hazelnuts**
- **1 cup sugar, divided**
- **¾ cup cold butter, cubed**
- **2 cups fresh blackberries**
- **2 cups fresh blueberries**
- **2 cups fresh strawberries, sliced**
- **3 tablespoons cornstarch**

1 In a large bowl, combine the flour, hazelnuts and ½ cup sugar; cut in butter until crumbly. Set aside 1½ cups crumb mixture for topping. Press remaining mixture onto the bottom and up the sides of an ungreased 9-in. deep-dish pie plate.

2 Place the berries in a large bowl; sprinkle with cornstarch and remaining sugar. Stir until well blended. Spoon into crust. Sprinkle with reserved crumb mixture.

3 Bake at 375° for 55-60 minutes or until crust is golden brown and filling is bubbly (cover edges with foil during the last 15 minutes to prevent overbrowning if necessary). Cool on a wire rack.

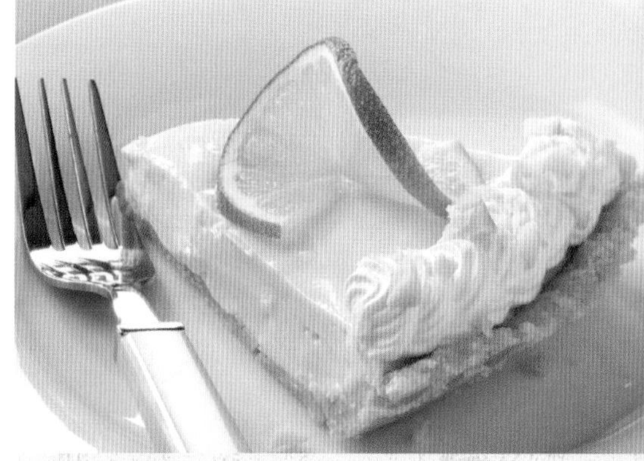

Key Lime Pie with Shortbread Macadamia Crust

PREP: 20 MIN. + CHILLING • YIELD: 8 SERVINGS

Key lime is my favorite pie. I make this at least four times a month during the summer! It's so refreshing. The shortbread crust gives a richness to the pie that a graham cracker crust doesn't.

Brynn LeMaire *Gueydan, Louisiana*

- **1 cup crushed shortbread cookies**
- **½ cup finely chopped macadamia nuts**
- **⅓ cup butter, melted**
- **¼ cup sugar**

FILLING:

- **1 package (8 ounces) cream cheese, softened**
- **1 can (14 ounces) sweetened condensed milk**
- **½ cup Key lime juice or lime juice**
- **1 cup heavy whipping cream, whipped**
- **¼ cup coarsely chopped macadamia nuts**

Lime slices, optional

1 Combine the cookie crumbs, macadamia nuts, butter and sugar; press onto the bottom and up the sides of a greased 9-in. pie plate. Refrigerate for 30 minutes.

2 For the filling, in a large bowl, beat cream cheese until smooth. Add milk and lime juice; beat until smooth. Pour into the crust. Refrigerate for at least 4 hours. Garnish with whipped cream, macadamia nuts and lime slices if desired.

Best Lime Tart

PREP: 35 MIN. • BAKE: 15 MIN. + CHILLING
YIELD: 12 SERVINGS

Look no further for a treat with the perfect balance between tart and sweet. The almonds in the crust are just wonderful, making it one of my husband's favorite desserts.

Charis O'Connell *Mohnton, Pennsylvania*

- **1¼ cups graham cracker crumbs**
- **5 tablespoons butter, melted**
- **¼ cup ground almonds**
- **3 tablespoons sugar**

FILLING:

- **4 egg yolks**
- **1 can (14 ounces) sweetened condensed milk**
- **½ cup lime juice**
- **2 teaspoons grated lime peel**

TOPPING:

- **½ cup heavy whipping cream**
- **1 tablespoon sugar**
- **½ cup sour cream**
- **1 teaspoon grated lime peel**

Fresh raspberries and lime wedges

1 In a small bowl, combine the cracker crumbs, butter, almonds and sugar. Press onto the bottom and up the sides of a greased 9-in. tart pan. Bake at 325° for 15-18 minutes or until edges are lightly browned.

2 In a large bowl, whisk the egg yolks, milk, lime juice and peel. Pour over crust. Bake for 12-14 minutes or until center is almost set. Cool on a wire rack. Refrigerate for at least 2 hours.

3 In a large bowl, beat cream until it begins to thicken. Add sugar; beat until stiff peaks form. Fold in sour cream and grated lime peel. Spread over tart. Garnish with raspberries and lime wedges.

Banana-Berry Pie

PREP: 30 MIN. + CHILLING • YIELD: 8 SERVINGS

Here's a gorgeous pie that really looks like you fussed. It features a crunchy graham cracker crust with a touch of ginger, a lovely fresh strawberry layer and tasty banana cream topping.

Julie Guntzel *Bemidji, Minnesota*

- **1¼ cups graham cracker crumbs**
- **5 tablespoons butter, melted**
- **2 tablespoons sugar**
- **1 teaspoon ground ginger**

FILLING:

- **¾ cup sugar**
- **2 tablespoons plus ¾ teaspoon cornstarch**
- **1 tablespoon strawberry gelatin**
- **¾ cup cold water**
- **2 cups sliced fresh strawberries, divided**
- **1 can (14 ounces) sweetened condensed milk**
- **1 package (8 ounces) reduced-fat cream cheese**
- **¼ cup cold 2% milk**
- **1 package (3.4 ounces) instant banana cream pudding mix**

1 Combine the graham cracker crumbs, butter, sugar and ginger. Press onto the bottom and up the sides of an ungreased 9-in. pie plate. Bake at 350° for 8-10 minutes or until lightly browned. Cool on a wire rack.

2 For filling, in a small saucepan, combine the sugar, cornstarch and gelatin. Stir in water until smooth. Bring to a boil; cook and stir for 2 minutes or until thickened. Cool slightly. Arrange 1 cup strawberries over crust. Pour gelatin mixture over strawberries. Refrigerate for 2 hours or until set.

3 In a large bowl, beat the sweetened condensed milk, cream cheese, milk and pudding mix for 1 minute. Spread over top of pie. Refrigerate for 2 hours or until set. Garnish with remaining strawberries. Refrigerate leftovers.

Rhubarb Meringue Pie

PREP: 50 MIN. + CHILLING • BAKE: 65 MIN. + COOLING
YIELD: 6-8 SERVINGS

My husband's grandmother was a great cook and didn't always share her secrets, so we are fortunate to have her recipe for rhubarb cream pie. I added one of my favorite crusts and a never-fail meringue.

Elaine Sampson *Colesburg, Iowa*

- **¾ cup all-purpose flour**
- **¼ teaspoon salt**
- **¼ teaspoon sugar**
- **¼ cup shortening**
- **1 tablespoon beaten egg**
- **¼ teaspoon white vinegar**
- **3 to 4½ teaspoons cold water**

FILLING:

- **3 cups chopped fresh or frozen rhubarb**
- **1 cup sugar**
- **2 tablespoons all-purpose flour**
- **Dash salt**
- **3 egg yolks**
- **1 cup heavy whipping cream**

MERINGUE:

- **4 teaspoons plus ⅓ cup sugar, divided**
- **2 teaspoons cornstarch**
- **⅓ cup water**
- **3 egg whites**
- **⅛ teaspoon cream of tartar**

1 In a small bowl, combine flour, salt and sugar; cut in shortening until crumbly. Combine egg and vinegar; sprinkle over crumb mixture. Gradually add water, tossing with a fork until a ball forms. Cover and chill for 1 hour or until easy to handle.

2 On a lightly floured surface, roll out pastry to fit a 9-in. pie plate. Trim to ½ in. beyond edge of plate; flute edges. Place rhubarb on crust. Whisk sugar, flour, salt, egg yolks and cream; pour over the rhubarb. Bake at 350° for 50-60 minutes or until a knife comes out clean.

3 In a small saucepan, combine 4 teaspoons sugar and cornstarch. Gradually stir in water. Bring to a boil, stirring constantly; cook for 1-2 minutes or until thickened. Cool to room temperature.

4 In a small bowl, beat egg whites and cream of tartar until frothy. Add cornstarch mixture; beat on high until soft peaks form. Gradually beat in remaining sugar, 1 tablespoon at a time, on high until stiff glossy peaks form and sugar is dissolved. Spread evenly over hot filling, sealing edges to crust. Bake for 15 minutes or until meringue is golden brown. Cool on a wire rack for 1 hour. Store in the refrigerator.

EDITOR'S NOTE: If using frozen rhubarb, measure rhubarb while still frozen, then thaw completely. Drain in a colander, but do not press liquid out.

Peanut Butter Pie

PREP: 25 MIN. + CHILLING • YIELD: 8 SERVINGS

Although I make this fudgy peanut butter pie regularly for luncheons at our church, I've yet to eat a full piece. Usually, there's nothing left but crumbs!

Lillibell Welter *Rainier, Oregon*

- **1 package (8 ounces) cream cheese, softened**
- **1 cup plus 2 tablespoons creamy peanut butter, divided**
- **½ cup sugar**
- **1 carton (12 ounces) frozen whipped topping, thawed, divided**
- **1 chocolate crumb crust (8 inches)**
- **⅔ cup plus 2 tablespoons hot fudge ice cream topping, divided**

1 In a large bowl, beat cream cheese until smooth. Beat in 1 cup peanut butter and sugar. Fold in 3 cups whipped topping; spoon into crust.

2 In a microwave-safe bowl, heat ⅔ cup hot fudge topping for 30 seconds. Pour over peanut butter layer and spread to edges of crust. Refrigerate for 2 hours.

3 Spread remaining whipped topping over pie. Cut into slices. Place the remaining hot fudge topping and peanut butter in two separate plastic bags. Cut a small hole in the corner of each bag; pipe fudge and peanut butter over each slice of pie.

Blueberry-Blackberry Rustic Tart

PREP: 20 MIN. + CHILLING • BAKE: 55 MIN. • YIELD: 8 SERVINGS

Blackberries and blueberries pack the crispy golden-brown cornmeal crust in this homey tart. It's a delicious dessert, treat between meals or late evening snack!

Priscilla Gilbert *Indian Harbour Beach, Florida*

- **2 cups all-purpose flour**
- **⅓ cup sugar**
- **¼ cup yellow cornmeal**
- **⅔ cup cold butter, cubed**
- **½ cup buttermilk**

FILLING:

- **4 cups fresh blueberries**
- **2 cups fresh blackberries**
- **⅔ cup sugar**
- **⅓ cup all-purpose flour**
- **2 tablespoons lemon juice**
- **1 egg, beaten**
- **2 tablespoons turbinado (washed raw) sugar or coarse sugar**

Whipped cream, optional

1 In a large bowl, combine the flour, sugar and cornmeal; cut in butter until crumbly. Gradually add buttermilk, tossing with a fork until dough forms a ball. Cover and refrigerate for at least 30 minutes.

2 On a lightly floured surface, roll dough into a 14-in. circle. Transfer to a parchment paper-lined baking sheet.

3 In a large bowl, combine the berries, sugar, flour and lemon juice; spoon over the pastry to within 2 in. of edges. Fold up edges of pastry over filling, leaving center uncovered. Brush folded pastry with egg; sprinkle with sugar.

4 Bake at 375° for 55-60 minutes or until crust is golden brown and filling is bubbly. Using the parchment paper, slide tart onto a wire rack to cool. Serve with whipped cream if desired.

Strawberry-Rhubarb Meringue Pie

PREP: 55 MIN. • BAKE: 40 MIN. + CHILLING
YIELD: 8 SERVINGS

This pie is a rite of spring at our house, and many people have enjoyed sharing it with us. We love that it's both sweet and tart, with a mild almond accent.

Jessie Grearson-Sapat *Falmouth, Maine*

- **½ cup all-purpose flour**
- **¼ cup whole wheat pastry flour**
- **¼ cup ground almonds**
- **½ teaspoon salt**
- **¼ cup cold butter, cubed**
- **2 tablespoons cold water**

FILLING:

- **1 egg, lightly beaten**
- **¾ cup sugar**
- **2 tablespoons all-purpose flour**
- **¼ teaspoon ground cinnamon**
- **2 cups chopped fresh or frozen rhubarb, thawed**
- **1½ cups sliced fresh strawberries**

MERINGUE:

- **3 egg whites**
- **¼ teaspoon almond extract**
- **6 tablespoons sugar**

1 In a food processor, combine the all-purpose flour, pastry flour, almonds and salt; cover and pulse until blended. Add butter; cover and pulse until mixture resembles coarse crumbs. While processing, gradually add water until dough forms a ball.

2 Roll out pastry to fit a 9-in. pie plate. Transfer pastry to pie plate. Trim pastry to ½ in. beyond edge of plate; flute edges.

3 In a large bowl, combine the egg, sugar, flour and cinnamon; stir in rhubarb and strawberries. Transfer to prepared crust. Bake at 375° for 35-40 minutes or until filling is bubbly. Place pie on a wire rack; keep warm. Reduce heat to 350°.

4 In a large bowl, beat egg whites and extract on medium speed until soft peaks form. Gradually beat in sugar, 1 tablespoon at a time, on high until stiff peaks form. Spread over hot filling, sealing edges to crust.

5 Bake for 15 minutes or until golden brown. Cool on a wire rack for 1 hour; refrigerate for 1-2 hours before serving.

Chocolate-Amaretto Mousse Pie

PREP: 15 MIN. + FREEZING • COOK: 20 MIN. + CHILLING
YIELD: 8 SERVINGS

My mother made this silky pie when I was a child. It was my father's favorite. The fluffy chocolate-almond filling is held in a thin chocolate shell. Be warned, it is so rich that you should only take a sliver.

Jamie Burkhart *Windsor, Missouri*

- **1 teaspoon plus ½ cup butter, divided**
- **2 cups (12 ounces) semisweet chocolate chips, divided**
- **1 can (14 ounces) sweetened condensed milk**
- **¼ teaspoon salt**
- **¼ cup water**
- **½ cup Amaretto**
- **2 cups heavy whipping cream, whipped**
- **¼ cup slivered almonds, toasted**

1 Line a 9-in. pie plate with foil and grease the foil with 1 teaspoon butter; set aside.

2 In a small saucepan over low heat, melt 1 cup chocolate chips with ¼ cup butter; quickly spread in an even layer in prepared pan. Freeze for 30 minutes.

3 In a small saucepan over low heat, heat the condensed milk, salt and remaining butter and chips until melted; stir until well blended. Gradually stir in the water; cook over medium heat for 5 minutes. Add Amaretto; cook for 5 minutes or until thickened, stirring constantly. Cool to room temperature.

4 Fold half of whipped cream into chocolate mixture. Using foil, lift chocolate shell out of pan; gently peel off foil. Return shell to the pie plate; spoon filling into shell. Garnish with remaining whipped cream; sprinkle with almonds. Chill for 3 hours or until set.

TIPS FOR WHIPPING CREAM

>> Before whipping cream, refrigerate the bowl and beaters for about 30 minutes. Pour the cream into a deep, chilled bowl; whip on high (with sugar if instructed) until soft peaks form if using as a garnish. Beat until stiff peaks form if frosting a cake.

Peanut Butter Chocolate Tart

PREP: 40 MIN. + CHILLING • YIELD: 16 SERVINGS

What better combination than peanut butter and chocolate, all baked in a chocolaty cookie crust? The taste reminds me of peanut butter cup candies, and is very easy to assemble.

Mary Ann Lee *Clifton Park, New York*

- **1 package (9 ounces) chocolate wafers**
- **½ cup peanut butter chips**
- **2 tablespoons sugar**
- **½ cup butter, melted**

FILLING:

- **1 cup creamy peanut butter**
- **½ cup butter, softened**
- **4 ounces cream cheese, softened**
- **1 cup confectioners' sugar**
- **¼ cup light corn syrup**
- **1 teaspoon vanilla extract**

GANACHE:

- **¾ cup semisweet chocolate chips**
- **½ cup heavy whipping cream**
- **1½ teaspoons sugar**
- **1½ teaspoons light corn syrup**
- **¼ cup chopped salted peanuts**

1 In a food processor, place the wafers, peanut butter chips and sugar; cover and process until finely crushed. Stir in melted butter. Press onto the bottom and up the sides of an ungreased 9-in. fluted tart pan with removable bottom. Refrigerate for 30 minutes.

2 For filling, in a large bowl, beat peanut butter, butter and cream cheese until fluffy. Add the confectioners' sugar, corn syrup and vanilla; beat until smooth. Pour filling into crust. Refrigerate while making ganache.

3 Place chocolate chips in a small bowl. In a small saucepan, bring the cream, sugar and corn syrup just to a boil. Pour over chips; whisk until melted and smooth. Pour over filling.

4 Sprinkle with peanuts. Refrigerate for at least 2 hours.

Strawberry Tart

PREP: 20 MIN. • BAKE: 10 MIN. + CHILLING
YIELD: 6-8 SERVINGS

Looking for the perfect ending to any summertime meal? Here's a swift-to-fix, creamy tart that boasts a crunchy chocolate layer tucked next to the crust.

Dawn Tringali *Hamilton Square, New Jersey*

- **1 sheet refrigerated pie pastry**
- **3 ounces German sweet chocolate, melted**
- **2 packages (8 ounces each) cream cheese, softened**
- **3 tablespoons heavy whipping cream**
- **2 teaspoons vanilla extract**
- **1¾ cups confectioners' sugar**
- **2½ cups sliced fresh strawberries**
- **¼ cup red currant jelly**

1 Press pastry onto the bottom and up the sides of an ungreased 9-in. fluted tart pan with a removable bottom. Place on a baking sheet. Bake at 450° for 10-12 minutes or until golden brown. Cool on a wire rack.

2 Spread melted chocolate over bottom of crust. Cover and refrigerate for 5-10 minutes or until almost set. Meanwhile, in a large bowl, beat the cream cheese, cream and vanilla until smooth. Gradually beat in confectioners' sugar. Spread over chocolate layer.

3 Arrange strawberries over filling; brush with jelly. Cover and refrigerate for at least 2 hours. Remove sides of pan before serving.

WINNERS CIRCLE

desserts

Did you save room for dessert? You'll wish you had after you view these irresistible finales. From classic standbys like Tiramisu to more inventive temptations like Strawberry-Lemon Crepe Cake, the recipes featured here offer a dazzling send-off after any meal.

FROSTED WALNUT BROWNIE CUPS, 287

Chocolate Peanut Butter Dessert

PREP: 40 MIN. + FREEZING • YIELD: 10-12 SERVINGS

When I want to splurge on a rich dessert, I whip up this chocolate-glazed frozen peanut butter mousse. It's so luscious, even a thin slice will satisfy. It tastes like a peanut butter cup.

Christine Montalvo *Windsor Heights, Iowa*

- **1¼ cups packed dark brown sugar**
- **1 cup heavy whipping cream, divided**
- **3 egg yolks**
- **1¼ cups creamy peanut butter**
- **6 tablespoons butter, softened**

GLAZE:

- **1½ cups heavy whipping cream**
- **2 tablespoons butter**
- **4 teaspoons dark corn syrup**
- **12 ounces bittersweet chocolate, chopped**
- **¼ cup coarsely chopped dry roasted peanuts**

1 In a small saucepan, combine the brown sugar, ½ cup cream and yolks. Cook and stir over medium heat until mixture reaches 160° and is thick enough to coat the back of a metal spoon. Cover and refrigerate for 3 hours or until thickened.

2 Line an 8-in. x 4-in. loaf pan with plastic wrap; set aside. In a large bowl, cream peanut butter and butter until light and fluffy. Add brown sugar mixture; beat until smooth. In small bowl, beat remaining cream until stiff peaks form. Fold into peanut butter mixture. Spoon into prepared pan. Cover and refrigerate.

3 For glaze, in a large heavy saucepan, bring the cream, butter and corn syrup to a boil, stirring frequently. Remove from the heat. Add chocolate; whisk until smooth. Set aside ⅓ cup glaze to cool. Place remaining glaze in a microwave-safe bowl; cover and refrigerate overnight. Spread cooled glaze over loaf; cover and freeze overnight.

4 Using plastic wrap, lift loaf out of pan. Place chocolate side down in a 15-in. x 10-in. x 1-in. pan; place on a wire rack. Discard plastic wrap.

5 In microwave, warm refrigerated glaze; stir until smooth. Pour over loaf; spread with a metal spatula to completely cover top and sides. Sprinkle with peanuts. Freeze for 1 hour or until glaze is set.

Tropical Macadamia Custard Dessert

PREP: 15 MIN. • BAKE: 40 MIN. + COOLING • YIELD: 12 SERVINGS

My husband's co-workers always love my desserts, especially the cookies and bars. So when I decided to enter a contest, I used them as my "guinea pigs." They nominated these bars for their unique flavor—and all asked for the recipe! Believe it or not, most of them are men.

Brenda Melancon *Gonzales, Louisiana*

- **1 package (16 ounces) ready-to-bake refrigerated white chip macadamia nut cookie dough, divided**
- **3 eggs**
- **1 can (20 ounces) unsweetened crushed pineapple, well drained**
- **1 can (12 ounces) evaporated milk**
- **1 package (7 ounces) dried tropical fruit bits**
- **⅓ cup packed brown sugar**
- **2 tablespoons all-purpose flour**
- **1½ teaspoons rum extract**
- **Whipped topping and maraschino cherries**

1 Let dough stand at room temperature for 5-10 minutes to soften. Press nine portions of dough into a greased 9-in. square baking pan. Bake at 350° for 10 minutes or until set. Let stand for 2 minutes.

2 Meanwhile, in a bowl, combine the eggs, pineapple, milk, dried fruit, brown sugar, flour and extract. Pour over crust. Crumble the remaining dough over filling.

3 Bake for 30-35 minutes or until top is golden brown. Cool on a wire rack. Cut into squares; garnish with whipped topping and cherries. Refrigerate leftovers.

Frozen Strawberry Delight

PREP: 20 MIN + FREEZING
YIELD: 10 SERVINGS

Simple, pretty and absolutely refreshing, this lovely dessert will become a family favorite in no time. Sprinkle in some fresh blueberries for a patriotic treat.

Barbara Christensen *Jacksonville, Florida*

- **1 can (14 ounces) sweetened condensed milk**
- **¼ cup lemon juice**
- **4 cups sliced fresh strawberries, divided**
- **1 carton (8 ounces) frozen whipped topping, thawed and divided**
- **8 Oreo cookies, crushed**

1 Line an 8-in. x 4-in. loaf pan with foil, letting edges hang over sides; set aside.

2 In a large bowl, combine milk and lemon juice; fold in 2 cups strawberries and 2 cups whipped topping. Transfer half of the mixture to prepared pan. Sprinkle with cookie crumbs; top with remaining strawberry mixture. Cover and freeze for 6 hours or overnight.

3 To serve, using foil, lift dessert out of pan. Invert onto a serving plate; discard foil. Spread remaining whipped topping over top and sides of dessert; garnish with remaining strawberries. Cut into slices.

Strawberry-Lemon Crepe Cake

PREP: 1 HOUR + CHILLING • COOK: 35 MIN.
YIELD: 10 SERVINGS PLUS 5 LEFTOVER CREPES

Each year for my husband's birthday I make him a different lemon cake (a tradition started by his mother). A couple years ago I made a lemon crepe cake. I later added fresh strawberries with fabulous results! I like to make the crepe batter and lemon curd the night before and assemble everything the next morning.
Lora Roth *Seneca, South Carolina*

- **1 teaspoon unflavored gelatin**
- **2 tablespoons cold water**
- **4 eggs**
- **1 cup sugar**
- **¾ cup lemon juice**
- **6 egg yolks**
- **2 tablespoons grated lemon peel**
- **6 tablespoons butter, cubed**

CREPES:

- **1¼ cups 2% milk**
- **3 eggs**
- **⅓ cup melted butter**
- **1 teaspoon vanilla extract**
- **¾ cup all-purpose flour**
- **½ cup sugar**
- **¼ teaspoon salt**

FILLING/TOPPING:

- **1½ cups heavy whipping cream**
- **¼ cup confectioners' sugar**
- **1 package (16 ounces) fresh strawberries, hulled and thinly sliced**

1 Sprinkle gelatin over cold water; let stand for 5 minutes.

2 In a small heavy saucepan over medium heat, whisk the eggs, sugar, lemon juice, egg yolks and lemon peel until blended. Add butter; cook, whisking constantly, until mixture is thickened and coats the back of a spoon. Remove from the heat; stir in softened gelatin until completely dissolved. Transfer to a large bowl; cool. Press waxed paper onto surface of lemon curd; refrigerate overnight or until chilled.

3 Meanwhile, for crepes, in a small bowl, whisk the milk, eggs, melted butter and vanilla. Combine the flour, sugar and salt; add to milk mixture and mix well. Cover and refrigerate for 2 hours or overnight.

4 Heat a lightly greased 8-in. nonstick skillet over medium heat; pour 2 tablespoons batter into center of skillet. Lift and tilt pan to coat bottom evenly. Cook until top appears dry; turn and cook 15-20 seconds longer. Remove to a wire rack. Repeat with remaining batter, greasing skillet as needed. When cool, stack crepes with waxed paper or paper towels in between.

5 In a large bowl, beat cream until it begins to thicken. Add confectioners' sugar; beat until stiff peaks form. Set aside 1 cup for topping; cover and refrigerate. In a large bowl, gradually whisk whipped cream into lemon curd.

6 To assemble, place one crepe on a cake plate. Spread with 3 tablespoons lemon curd mousse and layer with 2 tablespoons strawberries. Repeat layers until 15 crepes are used (save remaining crepes for another use). Cover cake and remaining lemon curd mousse; refrigerate until serving.

7 Just before serving, top cake with whipped cream. Garnish with remaining strawberries. Serve with additional lemon curd mousse.

Chocolate Peanut Torte

PREP: 35 MIN. • BAKE: 30 MIN. + COOLING
YIELD: 16 SERVINGS

The smooth peanut butter layers and fudgy topping of this rich and impressive dessert are always a hit with my family and friends.

Crystal Christopher *Hustonville, Kentucky*

- **1¾ cups all-purpose flour**
- **1 cup sugar**
- **¾ cup baking cocoa**
- **⅓ cup sugar blend**
- **1½ teaspoons baking powder**
- **1 teaspoon salt**
- **¼ teaspoon baking soda**
- **1 cup fat-free milk**
- **½ cup egg substitute**
- **¼ cup canola oil**
- **2 teaspoons vanilla extract**
- **1 cup boiling water**

CREAMY PEANUT FILLING:

- **1¾ cups plus 2 tablespoons cold fat-free milk, divided**
- **1 package (1 ounce) sugar-free instant vanilla pudding mix**
- **¾ cup reduced-fat creamy peanut butter**

TOPPING:

- **1 ounce unsweetened chocolate**
- **3 tablespoons butter**
- **½ cup confectioners' sugar**
- **2 tablespoons fat-free milk**

1 Coat two 9-in. round baking pans with cooking spray; line with waxed paper. Coat the paper with cooking spray and sprinkle with flour; set aside.

2 In a large bowl, combine the first seven ingredients. In a small bowl, combine the milk, egg substitute, oil and vanilla; add to flour mixture. Beat for 2 minutes. Stir in water. Pour into prepared pans.

3 Bake at 350° for 30-35 minutes or until a toothpick inserted near the center comes out clean. Cool for 10 minutes; remove from pans to wire racks. Cool completely.

4 In a large bowl, whisk 1¾ cups milk and pudding mix for 2 minutes; let stand 2 minutes or until soft-set. In a small saucepan over low heat, stir peanut butter and remaining milk until smooth. Fold into pudding.

5 Place bottom layer on a serving plate; spread half of filling over cake layer; top with second layer and remaining filling. Chill for 1 hour or until serving.

6 For topping, in a microwave, melt chocolate and butter; stir until smooth. Stir in confectioners' sugar and milk until smooth. Cool until spreadable. Spread frosting over top of cake.

EDITOR'S NOTE: This recipe was tested with Splenda sugar blend.

Dipped Brownie Pops

PREP: 45 MIN. • BAKE: 35 MIN. + COOLING
YIELD: 16 BROWNIE POPS

I had to have a quick school fundraiser for a student organization, so I made these brownie pops—I sold more than 200 in an afternoon! To make s'mores brownie pops, add crushed graham crackers to the dipped chocolate.

Jamie Franklin *Murtaugh, Idaho*

- **1 package fudge brownie mix (13-inch x 9-inch pan size)**
- **16 Popsicle sticks**
- **⅔ cup semisweet chocolate chips**
- **3 teaspoons shortening, divided**
- **⅔ cup white baking chips**
- **Assorted sprinkles, chopped pecans and/or miniature marshmallows**

1 Line an 8- or 9-in. square baking pan with foil; grease the foil and set aside. Prepare and bake brownie mix according to package directions for the size baking pan you use. Cool completely on a wire rack.

2 Using foil, lift brownie out of pan; remove foil. Cut brownie into 16 squares. Gently insert a Popsicle stick into the side of each square. Cover and freeze for 30 minutes.

3 In a microwave, melt chocolate chips and 1½ teaspoons shortening; stir until smooth. Repeat with white baking chips and remaining shortening.

4 Dip eight brownies halfway into chocolate mixture; allow excess to drip off. Dip remaining brownies halfway into white chip mixture; allow excess to drip off. Sprinkle with toppings of your choice. Place on waxed paper; let stand until set. Place in bags and fasten with twist ties or ribbon.

Berry & Cream Chocolate Cups

PREP: 50 MIN. + CHILLING • YIELD: 1 DOZEN

These cute chocolate gems make a great ending to a summer meal. The cool pastry cream filling is to die for, but this treat also tastes wonderful filled with ice cream or chocolate mousse.

Amy Blom *Marietta, Georgia*

- **1 package (12 ounces) dark chocolate chips**
- **2 ounces cream cheese, softened**
- **½ cup sour cream**
- **⅓ cup sugar**
- **2 tablespoons cornstarch**
- **1½ cups milk**
- **2 egg yolks, lightly beaten**
- **1½ teaspoons vanilla extract**
- **1½ cups thinly sliced fresh strawberries**

1 In a microwave, melt chocolate chips; stir until smooth. Spread melted chocolate over the bottoms and up the sides of 12 foil muffin cup liners. Refrigerate for 25 minutes or until firm.

2 In a small bowl, beat cream cheese until fluffy; beat in sour cream until smooth. Set aside.

3 In a small saucepan, combine sugar and cornstarch. Stir in milk until smooth. Cook and stir over medium-high heat until thickened and bubbly. Reduce heat to low; cook and stir 2 minutes longer.

4 Remove from the heat. Stir a small amount of hot mixture into egg yolks; return all to the pan, stirring constantly. Bring to a gentle boil; cook and stir for 2 minutes. Remove from the heat; stir in vanilla and reserved sour cream mixture. Cool to room temperature, stirring occasionally. Refrigerate until chilled.

5 Carefully remove foil liners from chocolate cups. Fill cups with pastry cream and strawberries. Chill until serving.

Frosted Walnut Brownie Cups

PREP: 30 MIN. • BAKE: 20 MIN. + COOLING
YIELD: 32 BROWNIE CUPS

Enjoy a taste of heaven with these mini brownie cups. They are always a huge hit and so simple to make.

Crystal Strick *Boyertown, Pennsylvania*

- **2 cups (12 ounces) semisweet chocolate chips**
- **1 cup butter, cubed**
- **1⅓ cups sugar**
- **4 eggs**
- **2 teaspoons vanilla extract**
- **1 cup all-purpose flour**
- **1 cup chopped walnuts**

GANACHE:

- **2 cups (12 ounces) semisweet chocolate chips**
- **¾ cup heavy whipping cream**

1 In a microwave, melt chocolate chips and butter; whisk until smooth. Cool slightly.

2 In a large bowl, beat sugar and eggs. Stir in vanilla and chocolate mixture. Gradually add flour; stir in walnuts. Fill paper-lined miniature muffin cups almost full.

3 Bake at 350° for 20-23 minutes or until a toothpick inserted in the center comes out clean. Cool for 5 minutes before removing from pans to wire racks to cool completely.

4 Place chocolate chips in a small bowl. In a small saucepan, bring cream just to a boil. Pour over chocolate; whisk until smooth. Cool for 30 minutes or until ganache reaches a spreading consistency, stirring occasionally. Spread over brownies.

GANACHE

>> A French term referring to a smooth mixture of chocolate and cream used as cake fillings, glazes and in candy-making. Traditionally, ganache is made by pouring hot cream over chopped chocolate and stirring until the mixture is velvety smooth. Flavorings can be added as well as corn syrup to give a shiny finish to a poured ganache. The proportions of cream to chocolate vary depending on the use.

Fudgy Peppermint Stick Torte

PREP: 25 MIN. • BAKE: 20 MIN. + CHILLING
YIELD: 16 SERVINGS

I created this recipe based on a chocolate cake a friend made for me several years ago. I love the fact that it has brown sugar instead of granulated sugar. It's a favorite around Christmas, not only because of the great flavors, but because it makes a spectacular presentation.

Mary Shivers *Ada, Oklahoma*

- **1½ cups butter, softened**
- **3¼ cups packed brown sugar**
- **4 eggs**
- **2 teaspoons vanilla extract**
- **4 cups all-purpose flour**
- **1¼ cups baking cocoa**
- **2 teaspoons baking powder**
- **1 teaspoon salt**
- **1 teaspoon baking soda**
- **2½ cups cold water**

FILLING:

- **1½ cups heavy whipping cream**
- **½ cup confectioners' sugar, divided**
- **¼ teaspoon peppermint extract**
- **1 package (8 ounces) cream cheese, softened**
- **1 cup crushed peppermint candies, divided**

1 In a large bowl, cream butter and brown sugar until light and fluffy. Add eggs, one at a time, beating well after each addition. Beat in vanilla. Combine the flour, cocoa, baking powder, salt and baking soda; add to the creamed mixture alternately with water, beating well after each addition.

2 Transfer to four greased and floured 9-in. round baking pans. Bake at 350° for 18-22 minutes or until a toothpick inserted near the center comes out clean. Cool for 10 minutes before removing from pans to wire racks to cool completely.

3 In a small bowl, beat cream until it begins to thicken. Add ¼ cup confectioners' sugar and extract; beat until soft peaks form. In another bowl, beat cream cheese and remaining confectioners' sugar until smooth. Fold in whipped cream, then ¾ cup crushed candies.

4 Place bottom cake layer on a serving plate; top with one-fourth of filling. Repeat layers three times. Refrigerate for at least 1 hour.

5 Just before serving, sprinkle remaining candies over the top.

Caramel Pumpkin Tiramisu

PREP: 35 MIN. + CHILLING • YIELD: 9 SERVINGS

I'm not fond of traditional tiramisu, so I used pumpkin and bourbon in place of coffee and it's absolutely fabulous. I always make extra sauce and eat it over vanilla ice cream. It's so good, I can't leave it alone!

Mary Filipiak *Fort Wayne, Indiana*

- **18 crisp ladyfinger cookies**
- **¼ cup maple syrup**
- **2 tablespoons bourbon**
- **1 cup heavy whipping cream, divided**
- **¼ cup sugar**
- **¾ cup solid-pack pumpkin**
- **1 teaspoon ground cinnamon**
- **½ teaspoon ground ginger**
- **¼ teaspoon salt**
- **4 ounces cream cheese, softened**
- **3 tablespoons confectioners' sugar**

SAUCE:

- **¾ cup caramel ice cream topping**
- **2 teaspoons bourbon**

1 Using a serrated knife, cut six ladyfingers in half widthwise. In a shallow bowl, combine maple syrup and bourbon. Dip six whole ladyfingers and six halves into mixture; arrange in a single layer in an 8-in. square dish.

2 In a small bowl, beat ½ cup cream until it begins to thicken. Gradually add sugar; beat until soft peaks form. In a large bowl, combine the pumpkin, cinnamon, ginger and salt; fold in whipped cream. In another bowl, beat the cream cheese, confectioners' sugar and remaining cream until thickened.

3 Spread half of pumpkin mixture over ladyfingers in the dish. Dip remaining ladyfingers; arrange over the top. Top with remaining pumpkin mixture and the cream cheese mixture. Cover and refrigerate for 8 hours or overnight.

4 In a microwave, heat caramel sauce; stir in bourbon. Serve warm with tiramisu.

EDITOR'S NOTE: This recipe was prepared with Alessi brand ladyfingers.

Apple Tarragon Granita

PREP: 10 MIN. + FREEZING • YIELD: 6 SERVINGS

Looking for a different twist on a classic Italian treat? Fresh tarragon complements the sweet, bright apple flavor of this icy grown-up dessert.

Debby Harden *Williamston, Michigan*

- **3 cups unsweetened apple juice**
- **½ cup sugar**
- **2 tablespoons coarsely chopped fresh tarragon**
- **4 teaspoons lemon juice**

1 In an 8-in. square dish, combine all ingredients until sugar is dissolved. Freeze for 1 hour; stir with a fork.

2 Freeze 2-3 hours longer or until completely frozen, stirring every 30 minutes. Stir granita with a fork just before serving; spoon into dessert dishes.

Raspberries with White Chocolate Sauce And Sugared Almonds

PREP: 10 MIN. • COOK: 10 MIN. + CHILLING
YIELD: 6 SERVINGS

With just a handful of ingredients, you can make a stunning dessert. The white chocolate ganache lightly coats the bright raspberries. Both my daughter and I enjoy this fabulous treat.

Cheryl Landers *LaTour, Missouri*

- **¾ cup slivered almonds**
- **2 tablespoons sugar**
- **½ cup heavy whipping cream**
- **6 ounces white baking chocolate, chopped**
- **¼ teaspoon orange extract**
- **3 cups fresh raspberries**

1 In a small heavy skillet, cook almonds over medium heat until toasted, about 3 minutes. Sprinkle with sugar; cook and stir for 2-4 minutes or until sugar is melted. Spread on foil to cool.

2 In a small heavy saucepan, bring cream just to a boil. Pour over chocolate; whisk until smooth. Stir in orange extract. Refrigerate until chilled.

3 To serve, divide raspberries among six martini glasses or dessert dishes. Top each with sauce; sprinkle with almonds.

WHITE BAKING CHOCOLATE

>> White baking chocolate is usually sold in 1-ounce squares in the baking section of grocery stores. You can substitute vanilla baking chips in place of squares, but be certain to use the same number of ounces called for in a recipe. One cup of vanilla chips is equal to 6 ounces of white baking chocolate.

Lemon Noodle Kugel

PREP: 25 MIN. • BAKE: 55 MIN. + STANDING • YIELD: 12 SERVINGS

Comforting kugel is a traditional dessert at our family's Polish Christmas Eve supper. Rich with butter, sugar, sour cream and cinnamon, it suits any special-occasion meal.

Romaine Smith *Garden Grove, Iowa*

- **5 cups uncooked egg noodles**
- **2 tablespoons butter**
- **4 eggs**
- **2 cups (16 ounces) sour cream**
- **2 cups (16 ounces) 4% cottage cheese**
- **1 cup milk**
- **¾ cup plus 1½ teaspoons sugar, divided**
- **1½ teaspoons lemon extract**
- **1 teaspoon vanilla extract**
- **½ teaspoon ground cinnamon**

1 Cook noodles according to package directions; drain and return to the pan. Toss with butter; set aside.

2 In a large bowl, beat the eggs, sour cream, cottage cheese, milk, ¾ cup sugar and extracts until well blended. Stir in noodles.

3 Transfer to a 13-in. x 9-in. baking dish coated with cooking spray. Combine cinnamon and remaining sugar; sprinkle over noodle mixture.

4 Bake, uncovered, at 350° for 55-60 minutes or until a thermometer reads 160°. Let stand for 10 minutes before cutting. Serve warm or cold. Refrigerate leftovers.

White Chocolate Brie Cups

30 min.

PREP/TOTAL TIME: 25 MIN.
YIELD: 15 SERVINGS

Try these unique little tarts as an appetizer before a special meal, or save them for a surprisingly different dinner finale. They're sweet, creamy, crunchy and very addictive!

Angela Vitale *Delaware, Ohio*

- **1 package (1.9 ounces) frozen miniature phyllo tart shells**
- **1½ ounces white baking chocolate, chopped**
- **2 ounces Brie cheese, chopped**
- **⅓ cup orange marmalade**

1 Fill each tart shell with chocolate, then cheese. Place on an ungreased baking sheet. Top with marmalade.

2 Bake at 350° for 6-8 minutes or until golden brown. Serve warm.

Burgundy Pears

PREP: 10 MIN. • COOK: 3 HOURS • YIELD: 6 SERVINGS

These warm spiced pears elevate slow cooking to a new level of elegance, yet they're incredibly easy to make. Your friends won't believe this fancy-looking dessert came from a slow cooker.

Elizabeth Hanes *Peralta, New Mexico*

- **6 medium ripe pears**
- **⅓ cup sugar**
- **⅓ cup Burgundy wine or grape juice**
- **3 tablespoons orange marmalade**
- **1 tablespoon lemon juice**
- **¼ teaspoon ground cinnamon**
- **¼ teaspoon ground nutmeg**
- **Dash salt**
- **Whipped cream cheese**

1 Peel pears, leaving stems intact. Core from the bottom. Stand pears upright in a 5-qt. slow cooker. In a small bowl, combine the sugar, wine or grape juice, marmalade, lemon juice, cinnamon, nutmeg and salt. Carefully pour over pears.

2 Cover and cook on low for 3-4 hours or until tender. To serve, drizzle pears with sauce and garnish with whipped cream cheese.

Marshmallow Monkey Business

PREP: 30 MIN. • COOK: 10 MIN. • YIELD: 20 SERVINGS

Just like kids, I love fun treats, and these really fit the bill. Plus, they are so easy to make and package! I wrap them in cello bags with twist ties. As a variation, use 3 tablespoons of peanut butter and reduce the butter to 2 tablespoons plus 1-1/2 teaspoons.

Susan Scarborough *Fernandina Beach, Florida*

- **1 package (10 ounces) large marshmallows**
- **3 tablespoons butter**
- **6 cups Rice Krispies**
- **½ cup chopped dried banana chips**
- **20 Popsicle sticks**

TOPPING:

- **2 cups (12 ounces) semisweet chocolate chips**
- **2 tablespoons shortening**
- **½ cup chopped salted peanuts**
- **½ cup chopped dried banana chips**

1 In a large saucepan, heat marshmallows and butter until melted. Remove from the heat. Stir in cereal and banana chips; mix well. Cool for 3 minutes.

2 Transfer mixture to waxed paper; divide into 20 portions. With buttered hands, shape each portion around a Popsicle stick to resemble a small banana.

3 In a microwave, melt chocolate chips and shortening; stir until smooth. Dip ends of "bananas" in chocolate; allow excess to drip off. Sprinkle with peanuts and banana chips. Place on waxed paper; let stand until set. Store in an airtight container.

Chocolate Almond Stacks

PREP: 30 MIN. • BAKE: 10 MIN. + CHILLING • YIELD: 2 SERVINGS

A yummy blend of almonds, whipped cream and chocolate sauce goes into this showpiece dessert. Lightly toast the almonds for extra flavor.

Leah Lyon *Ada, Oklahoma*

- **1 ounce bittersweet chocolate**
- **3/4 cup heavy whipping cream, divided**
- **1 egg**
- **3 tablespoons sugar**
- **1 teaspoon vanilla extract**
- **2 tablespoons all-purpose flour**
- **1/3 cup semisweet chocolate chips**
- **1/2 cup sliced almonds**
- **1/8 teaspoon almond extract**

1 In a small saucepan, melt chocolate with 1 tablespoon cream; stir until smooth. In a small bowl, beat the egg, sugar and vanilla on high speed for 5 minutes or until thick and pale yellow. Fold in flour and melted chocolate. Pour into two 5-in. x 3-in. x 2-in. loaf pans coated with cooking spray.

2 Bake at 350° for 8-10 minutes or until cake springs back when lightly touched. Cool for 5 minutes before removing from pans to wire racks. Cut cakes in half widthwise.

3 In a small saucepan, melt chocolate chips with 3 tablespoons cream, stirring constantly. Spread over top of cakes; sprinkle with almonds. Refrigerate for 15 minutes.

4 In a small bowl, beat almond extract with remaining cream until stiff peaks form. Spread half of the whipped cream on top of two cake squares; top each with a remaining cake square and remaining whipped cream.

FROZEN WHIPPED CREAM DOLLOPS

>> Try this handy tip! Drop rounded spoonfuls of leftover whipped cream on a cookie sheet and freeze. Once frozen, drop the dollops into a small resealable plastic bag and return them to the freezer. When company visits, you'll have the perfect amount of whipped cream at the ready—and a unique presentation—for hot chocolate or coffee beverages.

S'mores on a Stick

PREP: 15 MIN. + STANDING • YIELD: 2 DOZEN

My kids love to take these treats everywhere. That's lucky for me since they are so easy to make. Beside the sprinkles, try mini candies for toppings.

Ronda Weirich *Plains, Kansas*

- **1 can (14 ounces) sweetened condensed milk, divided**
- **1 cup miniature marshmallows**
- **1½ cups miniature semisweet chocolate chips, divided**
- **24 whole graham crackers, broken in half**

Assorted sprinkles

- **24 Popsicle sticks**

1 In a small microwave-safe bowl, microwave ⅔ cup milk on high for 1½ minutes. Add marshmallows and 1 cup chips; stir until smooth. Drop by tablespoonfuls onto 24 graham cracker halves; spread evenly. Top with remaining graham cracker halves; press down gently.

2 Microwave remaining milk for 1½ minutes. Add remaining chips; stir until smooth. Drizzle over cookies; decorate with sprinkles. Let stand for 2 hours before inserting a Popsicle stick into the center of each.

Sweet Potato Cheesecake Bars

PREP: 20 MIN. • BAKE: 25 MIN. + CHILLING • YIELD: 2 DOZEN

Your whole house will be filled with the aroma of pumpkin spice when you bake these wonderful bars. They look complicated but are so easy, you can whip up a batch anytime.

Nancy Whitford *Edwards, New York*

- **1 package (18¼ ounces) yellow cake mix**
- **½ cup butter, softened**
- **1 egg**

FILLING:

- **1 can (15 ounces) sweet potatoes, drained**
- **1 package (8 ounces) cream cheese, cubed**
- **½ cup plus ¼ cup sugar, divided**
- **1 egg**
- **1½ teaspoons pumpkin pie spice**
- **1 cup (8 ounces) sour cream**
- **¼ teaspoon vanilla extract**

TOPPING:

- **1¼ cups granola without raisins**
- **½ cup white baking chips**
- **¼ teaspoon pumpkin pie spice**

1 In a large bowl, beat the cake mix, butter and egg until crumbly. Press onto the bottom of a greased 13-in. x 9-in. baking dish.

2 Place the sweet potatoes, cream cheese, ½ cup sugar, egg and pie spice in a food processor; cover and process until blended. Spread over crust.

3 Bake at 350° for 20-25 minutes or until center is almost set. Meanwhile, in a small bowl combine the sour cream, vanilla and remaining sugar. Spread over filling. Combine topping ingredients; sprinkle over top. Bake 5-8 minutes longer or just until set. Cool on a wire rack.

4 Refrigerate for at least 2 hours. Cut into bars. Refrigerate leftovers.

Toffee Cheesecake Tiramisu

PREP: 30 MIN. + CHILLING • YIELD: 12 SERVINGS

I accidentally discovered this recipe when making tiramisu for my friend's rehearsal dinner a couple of years ago. I did not have enough Mascarpone so I decided to substitute cream cheese, and the result was a huge success. It tastes like cheesecake and tiramisu mixed together.

Tracy Wheeler *Bridgton, Maine*

- **1¼ cups brewed espresso**
- **4 tablespoons rum, divided**
- **4 tablespoons coffee liqueur, divided**
- **1 package (7 ounces) crisp ladyfinger cookies, divided**
- **1 carton (8 ounces) whipped cream cheese**
- **1 carton (8 ounces) Mascarpone cheese**
- **½ cup sugar**
- **1 cup heavy whipping cream, whipped**
- **2 teaspoons baking cocoa, divided**
- **¾ cup toffee bits**

1 Cool espresso to room temperature. In a shallow bowl, combine the espresso, 2 tablespoons rum and 2 tablespoons liqueur. Quickly dip 12 cookies in half of the espresso mixture. Arrange in an ungreased 11-in. x 7-in. dish

2 In a large bowl, combine the cream cheese, Mascarpone cheese, sugar, remaining rum and liqueur. Fold a fourth of whipped cream into the cream cheese mixture, then fold in remaining whipped cream.

3 Spoon half of cream cheese mixture over ladyfingers; spread evenly. Dust with 1 teaspoon cocoa. Dip another 12 ladyfingers in espresso mixture; repeat layers. Sprinkle with toffee bits. Cover and refrigerate for at least 4 hours or overnight.

EDITOR'S NOTE: This recipe was prepared with Alessi brand ladyfinger cookies.

Miniature Pumpkin Cake Towers

PREP: 50 MIN. • BAKE: 20 MIN. + COOLING
YIELD: 10 SERVINGS

I make these pumpkin treats every autumn, and they are gone in minutes. The spice combination is perfect for fall's crisp weather.

Deb Lyon *Bangor, Pennsylvania*

- **1 can (15 ounces) solid-pack pumpkin**
- **2 cups sugar**
- **¾ cup canola oil**
- **4 eggs**
- **2 cups all-purpose flour**
- **2 teaspoons baking powder**
- **2 teaspoons ground cinnamon**
- **1 teaspoon ground nutmeg**
- **½ teaspoon salt**
- **½ teaspoon ground ginger**

SPICED CREAM CHEESE FILLING:

- **1 package (8 ounces) cream cheese, softened**
- **½ cup shortening**
- **½ cup butter, softened**
- **1 tablespoon 2% milk**
- **1 teaspoon ground cinnamon**
- **1 teaspoon vanilla extract**
- **3 cups confectioners' sugar**

Hot caramel ice cream topping, warmed

1. In a large bowl, beat the pumpkin, sugar, oil and eggs until well blended. Combine the flour, baking powder, cinnamon, nutmeg, salt and ginger; gradually beat into pumpkin mixture until blended. Transfer to two greased 15-in. x 10-in. x 1-in. baking pans; spread batter evenly in pans.

2. Bake at 350° for 20-25 minutes or until a toothpick inserted near the center comes out clean. Cool on wire racks.

3. For filling, in a large bowl, beat the cream cheese, shortening and butter until light and fluffy. Beat in the milk, cinnamon and vanilla. Gradually beat in confectioners' sugar until smooth.

4. Using a 3-in. round cookie cutter, cut out 30 circles from cakes. Spread 1 cup filling over 10 cake circles. Repeat. Top with remaining cakes. Pipe remaining filling over tops. Store in the refrigerator. Garnish with ice cream topping.

Crescent Apple Dessert

PREP: 25 MIN. • BAKE: 20 MIN. + COOLING • YIELD: 12 SERVINGS

My family loves any dessert that tastes like apple pie. This one's so easy, even children can help make it. My four grandchildren love helping "MawMaw" make this tasty treat.

Judy Taylor *Kenna, West Virginia*

- **1 tube (8 ounces) refrigerated crescent rolls**
- **1 cup chopped walnuts**
- **¾ cup sugar**
- **½ teaspoon ground cinnamon**
- **¼ teaspoon ground nutmeg**
- **1 can (21 ounces) apple pie filling, chopped**

TOPPING:

- **½ cup all-purpose flour**
- **½ cup packed brown sugar**
- **¼ cup cold butter**
- **1 cup flaked coconut**
- **¼ cup chopped walnuts**

1 Unroll crescent dough into an ungreased 13-in. x 9-in. baking pan; seal seams and perforations. Bake at 375° for 10 minutes.

2 Combine the walnuts, sugar, cinnamon and nutmeg; sprinkle over crust. Spread with pie filling.

3 In a small bowl, combine flour and brown sugar; cut in butter until mixture resembles coarse crumbs. Stir in coconut and walnuts. Sprinkle over filling.

4 Bake at 375° for 18-22 minutes or until golden brown. Cool on a wire rack.

Granola Banana Sticks

**PREP/TOTAL TIME: 20 MIN.
YIELD: 6 SERVINGS**

My daughter and I won an award at our local fair for these peanut-butter-and-granola bananas. Sometimes we substitute rice cereal as a crunchy alternative to the granola bars.

Diane Toomey *Allentown, Pennsylvania*

- **¼ cup peanut butter**
- **2 tablespoons plus 1½ teaspoons honey**
- **4½ teaspoons brown sugar**
- **2 teaspoons milk**
- **3 medium firm bananas**
- **6 Popsicle sticks**
- **2 crunchy oat and honey granola bars, crushed**

1 In a small saucepan, combine the peanut butter, honey, brown sugar and milk; cook until heated through, stirring occasionally.

2 Peel bananas and cut in half widthwise; insert a Popsicle stick into one end of each banana half. Spoon peanut butter mixture over bananas to coat completely. Sprinkle with granola. Serve immediately or place on a waxed paper-lined baking sheet and freeze.

Lemon Icebox Dessert

PREP: 40 MIN. + CHILLING • BAKE: 20 MIN. + COOLING
YIELD: 12-16 SERVINGS

Perfect for summer, my dessert has a nice, light lemon flavor with a tender, flaky crust. It's an ideal finish to a potluck or backyard cookout.

Corene Thorsen *Oconomowoc, Wisconsin*

- **1½ cups all-purpose flour**
- **4½ teaspoons sugar**
- **¾ cup cold butter**

FILLING:

- **8 eggs, separated**
- **2 cups sugar, divided**
- **⅔ cup lemon juice**
- **3 tablespoons grated lemon peel**
- **1 tablespoon unflavored gelatin**
- **½ cup plus 2 tablespoons cold water, divided**
- **½ teaspoon cream of tartar**

TOPPING:

- **1 cup heavy whipping cream**
- **1 tablespoon confectioners' sugar**
- **1 cup flaked coconut**
- **1 tablespoon grated orange peel**

1 In a small bowl, combine the flour and sugar. Cut in butter until crumbly. Press into a greased 13-in. x 9-in. baking dish. Bake at 350° for 18-22 minutes or until lightly browned. Cool on a wire rack.

2 For filling, in a large heavy saucepan, combine egg yolks, 1 cup sugar, lemon juice and peel. Sprinkle gelatin over ½ cup cold water; let stand for 1 minute. Add to the egg yolk mixture. Cook and stir over medium heat until mixture reaches 160° and coats a metal spoon. Remove from the heat; cool completely.

3 In another large saucepan, combine egg whites, cream of tartar, and remaining sugar and water. Cook over low heat, beating with a hand mixer on low speed until mixture reaches 160°. Pour into a large bowl; beat on high until soft peaks form. Gently fold into yolk mixture. Spread over crust.

4 For topping, in a small bowl, beat the cream and confectioners' sugar until soft peaks form; spread over filling. Combine coconut and orange peel; sprinkle over top. Cover and chill for 4 hours or overnight. Refrigerate leftovers.

Sensational Tiramisu

PREP: 25 MIN. • COOK: 10 MIN. + CHILLING • YIELD: 12 SERVINGS

My lightened-up version of the popular Italian dessert is moist and creamy, and cuts so well into pretty layered squares. You'll love the blend of coffee, liqueur and cream cheese flavors.

Mary Walters *Westerville, Ohio*

- **1 package (8 ounces) reduced-fat cream cheese**
- **⅔ cup confectioners' sugar**
- **1½ cups reduced-fat whipped topping, divided**
- **½ cup plus 1 tablespoon sugar**
- **3 egg whites**
- **¼ cup water**
- **2 packages (3 ounces each) ladyfingers, split**
- **½ cup boiling water**
- **2 tablespoons coffee liqueur**
- **1 tablespoon instant coffee granules**
- **½ teaspoon baking cocoa**

1 In a small bowl, beat cream cheese and confectioners' sugar until smooth. Fold in 1 cup whipped topping; set aside.

2 Combine ½ cup sugar, egg whites and water in a small heavy saucepan over low heat. With a hand mixer, beat on low speed for 1 minute. Continue beating on low over low heat until mixture reaches 160°, about 8-10 minutes. Pour into a large bowl. Beat on high until stiff peaks form, about 7 minutes. Fold into cream cheese mixture.

3 Arrange half of ladyfingers in an ungreased 11-in. x 7-in. dish. Combine the boiling water, coffee liqueur, coffee granules and remaining sugar; brush half of mixture over ladyfingers. Top with half of cream cheese mixture. Repeat layers. Spread remaining whipped topping over the top; sprinkle with cocoa. Refrigerate for 2 hours before serving.

Grilled Bananas Foster

30 min.

PREP/TOTAL TIME: 20 MIN.
YIELD: 4 SERVINGS

I worked at a bed and breakfast a few years back, and bananas Foster was a dessert that they often served with dinner. This wonderful version can be prepared on your outdoor grill. Once it is grilled, just add ice cream and you have a heavenly dessert without heating up your kitchen.

Kathleen Hedger *Fairview Heights, Illinois*

- **⅓ cup packed brown sugar**
- **¼ cup butter, melted**
- **2 tablespoons rum or unsweetened apple juice**
- **4 medium bananas**
- **2 cups vanilla ice cream**

1 In a small bowl, combine the brown sugar, butter and rum. Cut each banana into 1-in. slices; place on a double thickness of heavy-duty foil (about 18 in. x 12 in.). Spoon brown sugar mixture over the bananas. Fold foil around banana mixture and seal tightly.

2 Grill, covered, over medium heat for 7-9 minutes or until bananas are tender. Open foil carefully to allow steam to escape. Spoon into four dessert dishes. Serve with ice cream.

General Index

30 MINUTES OR LESS

30 min.

Appetizers

Beverages

Breads

Breakfast & Brunch

Desserts

Main Dishes

Salads

Sandwiches

Side Dishes

Soups & Chilis

APPETIZERS

Cold Appetizers

Dips & Spreads

Hot Appetizers

Salsas

NUTS & NUT BUTTERS

OATS

OLIVES

ONIONS

PASTA

PASTRY & PHYLLO DOUGH

PLUMS (see Nectarines, Peaches & Plums)

PORK

Main Dishes

Sandwiches

Soups

POTATOES

PUDDING

PUMPKIN

QUINOA

RASPBERRIES

RHUBARB

Alphabetical Index

D

E

F

G

T

V

W

Z